Women Workers and Globalization

WOMEN WORKERS AND GLOBALIZATION

Emergent Contradictions in India

Indrani Mazumdar

Centre for Women's Development Studies, Delhi

Stree

WOMEN WORKERS AND GLOBALIZATION
EMERGENT CONTRADICTIONS IN INDIA
was first published in April 2007 by STREE,
and imprint of Bhatkal and Sen,
16 Southern Avenue, Kolkata 700 026.

First reprint January 2010

ISBN-81-85604-84-3

Rs 600.00

Designed by S. Rangarajan and STREE,
Typesetting by S. Ranjagajan,
and Printed by Webimpressions (India) Pvt. Ltd.,
34/2 Beadon St., Kolkata 700 006.

Printed by Mandira Sen for STREE,
an imprint of Bhatkal and Sen
16 Southern Avenue, Kolkata 700 026

To
women as workers,
those whose thoughts have been drawn upon,
and those—many more—
who may not appear before the reader
but whose aspirations, vision,
lives and experiences have inspired me.

Contents

Acknowledgements

The support for this study from UNIFEM is most gratefully acknowledged. In particular, I would like to thank Sumantra Guha and Meenakshi Ahluwalia whose active interest led to UNIFEM sponsoring the study and Narayan Banerjee, Director, CWDS, who extended institutional support.

Sona Mitra, Poulomi and Puloma Pal provided research assistance and companionship in field work, data collection and entry, which I gratefully acknowledge. The manifold day-to-day support of the administrative staff of the CWDS certainly allowed me to focus on completing and writing up the study, and I would particularly like to thank Prakash for his contribution in the efficient management of funds and accounts, Nandan and Sundaresh for dealing with computer problems, and Usha and Swapna for checking and formatting the first draft. The excellent services offered by the CWDS library are well known and made the task of finding and accessing literature from a wider range of libraries so much easier. My colleagues in the faculty of the CWDS have uncomplainingly tolerated a messy clutter of papers and books through which the project proceeded, and whenever pestered with questions unstintingly offered clarifications from their own experience and areas of expertise. I am particularly indebted to N. Neetha for help in updating the macro-employment tables when the study was being prepared for publication.

For a non-economist like me, dealing with the data was a difficult proposition and I take this opportunity to thank C. P. Chandrashekhar and Jayati Ghosh for instant personal advice and clarification whenever I faced problems in this area, quite apart from the immense value and influence of their prolific writing available in the public domain. Vina Mazumdar, Indu Agnihotri and Subodh Varma were, of course, constant companions throughout the endeavour and offered critical discussions. Professor Sabyasachi Bhattacharya was the first to read through the complete draft and gave his recommendation, without which the study may never have been published. I am deeply indebted and grateful. His detailed comments on the study as well as those of the publisher's referee (anonymous), have immensely helped in making a study that was initially not conceived of even as a full scale manuscript into a book. To Stree goes the credit of gracefully transforming the study into this book.

Finally, this book is about and committed to women as workers, and ultimately it is the product of hundreds of contributors. Some make an appearance only as nameless numbers in survey results; others remain unrecorded and invisible. Yet it is they who constituted the foundational base from which the author drew both inspiration and perspective. To them I cannot pay in words even a fraction of my real debt.

New Delhi,
January 2007

Indrani Mazumdar
Centre for Women's
Development Studies

Introduction

From 1991 onwards, 'economic reforms' aiming at a restructuring of the basic policy framework that had been established in India at independence, ushered in the Indian government's accession to the prescription of integration with the project of globalization. It was assumed that liberalization, and the greater integration of the Indian economy with world capitalism, would lead to expanded international trade and large inflows of capital and investment from across the globe. This would in turn stimulate growth and expansion of the production base and work towards material betterment in conditions of living. It was also widely propagated that this process would lead to a general convergence of incomes and living standards. Unfettered global market forces, and the reduction of state protection, support and direct investment in production, and even social welfare, were to be the vehicles of advance of the restructured economy.

Since then, although the effect of such 'reforms' on overall 'growth' is a contested issue, there can be little doubt that some sections of India's businessmen, industrialists and their associates in the upper echelons of the middle classes have been propelled to high fortune. Simultaneously, global brand names, financial interests, and commodities (including the cultural variety), have carved out commanding spaces for themselves in the Indian market, particularly, the metropolitan urban market. As the presence of global players has become more visible, and access to a global range of commodities become easy for the Indian elite, changes have taken place in the aspirations and living patterns of the middle and upper classes. The life styles of some of them, no longer carrying the opprobrium of ostentation as earlier, now compare more closely with the first world than with their compatriots in the overwhelmingly third world foundations of Indian society. It has also led to a growing perception of coalescence of their interests with that of big business in India and in the metropolitan core countries of world capitalism.

At the other extreme, a combination of disturbances and swings in wage and self-employment, following India's integration into the world market, declining availability of public services, and higher prices of basic necessities, have devastated the lives of many at the lower ranks of the social order. Neither uniform nor even, the changes introduced by globalization have led to the overall sharpening of several features of social and economic disparity in India, evoking strong reactions from the women's movement. Basing themselves on a wide range of women's experiences, and arguing that women have been 'the worst affected by the policies of globalization, liberalization and privatization', women's organizations in India have been pointing to the need to draw 'the links between violence, poverty and globalization'.[1]

Studies in different parts of the developing or underdeveloped world, whether supportive or critical of the globalization project, have all pointed to its effects of increasing women's vulnerabilities and insecurities. It is widely accepted that the advance of globalization has been marked by expanding forms of violence, insecurities and greater pressures in the sphere of work, increased compulsions towards migration, greater vulnerability to economic and social exploitation, and generally harsher conditions of life for the poor, the unskilled and the uneducated. While there may be dispute on the actual features, causes and processes, there is a consensus on the emergence of many new areas of concern consequent to the changes in women's lives being brought about by globalization.

In relation to women and work in the era of globalization, influential theories and propositions have been thrown up, often based on observation of partial or temporary phenomena. Some perhaps need to be reevaluated in the light of current evidence. The thesis, for example, that globalization leads to the feminization of labour led the field of enquiry for many years. As such, the elements of counteraction to growth of female employment flowing from high levels of male unemployment, stagnation or deceleration in growth of employment, or the causes and effects of generalized swings in overall employment on women workers, remained relatively neglected areas of investigation. Similarly, with the shrinking of more stable and relatively protected jobs in the organized sector, a universal characteristic of globalization, the large majority of working women in developing countries are getting even more concentrated in what is generally referred to as the informal sector. This has fuelled much discussion on the employment-generation capacities of the informal sector as compared to the formal sector, and greater advocacy of promotion of informal employment as a survival strategy for women in poverty. The destabilizing effects of globalization on both incomes and employment in the informal sector, the profoundly exploitative tendencies in 'perennialization' and expansion of such informality, and the hardening of such characteristics, are increasingly being removed from the reckoning in the formulation of various strategies for the informal sector.

Advancing the debate on these issues on the basis of empirical and experiential analysis is not a matter of mere academic interest. It has become a crying need for those involved in organizing women at various levels. Within the women's movement in India, there is growing consciousness of the relatively untapped potential of working women's organization in the broader movement for equality and emancipation. Bearing the weight of organizing women within an enormously expanded range of issues, with often invisible interconnections, many a tired grass root organizer is desperately searching for information and explanations to advance the movement's capacity to provide informed perspective and leadership in relation to women workers. This is even more true for those working in the major cities, where the rapid pace of events constantly threatens to overtake and allows little time or space for women organizers to collate information, assess, review, and work out appropriate and relevant strategies.

The hunger for explanations, information and articulation of women's needs is not limited to the organizational leaders alone. It is a hunger that emanates from the hearts and minds of ordinary women who are experiencing deep and often devastating changes in their lives. Many have been uprooted and dispossessed. Others have been drawn into a vortex of unstable social and economic relations that are dependant on the vicissitudes and vagaries of international market forces, which seem distant and whose nature is difficult to discern. They too are searching for pathways to deal with the changes in their lives, for ways to control their own destinies, and they too are entitled to know where and how they are being pushed. In the absence of the perspective of the women's movement being brought to bear on their experiences, passive fatalism, reconciliation and surrender to growing inequalities and exploitation, and a dangerous susceptibility to socially retrogressive ideologies inimical to women's social emancipation are all likely to gain ground.

This study investigates the impact of globalization on women workers in India, in some of the sectors that are either considered to be among the most globalized or prominent in global discourses around women's work. It takes as its starting point the need to demystify the phenomenon of globalization. The first chapter, therefore, attempts an overview of the prime drivers, processes, and forces behind the ascendance of globalization. The range of literature that has grown around the subject is, of course, immense and diverse, spanning several aspects including culture and even philosophy. However, the overview presented here essentially focuses on the economic processes, and is directed at establishing the general impact of globalization on employment, labour and women workers in particular, with a special focus on the Indian experience.

The overview is followed by four sectoral studies of women workers in India, two covering factory workers in garment exports and electronics, one of home-based workers in a range of manufacturing processes and industries, and one of more middle class women working in Information Technology Enabled Services (ITES). For each sector, primary surveys were conducted across 2002-2004, among women workers in and around Delhi. These locale-specific primary surveys constitute the basis of identification of the main issues and concerns of women workers in these sectors. However, using secondary sources, the studies have attempted to link the experiences of Delhi-based women workers with their counterparts in the same sectors in other parts of the country, for a more general understanding of the impact of globalization. The overall objective was to delineate the principal trajectories of women's employment in each of the sectors across the period of 'reforms,' outline the effects of the changed policy paradigm on their conditions of work, and analyse causative linkages with the processes of globalization. Further, in garment exports, electronics and IT services, which are clearly linked to global production and service networks, global sectoral trends and their ramifications have also been discussed. The study of home-based workers, on the other hand has focussed more on the policy framework towards this particular section of workers and the changes in perspective that have accompanied the liberalization process.

The primary surveys covered some 500 women workers of the capital city of Delhi (i.e., the National Capital Territory of Delhi), and its satellite townships of Noida (Uttar Pradesh) and Gurgaon (Haryana), through a combination of structured questionnaires, individual and group discussions. The structured questionnaires covered a total of 410 women workers, of which 150 were from garment export factories, 150 were home-based workers, 60 were working in electronics factories, and 50 were employed in ITES, principally in call centres. These questionnaires were filled mostly across residential colonies and settlements in the region, while some were filled in industrial areas but not within any factory or enterprise premises. Such a method of data and information collection was felt to allow greater freedom to the women workers to express themselves and was in any case necessary since most enterprise managements are averse to such enquiries. Further, unstructured interviews, and group discussions through a series of semi-formal workshops across several areas provided additional insights and information.

It must be mentioned that the areas of survey were selected on the basis of prior personal knowledge of the region, and experience of local mass work among women and workers over some twenty years. Thus, the survey of garment export workers, which is the most significant and extended industry employing women in the region, covered six of the nine districts in Delhi apart from the two industrial districts of Noida and Gurgaon. On the other hand, electronics factories were found to have become concentrated in Noida, as many of the earlier factories covered by an earlier study in 1997 had closed down or relocated in Noida. The smaller concentration of electronics factories employing women was reflected in the fact that workers were from just four districts, of which three were located in the National Capital Territory of Delhi and the fourth was Noida. The survey of home-based workers was confined to the National Capital Territory of Delhi covering seven of its nine districts, while the call centre workers, although the smallest in terms of number of surveyed workers, also came from seven of the Delhi districts as well as Noida and Gurgaon.

Apart from the geographical distribution, there were conscious attempts towards making the samples as wide and representative as possible, by covering the entire range of settlements. Thus, for the garment, electronics and home-based workers, the various types of worker settlement, namely the *jhuggies* (shanty settlements), the resettlement colonies, the urban villages and unauthorized colonies as well as regular worker colonies, which constitute the universe of working class residence in the area, were all covered.[2] Call centre workers, on the other hand, were all located in middle-class colonies. Overall, in place of conventional sampling methods, a combination of methods of approaching workers was used. In some cases, it was through prior contacts among trade union and women's organization activists who put us in touch with workers, in others by just looking for workers where they were most likely to be found (in both residential and factory areas), and in the case of call centre workers through university students, placement agencies and again by general asking around. Given the small size of the samples, it is clear that larger employment trends cannot be extracted from the primary surveys; however, we believe that the samples are sufficiently representative for identifying most of the range of issues that affect women in each sector.

Larger employment trends have been drawn out of secondary data from government and in one case, private surveys. General employment data for India including at industry level have been taken from the larger rounds of the National Sample Survey Organisation (NSSO), which cover both organized and unorganized sector workers, while the Annual Survey of Industries and various Ministry of Labour reports have been used for the organized sector. In the case of garments and electronics industries, industry-specific government reports have also been looked at, which provide more detailed and nuanced sets of date, but in the case of the latter, gender-disaggregated data were not available in such reports. In the case of IT-enabled services, on the other hand, more data were available from private industry association sources, which, in fact, is the source of much that appears about the sector in government reports as well. For home-based workers, two government-constituted commission reports have been used as the main sources of information.

In introducing the studies, a few clarifications are perhaps in order. The first is that paid work has been the focus of enquiry. This is so not because other aspects of women workers' lives, including the sphere of unpaid domestic or subsistence work are not considered equally important. They are, and have legitimately been, the subject of much of the theoretical and empirical research regarding the impact of structural adjustment on women including their role in shaping the gender-based inequalities faced by women workers in the labour market. An important aspect of the economic reform package that has been of special concern to women, is its intrinsic orientation towards reduction of social-welfare components of state budgets, those areas of state support that stretch beyond the realm of the economic production processes to the spheres of unpaid work in reproduction and care, traditionally the sphere where women predominate. An inevitable consequence has been increased pressures on women, not only within the domestic sphere, but also adding further weight to the inherited burden of inequalities that women carry into the sphere of their participation in paid employment. In India the benefits of welfare were even earlier generally not accessible to all; nevertheless the reduction of those limited welfare provisions by the state has been universally acknowledged to have had adverse effects on the lives of women, particularly on the majority who eke out their subsistence in conditions of overall poverty.

In this study, however. these aspects and their bearing on the sphere of paid work have not been elaborated. It has been taken as given that social inequalities and the disproportionate weight of unpaid work on the lives of women, aggravated by declines in social sector government spending (associated with structural adjustment policies), have in turn aggravated their unequal status in the world of paid work. The special focus on paid work was felt necessary because of the urgent need of the times for a more informed engagement of the women's movement with this sphere and the deeply exploitative relations that are therein being fashioned by globalization. Greater closeness and mutually supportive action by the women's movement with workers' organizations from within and without trade unions is perhaps more necessary than ever before in this era of erosion of labour rights and increasing involvement of women in wage labour.

Secondly, gender relations in the domestic social sphere have not been explored. Studies of increasing violence against women and deterioration of relations between the sexes, of expansion of iniquitous social practices such as dowry and other elements of social regression in contemporary times often point to their being fueled by economic, social and cultural processes that are inherent in globalization. This study, however, concentrates on only employment-related inequalities and issues. A few other aspects of gender relations are touched on only occasionally and on the basis of some of the perceptions of the workers surveyed. It perhaps merits mention that many qualitative aspects of women workers' life experiences would get missed out in the method of quantitative analysis that underpins this study. In its underlying perspective, however, the study assumes that other forms of social inequality provide the broader context of women workers' lives and also takes for granted the historical experience that while economic independence of women may be an essential prerequisite for emancipation, it does not automatically end patriarchal oppression in either the domestic or broader social spheres. What remains to be said is that there is also a need to give due importance to the issues of employment, around which organization by women has an intrinsic potential for contributing to the creation of subjective conditions necessary for the longer haul for the elimination of patriarchy.

Thirdly, as a measure of the study's quantitative limitations, it must be emphasized that both the sectoral studies and the primary surveys are located in the urban experience and clearly need to be supplemented with similar studies of the much vaster numbers of women workers in rural India and in particular among the peasantry, where the proportions of women have visibly increased.[3] Nevertheless, the four case studies when taken together have highlighted several issues that we believe require to be brought to the centre of the general debates on the impact of globalization on women. It is hoped that the detailed empirical findings of the primary surveys, which might appear tedious to many, will be of use in identifying the concrete issues around which women workers may be organized in each sector. Bearing in mind the limitations of individual interpretation and biases, the attempt has been to provide the primary data in as complete a manner as possible and in tabular form, for readers to use to draw any conclusions other than those given in this study as well. Even where the data might not seem to have any direct relevance to the subject of the impact of globalization, it was felt that the discoveries of the surveys should be made available for social analysis.

Each sectoral study, of course, threw up specific unanticipated questions and lines of enquiry, as the underlying design and interconnections of life processes do not always appear fully in survey- or data-based research. Not all of such questions could be followed through satisfactorily. However, in following up such lines of enquiry, and quite without any preconceived design, each study seems to us to have highlighted one or other aspect of the more general processes taking place in the era of globalization in relation to women's employment.

Thus, for example, the case of garment export workers shows that in general, multilayered local sub-contracting by independent Indian exporters was the framework in which the initial growth of the industry took place from the 1970s. It is increasingly being replaced or is relatively declining in the face of a general trend towards consolidation in the industry and a rise in the numbers and weight of organized-sector larger manufacturing exporters. Such large manufacturer exporters are more closely linked to the concentrating and monopolistic retail industry buyers in western countries who appropriate the lion's share of profits. In the Delhi region, the growth of larger manufacturers has been accompanied by some shifts in the earlier patterns of gender-based occupational segregation. Earlier, particularly in unorganized production, women were generally concentrated either at the lowest unskilled level of helpers or in the more skilled tasks of checking but excluded from the largest employment category of tailors. In the larger manufacturing units, as deskilled assembly of garments has replaced earlier systems of more skilled tailoring of whole garments, women do tend to be recruited as tailoring operators in larger numbers; however, quite high rates of unemployment among garment workers appeared to be common with reports of several garment factories closing down, retrenching or relocating. This had affected both women and men. Since the consolidation of larger manufacturing units has been at the cost of the earlier unorganized sub-contractors, whose male tailors became available as experienced but cheap labour, the recruitment of women even in the larger units of Delhi has been much more limited in comparison to other parts of India. Further, a clear association between low wages and higher share of women in employment in the industry appeared in cross-regional comparison in the organized sector of the industry. Greater proportions of women workers (in fact, the majority as far as the organized sector is concerned) were found in precisely those areas (Tamilnadu and Karnataka) where wage rates are comparatively much lower than Delhi and where women workers' wages relative to male workers' wages were also substantially lower. In Delhi, on the other hand, where wage disparities between men and women did not appear in organized sector wage data for the industry, the proportions of women workers appeared to be even lower than existed earlier when unorganized manufacturing was more dominant. At an all India level, while the numbers of women workers in the manufacture of wearing apparel seemed to have increased substantially between 1993-1994 and 1999-2000, their share of employment (principal usual status) in the sector actually showed a steep decline from 29 per cent to 20 per cent across the same period. Clearly where consolidation in larger manufacturing units accompanies large-scale displacement of both men and women from other smaller units, as has been a feature of the industrial scenario under liberalization, women's employment share becomes even further circumscribed tending towards decline. Although the most recent employment data for 2004 again shows a rise in share of women workers in the garment industry to 28 per cent, women's share still remains marginally below what was seen in 1993-1994. Since garment exports between 2000 and 2004 showed no significant increase, it appears that fluctuations in the share of women's employment seems to be more indicative of a continuous cycle of absorption and shedding of labour within an overall drive to lower wages, and in part, perhaps, due to the greater absorption of women workers into the changing structure of the domestic market for readymade garments.

In the case of the electronics industry, where the organized sector constitutes more than one-half of women's employment in the industry, sharp swings in both male and female employment were clearly evident. A few thousands of women suddenly gained jobs in one state (Maharashtra) over an eight-year period beginning 1987 during which male workers lost their jobs also in thousands. In the next two years, the process reversed with thousands of women losing jobs, while men gained employment. In another state (Karnataka), both men and women gained employment between 1995-1996 and 1998-1999 and again both lost jobs on a large scale in the following year. In a third state (Uttar Pradesh, where Noida is located), huge swings were visible in male employment while women's employment showed no increase and their share declined. These three states, which accounted for more than three-quarters of women's employment in electronics in the mid-1990s are a fair indicator of the overall volatility and insecurity that have affected both men and women working in the electronics industry even in the centres of its expansion. The volatility itself indicates a level of crisis in the electronics industry. Widespread closures have been the result of policies of liberalization of hardware imports or promotion of software exports at the cost of local hardware manufacturing. Multinational producers who are directly investing in consumer electronics and a retreating public sector have the impact of a strong displacing force that has adversely affected employment in the sector. In the Delhi Noida region, in the late 1980s and early 1990s, electronics employment had pulled in migration of several women from the far south of India. Large-scale closures were now leading to reverse flows as many of them had been displaced from employment. Consolidation among fewer manufacturers was also visible in electronics as also a greater weight of multinational producers. Some of even these had also closed down or were in the process of reducing their workforce over the last five years, while the most flourishing of them were working their workers ten hours a day seven days of the week in a highly oppressive atmosphere. Such a pace of work naturally reinforced the tendency for women workers in electronics to be young and single, with a somewhat higher proportion of them being divorced, separated from their families or, as in the case of some of the unmarried, just not able to get married.

Recording the products, labour process and labour time by broad industry division and rates of remuneration among home-based workers highlighted several relatively less-discussed features of home-based work in the era of globalization. The wide range of modern products being produced by these workers was directed mostly at the domestic (but not local) market. The labour involved, although arduous, in general required little skill. The availability of piece rated home-based work in Delhi was due to the existence of a wide range of factories and wholesale markets in the city. Most of the workers were involved in more extended and socialized forms of manufacture (only a part process was farmed out to them in their homes), and the products were non-marketable by the workers themselves. Profit margins from their work, which, of course, are appropriated either by factory owners, wholesale traders, and a range of intermediaries in between, tend to be quite small and reasonable incomes accrue only to those who deal in volume. In other words, elimination of the middleman, the factory owner or the merchant, and establishment of a direct link between the worker and the product market would almost in no case lead to even subsistence incomes for them. Perhaps one of the greatest wholesale tragedies of the present era is that these large numbers of women working in both social and economic confinement at pittance wage rates on an average of a little over Rs 2 per hour, are facing even greater difficulties as a result of the shrinking availability of work, declining incomes, and in some important areas a decline in nominal piece rates. Declines in work availability is at once linked to consolidation of work organization within factories (as in the case of garment exports) and mechanization in some spheres, the crisis faced by several of the smaller local manufacturers who have been closing down on a large scale, as well as the overall situation of crippling demand constraint that has grown with greater vengeance during the period of liberalization.

The last of the sectoral studies covers a different class of women workers in new forms of employment in the service sector, whose rise has led to much euphoric celebration of globalization among some sections of the business and middle classes. IT-enabled services, the product of the digital age, are seen by globalizers as being singularly important for employment generation as well as in terms of potential to transform India from a still largely backward and overwhelmingly poor country into the 'superpower' league. What emerges from the study is the overwhelmingly dependent status of this form of employment, which largely provides real-time computer telephony or call centre services to consumers in western countries, for firms also located or headquartered there, by workers located in India. In the process, night-work and a degree of cultural degradation (since these employees have to affect the accents of service-receiving countries and often to change their names to western names) are conditions of service in the sector, none of which can be a cause for great celebration. Further, in its essence, the nature of the work has been part of a larger trend towards industrialization of white-collared work in western developed capitalism, characterized particularly by subalternization of white-collared women workers. In the call centre industry, new technology in fact plays a key role in pushing productivity to superhuman levels along with maximization of supervision, both of which lead to quick burnout among a generally very young workforce. This intensification of the labour process is of course a universal phenomenon, not only in services but also in manual production-based industries, and emerged as a feature in the case studies of other sectors as well. Its adverse effects on the health of workers appears prominently even among the class of more privileged employees in call centres.

In the concluding section, some aspects of the local context and background of the workers covered by the primary surveys have been discussed, and some of the general issues emerging from the sectoral studies when taken together have been summed up. Although the attempt throughout has been to try and capture the larger picture, any such claim has to be tempered by the fact that the specific sectors for which primary surveys were conducted employ perhaps less than 5 per cent of working women in the country. Broad macro-data based employment trends from 1993-1994 to 2004 across all major sectors and inclusive of agriculture is of course presented and analysed in Chapter 5, which is why that chapter appears somewhat longer than the others. But the more detailed descriptions and analysis of sectoral issues have obviously been possible only where the macro-data are backed by the primary surveys and not for the other sectors. Nevertheless, we hope that the study as a whole will be of some use to organizers and leaders of the women's and workers' movement as well as those in the government and other organizations who seek to counter the negative and unjust impact of the contemporary dynamics of globalization.

The overall picture that emerges from the studies points to the emergence of multilayered contradictions in the sphere of paid work by women. On the one hand, some processes associated with globalized organization of production have led to the drawing in of women into forms of employment to which they might earlier not have had such access, but such a phenomenon has tended to be highly circumscribed by the larger trend of falling work participation rates among women and higher levels of unemployment. On the other hand, large-scale displacement of women from employment has also been observed, both in sectors where export markets are seen to be expanding as well as sectors where women workers are being weeded out due to the deindustrializing effects of liberalization. At the same time, within their spheres of work, new developments are taking place in the nature of women workers' relations with their employers. If in the export-oriented garment industry, exploitation by job work fabricators and local manufacturers is now being subsumed within indirect pressures from multinational retailers or buyers in the developed countries, in the electronics industry more direct contradictions are developing in relation to multinational corporations. In the IT-enabled sector, new avenues of employment can be seen combining with new forms of cultural degradation, with technology itself becoming an instrument of closer and more oppressive systems of social control. Among home-based workers, on the other hand, loss of work that was earlier available and falls in income are linked to crisis and decline in local small-scale industry. In general, losses of employment contrast sharply with the fairly generalized intensification of the labour process, both of which have become the hallmarks of globalization. Increasingly it is becoming clear that the destiny of women workers across the board and not only in the sectors covered by this study will depend on how the processes associated with globalization will be played out or dealt with by policy in the years to come. It is hoped that the information and analysis presented in this book will help extend the understanding of the links between the immediate experiences confronting women workers and the globalized processes that have influenced and shaped them.

Notes

1 'Womenspeak, United Voices Against Globalization, Poverty and Violence in India,' March 2000. This document adopted at a convention organized in Delhi by six national women's organizations in 2000 and supported by several other regional organizations and groups, outlines the approach towards globalization for the major part of the women's movement in India, representing perhaps around six million women. The largest of the national organizations, All India Democratic Women's Association (AIDWA), alone has a membership of over five million.

2 Resettlement colonies are areas where *jhuggi* dwellers were resettled (generally on plots of 25 square yards) after their *jhuggies* were demolished in successive waves from the late 1960s onwards. The term 'urban villages', refers to the remnants of what were originally clusters of village residences and therefore protected by law from acquisition by the urban development authorities. Many of them, particularly those located close to industrial areas, have become areas where migrant workers have clustered in rented tenements. 'Unauthorized colonies' refer to colonies carved out of arable land, not authorized by Delhi's Master Plan or government, and where generally roads, lighting and municipal water supply are not available. For a brief description of the type of settlements, see Chapter 2.

3 As per census figures, the share of female cultivators among total cultivators has risen from 20 per cent in 1991 to 32.4 per cent in 2001.

ONE

Emergent Contradictions: Overview on Globalization

'Globalization' is generally used as the term of choice to describe the current processes of growing integration within the world economy through increased cross-border movement of capital, goods and services and establishment of global production networks. It has undeniably become the most powerful force determining current national and international policies and outcomes. Despite differing interpretations of and attributions to it—and despite its sources of continuity in the earlier history of capitalism—the phenomenon of globalization that we have experienced over the last quarter of a century is defined by some qualitatively new features. Further, its advance has been inextricably linked with its enabling prescriptive elements of policy shifts towards liberalization and deregulation of national markets. The changes so effected have been based on the neo-liberal precepts of curtailment of state expenditures and removal of regulatory restrictions on the operations of private business and capital and the belief that free markets lead to the most efficient and productive allocation of resources. With the universalization of such policy shifts across the world, an almost mystical perception of the inevitability of globalization has swept across countries, projecting absolute faith in the power of the unrestricted market to resolve the fundamental problems of the human condition at global, national and local levels.

A VIEW FROM HISTORY

According to some commentators, globalization is nothing new. For example, it has been pointed out that when defined as a process of global economic integration through increases in movement across national borders of some combinations of goods and services, capital, labour and financial capital, the late nineteenth century could be referred to as a period of globalization;[1] however, the term that most appropriately emerged then (from both its supporters and detractors), and that has since defined the historical stage set by that age, was not globalization but imperialism.

The concept of imperialism was not considered as co-terminous with colonialism, whose long history stretched way back beyond the nineteenth century into the period before capitalist industrialization in Europe. On the other hand, the word 'imperialism' first became part of the political and journalistic vocabulary during the 1890s as a term to describe what was considered at the time as a new or novel phenomenon.[2] It was then delineated and clarified as having economic roots in a specific new phase of capitalism in which overseas economic expansion and the exploitation of the overseas world were crucial to capitalist countries. Imperialism was identified with the phase of capitalist development engendered by enormous concentration and centralization of capital in the industrialized countries from the late nineteenth century onwards. Such centralization took place through formation of cartels, a coalescence of finance and capitalist industry, and the emergence of powerful monopolies or oligopolies on the world stage. It compelled an expansionist scramble for markets for capital and goods as well as control over sources of raw material, and led to the intensified exploitation of weaker nations by a handful of the richest and most powerful capitalist powers, either along the colonial route or through establishment of less politically defined 'spheres-of-influence'.[3]

The features of centralization of capital through the combination of already existing capitals, an important share of external trade in national incomes, vast cross-border flows of capital and rapid integration into a single world economy are common to both. Even the 'tightening web' of transport and communications (extension of railways, transcontinental telephone lines, and so on) that had enabled integration in the earlier period could be considered to have played a role then similar to that played by information and communications technology today. Further, what historian Eric Hobsbawm referred to as the domination of the advanced and developed capitalist core over the backward nations, and the profoundly unequal and highly asymmetrical relationship between metropoles and their dependencies that defined the earlier period, are characteristics that can hold equally true today. What is different and what in a sense defines and makes globalization a new phenomenon is, first of all, the differences in developments and context wrought by intervening history. Globalization, today, cannot be understood without reference to the changes that it has brought about, changes that cannot themselves be understood without reference to the developments of the period preceding its ascendance.

The Pre-Globalization Context: Advancing Decolonization

The world economic order that is being changed by globalization is one that had witnessed the collapse of the political hegemony of the colonial empires of the earlier period and the growth of forces that sought restriction of economic imperialism. The first half of the twentieth century had seen two world wars, interspersed with revolution and establishment of socialism in the USSR, and a great depression in the capitalist world, following which national liberation movements leading to decolonization had brought into existence several new independent states. These momentous events had clearly altered the context of the world economy, and in the new configurations that emerged, in every single country, the state had emerged as an important interventionist and regulating agency directing the economy.

Towards the end of World War II, by which time the United States had replaced Britain as the foremost capitalist power, an international financial architecture, designed by consensus among the major powers at the Bretton Woods Conference of 1944, had established the US dollar as the medium of international trade on the basis of a fixed rate of its exchange against gold (US $35 per ounce of gold). Having escaped any real ravages of war, the United States had by then emerged as the richest country (in 1950 it contained 60 per cent of the capital stock of the advanced capitalist countries and produced 60 per cent of their output). The Bretton Woods Conference gave birth to both the International Monetary Fund (IMF) charged with preventing another global depression, and the International Bank for Reconstruction and

Development (World Bank) to finance reconstruction of the countries that had been ravaged by the war. While maintenance of stability of economic relations between the main powers was among the IMF's articles of purpose,[4] in the background of the experience of the great depression (1929-1933), its objective was also to ensure that individual states functioned effectively to ensure adequate *global aggregate demand*, to prevent any of these economies from going into a slump, and to '*provide liquidity* in the form of loans to those countries facing an economic downturn and unable to stimulate aggregate demand with their own resources'.[5] It might be recalled that among the key participants at the Bretton Woods conference who played a role in the conception of the IMF was the British economist John Maynard Keynes, whose ideas regarding the need for government stimulation of aggregate demand through its own expenditures towards maintaining high employment had become influential by then.

Addition of Welfare Dimensions to the Role of the State: The Golden Age

Across developed capitalist countries, state regulation of the overall economy of private business and employment and provisions for social welfare became the dominant policy paradigm, emerging from the experience that if market forces were given completely free reign, self-destructive crises or a social revolution could overtake them. Direct intervention of the state in the production economy, in both industry and services, enabled expansion of national economies beyond the limitations of purely private economic activity, and additionally provided employment to large numbers, ensuring that aggregate demand did not fall. Prevention of mass unemployment or promotion of 'full employment' became an object of state policy in the developed world.

On the other hand, across the underdeveloped regions, as several countries threw off the yoke of colonial rule, the state had emerged as an important instrument for their independent industrialization and economic development and, in many cases, came to play the role of a bulwark against domination by metropolitan capital. Import substitution policies, some degree of protection of internal markets from imported goods, controls on foreign investment, and a strong presence of the state in the development process were practically universal and most significant in those countries where industrialization advanced more rapidly. Long-term drains on their resources during the colonial era had left these regions impoverished, and their attempt was to industrialize independently and liberate themselves from the retarding effects of imperialism on their development. If in the socialist world, in any case, the state was the supreme agency of economic development, *mixed economies*—where the public sector and private business and industry grew with a degree of mutual reinforcement within national borders—had became the new context in which capitalism continued to develop. It is this form of development and its attendant social and economic correlations within and between nations that is being changed by neo-liberal policy and advancing globalization.

An important element of the form of state regulation was in the sphere of relations between capital and labour. In differing degrees based on differing levels of development, resources and capacities of the individual states and actual national political correlations, most capitalist-dominated states had put in place a set of regulatory mechanisms that allowed for a degree of job security and collective bargaining for labour where they were organized.

It was within the framework of such state interventions and regulations that what is often referred to as the 'golden age' of capitalism unfolded, when powered by technological revolution, world output of manufactures quadrupled (between the early 1950s and the early 1970s) and world trade in manufactured products grew tenfold.[6] It was an age when in the developed capitalist countries, whose strides in industry, trade, and more generalized affluence defined the golden age (the developed capitalist countries represented about three quarters of the world's production and over 80 per cent of its manufacturing exports in this period), a combination of rising profits and rising non-business incomes in the form of wages and social security and social welfare benefits were made possible by policies of individual states.[7] For developed capitalism, this particular phase of more advanced industrialization and expansion of trade, augmented and enhanced by the role of their states in pushing for full employment, propelled greater *popular affluence* and expanding markets, both internal and through mutual trade, which for quite some time more than made up for their loss of colonies.[8] A feature of this period in the developed world noted by Hobsbawm was 'the mass entry of married women—largely mothers—into the labour market'. He gives the example of the United States, where married women living with their husbands and working for pay formed less than 14 per cent of the total female population in 1940. By 1980 their number rose to over 50 per cent. The percentage had just about doubled between 1950 and 1970. Further, according to him, it was this along with the striking expansion of higher education that formed the background, at least in the typical developed Western countries and the United States, to the impressive revival of feminist movements from the 1960s on.[9]

The Closing of the Golden Age

By the early 1970s, however, the edifice of the international financial system established at Bretton Woods crumbled and finally collapsed. The fixing of the US dollar as the medium of trade at Bretton Woods had given the state policy of the United States exceptional leverage, enabling it freely to print dollars to finance its own policy-driven loan programmes and also to finance its several military interventions over the following decades in several parts of the world.[10] In fact, the United States printed and put in circulation far more US dollars than could be backed by their gold reserves, and when in 1968, President De Gaulle of France asked for the French US dollar holdings to be honoured in gold it was clearly impossible (even though the United States held three-fourth of the world's gold, there was nothing like enough to match the quantity of US dollars circulating in the world economy at US $35 per ounce). This led to France and Germany then devaluing their currencies against the dollar followed by unilateral devaluation by the United States from US $35 per ounce of gold to US $38 per ounce in 1971. Faced with the threat of an escalating round of competitive devaluations, the Dollar Standard was finally abandoned and gold was floated in August 1973.[11] After 1973, one country after another had to abandon efforts to completely control the exchange rate of their own currency.

Concurrent to the events leading to the collapse of the Bretton Woods financial system was the rise to international prominence of the

Organization of the Petroleum Exporting Countries (OPEC), as its Member Countries (comprising major petroleum exporting countries in the developing world and spearheaded by the Arab countries) took control of their domestic petroleum industries and acquired a major say in the pricing of crude oil on world markets. Much of the industrial advances made by the developed countries during their golden age had been premised on the easy and cheaply available supplies of oil. By the early 1970s, however, the continuing monopolistic domination of the international oil market by western conglomerates was suddenly challenged by a unified block of developing country producers, intent on establishing their own interests. In the context of a fall in oil prices caused by the United States devaluation of the dollar and the concomitant increase in the price of imports of developing countries including oil producers, an assertion by Arab countries in OPEC led to a quadrupling of world oil prices between 1973 and 1974 popularly known as the oil shock.[12] Following the collapse of the Bretton Woods international financial system, the quadrupling of the price of oil, and massive increases in the world's money supplies (see globalization of finance, p 22) came a sudden slump of industrial production in the developed countries by 10 per cent and international trade by 13 per cent between 1973 and 1975, bringing the long post-war boom to a close and heralding the end of an era.

Thereafter, the pace of economic growth slowed down, with booms becoming shorter followed by severe slumps such as in 1980-1982 and again at the end of the 1980s. Further, although international trade accelerated again in the 1980s to levels comparable with the 'golden age', endemic unemployment once again came to haunt the developed countries and continued at high levels even during the times of boom. Governments increasingly found their finances strained, with welfare payments (including extra burdens from higher unemployment levels) rising faster than revenues in slowed down economies. Without going into the generic factors responsible for the reappearance of instability in developed capitalist countries, or the increasing inability of their governments to manage their economies during 'the crisis decades' after 1973, what is of note here is that neo-liberal policies brought about deliberate changes in the state's role in relation to labour and employment.

The Globalization of Neo-Liberalism

It may be recalled that the global shift in policy towards neo-liberalism was started in the United States and the United Kingdom, under Ronald Reagan (1980-1988) and Margaret Thatcher (1979-1990), respectively.[13] It was then universalized across several developing countries through aggressive conditional lending practices by the IMF and the World Bank under whose twin patronage, from the 1980s onwards, neo-liberal policies of structural adjustment and liberalization were put in place across the third world.[14] Liberalization entailed shifts in macroeconomic policy towards privatization, cutting government expenditures in employment and social welfare (in the name of reducing fiscal deficits) and shifting the focus of policy to providing an enabling environment for freer capital movement and unrestricted play of market forces. Privatization of several state concerns, cutting costs in both public and private sectors through downsizing or shedding of labour, and lifting of national controls on capital movements in financial markets were effected across the developed OECD countries, albeit in somewhat differing degrees. State protections for labour were increasingly replaced by retrenchment drives; and the shifting pecuniary interests of individual business concerns were given priority over the 'full employment' objectives of state regulation.[15] They paved the way for a general curtailment of the rights and collective bargaining power of labour vis-à-vis capital.

In the developed world, higher rates of unemployment, declining real incomes accruing to labour, and growth of new extremes of poverty and wealth at the expense of the range of intermediate incomes became the defining features of the liberalization era. Moreover, with production systems being made more 'flexible' in response to variations in product demand and 'market turbulence', reductions in the full-time workforce and increasing weight of part-time, temporary and contingent workers led to a generalized erosion of job security. A disproportionate number of such precariously situated contingent workers were women.[16] Nevertheless, despite visible signs of general instability, of higher levels of poverty, squalor and homelessness and a striking growth of social and economic inequality, welfare and social security systems in developed countries could not be completely dismantled and therefore provided some cushioning. Nor was the neo-liberal object of lowering taxes and curtailment of government expenditures and the fiscal deficit adhered to, even by its most ardent advocates there.[17] Further, despite anti- statist free market theorization, the United States, in particular (during the Reagan era), continued periodically to resort to deficit financing on a large scale to boost economic activity and Britain under Margaret Thatcher ultimately taxed its citizens more than before, although ensuring less protective mechanisms for labour and a lesser role for the state in income transfers to workers. It was in developing countries, where conditional lending by the IMF and the World Bank left fewer choices, that the reversals in policy had far more generalized and severe effects when the policies designed to advance the decolonization process began to be rolled back.

The Pre-Liberalization Focus in the Third World: Decolonizing Development

An inheritance of mass poverty, unemployment or underemployment, and a relatively small and uneven base to industrialization, had of course continued to operate in the pre-liberalization era in most of the developing countries. Nevertheless, although slow, and with some lagging more than others, efforts at independent industrialization enabled by public investment and/ or credit were made possible through decolonization and import substitution policies that allowed for dispersal of some benefits to a relatively wider swathe of the population than before. Such policies had expanded and created new industrial bases in several developing countries. By the mid-1980s, seven countries located in the third world alone consumed 24 per cent of the world's steel and produced 15 per cent of it. (They were China, South Korea, India, Mexico, Venezuela, Brazil and Argentina).[18] Ironically the development of such industrial bases through decolonization and resistance to imperialist incursions now appeared to create more appropriate conditions for fulfilment of resurgent expansionary needs and globalization interests of metropolitan capital.

For some two and a half decades after the war, the developing countries that achieved major advances in industrialization did so through state policies driven primarily by their home market considerations, markets that they largely kept protected. This was true for those who maintained a stance in favour of national liberation or self-reliance and non-alignment, as well as some more closely politically allied with western powers. It was made possible by a context engendered by the existence of the USSR as an economic counterpoint to western imperialism and the politics of the cold war. According to A. Singh, 'the period of 1950 to 1980 was also—and in an important sense—the Golden Age of development for the poor countries of the world', when the 'South' bettered the record of the 'great transformation' in the developed countries of the 'North', during the nineteenth century. He observed that 'the South did this in half the time, at twice the growth rates, and with five times the North's population in the nineteenth century'.[19]

Such a statement of course requires several qualifications, including, as in India, the innate contradictions of state-led industrialization in conditions of highly skewed initial distribution of assets and incomes being left intact.[20] Non-redistribution of concentrated land assets had constrained generalized growth in agriculture and continued impoverishment in rural India. Although capitalist investment in 'Green Revolution' pockets supported by state investment in irrigation and overheads led to remarkable agricultural output growth from the 1960s to the 1980s, it was accompanied by sharp declines over time in employment, in terms of labour days in crop production, owing to mechanization.[21] Non-mobilization of sufficient resources by the state from large privately held economic surpluses (through direct and effective taxation of the wealthy owners of capital) ultimately led to fiscal crisis, stagnation in public investment (in real terms) for nearly a decade after the mid-1960s, 'with a tendency to place its burdens on the consumption of the working people through additional and highly inequitous indirect taxation'.[22] It also led to spiralling public debt. As the contradictions of such an economic path approached denouement, manufacturing growth dropped from an annual rate of 7.8 per cent between 1951 and 1965 to 3.3 per cent in the latter half of the 1960s and remained at 4 per cent over the 1970s. At the same time private economic surpluses had been allowed to increase persistently over time through budgetary concessions of all kinds, as had concentration of wealth and economic surplus in the hands of monopolistic capitalist sections. As pointed out by Prabhat Patnaik, 'a rise over time in the share of private economic surplus must entail either a decline in what is available to the state for its expenditure and investment, or a decline in the share of the working people', which in some sectors might be offset by productivity increases or militant organization by workers. But overall it meant 'impoverishment for those sections of the working people who are weak or unorganized, together with a slowing down of the growth of public investment, and with it a slowing down of the pace of industrialization'.[23] Given a degree of diversity of actual conditions, with varying levels of factor emphasis, the essentials of this argument would probably hold true for many of the developing countries. Nevertheless, there can be little doubt that state investments in the process of industrialization and import substitution policies of developing countries were necessary for any country advancing the decolonizing agenda, and took place despite constant pressure from international financial institutions such as the World Bank not to do so.[24]

Liberalization's Paradigm Shift: Reversing of the Decolonizing Agenda

The fiscal problems faced by most developing country states by the 1970s came to be increasingly dealt with through international borrowings. This was facilitated by the increasing propensity of commercial banks located in the developed countries to lend to them at relatively high rates of interest (on an average of 9.6 per cent in 1982).[25] The banks themselves were flush with far greater funds than could be absorbed by profitable investment in the slowing down economies of the developed world. From 1972, when the value of the overseas loans extended by these banks was estimated to have been US $2 billion, it rose to US $90 billion in 1981.[26] Inevitably, several countries reached situations when they could no longer service their foreign debts, beginning with Mexico, Brazil and Argentina (Latin America had absorbed well over 60 per cent of such bank loans) in the early 1980s and reaching India in 1991. It created conditions for the stepping in of the IMF and the World Bank (and in some cases the US government directly) using conditional loans to governments facing such crises, to bring about major and universalizing shifts in policy.

Economies of developing countries were thus restructured and directed towards neo-liberal 'reforms', i.e., away from state investment-led industrialization towards wholesale liberalization and opening up to international trade and capital flows. As country after country was pushed into undertaking deep unilateral liberalization and opening their economies to both trade and foreign investment, the earlier attempts at independent development and delinking from domination by metropolitan capital through expansion of state investment were brought to a close for many countries in the developing world. It gave way to 'control of fiscal deficits' by curtailing government spending and what has been termed the 'deflationary bias' that accompanies liberalization, and which, in effect, 'keeps employment and output growth below their potential'.[27]

Such a shift could not, however, have taken place without the acquiescence and even, in several cases, enthusiastic support from the ruling sections within the developing countries, although in some of the earlier liberalizing countries, it was forced through by military means.[28]

Internal Support Base of Liberalization in a Developing Country: The Case of India

In the case of India, many had long argued (during the state led industrialization period) that the absence of basic land reforms or the redistribution of agricultural surpluses would set limits to the growth of the domestic market and domestic industry and ultimately constrain the path of industrial development. Some had also argued that the narrow social base of the Indian capitalist class had led to an alliance with landed feudal elements that predetermined the failure of land reform. It was further argued that in the first two decades after independence, the nature of state led capitalism had favoured the growth of monopolistic sections, who maintained a dual relationship of conflict and increasing collusion with metropolitan capital.[29] The latter arguments were, in the main, articulated at a political level and often dismissed by acadaemia in the heyday of import substitution, state regulation and investment in industrial development, when economic ties with the USSR and non-alignment as foreign policy was accompanied by socialist rhetoric. Recent analysis, however, suggests that the early argument about a dual relationship with metropolitan capital was not as far-fetched as used to be made out.

As argued by Ghosh and Chandrashekhar, the processes that led to a change in the stance of Indian capitalists towards embracing the neo-liberal programme included 'the sluggish growth of the home market in the 15 years starting in the mid-1960s'.[30] They argue that the entrenched monopolistic interests, which had benefited the most and grown under the earlier regime, then sought a new stimulus to industrial expansion and a new basis for their capital accumulation by entering export markets. This entailed and therefore inclined them towards collaboration with metropolitan capital as a junior partner, and acceptance of some loosening of the frontiers of Indian markets in return. The proliferation of the capitalist class that had taken place during the import substitution era included sections that came up in product groups and areas outside the traditional bases of existing monopolistic groups or in ancillary sectors. Some of them had accumulated capital through trade (particularly in sectors where high profits were available through the black market). Others accumulated substantial sums from speculation in the stock market which 'came into its own' in the late 1970s. Some grew out of the small-scale sector for which 870 products were reserved and even new regional business groups had emerged in agriculturally successful districts. Among these sections there were many who 'were interested in the abolition of state regulations which offered protection to traditional oligopoly and wanted to use foreign collaboration as a means of entry into the industrial sector'. Some had accumulated sufficient capital for large-scale production and were less averse to import competition. Further, the urban middle classes and more prosperous rural farming groups along with a 'qualitatively significant number of people from among the Indian elites' actually becoming residents abroad contributed to consumerist demands for opening up the economy. Since such developments took place in the context of an economy with low but unequally distributed incomes and low purchasing power among a major part of the population, higher returns were sought in new products (with greater import content) catering to higher income groups. All this fed a growing predilection among emerging powerful groups and classes towards deregulation and opening up of the economy.

At the same time, proliferation of the capitalist class within the country, while contributing to 'a broadening of the base upon which the entire capitalist order rests', had also led to 'a relative decline of the weight of established big business'. In seeking reversal of such a decline, established big business also sought opening up of economic space within the economy through the elimination of anti-monopoly legislation, removal of licensing requirements, removal of reservation for small capitalists and the public sector, privatization of profitable public sector units, and so on. These were, in fact, the very substance of the reforms in industry that were introduced in 1991 that formally pushed through the changed policy paradigm. It bears mention that neo-liberal policy prescriptions were brought in and applauded by the very sections who had earlier been the votaries and adherents of the earlier import substitution and state regulation oriented regime, suggesting that the long standing arguments regarding the dual character of the Indian capitalist class had some basis. At the same time it opens the doors of debate as to whether the national capitalist classes in developing countries are today willing or capable of deepening the decolonization process or promoting an independent growth and development trajectory.

FROM DECOLONIZATION TO LIBERALIZATION: THE SITUATION OF WORKERS IN INDIA

Despite a degree of resistance and contention among sections of the above-mentioned groups regarding some specific aspects of neo-liberal reform policies, such as withdrawals of agricultural subsidies or the specifics of tariff reductions on imports, one issue that united all of them was liberalization's reform agenda in relation to labour laws. This unanimity appeared again and again in the several reports on Indian industry and the economy, from committees constituted by the government as well as various chambers of commerce and industry and other such associations.[31] All of them advocated curtailment of the rights of trade unions, lifting of prohibitions on use of contract labour even in perennial forms of work, removal of legal restrictions on retrenchment and closures of factories and, generally, opposition to regulation of their dealings with workers by labour law enforcement inspectors.

Organized Labour

The evolution of these labour laws in independent India had its roots in the several phases of working class unrest from the 1920s onwards, which dovetailed into the national movement for independence. In particular, the dramatic upsurge in industrial actions in the 1940s had played an important role in placing workers' rights on the agenda of independent India's government policy. This was reflected in the Constitution as part of the 'Directive Principles of State Policy', aspects of which were translated into legislation. Where enforced, it was mostly due to the presence of organizations of workers and where conditions favoured greater bargaining powers for them. In essence, this meant relatively large-scale industries and services, which by virtue of being covered by state records and regulations came to be known as the organized or formal sector.[32] Constituting the principal area of growth in the early state-led industrialization period, large-scale or organized industry had doubled its number of workers from 3 million in 1961 to 7.78 million in 1981, and its share of industrial employment had grown from 15 per cent to 31 per cent across the same period.

Women workers had been largely excluded from such independent industrialization generated employment and increasingly marginalized in the larger industrialized sectors inherited from the colonial era, such as textiles or mines, although they continued to predominate in plantations.[33] For women in India, it was essentially education in particular, higher education, and not employment that brought access to the development engendered by independence. State-guided development accorded an important role to the state in promoting education and, in a sense, education was perhaps the principal avenue through which women were drawn into the modern forms of employment, increasingly in the service sector. Since education did not generally reach anywhere near universal levels and was not free of class, caste and gender bias, in terms of both access and content, its benefits reached a relatively narrow strata of women in a narrow range of occupations. Thus in the organized sector, community, social and personal services had become the principal employment category for women, accounting for well over half of women's jobs in the organized sector. The significant expansion of public sector services in areas such as the banking industry also opened opportunities for educated women to reach critical mass levels of employment, visible at least in the teaching and white-collar clerical occupations within the organized sector. Further, with the growth of modern light industries, some doors to entry into industrial employment had also opened for women by the 1980s, particularly in garments, electronics and pharmaceuticals.

From the mid-1960s, as the pace of industrialization slowed down, private capital sought to move out of many of the older and large employer industries in search of greater profits in new sectors, including conversion of productive assets into commercial real estate for quick gains. At the same time, mounting corporate tax arrears and a flourishing parallel black economy added to the weakening of the state's resource ability to push industrialization and generate greater demand for manufactured goods, compounded by recession in the advanced capitalist world in the 1970s. Half-hearted attempts to bring internal discipline within the capitalist class remained relatively ineffective and a drive for closures, retrenchment, and falling real wages generated conditions for widespread industrial unrest. These were dealt with in part through legislation restricting retrenchment and closures and in part through repression on workers' agitations.[34] From the watershed years of the 1970s, the 1980s saw declines in the proportions and influence of organized sector workers. It was a period marked by attrition in industrial relations and protracted lockouts and strikes in several industries. Staying power determined the final outcome, which was widespread retrenchment and closures of several major industries from the late 1980s into the 1990s, strikingly illustrated by the closure of textile mills in all the major centres of the industry.[35] As the strength and influence of the organized sector itself declined, the balance of power shifted further away from organized labour. By the 1990s, the sphere of influence of organized labour had, to a great extent, become confined to the public sector, where workers and employment were now threatened by the privatization drive. Supporters of liberalization thus targeted what was in fact only a skeleton of protections for labour in the form of labour laws, which now came principally to embody potential protections for the informal and contract workers on the fringes of large-scale industry, and the increasing numbers of largely yet-to-be-organized workers in the new medium and small-scale industries.

Nevertheless, in testimony to widespread popular resistance to such reforms, outright deregulation in the sphere of labour laws through parliamentary legislation has proved difficult for liberalizers, even as overall economic policies, and close links between the bureaucracy, political elites and private business interests have been undermining the ability of workers to resist backdoor or de facto deregulation. Despite its weakening force, there can be little doubt that organized labour in India has become the principal spearhead of mounting opposition to the liberalization policies over the last ten years. A striking feature of organized labour's resistance, particularly against privatization, has been the visibly increased numbers and presence of women workers in the several protest actions from local to national levels that have marked the period of economic reforms in India.

Unorganized Sector Workers

The situation of workers in the unorganized sector has of course always been less visible, being more atomized and dispersed. Despite their heterogeneity and scale of employment far outstripping the organized sector, it is necessary to recognize that the conditions of work, the nature of work, and wages in the unorganized sector are linked in several fundamental ways to developments in organized industry, to the path of development and industrialization and to the role of the state. In agriculture, state-aided private investment within an unreformed agrarian structure had led to a situation of regional concentration of growth, with a minority of capitalist landlords and rich peasants raising their level of income, while the majority of labourers and poor peasants stagnated at the margin of subsistence. This, in turn, made for debt and bondage at one extreme, and at the other, the emergence of an exploitative labour contractor regime to supply seasonal workers from more backward regions to more commercially developed areas of agriculture. In traditional manufacturing industries such as handloom, with the state providing only limited fund support and marketing facilities, wage and income levels sank even lower than of agricultural labour, creating conditions for 'downward occupational mobility and degradation of human resources, de-skilling and ruthless exploitation'.[36]

From the 1970s, however, employment in small-scale unorganized industries began to rise rapidly, topping large-scale industries by 1.76 million in 1981 and by 5.46 million within the next decade to form 48 per cent of all industrial employment and over 62 per cent of industrial wage employment by 1991.[37] By 2001, unorganized manufacturing accounted for the employment of around 85 per cent of manufacturing workers.[38] A significant portion of unorganized industry has grown around the periphery of modern industrial organizations through subcontracting (including into the home-based sector), utilization of machines from organized industries, and is dependent on large-scale industries for much of the raw materials utilized in production. It also acts as a pre-processing conduit for the supply of raw materials to modern industry, such as in the case of leather products. Further, it has a significant role to play in manufactured exports such as garments. Nevertheless, it is universally characterized by evasion of labour laws and degraded conditions of work and wages.

Through the years of state-led industrialization, the majority of women workers lived and worked in a mix of semi-marketized, semi-monetized, non-contractual or only partially contractual economic subsistence activities. Such activities and relations within and outside their household, were concentrated in agriculture or petty production and services, and the benefits of industrialization were at best peripheral to their situation and perhaps reached them only via their menfolk or through relatively limited forms of state support to small producers and welfare organizations. Initial avenues of development- generated wage employment for uneducated women could perhaps be located in the highly exploitative and unorganized construction and related sectors. In general, even such employment reached them over relatively more tortuous depths of immiserization and displacement from the traditional economy that have since delineated women's subaltern status in employment structures. It was such a situation that led to the disproportionate weight of the unorganized sector in the female labour force, which came to be recognized as a defining feature of women's employment from the mid-1970s onwards.

Whereas in organized sector manufacturing, women now account for 18 per cent of employment (in 2004), in unorganized manufacturing their share is around 34 per cent, showing a decline of half a percentage point over the 1990s. Of course, most of the women workers in unorganized manufacturing fall into the category of unpaid family workers; however, even among hired workers, their number is 1,308,285, accounting for 93 per cent of all hired women workers in manufacturing.[39] The reality is that many of the existing labour laws should be (in terms of their own definitions) applicable to most of the workers in unorganized manufacturing. In fact, poor enforcement has ensured that they are not applied even in urban areas, and urban manufacturers have been among the most vociferous in demanding curtailment of inspection by the labour law enforcement machinery.

Impact of Liberalization on Employment

At an overall level, the period of reforms has witnessed a sharp decrease in the rate of employment generation in India. In rural India, the rate of employment growth was 'as low as two-thirds of a per cent over the period 1993-1994 to 1999-2000 . . . less than one- third the rate of the previous period 1998-1988 to 1993-1994, it was also less than half the rate of growth in the labour force in the same period . . . [and] the lowest rate of growth of rural employment in post-Independence history'.[40] But even in urban areas the rate of growth of employment came down from 3.39 per cent per annum between 1987-1988 to 1993-1994 to 2.27 per cent between 1993-1994 and 1999-2000, while the pace of urbanization slowed down.[41] Clearly export growth in manufactures, which did increase in the 1990s, and enlargement of private corporate investment ('by enough to increase the overall investment rate despite sizeable reduction in the share of public investment in GDP') have not led to increases in employment growth rates. This is especially reflected in the decline in the industry's share of total employment, 'with manufacturing employment stagnant in the unorganized sector, an increase in smaller classes of organized-sector firms (across a wide array of industries), and a decline in the largest organized sector'.[42] The downward pressures that such an employment scenario has exerted on the incomes and work conditions of workers, particularly in the unorganized sector, has been documented by several field studies.[43] Its adverse effects on women workers appear quite starkly in the data collected for this study.

At one level, such a closure of earlier employment expansion in rural areas in India has been attributed to a combination of liberalization policies that had reversed the public programmes and policies of the 1980s that had contributed to more employment in rural areas across that decade. Cuts in social spending, particularly in education, health and sanitation, had reduced what had become an important source of employment, and financial liberalization measures effectively reduced the availability of rural credit.[44] Additionally, with import liberalization, deteriorating conditions have also been attributed to a 'macroeconomic consequence of globalization in the downward pressure on agricultural prices at a world level'[45] (whose adverse effects on developing countries have been compounded by continued and large state subsidies to agriculture in the developed countries, while developing countries have been forced to withdraw their own subsidies under the World Trade Organization (WTO) regime). At the same time, increasingly clear evidence has emerged of a steep decline in the levels of food absorption in India across the 1990s, to levels 'last seen during the early years of the Second World War, which included the years of the terrible Bengal famine'.[46] A key policy element responsible for such a situation was of course the erosion of the public distribution system in the 1990s under neo-liberal prescription, but it also reflects the real decline in income to below subsistence levels of very large segments of the country's labouring poor.

In urban areas too, despite growth of exports and emergence of new industries, the ground realities of experience of workers in India have been of large-scale closures. A significant if not the sole reason has been import penetration following the lifting of quantitative restrictions and lowering of tariffs on imports. It is often argued that any displacement in local industry would be countered by overall growth-generated employment. That this has not occurred is evident from the employment statistics. But even more importantly, such an argument ignores the fact that those who get displaced are not necessarily, and in fact not generally, the same as those who find employment in new sectors. The deep social and economic degradation experienced by displaced workers and its effects on their entire families where the labour of many in far worse conditions tends to replace the labour of one or two is a reality that remains invisible in the statistics. In fact, what is worse is that often even that option is not available.

Fears of displacement and deindustrialization due to increasing import penetration had been dismissed by some on the grounds that after an initial surge in imports between 1993-1994 and 1995-1996, thereafter import growth decelerated in value terms, and India's trade balance seemed to improve towards the end of the 1990s.[47] As shown by Chandrashekhar and Ghosh, however, 'the quantum index of imports more than doubled' between 1996 and 1999, the actual volume of commodity imports thus increased substantially, and 'in real terms the flow of imports was stronger than the flow of exports after the mid-1990s'.[48] Such a phenomenon having occurred even in a period of narrowing trade deficit could only be explained by a sharp fall in the unit value of imports into India. It has been argued that in the case of manufactured commodities, this was due to 'imports of capital goods, raw material, intermediates and components being sourced from abroad by transnational producers'. Some of these corporations had established themselves in the early half of the 1990s and 'displaced Indian brands based on manufacturing facilities established in India', but 'ended up creating production or assembly capacities that were far in excess of what was warranted'. For them 'it is possible that the transfer prices on imports, sourced from the parent or a third country subsidiary, were reduced to facilitate the drive to retain and increase market shares in the sluggish domestic market'.[49] In other words, there was a double displacement of workers in local industry at the finished goods level through entry of multinational producers, as well as of other local producers including ancillary industries through imports of intermediaries. Such an argument reflected and still reflects ground realities of the new dominance of multinational brands in the India, as well as widespread displacement of workers, some evidence of which also comes out in the sectoral studies in this volume.

GLOBALIZED PRODUCTION AND THE INTERNATIONAL DIVISION OF LABOUR

A significant growth of firms based in one country but operating in several, or the rise of multinational corporations, was one of the features of the post-war developments in capitalism in the developed world. For example, the number of foreign affiliates of US corporations had risen 'from about seven-and-a-half thousands in 1950 to over twenty-three thousands in 1966, mostly in Western Europe and the western hemisphere'.[50] But in the following period, the sheer scale of operations of some of these firms reached gigantic international proportions. Such expansion was facilitated by the technological revolution, which now allowed for 'centralized coordination' of geographically dispersed production units and the growth of 'a transnational process of manufacture', while reducing costs of transport and communication made it economically feasible. This naturally reinforced the tendency of capital to concentrate on an international scale, and much of what appeared as imports and exports across national frontiers was in fact internal trade within individual multinational corporations. By 1960, estimates placed the share of the sales of the two hundred largest firms as 17 per cent of the GNP of that sector of the world, and by 1984 at 26 per cent.[51] Further, the increasing practice of 'locational break up' of production by such corporations, the separation of its elements according to different types of skill requirements or the 'segmentation of production processes' into geographically dispersed parts was also associated with increased intra-industry trade across borders.

Manufacturing Exports from Developing Countries and the 'New International Division of Labour'

Till the 1970s the share of sale of manufactured products between industrialized developed countries themselves had continued to rise. Some three-fifths of their manufactures were sold to each other in the mid-1950s, rising to three-quarters in the early 1970s.[52] But then the developed world began to export somewhat more of its manufactures to developing countries and also import a part of its manufactured products from there. From the mid-1960s, corporations located in the developed countries had already begun to expand some of their manufacturing activities in the developing world as well. This was particularly so in some labour-intensive industries, such as textiles, garments and electronics assembly, where a tendency to employ women workers was marked, and where possibilities of reducing relative wages in their own countries through technological enhancement of labour productivity were limited. By the early 1980s, this phenomenon led to the thesis that a 'new' international division of labour (NIDL) had emerged. This was seen as replacing the 'old' international division of labour under colonialism, where the imperialist powers produced manufactured goods and the colonial world was exploited for its raw materials. The new division was held to be a consequence of the generation of 'a world market for production sites and for labour which embraces both the traditional industrialized and the underdeveloped countries'.[53] Developing country manufactured exports directed at the 'world market' dominated by the developed world were of course recognized to be largely limited to a few labour-intensive sectors where clearly cheaper wages were the main attraction for shifting production sites there by developed country firms.

However, the capacities and actual diffusion of such production sites in terms of developing regions and countries, were much more limited and uneven than was assumed in NIDL theories. On the one hand, 'the world market factories' in the developing world were largely peripheral to the accumulation process in the developed world, which continued to be either predominantly in the technologically advanced industrial sectors and in the controlling processes which were located within the industrially advanced countries and increasingly through speculation and the operations of internationalized finance. On the other hand, their role even within the economies of the developing world, with a few exceptions, was not central to the production or accumulation process there, where home markets and the state continued to play an important role in industrial development and capital accumulation. In fact, even in the 1990s, by the end of which transnational production was seen to have further expanded, it was pointed out that 'when taken as a whole internationalized production is still quite modest, at most 10 per cent of total production'.[54] In any case, 'world market factories' did not and still do not employ more than a small fraction of the labour force in developing countries, whose larger layers, overall characteristics (particularly in relation to gender) and relations with domestic classes—including the continuing force of semi-feudal or pre-capitalist social relations in most countries—found no place in NIDL theories.

Nevertheless, there can be no denying that some relocation of manufacturing from developed to developing countries was taking place along the subcontracting as well as foreign direct investment routes, and at somewhat greater pace from the latter half of the 1980s as trade liberalization became more widespread. If between 1970 and 1983, the share of developing countries in manufacturing exports more than doubled, from 5 per cent to over 10 per cent, by 1997 it was more than 26 per cent. Of some note, however, is the fact that despite the decline in the share of developed industrial countries in world manufacturing exports from 82 per cent to 71 per cent between 1980 and 1997, their share in world manufacturing income rose in the same period from 64 per cent to 73 per cent. [55]

Apart from the labour-intensive and therefore comparatively 'lower value-added' nature of developing country manufacturing exports, one of the reasons advanced for this growing disparity in income has been increased competition among developing countries for a share in a market for manufactures that is bounded and controlled by firms from the developed world. Thus, accompanying the spread of such export manufacturing across a larger number of developing countries, the unit values for many of their exports actually fell in the above period, which of course has adverse implications for their workers in several ways.[56] The other aspect of the low value of exports, where driven by foreign direct investment (FDI), was also that in such cases 'a significant part of the value added effectively accrues as profits to the multinational corporations that organize such production'.[57] Further, it is also clear that the major increases in manufacturing exports are confined to a relatively small number of developing countries. For example, it appears that just thirteen countries accounted for 88 per cent of manufactured exports of developing countries in 1996 from an already high 73 per cent in 1980.[58]

Fallout of Export Orientation: Resurgence of Old Colonial Patterns

The growing emphasis on export orientation in developing countries has another side relating to primary agricultural commodities, which has been more pervasive in its influence. Agricultural trade still accounts for a very significant proportion of exports of developing countries, and is being presented by liberalizers as an important avenue of development today. This is quite in contrast to the post-war decolonization era, when developing countries were trying to break out of primary commodity export dependence and seeking to diversify their economies in various ways, in order to avoid the problems of volatility, secular price declines and so on that were seen to be typical of primary commodity markets in world trade (quite apart from the felt need to focus on feeding their own populations). In fact, the Uruguay Round GATT agreement that brought the WTO into existence was actually negotiated with the dominating perception of agricultural exports (and also textiles and garments exports) as the principal means to increase incomes and employment in the developing world.

At the same time, a feature of trade liberalization and 'loan-conditional adjustment' that has been observed by Utsa Patnaik is the reappearance, from the 1980s, of 'an inverse relation between primary exports and domestic absorption of food grains' as happened during colonial times, suggesting that some of the features of the 'old' colonial division of labour are being revived.[59] The reasons for such a reappearance have been attributed to 'non-expansionary economic policies of the neo-liberal regime', which imply cuts in rural investment expenditures in developing countries. The argument is that growth of domestic demand is restrained by income-deflating policies and by opening the agricultural sector to the restructuring pull of 'global demand patterns'. Such global demand is 'asymmetric' and concentrated in the 'high-income developed countries' which enjoy a 'highly diversified consumption basket' largely drawn from the tropical or sub-tropical regions, where the earth's 'botanic diversity' is concentrated. This then leads to a diversion of resources in developing countries in these regions to export crops at the expense of food grains consumable by the mass of their population and results in fall in per head consumption of food grains, which is similar to what happened in colonial times.[60]

If export orientation in agriculture has shown a resurgence of one aspect of old colonial patterns, import liberalization, which characterizes the new global trade regime under the WTO, has seen a resurgence of the old deindustrialization process in several developing countries, as imports from the developed world displace local manufactures and local employment. Deregulated imports into the South have been displacing 'small-scale and highly employment intensive domestic producers' who are unable to compete in international markets. In most developing countries, the consequent job losses have simply not been compensated for by expansion in export employment, even where exports have grown significantly. Thus, it is argued that 'the net expansion in manufacturing employment becomes low, or even negative, because of the effects of import penetration'.[61] Additional displacement of local producers for the domestic markets by more capital intensive and therefore less employment generating FDI driven production, has also contributed to large-scale losses of employment. While many tend to overemphasize the importance of FDI to developing countries, what perhaps also needs to be noted is that despite bursts of FDI inflows into some developing countries, the 'historical pattern of the North largely investing in the North' has not been altered.[62] Liberalization-inspired globalization in the current era therefore carries within its ambit both old and new patterns of division of labour between the advanced capitalist core countries and the underdeveloped regions of the world, within an intrinsic pattern of expanding domination by and for the metropolitan core.

Globalization of Finance

Superimposed and spread over the developments in global production organization has been the enormous growth of a form of finance capital that is relatively autonomous of direct linkages with actual production and merchandise trade. With only 2 per cent of cross-border financial flows being trade-related, and with the daily volume of foreign exchange transactions having risen to the order of U.S. $1.49 trillion per day by the late 1990s (more than ten times world GDP in 1998), in it is now widely accepted that the driving force and new feature of the current period of increased interaction and interdependence between economics has been the emergence of the globalization of capital in the form of finance. What has been termed as the 'pyramidal growth of finance', the 'fluidity' of its movement across the globe and its rise to 'a position of dominance' has become the unique feature of globalization, distinguishing it from earlier phases of global integration.[63] It is worth noting here that the enormous influence that is exerted by proponents of neo-liberalism in directing policy in so many countries is based precisely on the force and power acquired by internationalized finance, whose interests have been furthered immensely by liberalization on a global scale.

Rise of the Private International Financial System

The phenomenal growth of the private international financial system from the 1960s was, of course, linked to a combination of factors including the rise of offshore finance, i.e., the holding of accounts in currencies that are not of the country in which the bank is located, which has been said to demonstrate vividly 'the way in which the capitalist economy escaped from national, or any other control'.[64] On the one hand, there was accumulation of an enormous amount of liquidity in metropolitan banks where the oil profits of OPEC countries were also generally deposited. On the other hand as discussed earlier, the build-up of dollar assets outside the United States particularly in 'offshore' centres in Europe (due to the unrestricted expenditures by the United States abroad particularly for military purposes), had led to the breakdown of the Bretton Woods system of pre-specified rates for the dollar against gold.[65] This in turn fuelled speculation in currency transactions and led to 'multiplying floods of unattached capital that washed round the globe from currency to currency, looking for quick profits due to which governments lost control over exchange rates and the world money supply.'[66] Increased liquidity propelled these banks to search for new avenues for keeping their capital in circulation. Initial avenues of investment were found in a consumer credit and housing finance boom in the developed industrial nations, and when 'opportunities there petered out,' they expanded their reach to high interest credit to developing countries. In the meantime, financial liberalization in the developed countries from the 1970s increased the *flexibility* of the operation of their banking and financial institutions, generated a whole new set of financial institutions that 'were not subject to regulations', provided space for *securitization*, or 'capital flows in the form of stocks and bonds rather than loans', and led to the 'autonomous creation' by the financial system of a whole range of speculative instruments through which high profits were earned.[67] With the slowdown in the productive economy of developed countries, capital and savings there tended to shift away from investment in production to investment in financial markets which now promised higher rates of return.

All this greatly increased competition within the financial system involving necessarily a search for new markets and new avenues of investment. It was at such a time that several developing countries acquired the status of 'emerging markets' for the global financial order, as when third world government debt reached crisis proportions and no longer appeared so attractive to investors, liberalization was pushed through (usually by the IMF sponsored Structural Adjustment Polices [SAP]). This opened developing country financial markets to international debt and equity flows into the private sector, including the privatizing public sector. And since the interest rates on foreign exchange deposits in developing countries are much higher compared to what prevails internationally, it has been pointed out that 'even the meanest rentier who is incapable of making a speculative 'kill' still does pretty well by bringing in finance into the third world economy'.[68]

International Finance and the Third World

The availability of international finance was seen as an opportunity by several developing countries that were otherwise strapped for foreign exchange, which in turn made them undertake a package of policies to provide an appropriately liberal environment all round in order to attract foreign investors. These included cuts in corporate taxes, liberalization of trade and reduction in import tariffs, all leading to further constraints in mobilization of resources by the state. It also meant cuts in public expenditure and investment, with adverse consequences for employment, growth rate, social expenditure, the state of infrastructure and so on, leading to or aggravating demand constraints within their economies. Since the stepping up of government investment gives rise to expectations of inflation and currency depreciation and a lowering of the value of financial assets held in that particular currency, international finance is inherently averse to any form of state interventionism in the form of expansionary public investment. As a result, where capital flowed in, retaining 'investor confidence' or fears of 'capital flight' ensured that even when in the midst of recession, governments did not step up expenditures to stimulate recovery. The possibilities of 'autonomous action by the state for promoting growth' in developing countries, was thus increasingly broken down, and as financial liberalization swept across a wide range of developing countries, it provided increased opportunity for volatile flows of 'hot money' to roam across wider spaces in search of quick and speculative gains, now able to instantaneously move across borders on the basis of differences in expected profitability.

Where globalization of finance capital initially took the form of metropolitan banks giving loans to countries including in the third world, liberalization then led to the opening of what were earlier protected economies to 'free movements' of not only goods but also of finance. This, in turn, gave rise to the ascendancy of 'the current form of international finance capital', with its 'enormous mobility' and 'appetite for speculative gains'. Although such finance capital remains dominated by the overwhelming weight of capital originating in the advanced capitalist countries (including speculative financial operations by MNCs that hold productive assets), it has drawn into its fold financial interests originating from developing countries as well. This in turn has led to further shifts in the stance of such interests away from autonomous development towards a common cause with internationalized finance capital. Primarily dislodged by such a shift were the remnants of redistributive developmental agendas in several third world countries that had grown out of the democratizing urges of decolonization. Neo-liberalism replaced such agendas, which were located in and dependent on the architecture of national economies and premised on the state playing an activist role in the economy, with increasing conservatism in relation to state investment and increasing libertarianism in relation to the operations of private capital of foreign and local origin. Both had and continue to have adverse repercussions on the conditions of life and work of the labouring poor in third world countries.

Intrinsic Dichotomies in the Globalization of Finance

That the globalization of finance has created conditions for stagnation in the real economy, including in the developed world, as the scope for earlier 'full employment' promotion or demand management by the state has receded, is quite widely accepted.[69] This has led to some believing that the imperialist characteristics of metropolitan core capitalist countries have receded with the growth of international finance. As argued by Prabhat Patnaik, however, 'in the era of global finance' there is inbuilt 'an intrinsically dichotomous effect upon the two segments of the globe', that is, between the metropolitan core capitalist countries and the third world. For while there was 'scope for growth of a certain nature in the advanced capitalist world … [its] nature was such that instead of pulling up the third world, it had the opposite effect of smothering the latter.' He argues that although the ascendance of finance and expanded earnings from financial and speculative investments acted as a dampener on real productive investment in plant and machinery in the developed countries leading to a shift from productive to financial asset holding, *demand* in the advanced capitalist countries increased owing to credit-financed consumption and also owing to extremely high fiscal deficits and government spending maintained by the United States in the Reagan era.[70] Further, he points out that although the United States was considered to be the 'locomotive' pulling up the activity of the world capitalist economy,[71] such a 'locomotive' theory was 'clearly inapplicable' to much of the third world, particularly Latin America and large parts of Africa, where output growth slowed down considerably, largely due to 'highly adverse terms of trade for primary commodities'. The basis of such an argument is that in the developed countries as a whole, even as additions to productive capacity were very little and in fact scrapping of productive assets took place leading to high and even increasing unemployment, 'the rate of capacity utilization increased and with it profit margins in the manufacturing sectors'. According to him, it is this rise in profit margins that was primarily responsible for 'the sharp shift in terms of trade against primary commodities' in the 1980s that 'unleashed economic retrogression in vast tracts of Africa and Latin America'.

The second dichotomous effect noted by him is caused by the fact that given the manner in which growth is achieved in the advanced capitalist centres (i.e., due to rising capacity utilization along with scrapping of productive assets) 'the system still remains demand constrained' both in times of boom and intensified in times of recession. 'There is in all seasons, therefore, an attempt to find markets elsewhere at the expense of other producers, producers who are smaller, weaker and with less staying power, that is, at the expense of producers in the backward economies'. This accelerates the pace of centralization of capital on a world scale which 'shows itself within the backward economies as a process of deindustrialization'. Such deindustrialization and centralization of capital in production 'dovetails' with the operations of finance whose independent operations in developing countries act as a spur. He points out that deindustrialization may be caused through provision of credit to investment projects by international finance in order to import equipment thereby displacing the domestic equipment producers. It may be through the pouring in of finance for purely speculative purposes, pushing up the value of the domestic currency and enlarging on the whole the magnitude of imports, which would necessarily entail deindustrialization. Further, when finance starts or threatens to move out, the country 'is forced to adopt a whole series of measures to entice foreign exchange to stay within its shores, measures which include selling off rights over mineral and other natural resources for a song, selling off public sector assets at throwaway prices, making prime land available to rentiers, etc.' or in other words a process of 'denationalization' of the country's assets.[72] In sum, he argues that the globalization of finance does not democratically distribute stagnation and retrogression across all countries, and in fact aggravates the 'hiatus' and inequalities between advanced and backward capitalist worlds while stripping the latter of their national assets, all of which has been the longstanding characteristic of imperialism.[73]

From the above argument, it would appear that the operations of globalized finance have anchored a process of expanding manufacturing incomes in the developed countries with adverse effects on developing-country primary commodity producers, accelerated centralization of capital on a worldwide scale and deindustrialization within backward economies, and compelled a process of denationalization of the assets of third world countries. Seemingly so distant, intangible and unrelated to the immediate world of the labouring poor in our own country, the effects of such activities of finance cuts deeply into their daily lives in several ways. In recent years, workers in the agricultural sector have been hard hit by the sharp fall in crop prices, while manufacturing workers, particularly small-scale and informal-sector workers have of course been adversely affected by deindustrialization in terms of loss of employment. Equally important for them are the effects of denationalization, as public resources are diverted away from actual and potential possibilities of providing for even basic necessities and infrastructure for the assetless and poor. For it is they who are most in need of provisions from public resources, their civic needs having become enhanced with the further waning of the natural economy in rural areas and the inevitable growth of their dependence on socially provided civic amenities in urban areas. Such needs, linked more often than not with natural resources, were more accommodated by nationalized public enterprise and systems of distribution. And since women generally bear the brunt of filling in for the lack of civic amenities with extra labour, they are amongst the most adversely affected.

Financial Crises and Their Effects on Women Workers

Several commentators have pointed to increased 'systemic risk' in the global financial system in recent years as increasingly 'the investment decisions of a few individuals in a few institutions virtually determines the nature of the exposure of the global financial system' with 'unregulated entities making huge profits on highly speculative investments' at its core. Even the more regulated entities such as banks are deeply entangled through increased lending to such unregulated entities, rendering 'the system more crisis prone'.[74] Across the 1990s there has been further consolidation and centralization of financial capital through mergers and acquisitions, and the series of crises that swept through several developing countries over the last ten years, have provided ample evidence of the increased 'systemic risk' inherent in globalization of finance, to which they have become exposed.[75] Providing a case study of the Asian financial crisis (1997-1999), the 1999 World Survey of Women in Development highlighted the effects of such crises on developing country workers in the form of large-scale retrenchment, sharp increases in urban unemployment, wage reductions alongside inflation, rising destitution in rural areas that were dependent on urban worker remittances and precipitous decline in purchasing power of the poor. On women workers, its adverse effects were 'amplified because of gender inequalities in labour markets', with the sectors and firms with concentrations of women workers being harder hit by the crisis, the overall tendency to fire women workers first, and fall in earnings in the informal sector as declining family incomes pushed more women into overcrowded informal sector work. Other commentators have highlighted the process of centralization of capital propelling such crisis within the realm of finance and leading to centralization of capital in the realm of the real economy, through takeover of productive assets (of both private and public sectors) by multinational corporations of the developed world.

CONCEPTUAL DISCOURSES ON GLOBALIZATION AND WOMEN'S EMPLOYMENT: THE INDIAN EXPERIENCE

Responses to the Discourse on Feminization of Labour

In the 1980s, the concept of 'feminization' of labour had emerged to somewhat loosely capture the characteristic features of changes taking place in what is called the labour market, as national statutory regulations gave way increasingly to market regulation and globalization. Particularly in the background of some developing countries emerging as export manufacturing hubs with increasing proportions of women workers in export-oriented garment and electronics industries, feminization of labour became a central concept around which much of the gender-oriented discourses on the impact of globalization proceeded.[76]

The conception of feminization of labour included two specific connotations. The first was of course identification of a sharp rise in the share of women in paid employment through either taking over jobs earlier done by men or, due to relatively faster expansion of sectors (particularly in manufacturing) where female workers predominated. The second connotation included the advance of more generalized precariousness in forms of employment. This was considered to be characteristic of 'flexibilization' policies, or the trend of employers (large and small) to respond to market uncertainties and increased pressure on costs by reducing their core workforce, and relying increasingly on irregular forms of employment in order to avoid paying wages to workers during economic downturns. The attributes of 'flexible' labour leant towards a casual nature of the work contract, lower rates of remuneration, lack of security provided, low access to skill, and so on, all 'characteristics associated with women's historical pattern of labour force participation'.[77]

More recently, studies have been pointing to the accumulating evidence of reversals in the trend of rising shares of female employment, particularly since the mid-1990s and in the very areas where the dramatic rise in female manufacturing employment had provided the initial stimulus for the feminization thesis. Such declines have been attributed to rising skill and capital intensities and technological changes affecting some of the labour- intensive industries, as well as the gradual closing of the gender gap in wages reducing the weight of an important element in the preference for female labour, namely, the lower female wage.[78] Following the East Asian financial crisis (1997-1999), additional evidence has emerged of greater job losses for women in times of crisis, when the 'flexible' characteristics of female employment made women the easiest to remove from employment. On the other side, from some other countries, evidence and arguments have been advanced that in fact defeminization of labour has been more pronounced in the liberalization era, as shifting industries and employment centres led to replacement of socially constrained and therefore less mobile women workers, by more mobile male workers.[79]

Despite a degree of academic debate on feminization in India, the instinctive core of the women's movement reactions to liberalization has continued to remain largely located in the more enduring discourse on marginalization of the majority of women in the industrialization process.[80] This is not without reason as demonstrated by the continuing pattern of low work participation rates of women in India, more pronounced in the urban areas (the seats of perceived enhancement of feminized manufacturing activities associated with globalization) and showing an overall decline in rural India. The percentage of principal status workers among women in the age group 15-59 actually declined from a low 18.7 per cent in 1983 to 18 per cent by 2004 in urban areas, and from 40.1 per cent to 36.3 per cent to in rural areas over the same period. Looking at the share of women in overall principal and subsidiary status employment for the period following the open declaration of liberalization, there too the share of women can be seen to have declined from 33 per cent in 1993-1994 to 32 per cent in 2004.

In March, 2000 (even before the NSS macro-data on falling work participation rates among women across the 1990s became available), reviewing their experience of the impact of structural adjustment policies and globalization on women's social and economic status, a joint platform of several women's organizations and groups identified loss of women's jobs through mechanization, cuts in government-initiated employment and reduction of local employment provided by domestic enterprises as the dominant phenomenon. They argued that 'SAP has had a differential impact and increased stratification among working women' with only 'a minority of urban educated women' having benefited from better employment opportunities.[81] The broad consensus among practically all women's groups in India is that more and more women are *in need* of employment or paid work. Such needs have reached critical levels in the globalization era as the subsistence and food economy of poorer households has become more pressurized due to increasing closure before advancing marketization in food production and distribution.[82] Not surprisingly, in a country where chronic hunger and malnutrition remains widespread, but where per capita food grain output and absorption has dropped in the liberalization era to below that of 50 years ago, growing food insecurity has been the central issue in the women's movement's response to liberalization.[83]

According to the above mentioned joint platform of women's organizations, 'because of their special place in the domestic economy' as the main providers of food within the family, women have to bear an 'unequal burden' of any reduction in food availability. And yet, coping with higher prices, higher unemployment and reduced food availablility has meant that women are looking for extra work often in most menial jobs, while simultaneously spending more time and effort in procuring food.[84] Among activist sections of the movement in India, the thesis of feminization of labour in the form of increased actual employment availability for women, thus, seems to have found little resonance.

Nevertheless, in more academic circles, the feminization debate has continued. Within the debates, supporters of liberalization and globalization have tended to emphasize (and search for signs of) the first connotation as a positive sign of employment opportunity gains for women. Equivocators generally perceive the changes under way as opening opportunities for some women and closing of the same for others, but conclude that the course of women's own agency and intervention must be directed towards exploration of perceived opportunities within the framework of liberalization. Opponents have emphasized the second connotation arguing that the forces that propel women into such exploitative conditions of work lie in the increasing burden of poverty or declining incomes of the majority in the era of liberalization, and called for fundamental change in policy.

The Informal Sector and Women Workers: Earlier Perspectives and Current Realities

Implicit in arguments regarding feminization as well as marginalization lies the related issue of expansion of what is termed the informal sector and its increasing size and weight in women's work and employment. Having evolved out of observation of self-employed forms of work and economic activity in the urban setting of some African countries by ILO employment missions, the informal sector was initially considered a defining feature of underdevelopment. Eluding any clear analytical definition, the informal sector 'became synonymous with the kaleidoscope of unregulated, poorly skilled and low-paid workers that the observer encounters when walking through the streets' of towns and cities in developing countries.[85] Its existence and characteristics were thus really defined in contrast and with reference to the formal sector which was supposedly characterized by regular and written contracts and therefore subject to state regulation.

Although before the birth of the concept of the informal sector, the unorganized sector and its workers had been a recognized category in India and even attracted legislative attention from the late 1960s, the concept of the informal sector held great appeal for those interested in bringing the issues of invisible women workers onto the agenda of national policy.[86] It seemed to be able to absorb within itself the experience of lack of clear definition or official record of not only several aspects of women's economic activity, but also major contingents of women workers such as home-based workers. In a sense, the concept played a role in highlighting the fact that vast contingents of working people in developing countries such as India had remained deprived of the benefits of the bare minimum employment security and labour rights that had been hammered into labour laws over years of industrial struggle in more large-scale industries. For women, it acquired even greater significance with the growing realization that declines in women's employment shares had accompanied the evolution of the formal sector in several important industries and that a disproportionately large majority of women workers were concentrated in the more backbreaking forms of labour and work that characterized the informal sector.[87]

Within current debates around the informal sector, however, surprisingly little attention has been given to the fact that across the liberalization decade in India, women's share of informal employment (non-agricultural) is also showing signs of decline. It came down from 21.5 per cent in 1993-1994 to 19.5 per cent in 2004.[88] It appears that the tendency of displacement of women workers in the informal sector has been accentuated under globalization. Advancing mechanization, removal of earlier protections for small-scale industry and alterations in the market for informal sector products because of penetration by large industry have all contributed to this process. Evidence has been piling up of mechanization displacing women in construction.[89] In the petty producer segment of the informal sector, such as handloom workers, liberalization has meant that the system of support for them instituted by the more regulatory regime was dismantled, driving more and more of them out of the market.[90] The beedi industry, where 80 per cent of the workers are women working at home, is facing stagnation and the number of workdays per worker has declined even as the number of beedi workers has increased. In all, it appears that even in harshly exploitative informal sector employment, women workers are facing increasing marginalization.

In the early years of discovery of the informal sector, the focus of women's groups was directed towards elimination of the exploitative conditions of work that characterized the sector through demands for state intervention, extension of labour laws and regulation for wage workers on the one hand. On the other hand, for self-employed women in the informal sector, demands were made for provision of low interest credit through extension of the priority lending schemes of public sector banks, and more supportive measures by the government to ensure supply of raw materials and marketing facilities. Such an approach has come under multiple pressures with the advance of liberalization.

Changing Tracks: Deregulation, Liberalization and Informal Sector Discourses

With the expansion of irregular forms of employment across the world, including in developed countries, and the increasing influence of the neo-liberal policy orientation, some distinct and interrelated changes in practice and approach towards the informal sector, or what is now called the informal economy, have become quite influential.

First, the 'flexibilization' of employment relations, leading to greater use of irregular and informal workers within the formal sector while downsizing more permanent workers, formed an integral part of the shift towards market regulation in place of statutory regulation. Such a shift touched underdeveloped countries, where the base of the formal industrial sector tends to be narrow, as well as the largely formalized industrialized countries of the metropolitan core. In several countries undergoing restructuring towards greater integration with the world market, 'labour market flexibility' was promoted through a series of measures supposedly directed at removal of 'labour market rigidities' and 'constraints' on the free operation of the market in allocation and reallocation of resources including labour. These 'reforms' amounted to little more than removal of job security provisions in labour laws and curtailment of bargaining powers of organized labour. To a greater or lesser degree across countries, with a range of actual deregulatory practices often preceding legislation or replacing the need for changing legislation, such 'labour market reforms' have been an intrinsic thrust of neo-liberal policy and globalization. Specifically targeting labour laws in developing countries, the World Bank, for example, has been arguing that 'In many Latin American, South Asian, and Middle Eastern countries, labour laws establish onerous job security regulations', while the well-known exploiters of informal sector migrant workers—the labour contractors—are viewed as efficient brokers who 'act as employment agencies and contribute to the flow of information across labour markets of neighbouring regions'.[91] An impression is sought to be given that dismantling of job security provisions for formal sector workers will somehow lead to expanding employment opportunities, better conditions and regular wage incomes for informal sector workers. It has driven a process of officially countenanced informalization of the hitherto formal industries (through increasing use of casual or contract workers and outsourcing practices), linked in several areas to employment of women at the informal bottom of the chain of international and national production networks.

Second, even as the informal sector has come to acquire an important identity and focus, in terms of collection of statistics, apart from the growing tendency to blur over the exploitative relations that operate within it, there is also a tendency to project the informal sector as a stimulus to entrepreneurial energies in developing countries. An additional tendency is to reinforce support for deregulation of national markets on the grounds that it provides an enabling environment for informal sector enterprises to flourish. An extreme form of this argument is that all the informal sector requires is legal recognition of the informal property assets of the poor, which can then be capitalized and thus release innate capacities for development and efficient and productive allocation of resources.[92] More influential, however, has been the projection of informal sector micro-enterprise as the solution to unemployment and the promotion of a kind of divisive and separate identity politics of informal sector workers as opposed to formal sector workers. Both arguments are generally accompanied by a marked tendency to avoid confronting overall policy choices that have been limiting employment growth in both formal and informal sectors.

The third pillar of the reconfigured approach to the informal sector under liberalization has been the promotion of institutionalized mobilization of informal sector workers' own resources as the principal source of funding their own 'social security' and credit needs, or in other words the resources of the poor being used to circulate among the poor. Such a conception of social security for unorganized workers, still in incipient form in terms of government policy and legislation in India, is based on the principle that the workers themselves must meet their requirements of social insurance through regular individual contributions. A social security scheme for unorganized sector workers based on such an approach was introduced in 2003 by the government of the day, but failed to endear itself to any section of workers, and had to be shelved after the 2004 elections led to a change in government.[93] Couched in a populist discourse of according priority to unorganized and informal sector workers, what was hidden was the shift in the labour and employment policy of the state, from providing direct employment or income transfers from employers (direct or indirect) to workers, to merely supervising and controlling a part of poor workers' actual and direct earnings.[94] The central problem of declining work opportunities with reasonable and regular incomes and the probable inability of unorganized workers to support such schemes, of course remained unaddressed in such an approach.[95] Similarly the possibilities of subversion of the benefits that are supposed to be spread to informal workers, in the absence of regular surplus income in their hands, were also ignored. At the present stage, the whole issue of legislation providing for social security for unorganized workers is up for public debate in the country and the pressure for greater support by the state is growing, although its final shape and destiny still remains somewhat unclear and will depend on the working out of actual political correlations thrown up by democratic processes.[96]

Organized credit-based mobilization through 'micro-credit' on the other hand, which especially targets women, has already become a more widespread material tool for moulding women's agency in the liberalized era. Widely projected as the panacea for women's income and employment needs, at an international level, micro-credit is visualized as an important method of promoting market-led growth, 'privatizing the economy' or 'bringing the vibrancy of the market economy to the poorest villages and peoples of the world'.[97] In India, the present strategy of micro-credit has gone hand in hand with financial liberalization, including a shift in the institutional structure of public sector banks away from development banking to market driven considerations of profitability, deregulation of interest rates, and decline in provisions for subsidized rates of interest for the poorer sections. Such a shift has entailed reversal of earlier objectives of providing the poor with preferential access to credit from the formal sector for production and self-employment (primarily through the public sector banks), led to a sharp rise in the share of informal sector loans in the debt portfolios of the poor, and spread money-lending as a major occupation in villages as well as a part-time or secondary source of income.[98] Declines in formal public sector credit for the poor have been sought to be substituted by micro-credit schemes which involve disbursement through privatized channels, of very small loans with no collateral, generally through the mechanism of NGOs and the formation of borrower groups from among the poor.[99] An element of the strategy is to organize self-help groups (SHGs) of 15 to 20 local residents, usually women, who meet regularly and circulate their savings as loans within their group.

Most women's organizations in India do not accept the micro-credit panacea to poverty approach promoted by international organizations. They acknowledge that micro-credit has been an instrument in the hands of many poor women to meet some of their credit requirements (particularly for consumption) in a situation where otherwise they would be completely dependent on usurious moneylenders. They also acknowledge the role of SHGs as a self-organizing tool and in drawing out latent leadership potential in women in some areas; however, in the sphere of income generation they point out that the record has been of a differential impact with the upper and middle income sections of the poor being able to respond relatively better to such assistance and argue that the issue of poverty cannot be resolved without more equitable distribution of wealth and resources. They have pointed out that thousands of co-operatives of traditional artisans have collapsed due to retreating support by the state as part of the liberalization policies of removing subsidies on raw materials and assistance in marketing. They forcefully articulate the central need for land and regular waged work on the basis of their experience of work among agricultural labour and argue that 'it is completely wrong to assume that the poor see self-enterprise as the best means of livelihood'. Finally, they point out that with liberalization policies, where small-scale enterprises are everywhere being swallowed up by large corporations, 'the future for micro-enterprises is, indeed very doubtful'.[100]

Towards a More Integrated Perspective

In general, while empirical evidence in India does not support the feminization of labour thesis in terms of any sharp rise in share of women in employment in manufacturing or services, debates around the concept have drawn attention to several inequalities and forms of exploitation faced by women workers. At the same time the sweepingly universalist position on feminization of labour, has not gone theoretically uncontested by women scholars at an international level. For example a feminist commentator has argued that 'restructuring of labour contracts and the altering of job boundaries are more likely to take place in a gender differentiated way than to be a force for overcoming the sexual division of labour' and 'that "flexibilization" does not necessarily lead to direct substitution of women for men in types of work traditionally done by men; nor does it necessarily lead to a rising female share in paid employment in manufacturing industries'. Further, 'the gender division of labour, which tends to confine women to relatively subordinate and inferior positions in the organization of monetized production, is not overridden by flexibility'.[101] Similarly, citing the case of India, it has been argued, that in a country beset by chronic unemployment, 'for flexibility and cheap labour contracts, women are by no means the only candidates'.[102]

Such perspectives have equal bearing on the informal sector, where women's share of employment is showing signs of decline in liberalizing

India. Most of the approaches and strategies for women workers in the informal sector have developed as containment strategies directed at what is called 'mitigating adjustment costs', which are universally recognized as being disproportionately borne by women. In general, such strategies have been unable to reflect the basic needs of employment and social security of women workers in the informal sector; these require much more fundamental changes involving not only redistribution of asset control and income shares within households but also reversal of the processes by which property and wealth has become further concentrated in the hands of a few within and between nations.

The projection of deregulated labour markets as being beneficial for employment of women is at one level empirically belied by the shrinking share of women in the unregulated informal sector. On the other hand, as has been argued at a more general level, regulatory legislation such as minimum wages for women workers 'can play a declarative and legitimating function, enabling women to avoid underselling their labour ... [and] can help to offset existing social distortions stemming from male bias'. Further, if regulations regarding maternity benefits or requirements of child-care act as a deterrent for employers to employ women, without such benefits, women themselves are constrained from taking up employment. The tendency to universally project a trade-off between workers' rights (given recognition in the form of state regulations) and employment in the arguments supporting deregulation for enhancing women's employment opportunities has also been challenged. For example Elson has argued that 'the trade-off between workers' rights and employment available is likely to depend on the overall state of accumulation. During a period of rapid growth and productivity improvements or when there are shortages of particular kinds of labour, the fact that workers have an extensive set of entitlements does not deter employment.' To this must be added the importance of the nature of growth which, if detached from democratic expansion of overall economic activity and employment and solely linked to increasing the profit margins of a select few large corporates, would also lead and does lead to a trade-off between workers' entitlements and employment opportunities. The issue of lack of employment opportunities is thus less related to existence of regulation in the sphere of workers' rights and entitlements and more to the overall nature and spread (or lack of spread) of growth processes.

The experience of women workers and the women's movement in India over the last two decades or so, has made it clear that enlargement of the organization of women workers, which is fairly universally recognized as necessary, is not in itself a sufficient condition for advancing employment and entitlements for women workers. Equally important is the perspective and focus of such organization. If it leads women workers away from intervention in the general economic policies affecting them, it is likely to build, at best, co-operative marginality; at worst, it would facilitate the transfer of their limited resources into the hands of the wealthy corporate sector. A perspective of intervention in fundamental policy directions by women workers must, of course, be linked to the need to rescue the economic sovereignty of the state and direct it towards a more redistributive led growth trajectory. In the words of Womenspeak, 'Our slogan is structural transformation towards equality—not structural adjustment to intensify inequality'.

Notes

1 For comparison with the late nineteenth century, see presidential speech delivered by Deepak Nayyar at the 78th Annual Conference of the Indian Economic Association, 1995. This is quoted in K. Singh, *Globalisation of Finance* (Delhi: Madhyam Books, 1998); see also United Nations, *1999 Survey of Women in Development, Globalization, Women and Work,* Chapter 1 (United Nations, 2000), and J. Ghosh and C.P. Chandrashekhar (eds), Introduction. *Work and Well-Being in the Age of Finance* (Delhi: Tulika, 2003).

2 E. Hobsbawm, *The Age of Empire*, New York: Vintage Books (1987).

3 Although the analysis of imperialism in the first two decades of the twentieth century was to a great extent focused on how it engendered conflict among the major capitalist powers, leading to World War I, its influence (notably Lenin's *Imperialism, the Highest Stage of Capitalism*)

was most marked on the national liberation movements that swept through many colonies or dependencies, right through till the 1960s.

4 The articles of purpose of the IMF, as stated in 1944, were: '(*i*) To promote international monetary cooperation through a permanent institution which provides the machinery for consultation and collaboration on international monetary problems. (*ii*) To facilitate the expansion and balanced growth of international trade, and to contribute thereby to the promotion and maintenance of high levels of employment and real income and to the development of the productive resources of all members as primary objectives of economic policy. (*iii*) To promote exchange stability, to maintain orderly exchange arrangements among members, and to avoid competitive exchange depreciation. (*iv*) To assist in the establishment of a multilateral system of payments in respect of current transactions between members and in the elimination of foreign exchange restrictions which hamper the growth of world trade. (*v*) To give confidence to members by making the Fund's resources available to them under adequate safeguards, thus providing them with opportunity to correct maladjustments in their balance of payments without resorting to measures destructive of national or international prosperity.'

5 Joseph Stiglitz, *Globalization and Its Discontents*, chapter 1 (New York: Allen Lane, 2002).

6 Hobsbawm, The golden years, in *The Age of Extremes* (New Delhi, Viking, 1995): chapter 9.

7 Ibid.

8 Of course the golden age of capitalism unfolded in the background of the cold war and the unprecedented militarization of the United States. If peacetime and the role of international *gendarme* assumed by the United States left Europe and Japan free to concentrate their expenditures in other spheres of commodity production, the United States was able to augment its industrial programme through demands of militarization, leading to what was popularly referred to as the military industrial complex.

9 Hobsbawm, *Age of Extremes*, chapter 10.

10 An example of how the United States used such loans as an instrument of state policy was in the aid provided for reconstruction of postwar capitalist Europe and Japan, while excluding and isolating the far more severely war ravaged USSR from such aid and trade.

11 Initially, in 1973 when gold was floated, its price soared to levels of U.S. $500 per ounce but then gold was allowed to trickle out of Fort

Knox and the panic subsided and the price fell back and gold now floats like any other commodity.

12 The spur to the formation of OPEC in 1960 and its fuller assertion in the 1970s was the growing realization by the oil producing countries (particularly the Arabs) that the West was increasing its energy use by 5 per cent annually, paying low oil prices, yet selling inflation-priced goods to the petroleum producers in the Third World. Matters came to a head during the 1973 Arab-Israeli War (6 Oct to 26 Oct 1973, between Israel and a coalition of Arab nations led by Egypt and Syria) in which the United States and some countries in Western Europe had supported Israel. The Arab countries imposed an oil embargo on the USA and the Netherlands which was lifted only in March 1974, by which time the OPEC had achieved a major increase in the price of its oil.

13 The earliest neo-liberal model, of course, came up in Chile in 1974 when backed by the United States, the dictatorial regime of Pinochet was established. Under Pinochet's regime, a group of economists known as the 'Chicago Boys' who were followers of Milton Friedman (generally known as the world's pre-eminent neo-liberal economist) were in charge of economic policy. Friedman, who himself met with Pinochet, was famously known to have described the military dictator's neo-liberal, monetarist economic reforms implemented in Chile as the 'Miracle of Chile'. This, however, did not yet have the globalizing force that the Reagan and Thatcher era brought about.

14 For a description of the shift to neo-liberalism and how the two Bretton Woods institutions acted in tandem to force policies on third world countries, see J. Stiglitz, *Globalization and Its Discontents.*

15 The 1970s epitomized the turning point from when both profits and non-business incomes could no longer rise without getting in each other's way, or in other words, maintaining a balance between the demands of capital and labour was no longer feasible within the framework of capitalism.

16 United Nations, *1999 Survey of Women in Development*.

17 According to Hobsbawm, *The Age of Extremes*, p. 408, 'In spite of substantial efforts, hardly any national governments in the rich countries, and certainly not those most hostile to public social welfare, managed to reduce the vast proportion of their expenditure for these purposes, or even to keep it in check.' He added the following figures, 'In 1972 fourteen such states spent a mean of 48 per cent of their central government expenditure on housing, social security, welfare and health. In 1990 they spent a mean of 51 per cent. They are: Australia

and New Zealand, the U.S. and Canada, Austria, Belgium, Britain, Denmark, Finland, Italy, the Netherlands, Norway and Sweden.'

18 Hobsbawm, *The Age of Extremes,* p. 414.

19 A. Singh, Global economic change, skills and international competitiveness, *International Labour Review* 133 (1994): 171-172.

20 It should be remembered that despite socialist rhetoric regarding the mixed economy model in India, an active role for the state in undertaking investments in order to plug gaps in the production structure had been advocated by the Bombay Plan drawn up by the leading captains of Indian private industry at the point of independence, clearly with their own interests in mind. Reluctant to part with their own resources for the state effort, the Bombay Plan had suggested that 40 per cent of the plan expenditure of the Indian state should come from deficit financing.

21 Utsa Patnaik, India's agricultural development in the light of historical experience, in: Terence J. Byres (ed.), *The State, Development Planning and Liberalisation in India* (New Delhi: Oxford, 1998).

22 P. Patnaik, On the political economy of economic 'liberalization', In: *Whatever Happened to Imperialism and Other Essays* (New Delhi: Tulika, 1995) p.183. He adds, 'according to the Indirect Taxation Enquiry Committee Report, 55 per cent of total indirect tax revenue in 1973-1974, the only year for which calculations have been made, came from households with monthly per capita expenditure less than Rs 100'.

23 Ibid, p.186-187.

24 For an account of the pressures exercised by the World Bank on India, see Patnaik *Whatever Happened to Imperialism,* pp.176-180.

25 E. Hobsbawm, *Age of Extremes.*

26 Estimates by S. Strange, quoted in J. Petras and H. Veltmeyer, *Globalization Unmasked* (New Delhi: Madhyam Books, 2001).

27 United Nations, *1999 Survey of Women in Development*, p. 46.

28 An example of where neo-liberal policy was forced through at gunpoint is Chile, when the elected President Salvador Allende was assassinated in 1974, the military captured power under General Pinochet and unleashed large scale repression.

29 See E.M.S. Namboodiripad, *Economics and Politics of India's Socialist Pattern* (New Delhi : People's Publishing House, 1966).

30 C.P. Chandrashekhar and J. Ghosh, The political economy of reform. *The Market That Failed,* chapter 4 (New Delhi: Leftword, 2002).

31 Details of these various reports are provided in I. Mazumdar and I. Agnihotri, Labour in times of closure. In U. Kalpagam (ed), *Labour and Poverty in Uttar Pradesh* (New Delhi: Segment books, 2004).

32 Directive Principles of State Policy included 'the right to an adequate means of livelihood', 'equal pay for equal work', 'protection of the health and strength of workers', 'the right to work, education and public assistance in case of unemployment, old age, sickness, disablement and any other types of undeserved wants', 'just and humane conditions of work and maternity relief', 'provision of work, a living wage, conditions of work ensuring a decent standard of life and full enjoyment of leisure and social and cultural opportunities'. See Articles 39(*a*), 39(*d*), 39(*e*), 41, 43 and 42 of the Indian Constitution. Of course the directive principles are in themselves non-justiciable.

33 In India, out of four major modern industrial sectors inherited from the colonial era where women wage workers could be found in fairly substantial numbers, i.e. textiles, jute, mines and plantations, the number and share of employment of women in the first three declined substantially.

34 Measures attempting to discipline the capitalist class in the 1970s included the appointment of the Monopolies and Restrictive Practices Commission (MRTP Act of 1971), tightening of licensing and restriction on the outflow of wealth through enactment of the Foreign Exchange Regulation Act (FERA) of 1972, while restrictions on retrenchment and closures were brought in as amendments to the Industrial Disputes Act. Repression on workers was unleashed through invoking the colonial Defence of India Rules (DIR), and then through the Maintenance of Internal Security Act (MISA), whose widespread use against all political opposition during the years of Emergency (1975-1977) ultimately led to its removal from the statute book in the following period.

35 Major centres of the textile industry such as Mumbai, Ahmedabad, Kanpur, and even a relatively smaller centre like Delhi witnessed the closure of textile mills.

36 *Shramshakti*, Report of the National Commission on Self-Employed Women and Women in the Informal Sector, (1988) p.72.

37 T. Roy, *Outline of a History of Labour in Traditional Small-Scale Industry in India*, NLI Research Studies Series No. 015/2001, VVGNLI.

38 Data source for the year 2001: Ministry of Labour, for the organized sector, and the NSSO Report No. 479 (56/2.2/3), for the unorganized manufacturing workers.

39 Calculated on the basis of Ministry of Labour reports, for the organized sector, and NSSO's Report No. 479 (56/2.2/3), for unorganized manufacturing workers.

40 Chandrashekhar and Ghosh, *The Market That Failed*, chapter 12.
41 Urban population growth dropped from 3.2 per cent per annum in the 1980s to 2.7 per cent in the 1990s; A. Sen, Globalization, growth and inequality in South Asia. In Ghosh and Chandrashekhar (eds), *Work and Well-Being.*
42 Ibid. p. 477.
43 See for example J. Breman, Urban poverty in the early twenty-first century. In *The Labouring Poor in India*, chapter 7 (New Delhi: Oxford, 2003).
44 Chandrashekhar and Ghosh, *The Market That Failed*, p.144.
45 A. Sen, Globalization, growth and inequality.
46 U. Patnaik, Rural India in ruins. 2004. *Frontline*, 12 March. According to her calculations, by 2000-2001, the average Indian family of four members was absorbing 93 kg less food grains compared with a mere three years earlier—a massive and unprecedented drop, entailing a fall in average daily intake by 64 gram per head, or a fall in calorie intake by 256 calories from food grains (which accounts for 65 to 70 per cent of the food expenditures of the poor).
47 The latter half of the 1990s was also a period of 'sharp deceleration of industrial growth' in India as the investment boom of the preceding three years, which had generated far greater productive capacity than could be absorbed, petered out. Private investment rates, did again increase from 16.0 per cent in 2001-2002 to 17.3 per cent in 2002-2003 and further to 17.4 per cent in 2003-2004, while public investment, after declining continuously since 2000-2001, improved from 5.4 per cent in 2002-2003 to 5.6 per cent in 2003-2004. Nevertheless, the trade deficit burgeoned to a record high in 2005, whose reasons perhaps require closer analysis than appears in the statements from government and commentators in the financial papers.
48 Chandrashekhar and Ghosh, *The Market That Failed*, pp 118-120.
49 Ibid. The stress on imports of capital goods in their argument is explained by the authors since 'in the case of a number of finished consumer goods, quantitative restrictions were removed only towards the end of the decade'.
50 Hobsbawm, *Age of Extremes*, p.278.
51 Ibid.
52 Ibid, p.279.
53 F. Frobel, J. Heinrichs and O. Kreye, *The New International Division of Labour* (Cambridge University Press, 1980), p.44.
54 J. Burke and G. Epstein, Threat effects and the internationalisation of

production. In Ghosh and Chandrashekhar (eds), *Work and Well-Being.*

55 Ibid, J. Ghosh, Exporting jobs or watching them disappear.

56 Ibid. Ghosh cites the case of Mexico whose share in manufacturing exports rose tenfold between 1980 and 1997, but whose share in manufacturing value added fell by more than one-third.

57 Ibid. Another aspect of of the results of FDI is the danger of 'outward net transfers'. For example, as clearly illustrated by observations in sub-Saharan Africa, 'profit remittances have exceeded net inflows of FDI every year since 1984'. K. Singh, *A Citizen's Guide to the Globalisation of Finance* (New Delhi: Madhyam Books, 1998).

58 Ibid.

59 U. Patnaik, On the Inverse Relation between Primary Exports and Food Absorption in Developing Countries under Liberalised Trade Regimes. In Ghosh and Chandrashekhar (eds.), *Work and Well-Being.* She has pointed out that under loan-conditional adjustment and trade liberalization from the late 1970s, a large number of the sub-Saharan African countries undertook what was considered a successful primary export thrust, which led to a negative food grains growth rate across the 1980s and 1990s and a situation in several countries where per capita total calorie intake declined even after accounting for food aid. Although her argument that this same feature would appear in India did not receive much support in the early 1990s, in recent years, evidence has now accumulated of both declines in per capita food output as well as food absorption in India, compelling more attention to her argument.

60 Ibid.

61 J. Ghosh, Exporting jobs or watching them disappear. In Ghosh and Chandrashekhar (eds.), *Work and Well Being.* Ghosh points out that the single exception to the relative stagnation of manufacturing employment in the South is China which has been host to the greatest amount of foreign direct investment in the South. One of the reasons for this is that China did much less in terms of import liberalization, quite apart from the fact that so much of China's industry still remains under state ownership/control permitting a range of domestic manufacturing to survive, as a result of which job losses in non-exporting sectors have been contained to some extent.

62 In terms of distribution, by 1914, 30 per cent of the stock of long-term foreign investment in the world was in Europe, 25 per cent in the United States, and 45 per cent in the underdeveloped world (20 per

cent in Latin America and 25 per cent in Asia and Africa). In comparison, in 1992 stock of FDI was far more concentrated in the industrialized countries (78 per cent) with developing countries receiving only 22 per cent. In 2002, developed countries accounted for 71 per cent of FDI inflows. Prabhat Patnaik has argued that FDI tends to come to developing countries only where, in any case, domestic savings are high. Since some 85 per cent of even FDI is accounted for by mergers and acquisitions, FDI flows which have risen sharply in the 1990s seem to reflect more of a tendency to centralization of existing capitals rather than expansion of investment in production.

63 Ghosh and Chandrashekhar (eds.), *Work and Well Being*, Introduction. An enabling element in the integration of global financial markets was the revolution in information and communications technologies which made cheap global communications and networking possible, and allowed for registration of transactions in real time and the 'instantaneous movement of digitally empowered capital'.

64 Hobsbawm, *Age of Extremes*, p.277. According to him the expansion of the private international financial system grew out of the tendency of finance to avoid taxes and other restrictions by moving into 'offshore' centres or into accounts in currencies that are not of those of the country in which the bank is located. For example, some time in the 1960s, the old international financial centre, the 'City of London' became a major offshore centre for 'Eurodollars'. Huge quantities of free-floating dollars accumulated in these accounts due to the unrestricted expenditures of the United States abroad, particularly for military purposes. The private international financial system also became the main mechanism for recycling what has been termed the 'klondike of oil-profits' from the OPEC countries which were mainly held in deposits with the international banking system based in and controlled by the developed world.

65 It has been argued by some that the acceptance of the U.S. dollar as the store of value by wealth holders was even earlier only theoretically linked to the promise to convert dollars to gold on demand at a fixed pre-specified price. In practice, however, it was the military might of the United States that generated confidence in the dollar. See C. P. Chandrashekhar, The imperialist war on 'terror' *The Marxist* 19, 3 (July-September 2003).

66 Hobsbawm, *Age of Extremes*.

67 Securitization converted cash-generating assets into marketable securities for sale to investors with the objective of separating business

risk from the risk of sold assets. Speculative instruments such as derivatives include futures and options whereby the risk associated with the underlying security is purchased or sold, and profits are made from fluctuations in value whose basis may be determined purely in the realm of investors' or speculators' expectations. In general, such instruments and the enormous amounts of fluid capital concentrated in the financial markets has led to hugely increased parasitic and speculative practices of engaging in business in order to make quick profits from fluctuations in prices, as opposed to the practice of investing in a productive enterprise in order to share in its earnings.

68 P. Patnaik, Globalization of capital and the theory of imperialism. In *Retreat to Unfreedom* (New Delhi: Tulika, 2003).

69 Such stagnation is inherent because any boosting of the economy by the state to levels close to 'full employment' gives rise to expectations of inflation and currency depreciation, leading to flight of finance capital.

70 Patnaik has argued that the reason that the United States was able to maintain such high fiscal deficits (in the Reagan era) was because the dollar remains 'the fulcrum of the international financial system' and 'already so much of the world's wealth is held [in dollars] that all countries have some vested interest in protecting its value' This allows greater latitude to U.S. government spending than others. Non-dollar currencies of the first world are also held in the conviction that the values of these other currencies will not decline in relation to the dollar and their governments actually intervene to take steps to ensure this.

71 Although Patnaik is here referring to the Reagan era, in recent years when the fiscal deficit of the United States under George Bush is again on touching record highs, we find an IMF mission to the United States in May 2005, again reiterating, that 'The United States has continued to be the main locomotive of global growth'. See http://www.imf.org/external/np/ms/2005/052505a.htm. In the 1990s, following an initial rise, there was a subsequent collapse of most crop prices in world trade with obvious adverse effects on the producers in developing countries who additionally were also less protected by subsidies than those in the developed world due to pressures from the inequitous Agreement on Agriculture under the WTO regime.

72 It may be recalled that gaining national control of national assets was one of the agendas of decolonization undertaken vigorously through the 1950s and 60s, and often in the face of even military opposition from former colonial powers.

73 See Prabhat Patnaik, *Retreat to Unfreedom*, pp. 21-25.

74 J. Ghosh and C. P. Chandrashekhar (eds), Introduction, *Work and Well Being*.

75 As outlined in the 1999 World Survey of Women in Development, the familiar sequence of events leading to such crises, are as follows. Large capital inflows into a developing country lead to increased bank credit and a subsequent increase in economic activity which eventually tends to spur inflation. As a result, domestic currencies become overvalued causing exports to decline and imports to rise. Foreign investors then begin to expect a currency devaluation precipitating capital flight. Bankruptcies, closures and selling-off of assets inevitably follow.

76 See United Nations, *1999 Survey of Women in Development*.

77 G. Standing, Global feminization through flexible labor: A theme revisited, *World Development*, 27, 3 (1999), p. 583.

78 See J. Ghosh, *Globalisation, Export Oriented Employment for Women and Social Policy*, UNRISD, 2002.

79 R. Assaad, Informalization and de-feminization: explaining the unusual pattern in Egypt, Paper Prepared for Presentation at the Conference Rethinking Labor Market Informalization:Precarious Jobs, Poverty, and Social Protection, Cornell University (October 18-19, 2002).

80 From the 1970s the marginalization thesis had acquired momentum, as the employment patterns established by the nature of the development path were found to have not been favourable to increased work participation rates for women.

81 *Womenspeak: United Voices against Globalization, Poverty and Violence in India,* March 2000. This document which acts as a basic charter for the movement was initiated by six national women's organizsations representing perhaps around six million women at the time (the largest of the organizations, AIDWA alone had a membership of over six million). Several other regional or smaller organizations and groups were also part of the convention where the document was adopted.

82 The recognition of the dire need for employment at least in rural areas dawned on the legislative class following the 2004 elections and it was this that led to the enactment of the National Rural Employment Guarantee Act in 2005.

83 Much was made of surplus food stocks that accumulated in government godowns in the 1990s. But as has been pointed out by many, such accumulation was due to inability of people to buy food-grain even from the public distribution system. Shockingly, when hunger was becoming widespread, food grain was being exported at rates lower than government rates for people below the official poverty line.

84 *Womenspeak.*

85 J. Breman, A question of poverty: *The Labouring Poor in India*, chapter 6 (New Delhi: OUP, 2003).

86 From the late 1960s through the 1970s, several new central laws targeting specific sections of unorganized workers were brought into existence, including The Beedi and Cigar Workers (Conditions of Employment) Act, 1966; the Contract Labour (Regulation and Abolition) Act, 1970; The Bonded Labour System (Abolition) Act, 1976 and the Inter-state Migrant Workmen (Regulation of Employment and Conditions of Service) Act, 1979, along with Welfare Cess and Fund Acts covering workers in the beedi industry, cine industry and in iron ore, manganese ore, chrome ore, lime stone, dolomite and mica mines. For women, this period saw the enactment of the Equal Remuneration Act, 1976.

87 Declining shares of women in formal sector industries was particularly marked in the textiles and mines in India, although in some service sector industries, such as banking, formalization enabled greater entry of women.

88 Based on estimates of male and female informal employment for 1999-2000 given in paper by J. Unni, Size, contribution and characteristics of iInformal employment in India. Paper presented in the workshop on Globalization and Its impact on Women Workers in the Informal Economy, UNIFEM and SEWA Bharat (December, 2002). The same method that she has used for calculating informal employment, that is, subtracting organized sector employment from NSS employment estimates, has been applied to the 1993-1994 and 2004 rounds for comparison.

89 See R. Jhabvala, Globalization, liberalization and women in the informal economy. In: V. Jha (ed.) *Trade, Globalisation and Gender–Evidence from South Asia* (UNIFEM, 2003). In the case of construction, Renana Jhabvala points out that the practice of global tenders for even government sponsored construction has brought MNCs into the construction sector in a big way with a whole host of machinery displacing the tasks traditionally carried out by women. She adds that in competition such machines have also been brought in by Indian construction companies and such processes are being supported by the government.

90 For example, according to an earlier policy, textile spinning mills had been obliged to provide for hank yarn for handloom weavers. Such obligations were withdrawn as part of the liberalization process in the textile industry, leading to sharp rises in the price of hank yarn. This, in

turn, led to a crisis for handloom weavers and, in the early 1990s, there were large numbers of suicides by weavers.

91 World Development Report (1995), *Workers in an Integrating World.*

92 The most extreme form of such a point of view comes from Hernando De Soto (from Peru), whose thesis rests on the presumption that the informal sector's only problem lies in lack of legal recognition of the property assets in the hands of the poor, thereby constricting capitalization of their assets and holding back the innate capacities for the development of capitalist industrialization. For a sharp critique of De Soto's arguments see Breman, *Labouring Poor in India.*

93 The 2003 'social security scheme' for unorganized workers was introduced at a pilot level in some specific districts. It had come in for sharp criticism from several workers' organizations on the grounds that the approach was flawed since it contains the premise that most informal sector workers have regular surplus incomes from which they can meet their insurance needs, and unless the government is prepared to contribute itself and raise resources from the employers or propertied classes who benefit from the labour of informal workers, the scheme can only end in defrauding workers. Since then, the general elections of 2004 saw an overturning of the government of the time and the scheme was abandoned.

94 In labour laws for the organized sector, there are clear provisions for employer contributions for health insurance, provident fund and so on. No such provision had been made in the 2003 insurance schemes for unorganized workers nor had there been any financial outlays on the part of the government. Following the elections of 2004 and the change in government, the National Commission on Enterprises in the Unorganised Sector has drafted a new bill on social security for unorganized sector workers. At the time of writing there had been no further movement on the draft from the Ministry of Labour.

95 The elections of 2004, however, seem to have pitch-forked the question of growing unemployment onto the centre of the political stage. As a result, the government that came into office in 2004 has enacted a National Rural Employment Guarantee Act, 2005, entitling applicants, on the basis of one person per rural household, to 100 days of guaranteed employment at minimum wages.

96 Although it is quite clear that the pressures for both employment guarantee and social security for unorganized sector workers has emerged from the distress reactions of common people manifested in political processes and the assertion of the electorate in 2004, it appears

that even among the pro-liberalization lobby there is some division on this question. While one group remains outright opposed to the state investing its resources on any scale for such schemes, another group argues that social security nets have to be put in place for which funds may supposedly raised by further liberalization, further opening up to foreign investment flows, curtailing of rights of organized sector workers (labour market reforms) and disinvestment in the public sector.

97 Quotes from M. Yunus, Grameen Bank, and World Bank President J. Wolfensohn referred to in V. K. Ramachandran and M. Swaminathan, Financial liberalization and rural credit in India. In Ghosh and. Chandrashekhar (eds.), *Work and Well Being.*

98 Ibid., V. K. Ramachandran and M. Swaminathan, whose conclusions are backed by field surveys of Gokalipuram Village (Tamilnadu) in 1977, 1985 and 1999.

99 See NABARD website for details of the micro-finance programme.

100 *Womenspeak*, pp.34-37.

101 D. Elson, Appraising recent developments in the world market for nimble fingers. In A. Chhachhi and R. Pittin (eds.), *Confronting State, Capital and Patriarchy*: (London Macmillan Press, 1996).

102 N. Banerjee, How real is the bogey of feminisation? In T.S. Papola and Atul Sharma (eds.) *Gender and Employment in India* (New Delhi, Vikas Publishing House, 1999).

TWO

Hierarchies of Exploitation and Multiple Inequalities: Women Workers in the Garment Export Industry

TWENTY-FIVE YEARS IN THE GARMENT EXPORT INDUSTRY: SUSHILA'S STORY

Thirty-five-year old Sushila has spent twenty-five years as a worker in Delhi. Separated from her husband within a year of her marriage, she is today the sole earning member in a household consisting of her mother, an unmarried sister, her presently unemployed brother, his wife and three children. Located in the slum resettlement colony of Inderpuri, on a plot of 25 sq yds, her home is the house that her late grandmother, a migrant construction worker from Rajasthan, built. Born in Delhi, she started her working life as a button-stitcher in a garment factory at the age of nine (along with her brother, aged eleven), in the first phase of growth of Indian garment exports.[1]

Literate but uneducated, she learnt her trade in the course of working in six garment export factories, rose from the position of unskilled helper to that of skilled checker and then, for a short while, was appointed as a supervisor, solely on the basis of application, personal efficiency and practical experience. In the early 1990s, she taught herself how to read English with the help of her two younger sisters, whom she and her brother (both with only primary education) have educated up to college level. She learnt the English alphabet in order to become a qualified measurement checker, a function role that she had already been playing for some years before (although without the designation), on the basis of her practical experience. This was during her twelve-and-a-half year stint in a prominent garment factory in the nearby Naraina Industrial Area, as a 'permanent' worker entitled to health insurance, provident fund, overtime at a double rate, and so on. It was a time when Naraina housed a number of garment export factories. Today most of them have closed down, while Sushila's own factory first shifted out of Delhi to Gurgaon (in the neighbouring state of Haryana) only to close down within two years there in early 2001.

After scouring various industrial areas in Delhi in search of a job for six months, she now works in Gurgaon, some 30 kms from her residence at less than half what she was earning earlier. After one year of work there, she is still a casual worker in a factory where even casual workers are increasingly being replaced by contract workers. In fact, there would be no record that she was even working there, since she receives her wage without a pay slip, and does not sign on a wage register or even a voucher. Thus is she prevented from having any legal entitlements and benefits from her employers despite her tenure as a worker for them. She leaves her house every morning, seven days a week, at 7.30 a.m. and returns at 10 p.m., after working for a minimum of ten hours and commuting for another four hours. She commutes because, as she found in her search for work in closer industrial areas, most of the bigger garment factories have moved out or closed down, and the ones that have remained seem to have widely fluctuating orders and pay too little. She stands all day at work, where earlier she would at least have been provided with a stool. A day off from work means no wage, something that she cannot afford in her present state. She has no health insurance, no provident fund or benefits of any other kind.

More than half of the settlement she received upon severance from her 'permanent' job[2] was used up for expenses incurred when her brother was hospitalized and required surgery in 2002. She thinks longingly of her earlier factory, which has restarted production, but with predominantly casual workers. When she was working there, she had 'no debts, no tension, nothing'. Five of Sushila's family have been victims of tuberculosis, and the expensive treatment remains a perpetual burden on the reduced family budget.

Sushila, although somewhat exceptional in initiative, experience, speed and skill in her work-life and representative of a relatively small proportion of women in the role that she plays in her family, is not an exception to the general condi-

> tions that are being faced by garment workers in Delhi today. Loss of steady or permanent employment to be replaced by harsher and more exploitative conditions, lower wages, excessive overtime, mostly uncompensated, are the characteristic features of the deteriorating conditions of life. Sanitation and civic amenities for the poor remain low priority in the globalization agenda of the metropolis that is her home. Rising costs of basic essentials for sustenance following the state's cutting down of the public distribution system and the lack of public health delivery have made the strains of declining income virtually unbearable. That such experiences are not exceptional is confirmed by the findings of a survey of some 150 garment workers in Delhi conducted in the last four months of the year 2002.
>
> Sushila has witnessed many changes. She says that most garment export companies now function with casual or contract labour–workers without minimum wage scales and without Employees State Insurance, Provident Fund or any other benefits. On the other hand, she observed that, increasingly, export houses are bringing all aspects of production 'in house' and even 'fabricators' are out of work. She says that her family and neighbours had for many years done embroidery, thread cutting, beadwork and so on, as home- based workers for the garment export industry. 'Such work is now no longer available or so rare as to be practically non-existent.'

According to the last comprehensive survey of the garment industry in India, conducted by the Textiles Committee of the Government of India (1989-1990), women workers in Delhi (220,000) accounted for 28 per cent of the total of 783,000 garment workers in Delhi. The concentration of the industry in Delhi at the time was such that more than half the women employed in the garment industry (57 per cent) could be found in the Delhi region. The findings of a field survey of women workers in Delhi's garment export industry conducted over four months in the latter half of 2002 are of some significance in analysing the changing scenario in the industry under globalization.

Through informal connections with women's organizations, trade unions and other sectional contacts, and personal experience of several years of mass work across the working class areas of the city, a sample of 150 women workers was obtained for this survey. The women were contacted and interviewed in a cross-section of industrial and residential areas. We believe that the sample is more truly representative of garment workers living and working in the maze of economic and social life in the metropolis of Delhi, than could have been achieved through more conventional or unidimensional methods of survey. At the end of the survey, the 150 women workers were found to be living in twenty-five colonies in six of the nine districts of Delhi plus Noida and Gurgaon and worked in ninety-nine garment export factories located in seventeen industrial areas.[3]

WOMEN WORKERS IN DELHI'S GARMENT EXPORT FACTORIES

Only 10 per cent of the surveyed workers were natives of Delhi in the sense that they were born here. All others were migrants, of whom the majority (63 per cent) were of rural origin. The mother tongue of 72 per cent was Hindi, including some special dialects such as Bhojpuri. Another 8 per cent hailed from the states of Punjab and Rajasthan. In all, workers of north Indian origin constituted 80 per cent of Delhi's garment workers. Of the remaining 20 per cent, the single largest group seems to be that of Bengalis, who accounted for some 14 per cent of the surveyed workers.

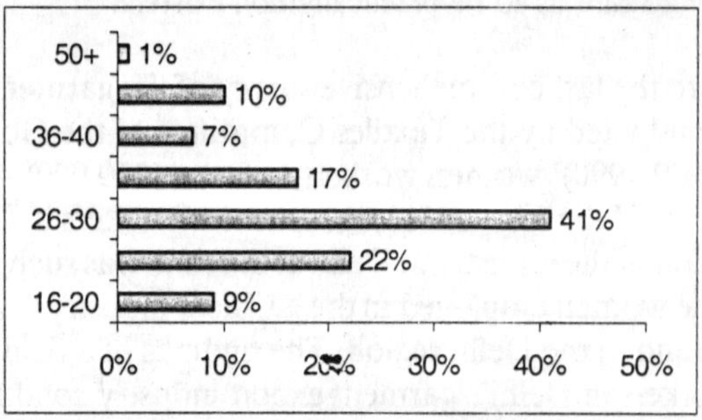

Figure 2.1. Age Distribution

The overwhelming majority of the women (83 per cent) were married, 5 per cent were widows, barely 2 per cent were separated or divorced and only 10 per cent were found to be unmarried. Most of the workers were young, with 63 per cent in the age group 21-30 (see Fig.2.1).

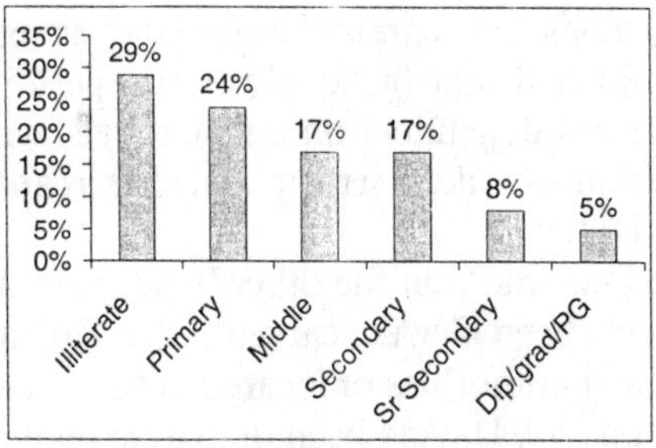

Figure 2.2. Educational Status

Less than 30 per cent were illiterate, while at the other extreme some 5 per cent were diploma holders or graduates with one worker who had a double MA. Figure 2.2 gives the educational breakdown of the sample. Thus the characteristic profile of women working in Delhi's garment export factories was found to be predominantly *young, literate* and *married* migrant workers from the rural hinterland of north India.

According to the survey, 15 per cent were residents of *jhuggies* (shanty cluster settlements) while close to 10 per cent lived in resettlement colonies of which the more longstanding ones go by the name of JJ (*Jhuggi Jhonpri*) colonies, clearly indicating the origins of those who had been resettled in these colonies. Another 12 per cent resided in urban villages, that is, the remaining residential bases of Delhi's original village inhabitants whose agricultural land had otherwise been acquired and urbanized by the Delhi Development Authority (DDA).[4] The majority of the garment workers (over 55 per cent) lived in the unauthorized *kacchi* colonies that have sprung up around the periphery of the metropolis and where the working classes of Delhi are located in increasing numbers, and only about 3 per cent were living in regular better quality colonies.[5]

Jhuggi settlements generally tend to be one-room shanties packed together alongside open drains or railway lines with little in the way of proper drainage facilities, the shanties themselves are without toilets, taps or windows and residents have to avail of public taps for their water supplies and even more limited forms of public toilets or open spaces for their toilet needs. Resettlement colonies tend to have more *pucca* housing built on plots in back-to-back series (generally of 25 sq yards) with common walls at the sides and back, leaving only the front side for openings. Open drains line the lanes along the plot fronts, with public taps for each lane (generally one tap per 25 plots). Most of the residents are still dependent on public toilets, while some have been able to build small toilets on their own plots as and when sewage pipes have been laid.

Unauthorized colonies, on the other hand, have a more uneven topography, having been illegally carved out of land acquired by the urban development authorities or located in the so-called green belt around the capital city. Having been drawn up by property dealers, often in association with land mafias, they have more variable plot sizes. Workers seeking some relief from the rigours of *jhuggi* and resettlement colony life occupy the smaller plots, although often their houses are *kuccha* and generally the areas of working class concentration are without any of the public civic amenities, such as safe drinking water, tarmac roads or sewers and so on. Close to three-fourths of the garment workers (72 per cent) lived in rented accommodation in the full range of settlements of workers mentioned above. These then are the workers who labour at the base of the hierarchy of the globalized garment industry.

THE GLOBAL CONTEXT OF THE GARMENT INDUSTRY

More than any other industry, garment manufacture has been at the centre of much of the debate, controversy and generalizations that have emerged regarding the impact of globalization on women's employment. This is not surprising, since more than two-thirds of the global labour force in the garment or clothing industry consists of women, and the industry accounts for almost one-fifth of the female labour force in manufacturing, worldwide.[6] The link between garment workers and gender consciousness perhaps has some emotive continuity stretching far back into the history of the readymade garment industry in Europe and North America. After all, the first forms of female organization in working class movements there developed out of the seamstress's unions. The debates on the impact of globalization, however, have emerged more from the current physical features of worldwide discontinuities in the production processes, rather than from the continuing fact of inherently higher levels of female employment in the garment industry. Many of these features are well known, having been publicized by a series of consumer-based campaigns emanating from North America and Europe, but it is still useful to look at the bigger picture to understand the driving global processes, as well as to arrive at a perspective about their influence on specific developments in the Indian garment export industry and the women workers associated with it.

Expansion of Trade and Exports and Changing Location of Production

Considered to be a leading sector of globalization, the world garment trade has grown faster than trade in manufactured goods as a whole. And as in other sectors, trade and export in clothing has expanded far more rapidly than has production. World exports of clothing, which accounted for U.S.$41 billion in 1980, rose to U.S.$177 billion in 1997, an increase of 335 per cent. In comparison, between 1980 and 1995, world clothing output rose by 59 per cent. In this period of expanding trade, however, a dramatic change has occurred in the relative importance of regions as well as individual countries in world production and exports of clothing. In 1980, Western European exports were higher than those of Asia. By 1990, Asia was ahead with 44 per cent of the total, as compared with 42 per cent for Western Europe.[7] And by 2001, Asia's share in world clothing exports stood at over 51 per cent as compared to that of the European Union, which was a little over 24 per cent.[8]

Between 1980 and 1997, where Asian output rose by 177 per cent, and that of the Americas rose by 67 per cent, European clothing output fell by nearly 13 per cent in U.S. dollar terms and its share of clothing output dropping from 48 per cent in 1980 to 26 per cent in 1995. The share of Asia, on the other hand, rose from 27 per cent to 46 per cent, while that of the Americas changed little—mostly because of an expanded share of the developing countries in Central and South America. In other words, there has been a shift in the production and exports of clothing away from the developed world towards the developing countries, seen in its most concentrated form in Asia. Already by 1996, the developing countries' share in world clothing exports was 73 per cent.

Following this dramatic reconfiguration, what is of note is that the value of world output of clothing stagnated between 1995 and 1998, remaining virtually unchanged. Increases in Asian and American output were offset by a 17 per cent decline in European output in the same period. In the Americas an increase of 14.3 per cent in their clothing production between 1995 and 1998, is largely explained by developments in Latin American countries; in the United States or Canada, there was a fall in the production of clothing.[9]

Despite all the above changes in the international production and trade map, the destination of world exports in clothing became increasingly concentrated in the most developed centres of capitalism. The dominance of the developed world in world clothing imports continued with the largest importing country, the United States, doubling its share in imports—from 16.4 per cent in 1980 to 32.4 per cent in 2001 (and Japan almost trebling its share: from 3.6 per cent to 9.3 per cent) in the same period. In all, the combined imports of the European Union, the United States and Japan constituted 80.4 per cent of world clothing imports in 2001, up from 74.3 per cent in 1980.[10]

Thus, while production activities in the clothing industry are worldwide, they are connected through various arrangements and strategic decisions principally to serve markets located in the developed countries. Changing characteristics of the economies of the developed capitalist centres have been the principal forces behind relocation strategies implemented by corporations hailing primarily from the United States and Europe which have become the major influences shaping the globalized features of production and trade in clothing.

Redrawing of the Global Employment Map and Instability of Employment

Despite trade expansionism, the total estimated world employment in both textiles and clothing changed relatively little between 1980 and 1995; however, the geographical distribution of employment changed radically. On the one hand, clothing employment in Asia rose considerably between 1980 and 1990, when it was nearly 35 per cent above its 1980 level. It subsequently slightly declined between 1990 and 1995 but increased again between 1995 and 1997, by which time its share in world employment stood at 62 per cent. On the other hand, clothing employment in the Americas fell steadily through the entire period from 1980 to 1998, and the United States, in particular, showed a substantial fall during the period from 1995 to 1998. Europe saw a more dramatic fall in employment—more than 50 per cent from 1980 to 1998—most concentrated in the period from 1990 to 1998, when the fall was 47 per cent.[11]

The sweeping changes that occurred over the last two decades of the twentieth century were not only in relative employment shares between countries, but in absolute terms within many countries as well. By 1995, clothing employment in the United States had dropped from its 1980 level by close to 40 per cent. Similarly, Japan saw a drop of a little over 27 per cent, while in Brazil, it dropped by over 44 per cent. Main among the countries which lost clothing employment between 1980 and 1995 were the United States, Hong Kong (China), Germany, Brazil, Poland, the United Kingdom, France and Japan. On the other hand, most of the countries that saw major increases in clothing employment during this period had very low starting points in 1980 (apart from China), such as Indonesia, Bangladesh, Thailand, Turkey, Sri Lanka and Morocco. What united all the countries showing increased employment, despite differing starting points or histories of their clothing industry, were their extremely low wage costs. As may therefore be seen, increases in clothing employment took place across a swathe of low-wage countries, while high-wage countries lost employment. As such, it has become increasingly clear that the principal drive behind the globalization of the garment industry is the ever widening search for cheaper labour. The process has at an initial stage led to widespread loss of clothing employment and worsening conditions of work in advanced capitalist economies,[12] and has sometimes been seen as advantageous to the developing countries in terms of increased employment opportunities. However, what needs to be understood is the extreme instability of both location of production centres and consequently of employment within and between the developing countries.

As an ILO report focusing on the clothing industry points out,

> Employment has fluctuated widely over the years in response to the changing comparative advantages of different countries and their relative international competitiveness. Investment, trade and, consequently, employment have moved in successive waves in response to relative changes in wages and other production costs. Jobs created in any one country cannot be regarded as a long-term gain. All the developing countries, and in particular those that are heavily dependent on international trade are facing fierce competition, particularly, in the labour-intensive activities where relative wage levels continue to play a significant role in determining relocation policies . . . Centres of development, production and trade are constantly shifting and taking jobs with them. The countries that *suffer most* as a result of this *instability* are those with *limited development alternatives* in the event of loss of competitiveness (emphasis added).[13]

Monopoly Retail, Brand Names, Finance and Appropriation of Value by Developed World Corporations

A prominent feature propelling globalization of production and trade in clothing has been the rising dominance of retail or purely marketing-based capital in the developed capitalist countries, particularly in the United States. Documented by a number of studies, it is well established that the global apparel industry is now mainly controlled by a few large retailers in the developed capitalist world who contract out the production of clothes under their own private labels.[14]

Initially, it was manufacturing capital in the advanced capitalist economies which began sourcing a substantial part of its output through contract manufacturing by small producers, many of whom were located overseas and particularly in East Asia.[15] But from the early

1970s such manufacturing capital was replaced by wholesalers and retailers who sought to bypass the manufacturers and began to source directly from overseas manufacturers. In this manner, retail profits in the major importing centres increased relative to manufacturing, the power and market control of corporate retail companies being immensely enhanced through mergers, acquisitions and consolidation and concentration of retail capital in general.[16]

While the growth of major retail chains has a long history, it was the onset of recessionary conditions in the 1970s that led to their new ascendancy and a generalized restructuring of the apparel industry. With the shrinking of the middle class in countries like the United States, traditional retailing, based on cost price and standard profit margins, gave way to new off-price and discount store chains and niche marketing.[17] What emerged through the economic downturn was, on the one hand, a more differentiated market, reflecting the increasing disparities in buying capacities within the core capitalist countries, with high priced up-market niches catering to the rich and severe downward pressure on prices in the mass market. On the other hand, the same countries witnessed the increasingly concentrated power of large-scale retailers who directly contracted out to low-cost suppliers in the developing countries.[18] Even the giants were however, competing for a greater share of a stagnant or slower growing market, and by the 1980s large retailers too faced a crisis of productivity and profitability.[19] As a result, in order to maintain and increase their rate of profit, the squeeze on manufacturing costs was made tighter, which in the case of the labour-intensive clothing industry meant a squeeze on the price of labour. Thus, the net of supplier countries in the developing world was further widened to even lower wage countries.

Along with the domination established by corporate retailers over the global apparel industry, from the late 1980s through the 1990s more and more apparel manufacturing companies in the core capitalist economies began to divest themselves of manufacturing responsibilities to become purely brand marketing companies.[20] On the one hand, this reflected the growing primacy of marketing over manufacture becoming the principal feature of the apparel industry in these economies. Equally, if not more importantly, and in spite of internal wage repression, profits drawn from apparel manufacture in the core economies with higher-value currencies had become less than from outsourced manufacture in countries with lower-valued currencies (as per exchange rates).[21] This was all the more true for apparel (even relative to textiles), given the absence of any major productivity enhancing technological breakthrough in the core economies.[22]

Through widening the net of international subcontracting in and between developing countries, the large corporations in the developed countries (both retail and brand name manufacturers who were no longer manufacturers), have been able to enhance their own profits. Competing suppliers from developing countries, with far less resources, could be forced to push down prices by paying lower wages. In addition, the corporations could cushion themselves from business cycles, since they could oblige these suppliers and their workers to absorb the unused capacity and the unemployment which accompanied business downturns. The fallout of such domination and exploitation of supplier countries by the core economy buyers has been a radical redistribution of costs and points of value appropriation in the global clothing industry (see Table 2.1). Today corporate retailers and brand names account for 75 per cent of the final price of apparel at one extreme, while the share of factory workers' wages has been reduced to 1 per cent.

Table 2.1. Cost structure of the apparel industry in the United States

Cost Components	Percentage
Retail shop profit and other costs (personnel, rent, administration and advertising)	50
Brand profit, overhead and promotion	25
Material costs and factory profits	13
Transportation/Taxes/Import costs	11
Factory workers' wages	1
Retail price	100

Source: Sweatshopwatch, as quoted in M.Vijaybhaskar, Garment industry in India in Gopal Joshi (ed), *Garment Industry in South Asia, Rags or Riches*, ILO/SAAT, 2002.

Such a specific series of developments in the apparel industry of the metropolitan core capitalist countries did not take place autonomous of the more general process of the rise to dominance of finance capital relative to manufacturing capital. Recent studies have detailed the particulars of corporate concentration in the clothing industry of the developed countries, particularly in the United States, pointing to their relationship with the financial markets and the resultant squeeze on the cost of manufacture propelling footloose global movement of clothing production.

When in the 1980s, financiers flush with funds to invest and in search of avenues for new investments had begun gearing up to finance a new wave of corporate consolidation, the retail industry was among those targeted, prompting a frantic wave of mergers and acquisitions, some led by real estate speculators. The retail industry emerged from this process larger and more concentrated than ever before with high levels of debt, as major retailers borrowed heavily to buy up their company's shares and prevent them from being taken over by speculators.[23] The pressure to reduce costs in order to maintain high stock prices and thus ward off any fresh attempts at takeovers became even more acute. Both for retailers and brand manufacturers, maintenance of high stock prices in volatile financial markets (which responded to ever-increasing returns on investment and market share rather than the value of physical assets), propelled a rush to lower the cost of production further and further by outsourcing to low-wage production centres.

The increasing appropriation of profits and value by non-manufacturing segments of the apparel industry, the concentration of market control in the hands of a few large corporations and the even more parasitic weight of finance on the global apparel industry have led to a worldwide squeeze on manufacturing costs. It is this squeeze that has created the conditions for enhanced exploitation and low wages in both developing and developed countries.

From One Form of Domination to Another: The Multi-Fibre Arrangement and Its Phaseout

Since the mid-1970s, the international trade in textiles and clothing was regulated by the Multi-Fibre Arrangement (MFA). The MFA was a specific arrangement between developed and developing countries. Brought into existence in 1974, it constituted a protectionist assertion by U.S. and European manufacturers to restrain large quantities of imports from some developing countries and protect their domestic clothing and textile industries. The MFA was not one agreement but consisted of a whole series of bilateral agreements, which were negotiated country-by-country, to set quota-based ceilings on the importation of textiles and clothing from individual developing countries to developed ones. Restrictions on imports through the quota regime of the MFA (revamped thrice since its creation, each directed at increasing the coverage and intensity of the restrictions) were combined with duty restrictions on textiles and textile products.

Under GATT '94, the Agreement on Textiles and Clothing (ATC) replaced the MFA, envisaging a phased withdrawal of all quantitative restraints and quotas so far imposed by the developed countries under the MFA by 2005. Protection of the domestic textile and clothing manufactures of Europe and the United States by their governments had been the principal propeller of the MFA, while their retailers were generally opposed to such restrictions. Studies have pointed out that organized lobbies of retailers, particularly in the U.S. had been lobbying for the removal of MFA for several years as it raised obstacles for their already established individual supply lines.[24] However, it is also a fact, that the MFA, through its quota restrictions on a country-to-country basis created the conditions for a movement of apparel production and even a degree of direct investment from quota-saturated countries to those who had unutilized quotas. Through such a process the net of supplier countries widened, which ultimately worked in the collective interest of the importing country buyers. Many of the developing countries who so effected entry into garment production for export were quota-rich (that is, they had large unutilized quotas) precisely because they had no established garment industry and thus had provided no threat to the interests of apparel manufacturers in the developed world.

In the final analysis, even as it restrained the quantities that could be purchased from an individual country, the MFA set the stage for the development of greater bargaining power of the principal importing countries' corporate buyers vis-à-vis the increased number of competing supplier countries. In the post-MFA period, footloose buyers from the developed countries, who now have the advantage of a wider competition among supplier countries than before, have been mounting pressure on exporting countries to lower prices, which in turn is having adverse effects on the wages and working conditions of the already-exploited garment export industry workers in several developing countries.

Primacy of Marketing over Manufacture: Insecure Employment and Intensified Pressure on the Labour Process

The overall production process in the garment industry can be broadly grouped into three stages: pre-assembly (design and fabric-cutting), assembly (sewing, washing, pressing, and so on) and post-assembly (distribution and retail). Technology advances in the industry have not fundamentally altered the sewing action, which remains the core of the assembly or manufacture of garments. Nor is any major breakthrough in sewing technology likely. Developments here have tended to be incremental rather than fundamental, such as the introduction of multiple stitching machines capable of more complex styles of stitching; sewing itself remains labour intensive in essence.[25]

The focus of change affecting labour processes in the globalizing garment sector has actually shifted from equipment and manufacturing to managerial systems and is driven by the post-assembly stage of distribution and retail. Variously termed post-Fordism, quick response, and lean or just-in-time production, the central aim is what is called 'market responsiveness'. This is accomplished through shorter product runs, greater diversification of product lines and quick-response inventory (maintenance of low inventory) systems. The emphasis on low inventories and just-in-time production has led to irregular employment patterns, which may be met through outsourcing production to the informal sector, or equally through increasingly moving even formal sector workers to being casual or informal. The quick-response system, consisting of short lead times (between order and delivery) and rapidly shifting volumes of production demands, operates through keeping open several supply lines and often requiring geographical proximity of some suppliers.[26] The pressure has thus become ever more acute on the manufacturing process. It is expected to produce and deliver faster, that too work of high quality, necessitating a degree of organization and minimum technology associated with greater capital investment, without necessarily having assured long term orders in any given line. This is what has led to the increasing tendency to 'flexible' employment practices, that is, the employment of labour who will not be paid wages or compensation during periods of low or no production. Thus importing buyers transfer their own risks onto the developing country supplier manufacturers, who in turn transfer it on to the workers. Over and above greater insecurity of employment, under the new managerial and marketing systems, an intense pressure is exercised on the labour process demanding both greater speed as well as longer hours of work.

Women's Employment in Clothing: A Perspective on the International Experience

A high share of female employment in the clothing industry has been an enduring feature since the inception of mass manufacture of garments in Europe and America in the nineteenth century. Such a concentration of women workers in the industry was of course predicated on the prevalence of lower wages for women embedded within the broad capitalist economy. Garment manufacture was characterized by lower levels of productivity and wages in comparison to the more capital-intensive industries whose workers were generally overwhelmingly male. At a global level 79 per cent of the jobs in clothing in 1980 were occupied by women; however, by 1995, their share had declined to 74 per cent.

The decline itself (however small), cannot be viewed as a matter of insignificance as a glance at what has been happening in various regions reveals. Apart from Africa, which saw an increase from 51 per cent to 64 per cent in the employment share of women over the period from 1980 to 1995, and Asia, where this share rose from 65 per cent in 1980 to some 71 per cent in 1995, in all regions there were falls in the female share of employment in the clothing industry.[27]

In a few countries of Western Europe, the decline in female share was steep (in Ireland the percentage of women dropped from 94 per cent in 1985 to 70 per cent in 1995). Figures on the share of female employment in the industry, often camouflage changes taking place in terms of real employment opportunities for women, in absolute terms as well as relative to their needs. For example, several European countries showed less dramatic drops in percentages, but far more significant losses of actual employment.[28] In Canada and the United States, the actual employment losses were even greater: the decreased share of women workers reflected cuts of altogether 320,000 women's jobs in both countries.

Within Asia, the Republic of Korea had a share of 76 per cent women in clothing employment in 1985, which fell to 70 per cent in 1995. This reflected a drop of more than 50,000 female workers in real terms.[29] Bangladesh, on the other hand, saw a rise in total employment as well as in the share of female employment from 17 per cent to 69 per cent. In Sri Lanka, female employment percentages fell from 89 per cent in 1985 to 87.5 per cent in 1995, although the number of female employees increased by more than 50,000. A similar trend was visible in Malaysia, where the percentages dropped from 89 per cent in 1985 to 82 per cent in 1995, with rising female employment in the sector. Even countries with low shares of female employment, such as Nepal, saw a significant rise in the number of women in the industry, although the women's share fell from 22 per cent to 17 per cent between 1985 and 1995.

At a worldwide level, increases in women's employment in apparel manufacture can be seen to have taken place in precisely those countries with the lowest wages per hour in clothing production (less than U.S.$0.30). The highest wages were in Western European countries (U.S.$10 or more per hour in 1995), followed by the United States and Canada (at U.S.$7.64 and U.S.$6.81 per hour respectively), where, as we have seen, there has been the most visible decline in absolute numbers as well as share of female employment. Some commentators have concluded that as employment shifts to countries with greater comparative advantage (a euphemism amounting to saying little more than that wages were relatively lower) some women will gain employment and others will lose their jobs. The point, however, is that any gain in women's employment is first of all inherently unstable. For the domination of metropolitan country buyers without any permanent structural links with their supplier manufacturers in developing countries, combined with their high levels of mobility facilitated by globalized trade, brings an attendant instability to production centres within any of these countries.

Further, the perceived gain in women's employment in the garment export industry in developing countries is inevitably a companion to a generalized and unrelenting pressure to lower wages, and harsher conditions of work relative to industrial workers in several other less globalized industries, even within the low wage developing country. The use of female labour to lower wages, often to be then dispensed with when it has achieved this function, has been a well-known feature of capitalist production and history in many parts of the world. When the gap between male and female wages is wide, more women tend to be brought in. If it narrows, many of them may be dispensed with or replaced. Thus the fluctuations in female share of employment in the garment industries of individual countries is probably a reflection of the differences in the location of the female wage relative to male wages in the industry within a given economy at points in time.[30]

Finally, on the one hand, through unrelenting cut-throat pressure on manufacturing costs to prop up immensely high monopoly profits, metropolitan country-based corporate retailers and brand names appropriate the major part of the value generated by the labour of developing country garment export workers. On the other, indigenous capital in the form of exporters also claims a substantial share. What is left for the workers in the form of wages and other benefits (or lack of them) often falls below subsistence levels, particularly when the overall opportunities for their employment is otherwise negligible.

THE INDIAN GARMENT EXPORT INDUSTRY

Initial Independent Growth and Development

Unlike most countries in the developing world, India did not enter garment exports as part of the international production chain fashioned by either manufacturing or retail capital in the developed capitalist economies. The country has the largest cotton acreage globally (27 per cent) and an evolved textile industry, which encompasses the entire value and supply chain from fibre to garment manufacture. Thus the investment, skills and entrepreneurship behind the initial spurt in garment exports came from the domestic industrial resources of the Indian economy. Manufacturing of readymade garments had its origins in India during World War II when units for mass production of military uniforms were set up. Domestic demand for ready-mades; however, was limited, and from the 1960s, the rapid growth of the industry was brought about through the rising growth of exports, which by the end of the 1980s accounted for more than 50 per cent of the total garment production in the country.[31] From virtually non-existent exports of garments in the early 1960s, it has grown to become one of the major export items for the country constituting roughly 13 per cent of India's total manufactured exports in the period 2003-2004.[32]

A series of government policies, including a compulsory export quota for textile mills and cash incentives drawn from cess on textile mills, duty drawbacks and so on, promoted garment exports in the 1970s.[33] These combined with the higher profit margins from exports in high value currencies compared to a severely demand-constricted domestic market to facilitate rapid expansion of garment exports. With the shift of emphasis in world trade from purchase of textiles to readymade apparel in the mid-1970s, cotton, which was popular but expensive in the West but grown, spun and woven locally and available cheap in India, became the basic fabric that led Indian garment exports. Initially, the fabric for garment exports was supplied by the handloom sector, but as the demands of garment production for exports outstripped the production capacities of handloom, increasingly, exporters turned to the power loom sector, which was growing rapidly from the 1970s, and, to a lesser extent, to the composite mills as their sources of cloth.[34]

Indian garment exports grew around the casual fashions of the late 1960s, when the 'India look' of handloom garments caught American and European fancy.[35] Thus, the first phase of growth, occurred between 1970-1971 and 1975-1976, when the share of clothing in the country's manufactured exports rose from 3.8 per cent to 11.1 per cent and its corresponding share in total exports from 2 per cent to 5 per cent.[36] In this phase, expansion took place through merchant exporters locating markets through informal connections, often through the Indian diaspora. The share of Western Europe and the United States in India's garment exports rose from a mere 8 per cent in 1967 to reach 66 per cent in 1974 and 78 per cent by 1978.[37]

From the mid-1970s, after its initial independent spurt, the quota regime instituted under the MFA became the prime mover behind the organization and development of the Indian garment export industry. Despite the restrictions imposed by the MFA, since the 1980s, it was the quota controlled markets in the United States and Western Europe that dominated the Indian garment export destinations, their share of total garment exports consistently above 70 per cent.[38] Indian garment exports was able to provide fashion garments, primarily cotton-based ones, at extremely low prices in times when cost-cutting in the MFA countries was further impelled by recession or slow-growing demand.

At the same time, structural constraints of low output and relatively high priced handloom production had begun to impose internal supply restraints on growth of Indian garment manufacture. The second phase of growth of exports commencing from 1983-1984 onwards, seems to have been driven by the rapid development of the power-loom and cotton knitwear sectors.[39] Unorganized power-loom manufacture, which grew around the offloaded machinery from the older and declining large-scale textile mill industry, had increasingly eroded the market for both handloom and the composite mills. The trajectory of growth of the market for Indian garment exports which had specialized in the low volume segments with greater fashion content, was thus as yet on the periphery of international mass retailing.[40] As compared to the excessive quantities available at economic rates from the larger mills or the too little and more expensive from the dispersed handloom industry, power-looms were able to provide appropriate quantities of cheap woven cotton fabric suitable to the specific needs of the local export industry. Similarly small-scale hosiery manufacturers supplied the fabric for cotton knitwear garments. With the worldwide shortage of cotton after 1986, India's cotton production base also proved advantageous for its garment exports, which were able to maintain their position in world exports of apparel.[41] And India's share of world clothing exports increased from 1.6 per cent in 1980 to 3.1 per cent in 2000. Although it's position dropped marginally by 2003, when its share stood at 2.9 per cent, India remained the fourth largest exporter of clothing in the world.[42]

Small-Scale and Unorganized Manufacturing Base of Merchant Exporter and Fabricator

The manufacturing base that underpinned the Indian garment industry grew within the parameters of small-scale industry for which garment manufacture was reserved for fifty years from 1951 to 2000.[43] Reliable data on the industry are hard to find, but according to the last comprehensive survey of the readymade garment industry conducted by the Textiles Committee in 1989-1990 (inclusive of domestic manufacturers), some 80 per cent of the units were small or cottage-sized (that is, with sewing machines ranging from below ten to twenty). Only 6 per cent of the units had fifty machines and above. Indian garment exports were dominated by merchant exporters, who contracted out production orders to a number of job work fabrication units of various sizes in the unorganized sector. More than 70 per cent of the machines (primarily sewing machines) and some 84 per cent of employment in the garment export industry were in fabricator units.[44]

Less than 6 per cent of the 17,546 exporters registered with the Apparel Export Promotion Council (AEPC) in 1990 were designated manufacturers, the others were all merchant exporters; although many of those designated merchants were also operating manufacturing units, often in the unregistered sector.[45] Thus, manufacturing for garment exports in India was characterized by widespread sub-contracting by exporters and domination of unregistered and unorganized manufacturing from its early days. Estimates of the share of unorganized manufacturing in garment production vary, but differences are marginal, with one estimate placing it at 80 per cent while another makes it 75 per cent.[46] The prevalence of unorganized and unregistered manufacturing created a foundation of pervasive informal employment relations largely outside the reach of labour laws, initially characterized by piece-rate wages and multi-layered contract work spread out in small units and often extending into home-based work. Over the last fifteen years, however, time-rated wages have become more the norm at factory level production. The general trend of replacement of piece-rate work by time-rate is additionally confirmed by organized sector data available in the occupational wage surveys. The share of time-rated workers in the organized sector of the garment industry increased from some72 per cent in 1977-1979 to 92 per cent in 1994-1995.[47]

Concentrated Centres of Production

Initially Mumbai (Bombay) was the major centre of garment manufacture for export but was rapidly overtaken by Delhi in the mid-1970s and ever since exports from the Delhi region have consistently been the highest in value terms.[48] From the late 1980s, breaking with the pattern of metro city domination, Tirupur, a small town near the old textile city of Coimbatore (Tamilnadu) has grown into an important cluster whose garment export volume (primarily in cotton knitwear) now exceeds all other individual centres in terms of quantity.[49] The older centres of Delhi and Bombay, however, seem to have retained a lead over Tirupur in terms of value of exports.[50] In 2000, Delhi, Mumbai and Tirupur together accounted for over 78 per cent of export manufacture in quantity terms and close to 75 per cent in U.S. dollar value terms. Bangalore and Chennai (Madras) although far behind, accounted for another 14 per cent of output and 19 per cent of exports in value terms.[51]

Eight Export Processing zones (EPZs) had been established in India by the 1990s, but the EPZs account for a very minor share of India's exports (about 3 per cent to 4 per cent)[52]. As such, the closed and restricted enclave system that characterizes EPZs has not been of any real significance in shaping the structure or contours of the Indian garment export industry. The overwhelming majority of manufacturing units are located outside the zones, although a number of merchant and manufacturing exporters outside also avail of duty-free import and investment concessions similar to those granted to EPZ units by registering as Export Oriented Units (EOUs).

The Quota Regime to its Phaseout: Subcontracting by Western Corporate Buyers, Decline in Local Outsourcing

One inevitable fallout of restraints on imports by the quota countries had been the heightened competition among Indian garment exporters for individual shares of the country's limited quotas. Thus, under the MFA regime, the AEPC, which was constituted in 1977-1978, became for all practical purposes, merely an agency for distribution of quotas among Indian exporters.[53] While several formulae for quota distribution were tried out over the years, an increasing weight was given to those who had stable orders and some 'past performance' in exports as well as a minimum export base. Equitable distribution of quotas among Indian exporters, being unviable as per the criteria, fell victim to MFA-imposed restraints, while attempts to independently establish themselves in the markets of the importing economies were stifled by the need to have proven orders to access quotas.[54] Under the MFA, all further development was tailored to the quota system, which favoured established importers rather than independent expansion by exporters.

The initial market trajectories and manufacturing base established independently by Indian exporters were of such an order that quotas were always restrictive. Quota-controlling merchandisers, however, had developed little stake in investment and improvement of manufacturing facilities, leading to a continuing and perhaps increased reliance on job-work fabricators. The high profits of the exporters under the quota regime thus remained linked to the proliferation of competing informal and often illegally established fabricating units with a low-paid and impermanent workforce, unprotected by labour laws. On the one hand, metropolitan country buyers were able to exploit the aggravated competition among local exporters caused by the restraints to their own advantage. On the other, due to quota constraints on expansion of markets, Indian exporters maintained and increased their profits by constantly seeking to lower the cost of production through practices of evasion of minimum wages and other labour laws.

An increasing importance of a few larger manufacturing exporters in India had begun to make itself felt in the late 1980s, further receiving an impetus in the 1990s from policy changes made by the government. For some years, units with 75 per cent exports were allowed to exceed the ceiling on investment on plant and machinery for small-scale industries. The condition for exceeding the ceiling was further brought down to 50 per cent exports in 1996, and finally the reservation for the SSI sector itself was withdrawn in 2000 for woven garments, facilitating an increase in proportions of manufacturer exporters from 6 per cent in 1990 to 16 per cent by 2001.[55] Garment export factories started becoming larger, while ownership became more concentrated.[56] But government policy provides only one half of this story. The other half is provided by the increasing influence and power of corporate buyers from the importing countries on Indian exporters. The major international corporations tend to maintain close links with larger and more technologically equipped manufacturers, although spread over many countries so that individual countries or suppliers have little bargaining power. Following the development of an export-oriented manufacturing base in the country by Indian exporters using their own resources, corporate buyers from the West began to source a part of their supplies from India, largely through manufacturing exporters.

The process of lifting of quotas having created conditions for heightened competition between developing countries, many Indian exporters reared on quotas began to feel that even their limited share of exports defined by quotas were now threatened by competitors from other developing countries. Thus major international buyers with market control have increasingly been able to utilize their enhanced insecurity to make greater demands for price reduction, more stringent quality controls, combined with direct intervention in management practices of local manufacturers.

In fact the campaigns by consumer organizations in the United States and Europe against sweatshops in the third world (however well-intentioned), have been appropriated by corporate buyers who now demand 'compliance' with standards set and supervised by them. Such supervision takes several forms including supervision of equipment and technology, and supervising factory conditions for labour is just one aspect. As was the case under the MFA system, where through their control over market access major buyers were able to appropriate quota restraints to enhance their power vis-à -vis competing exporters, so also they have been able to appropriate demands for compliance with 'labour standards' to acquire enhanced powers to intervene in the internal management of export houses. Unsurprisingly, such interventions are not backed by any acceptance of the higher prices which 'compliance' would entail.

Many Indian manufacturing exporters are perforce moving away from their earlier independent position, becoming more subordinate and locked into the buyer-governed international supply chains of brand names and large-scale retailers in the importing countries, with their entire manufacturing procedures being brought under scrutiny and inspection by their buyers. As part of such a process, along with technological modernization, increasingly all aspects of the manufacturing process are being brought in-house by them to meet the inspection and supervision standards set by buyers.

Such manufacturing exporters are still a numerical minority among the listed garment exporters, and even they continue to require a back-up from fabricating units when volumes exceed their own manufacturing capacities. Yet their growing importance seems to be a mark of what may be termed a shift away from local sub-contracting by independent Indian exporters toward domination of international sub-contracting by importing countries and their principal corporate buyers. Now Indian manufacturing exporters, with more modern units and more expensive and, largely, imported machinery, are the ones on the risk front-line, and it is their workers who are being forced to absorb the consequences of unused capacity which accompanies business downturns of the multinational corporate retailing industry. Inevitably this process has seen the demise of several fabrication units in the unorganized sector, leading to loss of employment there; it has simultaneously led to greater use of dispensable casual and contract labour in larger manufacturing units.

Technology, Increasing Imports, Intensification of the Labour Process

The production of garments essentially involves a sequence of designing, pattern-making, fabric processing and testing, cutting, stitching, zipping/button-work, trimming (thread-cutting), checking and finishing (washing, spot-removing, ironing and packing). Embroidery is done either before or after stitching. Of all these, stitching is the major operation and sewing machines constitute around 87 per cent of the total machinery deployed in the industry.[57] The broad categories of machines are cutting machines, sewing machines, specialized machines (overlock, buttonholing, embroidery and so on) and processing machines (ironing, washing and so on).[58] Less than 10 per cent of all categories of machines were imported in 1990–1991 . Roughly 88 per cent of the sewing machines in the Indian garment industry were then indigenous, most of them low speed manually driven, but over 70 per cent of the high-speed power driven sewing machines were also indigenous.[59]

All recent studies, however, have pointed to a substantial increase in the use of imported machinery in all categories, mostly driven by the manufacturer exporters.[60] Increasing imports have been considerably facilitated by the Export Promotion Capital Goods Scheme (EPCG) of the government under which machinery for export-based industries can be imported duty-free. The growing emphasis on imported machinery is, of course, largely driven by the standards and demands of corporate buyers and has increased the capital intensity of garment manufacture. As one report states 'the major reason for investing in the most state of the art sewing equipment has been to impress the customer, rather than cost effectiveness'.[61] For example, according to the same report, between hand embroidery, the use of simple embroidery machines (hoops and single-needle chain stitch machines) and highly up to date multi-needle multi-head computerized embroidery machines, there is very little cost differentiation for the exporters. Increasingly, the monolithic views and power of metropolitan country corporate buyers are intervening in and moulding the processes of manufacture to a standard increasingly distant and destructive of the intrinsic qualities that had led to the growth of Indian garment exports.

At the same time, manufacturing exporters also seek to maximize the returns on their more expensive and imported machinery by extracting more from their labourers. Not only do they demand increased output per day per worker through intensified labour (in classical Taylorist style), but they also tend to expand the number of hours of work. Such an extension of the working day is essentially the product of the manufacturers' drive to ensure maximum output from their machines, without employing any more workers. One of the fallouts of the intensified pace of work is the tendency to dispense with or discriminate against older workers who naturally find it more difficult to keep pace with the young.

WOMEN WORKERS IN INDIA'S GARMENT EXPORT INDUSTRY

Despite being a large employer of women, the proportions of women workers in India's garment export industry are, even today, far below the international average. Broad-range data from National Sample Surveys (NSS) on employment inclusive of unorganized manufacturing, on the one hand, and Labour Bureau Occupational Wage Surveys or Annual Surveys of Industries (ASIs) that are confined to the registered factory sector, on the other, are able to give us an idea of general trends over time regarding employment and women's share in the readymade garment industry. However, the Textiles Committee Survey of 1989-1990 provides a more detailed and nuanced range of information, particularly for export-oriented garment manufacture, although in the absence of any more recent survey, some of the information is considerably dated. Nevertheless, the details of the structure of the industry provided by the Textiles Committee Survey gives us a contextual framework in which to place current trends and practices observable in NSS and ASI data combined with field-based micro-studies of more recent origin.

Varying Degrees of Female Intensity in Employment

The Textiles Committee Survey data showed that although higher than the 13 per cent share of women in domestic garment manufacturing units, women's share in garment export employment was just 28 per cent in 1989-1990.[62] With 86 per cent of total employment and 88 per cent of women's employment in the garment export industry at the time being concentrated in Delhi and Mumbai, these two centres were the principal determinants of this all India average. In Chennai, which accounted for less than 10 per cent of female employment in India's garment industry, women constituted a high 65 per cent of the workforce. The varying degree of female intensity in employment in the industry could be observed not only across regions but also between the different types of factory units (see Table 2.2).

Table 2.2 Share and distribution of female employment in the garment export industry (1989-1990)

Region	Fabricators [A]		Manufacturer Exporters (Factory) [B]		Merchant Exporters (Factory) [C]		All [A]+[B]+[C]
	Percentage of women workers in total (male + female) workers	Percentage share in women's employment in garment export units of all kinds	Percentage of women workers in total (male + female) workers	Percentage share in women's employment in garment export units of all kinds	Percentage of women workers in total (male + female) workers	Percentage share in women's employment in garment export units of all kinds	Workers in total workers in all types of units
Delhi	29	89	22	6	29	5	28
Bombay Mumbai	28	86	36	14	25	<1	29
Madras Chennai	42	15	71	85	-	-	65
Bangalore	16	43	40	57	-	-	24
All India	26	80	40	17	21	3	28

Source: Percentages (all rounded off) calculated from Textile Committee Survey (1989-1990) data given in S.L.Batra, *Employment for women.*

Apart from Delhi, whose specific characteristics are discussed in a later section, the broad trend of a higher intensity of female employment in the factories of manufacturing exporters becomes apparent from Table 2.2. Women constituted 40 per cent of the workforce in manufacturing exporter units, in comparison to 26 per cent and 21 per cent in fabricator and merchant export units, respectively. In fact, the much higher proportions of women in Chennai is also to some extent due to the fact that manufacturing exporters contributed close to 78 per cent of total (male amd female) garment export employment there in comparison to just 11 per cent in Mumbai or 8 per cent in Delhi. Clearly systems of production organization in the manufacturer exporter units were more female-intensive and led the way in Chennai, while fabricating units, contributing an overwhelming 88 per cent of total employment in Delhi and Mumbai, established the dominant pattern of much lower proportions of women workers in those centres.

Traditional exclusion of women from skilled tailoring

Tailors or stitching operators constitute close to 80 per cent of the work-force in the garment industry.[63] It was the exclusion of women from tailoring in the fabrication units that probably accounts for their relatively low employment proportions in the industry as a whole. Studies in the 1980s have documented the prevalence of only male tailors (initially working on piece rates) in fabricating units of Delhi when the practice was still largely for a single tailor to stitch a whole or major part of any garment.[64] Such exclusion reflected a carryover of the prevalent social tradition in professional tailoring. But it was also reinforced by the lumpenized conditions of work and residence in many unorganized fabrication units as the expansion of production led to more captive low-waged male migrant labourers hailing from the rural hinterland, replacing or supplementing the initial class of more urbanized and skilled professional tailors.[65] Women were introduced into the garment export industry in Delhi and Mumbai in the specific occupations of checkers (of stitches, measurement and so on),[66] multi purpose helpers, and thread cutters (trimmers).[67] In contrast, Chennai had a very high share of women in stitching/tailoring bringing up their overall employment share (see Table 2.3).

Given the fact that stitching operators/tailors account for four-fifths of the workforce in the industry, the exclusion of women from tailoring in the principal centres of the export industry, such as Delhi, provides some explanation for their relatively low employment share at the national level.

Table 2.3 Share of female employment in stitching/tailoring (1995)

	Fabricators		Merchant exporters		Manufacturer exporters	
	Women among tailors %	Women in total work-force %	Women among tailors %	Women in total work-force %	Women among tailors %	Women in total work-force %
Delhi	1	5.4	4	25.7	22	25.5
Mumbai	10	24.4	16	29.3	21	23.3
Chennai	83	69.6	94	86.4	95	72.9

Compiled from survey data in S.L. Batra, *Employment for women.*

Over the years, assembly line manufacturing, where parts of a garment are stitched along a chain of stitching operators, has been replacing the earlier system where a single tailor would stitch almost the complete garment. Such a changeover was led, in the first instance, by the organized manufacturer exporters. The chain system (as it is referred to by workers) opened the doors to a degree of increased employment of women as tailoring operators, extending into even fabrication units in Chennai and Tirupur. Nevertheless, of the 382,000 women[68] in the garment export industry in 1989-1990 at an all India level, some 298,000 (78 per cent of the industry's female workforce) were working for fabricators in Delhi and Mumbai where the general practice of hiring men for tailoring remained dominant. Thus, despite their low share of employment within these fabricating units, the fate of the continued employment of the several thousands of women already employed in the industry was inevitably linked to the survival of these fabricators.

Discrimination as Tool of Wage Repression and Exploitation : Evidence from the Organised Sector

Compared to unorganized manufacturing, the organized sector in the garment industry at an all India level (for which trend data may be found by comparing the Ministry of Labour's Occupational Wage Surveys (OWS) for 1977-1979 and 1994-1995 and the Annual Survey of Industries (ASI) for 1999-2000 and 2002-2003), shows a much more significant share in employment of women workers. It rose from 36 per cent in 1977-1979 to about 65 per cent in 1999-2000, and although it dropped to 61 per cent in 2002-2003, it is clear that women workers now are the numerical majority in organized sector garment production.[69] A look at the state-wise distribution (see Table 2.4), however, reveals that by 1999-2000 about 74 per cent of all workers and 88 per cent of women workers in the organized sector of the industry were concentrated in the two southern states of Tamilnadu and Karnataka, where the share of women was far above the all India average. By 2002-2003, although Tamilnadu saw a drop in numbers of workers and Karnataka emerged as the largest centre for the organized sector, 88 per cent of the women in the country's registered garment factories remained concentrated in the two southern states. In contrast, Delhi's share of organized sector garment employment was less than 10 per cent in 2002-2003, within which the share of women turned out to be an extremely low 12 per cent.[70] This, as can be seen, is less than half the share of women in the industry in 1989-1990 as per the Textiles Committee survey, which had included the unorganized sector.[71]

The phenomenon of a higher share of women in industrial employment in the southern states, particularly in the organized sector, is not confined to the garment industry alone. Obviously social differences in the overall situation of women (including perhaps relatively less seclusive traditions and relatively higher educational levels in the south) would be a contributory factor. No less important are the sharp differences in wages between the centres where women predominate and those where they are in a minority, as revealed in the Occupational Wage Survey data given in Table 2.5.

Table 2.4. Women's share of employment in the organized sector of garment industry (1994-1995 and 1999-2000)

	Estimated total number of workers in 1994 as per Labour Bureau Occupational Wage Survey	Women workers %	Estimated total number of workers in 1999-2000 as per Annual Survey of Industries*	Women workers %	Estimated total number of workers in 2002-03 as per Annual Survey of Industries*	Women workers %
Uttar Pradesh	25,766	35	8,569	28	9,022	16
Tamilnadu	67,388	76	89,139	82	80,180	79
Delhi	41,546	15	18,706	18	25,440	12
Maharashtra	23,963	34	12,859	31	9,805	27
Gujarat	11,590	65	5,659	51	4,872	40
Other states	9,734	43	16,933	35	29,280	33
Total	246,392	55	237,330	65	265,834	61

* Refers to the number of directly employed workers and excludes contract workers for whom sex disaggregated figures are not available in the ASI report.

Table 2.5: Percentage share of women's employment and wage rates by sex : reference period 1994 –1995

State	Employment share of women workers %	Average Daily Minimum Wage Rates (Rs)			Average Daily Maximum Wage Rates (Rs)		
		Men	Women	Overall	Men	Women	Overall
Tamilnadu	76	33.63	22.37	25.10	52.35	31.71	36.72
Karnataka	73	48.81	37.12	40.26	68.28	43.89	50.44
Delhi	15	66.01	67.61	66.26	80.63	85.47	81.38
Uttar Pradesh	35	49.85	50.24	49.98	58.15	59.32	58.56
Maharashtra	34	81.54	60.05	74.16	110.72	76.95	99.13
Gujarat	65	55.09	40.38	45.59	101.18	41.92	62.94
Other states	43	51.71	42.73	47.80	69.71	51.72	61.88
Total	55	57.15	35.60	45.36	75.58	44.43	58.53

Source: Occupational Wage Survey, Fifth Round, Report on the Textile Garments Industry, 1995-1996 Percentages rounded off.

From Table 2.5 the relationship between low wages and higher share of women's employment is too starkly self-evident to require much further elaboration. The lowest overall wage rates occur precisely in those states where the female share of employment is the highest and conversely in the higher wage regions the share tends to be much lower. At the same time, with the exception of Delhi (which also shows the lowest proportions of women workers) and its neighbouring state Uttar Pradesh, in all other states, women workers' wage rates are considerably lower than male workers.[72] Unsurprisingly, the widest gap between male and female wages at the lower level (average minimum wage rate) can be seen in the state with the highest share of female employment (Tamilnadu), where women's wages were on an average some 33 per cent lower than men's. And the least gap (in fact almost equal) appears in the state with the lowest share of women (Delhi). Similarly, along with the broad tendency for the wage gap to be wider at the higher end (average maximum wage), again it is clear that lower wages for women is associated with higher shares of women's employment. It might be argued that regional differences in living costs explain the differences in overall wage rates, but this can hardly be advanced as an explanation for wage differentials between men and women of the same region.

Despite the actual discrimination against women evident in the wage rate data, the official conclusion has been that they do not indicate the violation of the provisions of the Equal Remuneration Act. The grounds for the wage gap are attributed to frequent change of jobs by women, differences in length of service, non-existence of any prescribed time-scale, merger of different levels of skills, inter-unit differences in wage rates, and, in the case of piece-rated workers variations in output between men and women.[73] While such conclusions are indicative of the inadequacy of the present law in defining and addressing the issue of gender-based wage discrimination, they nevertheless reveal several aspects of the manner and consequences of discrimination.

Among the causes of frequent change of jobs, causing shorter lengths of service, could be interruptions in women's working lives due to marriage, children and so on, just as output differences among piece-rated workers could be due to the time required by women to fulfil their domestic duties. Thus some causes might be rooted in social factors external to direct employer practices; however, equally probable causes would be the greater use of women in casual or contract work by employers and service interruptions due to their dispensability or 'flexible employment contracts'. At the same time there is some evidence that women are excluded from the higher paid piece-rated work, such as more skilled tailoring and confined to the low-paid tiers of piece-rated work.[74] Similarly, inter-unit differences put forward as a cause of differences in average wage rates would indicate that where the numbers of women are more, the wage rates are lower. Therefore, it is reasonable to assume that discriminatory practices by employers are also a significant factor in the wage-rate inequality experienced by women in the industry. In sum, such discriminatory practices not only ensure that women's wages are lower than men's, they also explain the link between increased women's employment with an overall lowering of wages in the industry.

The all-pervasive prevalence of unequal wages for women are further reflected in the fact that in both time-rated and piece-rated wage rates women's wages are lower than men's. Some aspects that emerge from the Occupational Wage Survey data on time-rate and piece-rate wages, sheds further light on some of the specificities of the use of inequality and discrimination as a tool for sharpening the general exploitative edge of capital over labour in the garment industry.

De-skilling, Time Rates and Lower Wages: the Exploitation of Women Workers

As mentioned earlier, the introduction of the chain system in tailoring has led to more women being employed as tailors. What perhaps needs to be added is that with chain or assembly line tailoring, the individual creative tailoring skill requirement is also eliminated, a classic case of de-skilling. A feature accompanying the process of deskilling of the tailoring occupation has been not only the expansion of time-rated work relative to piece-rated, but also lower wage rates of time-rated work in comparison to piece-rated. Most striking is the fact that in the principal occupation of tailor (specialist), the gap between overall wage rates of time-rated and piece-rated workers is the widest.[75] The average daily minimum wage rate was Rs 38.96 for time-rated specialist tailors, as compared to Rs 61.78 for those on piece rates. Similarly, the maximum wage rate was Rs 46.81 for the former in comparison to Rs 109.19 for the latter.[76]

More than in any other occupation in the garment industry, the lowering of wages in tailoring has been linked with bringing women into this occupation from which they were earlier excluded. In fact, it could be said that the object of bringing in women has been precisely to lower the overall wage. In this the shift from piece-rate to time-rate wages has been a factor. Generally speaking, time-rates are distinctly preferable to piece-rates as they are linked to greater security and continuity of employment, as well as better possibilities of regulation and restriction on excessive working hours; however, particularly in skilled occupations, time-rates have often been introduced with the specific objective of lowering the wage rates and curtailing the bargaining power that some groups of piece-rated workers might have acquired. This is what seems to have occurred most markedly among tailors in readymade garment manufacture and to a lesser degree even among helpers, as can be seen from Table 2.6.

On the other hand, among checkers where women have been around for a longer period, their piece-rate wage rates are less than half the time-rate for both minimum and maximum wage rates. In other words, whereas in tailoring time rates and the employment of women were linked for the purposes of reducing the wage bill, in the case of checking, piece rates are used to further depress the wages of women workers.

If the limited object of employment of women was for disrupting any growing bargaining power of the more skilled piece-rated male tailors, and lowering the wage rates, it seems to have been largely accomplished through the 1980s and early 1990s. It should then not come as a surprise that the broader data sources showed that by the end of the 1990s, women's share of employment in the apparel industry has declined.

National Sample Survey Revelations: Low and Fluctuating Share of Women's Employment, Unemployment and Casualization

A comparison between the 50th (1993-1994), 55th (1999-2000) and 60th (2004) rounds of the NSS shows an overall increase in employment in the manufacture of wearing apparel for both men and women, see

Table 2.6: Average daily wage rates for main occupations in textile garment industry (1995-1996)

Occupation	Average Daily Wage Rates for time-rated workers (Rs)				Average Daily Wage Rates for piece-rated workers (Rs)			
	Minimum		Maximum		Minimum		Maximum	
	Men	Women	Men	Women	Men	Women	Men	Women
Tailor (specialist)	46.35	35.02	54.43	42.74	68.24	43.45	125.04	64.24
Helper	47.20	30.22	56.58	38.23	61.59	-	66.18	-
Checker	51.37	37.27	60.97	46.31	33.86	17.72	33.86	22.58
All occupations	55.65	35.13	68.98	43.24	67.25	47.63	119.93	74.78

Source: Occupational Wage Survey, 1995-1996

Table 2.7. In contrast, however, to the rising graph of women's employment share in the registered factory sector of the garment industry between 1994-1995 and 1999-2000, NSS data, which includes the unregistered sector, shows a sharp decline in the share of principal status female employment in the manufacture of wearing apparel between 1993-1994 and 1999-2000. This was then followed by an increase in women's share till 2004, although at the end of the decade beginning 1993-1994, the share of women workers was still marginally less than at the beginning.[77] Since principal usual status worker applies to a person who was engaged in work-related activities for a relatively longer time of the period of 365 days preceding the date of survey, it is most likely to capture the segment of factory workers in the export sector. In this category, women's share in employment fell steeply from 29 per cent in 1993–1994 to 20 per cent in 1999–2000 and then rapidly increased again to 28 per cent in 2004.[78]

Table 2.7. Employment in manufacture of wearing apparel as per 50th, 55th and 60th NSS rounds

Year, NSS round and NIC code*	Principal status workers			Principal + Subsidiary status workers		
	Male	Female	Share of- female %	Male	Female	Share of female %
1993-1994, 50th round, NIC 265	578,600	233,307	29	589,231	291,925	33
1999–2000, 55th round, NIC 181	1,672,491	430,831	20	1,693,539	643,533	28
2004, 60th round, NIC 181	3,622,476	1,469,248	28	3,632,741	2,162,575	36

Source: Employment and Unemployment in India, 1993-1994, 1999-2000, and 2004, NSSO, Dept. of Statistics, Govt. of India.

*NIC refers to National Industrial Classification. NIC codes were changed in 1998. Accordingly for the 1993-1994 survey the codes of 1987 have been used, and the 1998 codes for the 1999-2000 and 2004 surveys.

On the other hand, in the category of subsidiary status worker, who is a person categorized as a non-worker (that is, unemployed or out of the labour force) who pursued the same economic activity in a subsidiary capacity, the share of women increased from 85 per cent to 91 per cent between 1993-1994 and 1999-2000, and reached 99 per cent in 2004, see Tables 2.8. In other words, disproportionately larger numbers of women are experiencing unemployment or short-term casual employment in the industry in comparison to male workers.

Table 2.8: Subsidiary Status Employment in the manufacture of wearing apparel as per 50th, 55th and 60th NSS rounds

Year, NSS round and NIC code	Subsidiary status workers		
	Male	Female	Percentage share of female
1993–1994, 50th round, NIC 265	10,559 (2%)	58,618 (20%)	85
1999-2000, 55th round, NIC 181	21,048 (1%)	212,702 (33%)	91
2004, 60th round, NIC 181	10,265 (0.2%)	693,327 (32%)	99

Figures in parenthesis show percentage of subsidiary workers to total Principal+Subsidiary workers

In the final analysis, NSS data reveal that most of the gains in women's employment in garments might have been offset by losses. Where the addition in employment of principal status women workers between the 1993-94 and the 2004 NSS rounds amounted to 1,235,941, at least more than half of that number (represented by the addition of 634,709 subsidiary workers) were also facing unemployment, under-employment or even displacement. Further, where the share of subsidiary status workers among male workers has remained marginal and declining from 2 per cent to 0.2 per cent, among women workers in the garment industry the share of subsidiary status workers has actually risen from 20 per cent to 32 per cent. Finally, the rather surprising leap in numbers of both men and women employed in the manufacture of wearing apparel (according to NSS estimates), particularly between 1999-2000 and 2004, is not explainable by growth of exports. In other words it seems that what appears as a reversal of the steep decline in proportions of women workers in garment manufacture after 1999-2000, and the vast increase in numbers of workers in the manufacture of wearing apparel, is probably more linked to the pressures of labour surpluses that are driving women into shifting from occupation to occupation in a desperate search for petty and irregular incomes.[79] This is further borne out by the fact that the sharpest rise in numbers has been among rural women and the share of rural women in the apparel sector crossed 50 per cent in 2004, up from 36 per cent in 1999-2000.

FIELD SURVEY: WOMEN AND WORK IN DELHI'S GARMENT EXPORT INDUSTRY

In the first part of this chapter, some of the contours of the field survey of women workers in Delhi's garment export industry and the profile of the workers have already been outlined. What is presented below are the findings of the field survey in relation to the universe of their employment and the trends and tendencies in relation to the nature of factories in which the women worked, the forms of their employment relations, and their conditions of work.

Factory Profiles

A view of the distribution of the factories in which the surveyed workers worked, indicates an increased concentration of garment factories in South Delhi, or to be more specific, in the Okhla Industrial Area, and Noida and Gurgaon in the neighbouring states, see Table 2.9. All these three industrial areas tend to have larger sized plot areas for factories than is commonly seen in several other industrial areas in Delhi.

Table 2.9: Distribution of surveyed workers by location of residence and location of factory

District	By location of residence	By location of factory
East Delhi	25	16
Northeast	18	11
Northwest	19	18
Southwest	32	17
West	14	9
South	27	29
Noida	12	25
Gurgaon	3	25
All	150	150

The information regarding the factory employment characteristics were gathered from the women workers themselves. Naturally, a few gaps exist in the information, and the unit workforce numbers in many cases would at best be approximations. Given the fact, however, that managements are notorious for fudging their figures (particularly in relation to employment), to avoid attracting labour law provisions, there is no reason to believe that the information from the workers would be in any way more unreliable than from more official sources.

More than half the factories in which the women worked had come into existence over the past decade (information on how old the factories were was available for seventy of the ninety-nine factories in which the women worked). Eleven (close to one-sixth) had been functioning for 20 years and more, the oldest unit having been there for 35 years. Twenty-two (a little less than one-third) ranged between 10 and 17 years, placing about half the factories at over 10 years old. Among the remaining units, seventeen were between 5 and 9 years old and twenty were from a few months to 4 years old. Among the older factories women constituted 26 per cent of the workforce as compared to 50 per cent in the newer units.

Only one of the thirty-three older units of 10 years and more was a fabricator unit. All the others were either merchant or manufacturing exporters, while fourteen of the twenty units of less than five years could be called fabrication units.[80] Thus, it would seem that although

Table 2.10: Distribution of surveyed workers by designation and workforce-size of factory

Surveyed women workers by designation	factories by size of total (male +female) workforce							In all factories	Percentage distribution of workers by designation
	1000-1500	500-805	300-455	200-290	100-195	50-95	7-49		
Helper	1	3	7	10	12	6	15	54	36
Thread-cutter	1	3	3	6	5	4	15	37	25
Checker	2	3	7	3	4	3	7	29	19
Tailor/operator	5	7	5	3	4	1	3	28	19
Other	-	-				1	1	2	1
All designations	9 (6%)	16 (11%)	22 (15%)	22 (15%)	25 (17%)	15 (10%)	41 (17%)	150	100

Table 2.11: Numbers of male and female workers in the factories as reported by workers

	Factories by size of total (male + female) workforce							All factories
	1000-1500	500-805	300-455	200-290	100-195	50-95	7-49	
No. of factories	4	10	11	21	18	11	23	98
No. of women workers	2033	2540	1255	731	649	183	258	7649
No. of male workers	2492	3565	3100	4109	1910	565	326	16067
Percentage share of women in total employment	45	42	29	15	25	32	44	32

older fabrication units have either graduated to becoming manufacturing exporters or been eliminated, new ones still seem to be coming into existence. The figures show that there is a trend towards increased employment of women in the 1990s, yet as far as fabricators are concerned, even in the newer units the female share in the workforce was a low 19 per cent.

Persistence of Inequality Despite Redistribution of Women Within the Industry

The survey revealed that a change has taken place in the distribution of women's employment in Delhi's garment industry in the globalization decade with a stronger presence of larger manufacturing units and a declining share of fabricators. Just a little over one-fourth of the workers were working in the small units of less than 50 workers, and in fact only some 37 per cent of the women were found to be working in the units below 100. The smaller factories are largely the fabrication units (whose workforce could rarely exceed 100),[81] which had accounted for 89 per cent of women's employment in 1989 according to the Textiles Committee Survey. Even if one assumes that some of the larger units were also of fabricators, the share of those units with 300 to 1,500 workers (who were clearly either merchant or manufacturer exporters) was close to 32 per cent of the surveyed garment workers in 2002 (see Table 2.10). Obviously the fabricating units have *declined in proportion* to the *rise in manufacturing or merchant exporters*. Accordingly the distribution of women workers among the different types of units has changed.

Further, the proportions of women in total employment in the ninety-eight factories (as reported by the workers) indicate that in the above 500 factories, women's share of employment (43 per cent) is quite significantly higher than the overall average of 32 per cent, see Table 2.11.

Going by the trends in recorded organized sector employment, apart from greater opportunities for women's employment, the rise of the larger units might also be seen by some as indicative of their access to more skilled categories of labour. Such a trajectory seems to be additionally borne out by the survey's finding that some 62 per cent of the women in factories employing 300 and above were working in the skilled categories of tailor operators and checkers. In contrast, some 71 per cent of the women working in the units with less than 300 workers were concentrated in the unskilled categories of helpers and thread-cutters.

A closer look at individual factory details, however, revealed that even in many of the larger manufacturing or merchant units, women remain a minority. On the one hand, women were a majority of the workforce (65 per cent) in eighteen of the ninety-nine factories of which eight were relatively larger manufacturers employing 500 and more workers. On the other hand in seventy-two of the units they constituted less than 20 per cent of the workforce of whom fifty-five had workforce sizes of more than hundred, including eight units with above 500 workers.

At a preliminary level, the reason for the *continuing low proportions* of women in the majority of the garment export factories in Delhi may be attributed to the fact that *tailoring operations* in most units still *remain male dominated.* This is further confirmed by the fact that only 19 per cent of the women workers were employed as tailor operators in an industry that is so overwhelmingly tailor dominated. In comparison 61 per cent were in the unskilled occupations of helpers and thread-cutters. It seems that if in the larger units women constituted a majority of the workforce, this was so because of a specific policy of preference in recruitment of women, particularly as tailoring operators.

At a more general level, it is true that the supply of male labour in Delhi still far exceeds that of female labour, which would account for the higher proportions of male workers in the garment industry, as in other industries. But given the fact that more than any other industry in the area, garment export manufacturing units have developed some tradition of employing women, and given also fairly high rates of unemployment among the women garment workers, supply shortages of female labour cannot be an adequate explanation for the extremely low proportions of women in so many units. One of the reasons for the continued domination of male workers in tailoring even in manufacturing exporter units may be sought precisely in the *decimation of several fabricator units* which has left thousands of trained male tailors without work, providing a *cheap source of labour* for the growing manufacturer exporters. Thus the opportunities offered by the rise of manufacturer exporters for a changeover from the exclusionist tradition in relation to tailoring that marked the earlier fabricator-dominated industry have not been substantial enough to counter the effects of a surplus of experienced male tailors in the labour market of the region.

High Level of Unemployment

A striking finding of the survey was the *spread* of unemployment among women garment workers in Delhi. On any given day, these unemployed workers can be seen (often in pairs) moving around in industrial areas in search of work. At the time of the survey, 30 per cent of the women workers were unemployed. Young and old workers had lost their jobs with one-third of them in their twenties, some two-fifths in their thirties, and a little less than one-fourth in their forties (see Table 2.12). At the same time, from the reports of the women, it is quite clear that the older women who lose their jobs face greater difficulty in finding new employment even where fresh recruitment takes place.

Of special significance was the fact that the majority of the unemployed were erstwhile casual or contract workers. Roughly one-third of them had been casual and close to another one-third were contract workers, both falling in the category of a 'flexible' workforce or in other words, a perpetually captive yet dispensable labour force.

Among the unemployed who said that they had been earlier employed as casual or contract workers, there were some who had put in 8 to 10 years of service and the overwhelming majority (four-fifths) had service tenures upward of a year.[82] Similarly, a little over one-third of those who had lost their jobs also considered their earlier employment fell in the category of permanent (which by law should have been somewhat protected), and had had relatively durable tenures ranging from a minimum of 2 years to 7 years (the exception to this overall trend was one worker who had actually put in 17.5 years of service in the same unit). Thus a significant section of the unemployed workers had earlier had relatively regular but obviously unprotected jobs.

Almost one-third of the unemployed workers, that is, fourteen out of the forty-five had lost their jobs due to closure of their factories. Five others were dismissed or thrown out because there was no work

Table 2.12 Erstwhile employment status and age of unemployed workers

Erstwhile employment status of unemployed workers	Age of unemployed garment workers				Unemployed workers by erstwhile employment status	Unemployed in each status category %
	20 - 28	30-37	40 - 45	50 -55		
Casual	4	7	3	-	14	25
Contract	5	5	3	1	14	35
Permanent	6	5	5	1	17	31
All	15	17	11	2	45	30

coming in to their units. Four more were forced to leave following relocation of their factories to Gurgaon and Noida. Two of them were just dismissed along with scores of their co-workers at the time of relocation, while two left because the new locations were too far for them to commute to. Two others were part of a general retrenchment of permanent workers in their factories who were being replaced by contract workers. Closures, declining availability of work in some units, relocation and mass dismissals thus accounted for over one-half (51 per cent) of the unemployed.

Of the others, eleven were just dismissed of whom three were permanent workers with 6 to 8 years of service, three were casual and five were contract workers. One of the casual workers was dismissed just at the time when she was to have become permanent, while four out of the five contract workers had served in their factories for more than a year each. Of the remaining nine who could be said to have voluntarily left their previous employment, one had not been paid wages for 3 months, one left due to pregnancy when she could not continue climbing stairs (she had no health insurance despite having put in 2 years of service) and two had left due to illnesses in their family requiring their care. One left because she had got married, another because she had small children and the overtime was too strenuous; two more left because they had moved to colonies at considerable distance from their earlier place of employment[83] and one because of a conflict with her supervisor.

In sum, the *causes* of unemployment among *over two-fifths* of the unemployed were *closures or no work* in their factories; for *two-fifths,* it was because of *flexible (easy to fire) employment practices,* and for *one-fifth* it was due to their *social conditions as women.* Yet all were in search of work, and all said that it was now much more difficult to find employment than earlier.

The brunt of termination of jobs and unemployment was clearly being borne by unskilled workers—63 per cent of those who had lost their jobs and were unemployed were unskilled workers. Of some note, however, was the fact that contrary to the general impression that skilled workers stand to benefit from the changing scenario, close to one-third (32 per cent) of the tailor operators and well over one-fifth (21 per cent) of the checkers were also unemployed. Further, loss of employment was experienced by workers in all sizes of factories, a sign of the general volatility of employment in the garment export industry. Table 2.13(a) gives the distribution of unemployed workers by designation and 2.13(b) by the size of the factory where they had been employed before termination.

Table 2.13.: Distribution of unemployed workers by
(a) designation (b) factory size

Designation of the person in factory where last employed	Percentage share of unemployed among all workers in each designation	Percentage share of each designation among unemployed	Work-force size of factory where last employed	Percentage distri- of unemployed by workforce size of factory where last employed
Thread-cutter	32	28	500–1025	18
Helper	30	35	300–455	18
Tailor operator	32	22	204–250	18
			100–190	25
Checker	21	15	18–60	21
All designations	30	100	All	100

The tragedy of unemployment was compounded for about one-third of the unemployed women whose husbands were also unemployed. Thus 30-year-old Israwati, hailing from a small peasant/agricultural worker family and having lived in Delhi for 15 years,[84] already painfully thin, was obviously close to starvation. Mother of six children, she spoke with quiet despair of how even neighbours from her *jhuggi basti* in Okhla, who had earlier been friendly, sympathetic and supportive, have stopped talking to her family because 'they fear we will ask for money from them'. She had been without work for 3 months as was the local contractor who used to employ her intermittently. Her husband had been unemployed for even longer and they were indebted to the tune of Rs 50,000. And then there is 34-year-old Bharati Bhattacharya, mother of three who has been a worker for

12 of her 16 years in Delhi. Together, she and her husband had over the years saved enough to build a small *kuccha* room in the urban village adjacent to the industrial area where both worked. For the last two years she had a job as a thread-cutter in a fabricating unit,[85] but lost it as there was no more work coming in to the unit. Her husband had lost his long-standing job some months before when his factory closed down. For the past six months, she had been trudging to various places in search of work for she has no money even to take a bus. She is now considering selling the small house for which her family toiled, scrimped and saved for years, but is nervous about what will happen after. These are just two among many garment workers whose toil has contributed to the profits of exporters and the export earnings of the country, but who are considered dispensable in the present era.

Increasing Casualization and Contractualization: The Squeeze on Wages

Earlier we have pointed to the decline in subcontracting or outsourcing to fabricators; however, in-contracting by exporters, that is, employment of workers within their own factory premises through labour contractors (thekedars) so as to avoid any direct legal relationship with the workers is not only widespread but on the increase. More than one-third of the factories were reported to be increasing the numbers of contract workers. Of them, a little less than one-half were older factories of 10 years and more where earlier permanent employment had been the norm. Of the fifteen units where contract workers were reported to be decreasing in number, in nine, overall numbers of male and female workers were being reduced, which gives an indication of downsizing rather than expansion of better-quality employment. In general, most workers felt that casual and contract work was on the rise and permanent jobs were being eroded.

More than three-fifths of the workers were themselves casual or contract workers—37 per cent were casual, and 25 per cent were on contract. It is often argued that the use of casual or contract labour as the most 'flexible' form of labour is essential for an order- or season-driven export industry; however, an investigation of the service tenure of the 'flexible' workers showed that the seasonal nature of orders was not the real reason for casual or contract employment of most of the workers. More than two-thirds of them (67.5 per cent) had been working in the same unit continuously for over a year with some having more than 10 years of service and by law they should have been made permanent or absorbed as regular employees, see Table 2.14.

Table 2.14. Service tenures and years of experience of workers (%)

Service	Casual workers	Contract workers	Permanent workers	No. of years as a worker	Casual workers	Contract workers	Permanent workers
>10	7	6	12	>10	12	9	12
5 – 10	12	3	42	5 – 10	12	3	46
1 – 4	49	58	38	1 – 4	49	58	34
< 1	32	33	8	< 1	27	30	8

On the one hand, there are several aspects of the legally defined labour contract with permanent workers that can be avoided through use of casual and contract labour, such as provisions for provident fund, health insurance, leave and so on. But what is usually left unstated by the propagators of flexible labour contracts and which is perhaps more decisive is the wage-depressed characteristic of casual and contract labour. It was found that where the average wage of permanent workers was Rs 2,306, for the 'flexible' workers it was considerably less, that is, Rs 1,793 for casual workers and Rs 1,536 for contract workers. Thus while even many permanent workers were being denied the legally stipulated minimum wage, casual and contract workers were being paid even less, see Table 2.15.[86]

Returning to the Dark Ages: The Regularization of Overtime Work

Well over one-half of the workers reported daily work hours ranging from 10 to 12 with on an average just 2 days off in a month. Such a killing pace of work has become acceptable to workers because eight-hour wages are so inadequate to meet their needs. The regularization of overtime work is one of the principal characteristics of garment export manufacture under globalization and has seared itself into the

Table 2.15. Average monthly wages of workers by designation and nature of employment contract

Designation	Casual		Contract		Permanent	
	No. of workers	Average wage (Rs)	No. of workers	Average wage (Rs)	No. of workers	Average wage (Rs)
Thread-cutter	14	1650	13	1412	10	2605
Helper	25	1480	16	1488	13	1875
Tailor operator	10	2443	3	2400	15	2366
Checker	7	2269	5	1500	17	2733
Others	–	–	–	–	2	2400
All	56 (37%)	1793	37 (25%)	1536	57 (38%)	2306

Table 2.16. Daily working hours

Daily work	Percentage of workers within each category of factory by workforce size						Percentage of workers
	500–1500	300–455	200–290	100–195	50–95	7–49	
10–12	43	52	63	47	50	69	56
9–9.5	10	8	5	11		3	6
8	47	40	32	42	50	28	38

consciousness of all workers. In most cases, it just becomes an extended shift since the requirement of double the regular hourly wage for overtime work is rarely implemented. Only 20 per cent of the workers were being given the double regular hourly rate for overtime.

Despite the legal bar on employment of women beyond 7 p.m., masses of women garment workers exiting their factories sometimes at 8 p.m. and sometimes as late as 10 p.m, is a common sight (see Table 2.16). Among the surveyed workers, such overtime was found to be *optional* for only *one-third* of the workers. For the others it was virtually a *condition* of service. The experience of late work as a condition of service among garment workers in a sense anticipates a similar consequence of the proposed change in law lifting the ban on *night work for women.*

It was found that rarely do employers provide their women workers, including those who work late hours, with transport. Company transport was available to only 5 per cent of the workers. Even among the women working 10–12 hours on a daily basis whose time away from home ranged from 12–15 hours, the proportion of those who had access to company buses was just 7 per cent.[87] For a detailed presentation of the relevant figures, see Table 2.17

Table 2.17. Mode of transport of workers

Daily hours	No. of workers		Mode of Transport*					
			Walking		Public Bus		Company Bus	
	No.	%	No.	%	No.	%	No.	%
12–15	46	31	24	52	19	41	3	7
11–11.5	32	22	11	38	20	63	1	3
10 – 10.5	26	17	9	35	17	65	-	-
9.5	23	15	13	57	9	39	1	4
8.5–9	23	15	15	65	7	30	1	4
All workers	150	100	72	47	72	48	6	5

* Two women who travelled by rickshaw have been incorporated into the walking category and one worker who went by a tempo has been added in public bus. Of the five workers travelling by company buses, three units were located in Noida and two in Gurgaon. In other words, company buses were there only when it would have been logistically impossible for workers to be available for work. Not one company bus was available for the Delhi workers.

Apart from the adverse health consequences of such long hours of work, often (as in Sushila's case), standing throughout, the consequences are also borne by the families and particularly the children of these workers. Of the workers surveyed, 83 per cent had children, one-third of whom had small kids or children below 5 years of age. And yet *not one of the units had a creche, which is a legal requirement.* Some of the more organized units had a room designated 'creche' which is usually nothing more than a showpiece for clearance of factory building plans or to impress international buyers.

Widespread Violations of Workers' Rights and Entitlements

Violation of labour rights *across the spectrum of labour laws* was found to be the normal experience of the overwhelming majority of women workers. Not surprisingly the maximum violation was in the sphere of minimum wages, with 78 per cent of the workers being denied their legal minimum wage. Again unsurprisingly, much higher proportions of casual and contract workers, 94 per cent and 97 per cent, respectively, were denied minimum wages. What is revealing is that among permanent workers, where more than 80 per cent had access to health insurance, provident fund and leave, less than 40 per cent had minimum wages. Table 2.18 gives the percentage of women workers among permanent, casual and contract workers with legally defined labour rights.

Table 2.18. Labour law implementation among permanent, casual and contract workers

Legal entitlement of workers	Among Permanent workers %	Among Casual workers %	Among Contract workers %	Among all workers %
Minimum wages	39	6	3	22
Health insurance	84	2	0	32
Provident Fund	80	4	0	32
Minimum Bonus	73	4	0	37
Leave	82	12	3	35

The category of checkers, being the older of the skilled-occupation categories open to women, were somewhat better off, particularly in relation to health insurance. They were also somewhat better organized with 36 per cent of them having union membership. On the other hand, the skilled tailor operators were the least organized with only 6 per cent of them being union members. In the case of the unskilled helpers, even union membership of 22 per cent could not ensure minimum wages for more than 8 per cent, although in the sphere of health insurance and provident fund, unionization seems to have ensured greater access to such entitlements. The *majority* of workers in all occupational categories (80 per cent) remained outside the fold of any union (see Table 2.19).

Table 2.19 Percentage of women workers with labour rights implementation among occupational categories

Legal labour rights	Among thread-cutters %	Among helpers %	Among tailor operators %	Among checkers %
Minimum wages	23	8	26	45
Health insurance	25	19	48	54
Provident Fund	28	21	54	45
Minimum Bonus	50	17	39	54
Leave	28	27	52	50
Union membership	20	22	8	36

Low rates of union membership are not seen only among women or garment workers in Delhi. In general, trade union membership in Delhi has not been expanding in the 1990s as compared to the 1980s; however, for the *'export workers'* one of the principal reasons for low union membership lies in the long and grinding work hours along with the few off-days. Such gruelling work hours leave little or no time for workers to collect, organize or gather outside their factories (that is, away from the eagle eye of their managements) without which the possibilities of joining or forming a union are limited.

An additional and growing factor restricting the growth of worker solidarity required for the establishment of unions (as reported in some of the meetings with unionized workers), is a growing tension between the older and younger workers. The context for such a tension is the pressure of managements to step up productivity through the sole mechanism of making the workers work faster. Thus many workers reported that daily production quotas had been doubled within the space of a few years, introducing a pace of work which only the young could maintain. Younger workers, eager to demonstrate their abilities, were often used by managements to push up productivity targets, thereby creating conditions for humiliation and sometimes exit of older workers unable to keep pace.

EMERGING ISSUES

As shown in the field survey, an increasing proportion of women workers are being concentrated in the larger and more consolidated garment export factories, even as decimation of the fabricator units has also led to losses of employment for many others. At the same time casualization and contractualization of employment through the increased in-contracting, which has accompanied the process of consolidation of manufacturing processes has been demonstrated to have a wage-depressing effect, a fall-out of the addition of further tiers to a hierarchy of exploiters (at the top through controls by monopoly retailers, and at the lower end through labour contractors.) The issues before women workers in this export industry include widespread denial of minimum wages and provisions for health insurance, provident fund and creches to which they are entitled by law. Further the more investment- and import-intensive production regime, in what is essentially a labour-intensive industry, has led to harsher conditions of labour including regularization of overtime work, mostly without full compensation, with extended hours of work into the night becoming virtually a condition of service.

It is such a situation at the ground level that provides the real context in which contemporary policy discussions that are taking place. The proponents of liberalization and their allies among the garment factory owners have been arguing that the changes taking place in the garment industry are part of a benign and progressive process whereby Indian manufacturers will be able to effectively utilize the withdrawal of the

MFA quota regime and become more competitive. To this end, government policy has been favouring consolidation, and the ire of the globalizing liberalizers is concentrated on existing national labour laws, with their demand for 'labour reform' assuming a high-pitched crescendo.[88] In the garment industry the pressure is on for legalizing the use of contract labour (quoting labour laws in other developing countries and ILO Conventions), especially in the units which provide 'at least 200 days employment to the labour in one year', for the employer's 'right' to adjust its workforce in line with 'structural changes' taking place, for allowing the employer to make workers work up to 60 hours in a week (in place of the present 48 hours), and for office bearership of unions to be restricted to the working employees.[89] The last demand is of course an attempt to isolate the garment workers from their class and the general trade union movement, and to ensure that dismissal of union leaders will decapitate any potential unions.

Such a demand for changes in the labour laws appears to be more political and propagandist, since in practice, as has emerged from the survey, the laws are not enforced effectively, the majority of the workers are not unionized and employment structures in the industry have an inbuilt impermanence. More reflective of the real situation is the political emergence, at the national level, of an elemental and aggressive social hostility to labour, pushed in the case of the garment exports by Indian manufacturing exporters whose social roots and habits lie more in mercantilist forms of accumulation rather than industrial.

It has to be admitted that women workers in garment exports, given their low rates of unionization, are as of now ill-prepared for the ongoing attack on their wages, conditions of work, and the declining share of their employment, a fact that is perhaps more true for the young and newer workers in the industry. The difficulty is compounded by the fact that as the older fabricator-driven garment industry moves towards consolidation, large masses of workers, male and female, are entering an expanding pool of the unemployed. This, as shown, has led to a tendency for the proportions of women workers to shrink, adding to the inherent pressure to socially marginalize women and women's specific needs, in their sphere of work. There is clearly a case for renewed efforts by trade unionists and women's organizations to bring together women workers in the garment industry, with a special focus on the young women, and to organize them around the twin agendas of improvement of wage and working conditions at the factory level on the one hand, and for protections against closures, retrenchment and unemployment at the other. Further, the view that 'labour market rigidities' have constrained growth is demonstrably untrue in the case of garment workers, and in fact the issue of concern is that actual 'flexibility' has allowed for enhanced exploitation and denial of basic labour rights of workers.

Notes

1 See Sushila, My story, *Seminar,* 1997 for a more detailed autobiographical statement up to 1997.

2 The settlement consisted of her provident fund and gratuity for just five years out of her service entitlement of twelve years and six months.

3 Such industrial areas included both those with formal legal status according to the Master Plan of Delhi (known as conforming areas) as well as the non-conforming areas where location of factories is illegal as per land use laws.

4 The residential areas of villagers known as *Laldora* areas were exempt from such acquisition.

5 See Introduction.

6 UNIDO, cited in S. Joekes, *Trade Related Employment for Women in Industry and Services in Developing Countries* (UNRISD, Geneva, Occasional paper 5,1995).

7 ILO, *Labour Practices in Footwear, Leather, Textiles and Clothing Industries* (Geneva: ILO, October, 2000).

8 WTO, International Trade Statistics, http://www.wto.org/english/res_e/statis_e/statis_e.htm see Annex.

9 Data sources: ILO, *Labour Practices*; Joekes, *Trade Related Employment for Women*; J. Delahanty A Common Thread: Issues for Garment Workers, paper for WIEGO, 1999.

10 Source: WTO, International Trade Statistics., op.cit

11 ILO, *Labour Practices.,* The largest employers in the industry in 1980, were the former U.S.S.R, with 2.3 million persons (23 per cent of the world total); China with 1.6 million persons (17 per cent) and the United States with 1.3 million persons, (13 per cent). They were followed

by Japan with 4.4 per cent, Brazil with 3.4 per cent and the United Kingdom, Hong Kong (China), Germany, Poland, Romania, France, the Republic of Korea and Italy, in that order.

12 See E.I. Rosen, *Making Sweatshops, The Globalization of the US Apparel Industry* (University of California Press, 2002).

13 ILO, *Labour Practices.*

14 E. Bonacich, L. Cheng, N. Chinchilla, N. Hamilton and P. Ong (eds), *Global Production: The Apparel Industry in the Pacific Rim* (Philadelphia: Temple University Press, 1994); N. Klein, *No Logo* (London: Harper Collins, 2000); Rosen, *Making Sweatshops.*

15 From the 1950s, apparel manufacturers started shifting production to Japan to take advantage of low wages there. Subsequently, when wages rose in Japan, production migrated first to Hong Kong, then South Korea and Taiwan, a process aided by a movement of Japanese apparel capital to offshore locations like South Korea. The 1980s witnessed the incorporation of other Asian countries with lower levels of development and lower wages signified in the fact that the share of the third world in clothing output increased from 11.7per cent in 1975 to 20.4 per cent in 1990.

16 Rosen, *Making Sweatshops.*

17 While some families moved up the economic scale, almost twice as many moved down—a process described for the United States in B. Harrison and B. Bluestone, *The Great U-Turn: Corporate Restructuring and the Polarizing of America* (New York: Basic Books, 1988).

18 Cheng and Gary Gereffi in Edna Bonacich et al. (eds.,) *Global Production.*

19 E. I. Rosen, *Making Sweatshops.*

20 The discarded factory, in Klein, *No Logo.*

21 One of the methods by which wages were often brought below legal minimum wages in the United States and even parts of Europe, was through employment of new wave immigrant workers (including 'illegals'), mostly women.

22 See Rosen, *Making Sweatshops,* p.116.

23 Ibid. Between 1980 and 1990, 80 per cent of the U.S. department store industry changed hands and nearly one-third of the discount department stores were involved in some type of merger and acquisition activity. Again, between 1990 and 1992, more than 100,000 retail firms filed for bankruptcy protection, a 60 per cent increase over the years 1984 to 1989. According to *http:www.sweatshopwatch.org/swatch/ industry /retailers.html*, over two-thirds of the U.S. garment imports is now controlled by the top ten retailers.

24 Ibid. Rosen has provided a detailed account of how from 1984 retailers and the apparel industry in the U.S. began lobbying to end the MFA and to secure the ATC, apart from actively supporting regional trade blocs such as NAFTA and the Caribbean Basin Initiative.

25 ILO, *Labour Practices.*

26 This is typified by the use of Mexico as a supply base for the U.S. market, or outsourcing to the low-wage transition economies of formerly socialist Eastern Europe for the European markets.

27 Such figures (ILO, *Labour Practices*) need, however, to be viewed with some caution. In the case of India (at least), which is included in the overall calculation, the figures are only of the organized sector while the bulk of garment manufacture is in the unorganized sector, where the proportions of women are much lower.

28 In Austria, for example, where the percentage of women workers only fell from 83 per cent in 1985 to 78 per cent in 1995, this was translated by a drop from 48,000 to 10,000 women employees, that is, a drop in women's employment in the industry by over 79 per cent Italy saw a similarly small reduction in terms of percentage, which included actual employment losses of some 80,000 female employees. Central and Eastern Europe even experienced some slight increases in the share of female employment—87 per cent to 88 per cent between 1990 and 1995, although the number of women employees dropped. Source: ILO, Labour Practices, op. cit.

29 It is worth mentioning that the high share of women workers in Korea's garment export industries constituted an empirical basis for much of the literature on export-oriented production and feminization of labour; however, as pointed out by analysts, the reversal of the process began in the 1990s, considerably before the Asian financial crisis. See J. Ghosh, *Globalization, Export-Oriented Employment for women and Social Policy*, UNRISD, 2002

30 This argument specifically applies to the garment industry context in the developing countries. In the advanced capitalist countries, more long-standing concentration of women workers in the garment industry may be attributed to the lower status of this labour-intensive industry in economies with a long period of relatively smaller reserves of unemployed labour. The indications of decline in the share of women workers is probably because of an increased level of overall unemployment.

31 Data source: Textiles Committee Report, 1991, Bombay Textile Research Association—In depth study of the Indian Apparel Industry

with special reference to steps to increase garment exports.

32 Board of Trade, Report of the Special Study Group on Textiles (Ministry of Textiles, Govt. of India , Sept 2005). In 2001, the value of Indian garment exports had reached Rs 25478 crores.

33 Additionally, capital constraints of small-scale exporters were progressively eased by the greater availability of loans from the massive mobilization of people's savings that took place through nationalization followed by expansion of the banking sector in India.

34 Source: Interview with Executive Secretary, Apparel Exporters and Manufacturers' Association (AEMA), New Delhi.

35 S. Bhatia, Indian garments industry in the post MFA period, *IIFT Occasional Paper* 7, 1997.

36 S. Chatterjee and R. Mohan. India's garment exports, *Economic and Political Weekly* (henceforth EPW), 28, 35, 1993.

37 This marked a break from the earlier period when the erstwhile Soviet Union and other Eastern European markets accounted for more than 60 per cent of the market share, 1970.

38 Source: Apparel Export Promotion Council.

39 B. Satinder, *Indian garments industry*; M. Vijaybhaskaran, Garment industry in India in G. Joshi, (ed.) *Garment Industry in South Asia, Rags or Riches* (ILO/SAAT, 2002).

40 K.V Ramaswamy and G. Gereffi, India's apparel sector in a global economy. *EPW*, 33 (3), 1998.

41 Chatterjee and Mohan, India's garment exports; and M.K Panthaki. Have quota restrictions increased garment exports? *Clothesline*, April 2001.

42 Source: WTO.

43 Small-scale industry is officially defined by a ceiling on investment in plant and machinery and not on employment.

44 As given in S. L. Batra, *Employment for Women, A Study of Export-Oriented Garment Industry* (New Delhi: CSD, 1996).

45 Data Source: *Directory of Apparel Exporters*, AEPC, New Delhi. Information on merchant manufacturers from interview with AEMA secretary and confirmed by S. L.Batra's survey of merchant exporting units. Merchant exporter units generally outsourced bulk tailoring operations to fabricators and kept some checking, finishing and packing operations in their own units.

46 See *Indian Cotton and Textile Industry: Reforming to Compete*, South Asia Rural Development Series, World Bank, 1999, for the former estimate and D. N. Sen Gupta, Effect of Policy on Export Competitiveness:

The Case of the Indian Garment Industry quoted in Vijaybhaskaran, Garment Industry in India.

47 Source: Ministry of Labour, Occupational Wage Survey, Fifth Round, *Report on Textile Garments Industry, 1995-96,* Labour Bureau, Simla.

48 The Delhi region now includes the industirial townships that have grown around Delhi in neighbouring states such as Noida in U.P. and Gurgaon in Haryana. Among the reasons for the emergence of Delhi as a principal centre was the presence of the central government which eased negotiation of several facilities including quota access. Equally important was the development of Delhi as the largest concentration of small-scale industry in the country already by 1967, and the availability of cheap labour in the form of large waves of migrant workers from the otherwise industrially backward north Indian hinterland. See I. Mazumdar, Unorganised workers of Delhi and the seven day strike of 1988. NLI Research Studies Series (V.V. Giri National Labour Institute, 2002).

49 A long-standing centre for handloom weaving, ginning and selling of raw cotton (*Tiruppu* means 'spin' in Tamil), the proximity of Tirupur to the textile mills of Coimbatore (most of which were spinning mills) facilitated the transformation of Tirupur into a major power-loom and hosiery product manufacturing centre. For a detailed description, see P. Cawthorne, The labour process under amoebic capitalism—a case study of the garment industry in a south Indian town, in I.S.A Baud and G.A. de Bruijne (eds), *Gender, Small-Scale Industry and Development Policy* (London: Intermediate Technology Publications, 1993; and N. Neetha, *Gender and Technology: Impact of Flexible Organisation and Production on Female Labour in the Tiruppur Knitwear Industry* (NLI Research Studies, 2001).

50 The lower unit values of Tirupur exports is of course an indicator of the general tendency to lower prices at an international level, although it is commonly attributed to the lower price of hosiery which dominates the Tirupur industry.

51 Source: Calculated from data in *Handbook of Export Statistics, 1998-2001* (New Delhi, Apparel Export Promotion Council).

52. See I. Mazumdar, EPZs and their workers in India: a study of the NOIDA Export Processing Zone, in A.S. Oberai, A. Sivananthisan, C.S. Venkataratnam (eds), *Labour Issues in Export Processing Zones in South Asia: Role of Social Dialogue,* (SAAT/ILO/IIRA, 2001).

53 From interview with executive secretary, AEMA.

54 It was reported that where equitable distribution was attempted, individual exporters would be allotted a ridiculous quota of five to ten

pieces.

55 In 1990, a total of 1,025 out of 17,546 exporters registered with the AEPC were manufacturers, compared to 4,247 out of 26,547 in 2001. A word of caution regarding the AEPC list of exporters—NCAER researchers (Navsharan Singh) have found that many of the exporters registered with the AEPC either no longer exist or have shifted out of the field. According to another observer, some 7000-8000 of the registered exporters are serious. Niki Tait Indian garment exports, moving towards 2005. *Clothesline* (April, 2001). In 2005, hosiery was also removed from the list of SSI reserved items.

56 Many exporters were owners of several factories.

57 T.A. Bhavani, echnological change in the Indian small scale industries, IDPAD Project Report, Institute of Economic Growth, 2001.

58 These are the categories given in S. Bhatia, Indian garments industry, IIFT. According to Niki Tait's report of 2001, CAD equipment is still relatively small in India.

59 Source: Percentages have been calculated from AEPC data given in S. Bhatia, Indian garments industry, IIFT.

60 See Bhavani, *Indian small scale industries,* 2001; Niki Tait, Indian garment exports, *Clothesline,* April 2001, SEWA-NCAER 2001.

61 Tait, Indian garment exports.

62 Source: Textiles Committee Report quoted in S. L. Batra, Employment for women.

63 Source:Textiles Committee Survey in S. L Batra, Employment for women.

64 R. Rao and S. Husain, Invisible hands: the women behind India's export earnings. In: N. Banerjee (ed.), *Indian Women in a Changing Industrial Scenario* (New Delhi : Sage, 1991). Interview with AEMA secretary.

65 Many workers lived on factory premises. For a description see Mazumdar, Unorganised workers of Delhi.

66 According to S.L. Batra's survey (1993–1994), over 70 per cent of checkers in fabrication and manufacturing and 58 per cent in the merchant units in Bombay Mumbai were women. Similarly 83 per cent of checkers in fabrication units of Delhi and 43 per cent and 66 per cent in manufacturing and merchant units respectively were women.

67 Of these occupations, as per notifications of the labour departments, only chekers are defined as skilled, the other two falling in the unskilled categories.

68 Out of a total of 1,389,000 workers

69 Occupational wage survey for 1977-1978 and *Annual Survey of Industries,* 1999-2000, vol 1.

70 Delhi's low share of organized sector employment was despite its remaining the largest contributor to garment exports in value terms. In fact as Table 2.4 shows, organized sector employment in garments in Delhi was substantially reduced during the 1990s.

71 Occupational wage survey data available till 1994-1995 shows that the sharpest rise in share of women's employment in the organized sector of the garment industry, took place between 1977-1979 and1987-1988, during which women workers' share rose from a little over 36 per cent to 53 per cent while the overall number of workers increased from 14,500 to 102,100.

72 The bulk of the garment units in U.P. are located in Noida and Ghaziabad, which are both actually industrial outgrowths of metropolitan Delhi and thus share several common social characteristics.

73 Ministry of Labour, Occupational Wage Survey, Fifth Round, *Report on the Textile Garments Industry, 1995-1996*, Labour Bureau .

74 A recent unpublished study by Sujana Krishnamurthy, Structure of the Garment Industry and Labour Rights in the Post-MFA Context: A Study, Centre for Education and Communication, New Delhi, has drawn specific attention to the exclusion of women from higher paid piece-rated tailoring as articulated by women workers in Tirupur. In other centres such as Delhi, the same phenomena have been noted in several earlier studies.

75 Tailor (specialist) is defined in the OWS as a tailor who prepares only a particular part of a garment—e.g., shirt collar, pocket, sleeves—on a machine.

76 Specialist tailors refers to the category of tailors involved in mass production. For women the average daily minimum wage rates were Rs 35.02 for time-rated workers in comparison to Rs 43.45 for piece-rated, and the maximum wage rates were Rs 42.74 and Rs 64.24 for the same categories, respectively.

77 A comparison between ASI employment figures and the NSS evidences the low share of the registered factory sector in total apparel manufacturing employment. Inclusive of its contract workers, the registered factory sector accounted for only 12 per cent of the industry's principal usual status employment in 1999-2000. Among women workers of the same employment category, the registered sector accounted for 36 per cent.

78 It should be noted manufacturing for the domestic market is included in NSS data.

79 A fuller discussion on this question may be found in chapter 5, pp.253-293

80 Broadly speaking, those units where the principal manufacturing activity of tailoring was outsourced have been viewed as merchant exporters. Manufacturing exporters' units on the other hand have both tailoring and finishing under one roof.

81 According to Batra's survey in 1993–1994, the average workforce size in fabrication units was twenty-four. S.L. Batra, *Employment for women*.

82 Service or tenure refers to employment in one unit, and in these cases refers to last employment.

83 They had moved from rented or *jhuggi* accommodations close to their factories to houses acquired or built by them in unauthorized colonies from where initially transport was a problem.

84 She lives in a *jhuggi* in the heart of the industrial area of Okhla.

85 She was one of four female and fifty male tailors.

86 The minimum wage for unskilled workers was Rs 2,668 at the time of the survey.

87 As per present law, employers are not allowed to work women beyond 7 p.m, and in the exceptional conditions where special permission may be obtained, they are required to provide them with safe transport.

88 For example, a recently released government report states, 'The most important and felt need of the textile industry, especially the garment sub-sector, is the amendment in the labour laws so as to create some flexibility in the seasonal nature of the production and to enhance productivity and quality. This factor has acquired added dimension due to the fact that many big buyers insist on "compliance,", major part of which is the meticulous observance of labour laws of the country in which the unit is located... The industry feels that lack of a proper Exit Policy in Indian labour laws and plethora of rules/regulations which give power (at least in theory) to the junior most government functionary to put the owner/promoter/director/manager in jail on pretext of a small violation, has discouraged any big house to invest itself in this labour intensive industry or from bringing FDI (foreign direct investment) in this sector.'

89 Report of the Special Study group on textiles set up by Board of Trade, Ministry of Textiles, Govt. of India (Thursday, September 29, 2005).

THREE

The Cutting Edge and Nimble Fingers: Women Workers in Electronics Manufacturing

Since the 'fusion of computing and communications' have broken the bounds of cost, time and distance, the electronics industry according to many people lies at the heart of developments in communication that sets this era of globalization apart from any other.[1] With a reputation for a historically unprecedented rate of technological progress, the pace of growth of electronics production had, by the 1990s, surpassed all other core industrial segments worldwide—the rapid pace of such changes fuelling and being fuelled by quick obsolescence and short product cycles. Among other features, is the visible dominance of micro-electronics–based information technologies (IT) up to a point where increasingly IT, despite being only a subset, is engulfing the whole of electronics.[2] At the same time, major transnational corporations in the industry have evolved globalized production systems to reduce costs as well as prise open new markets. As a result, some commentators believe that more than in any other industry, competition in the electronics industry today cuts across national and sectoral boundaries.[3] All these developments have introduced new complexities, bringing about shifts and changes in the profile and organization of the sector at such break-neck speed that social registration and analysis, particularly in relation to effects on women's employment, have experienced difficulty in keeping pace.

The great boom in micro-electronics in the early 1990s had caused worldwide euphoria, with many new age economists arguing that traditional business cycles had become outdated. Additionally, the substantial rates of growth in several developing countries, which were to a great extent based on exports of electronics manufacture, were central to the successful propagation of globalization and the view that greater integration with the global economy could be of benefit to third world countries.[4] At the beginning of the new century, however, the impact of slowing rates of growth in the advanced capitalist centres was felt most markedly in manufacture and trade in electronics. Electronic hardware production, which had reached its peak with 1336.369 billion U.S. dollars in 2000, fell abruptly to 1210.341 billion U.S. dollars in 2001; the most significant fall was that of electronic data processing (EDP), telecom and office equipment, that is, the very same products that had driven the phenomenal growth of the electronics industry and trade in the 1990s.[5] While the value of world exports in office and telecom equipment dropped from 940 billion U.S. dollars in 2000 to 828 billion U.S. dollars in 2001, its share in total world merchandise exports dropped from 15.2 per cent to 13.8 per cent.[6] The world began to sit up and take note of the fact that globalization-led 'growth', and technological development did not offer immunity from business cycles or crises in either developed or developing countries. Convulsions in the employment scenario in electronics began to appear as a feature to be contended with as the established architecture of the production economy in electronics began to waver.

For decades the established worldwide trend in electronics was seen to favour employment of women due to a notion that their 'nimble fingers' were particularly suitable for the fine and minute manual work required in electronic assembly. Across the world, women could be found in large numbers in the electronics industry (although generally in the lowest rungs), in contrast to traditional male-dominated engineering industries. In the industrializing developing world, also, export-oriented electronics manufacturing units were seen as 'massing together' hundreds of women workers. In fact, the electronics industry is regarded as a leading example of feminization. But with the extension of miniaturization of electronic components beyond manual capacities, in many areas manual work is perforce giving way to automation. At the same time, an emphasis on product innovation, rapid technological obsolescence and pressures to reduce cost of production have been accompanied by a continuous process of relocation of centres of production, leading to loss of jobs and instability of employment on a worldwide scale.

Although there is no comprehensive data on women's employment in the electronics sector at a global level, some tendency towards a decrease in women's share of employment has been observed in at least some countries. In the Republic of Ireland, women's share of employment in foreign-owned electronics plants fell from around 62 per cent in 1973 to 51 per cent in 1983. In the United States, women's share in semi-conductor production has been falling as automation of wafer fabrication has reduced the requirement for assembly workers. In the first instance, this is happening at many traditional sites of production located in the advanced economies. But a similar effect has increasingly been observed in those developing countries that had become central to international production chains in electronics through the 1970s and 1980s. In Mexico, for example, the share of unskilled assembly workers (where women were concentrated) fell from 84 per cent to 78 per cent in electronics assembly and from 85.7 per cent to 79.5 per cent in electronic components.[7] A similar trend was observed in the Republic of Korea, Singapore and Malaysia.

Often such job losses in electronics or IT manufacturing are discounted as minor, giving the argument that the overall growth of IT is leading to new opportunities for women in the vastly expanded and globalizing service sector. Such an argument glosses over the fact that generally those who lose their jobs in electronics manufacturing are not necessarily the same as those who would be acquiring them in IT services. Apart from the need for higher levels of education than what prevails among manufacturing workers, importantly, among the requirements for the new IT based service jobs are social qualifications. that is, belonging to higher levels of a stratified social structure.

This sectoral study seeks to collate and analyse trends in women's employment in India's electronics manufacturing industry within the context of global processes and to delineate the contours and trajectories of the impact of globalization on women working in the industry. A primary field survey-based case study of the Delhi region is situated within a broad description of all India policies and trends based on secondary sources.

EVOLUTION OF THE INDIAN ELECTRONICS INDUSTRY

Up to the early 1970s, the structure of the electronics industry in India essentially consisted of consumer electronics dominated by the private sector (largely small-scale industry assembling radios, supplied by an indigenous small-scale components industry) and of telecommunications and defence undertakings reserved for the public sector (large-scale public sector undertakings). In the 1970s, the public sector expanded in telecommunications, with specialized industrial electronics firms and in large engineering firms with important electronics activities.[8] The 1970s also saw the emergence of state-level public sector electronics corporations.[9] In this period, growth in the electronics industry was fundamentally driven by the public sector, where policy favoured non-discrimination against women. Thus recorded women's employment in electronics grew faster than in other sections of the formal industrial economy. In the context of the disturbing trend of declining numbers of women workers in several other industries such as textiles, it was therefore easy to conclude that, as in most other countries, the deployment of electronic technology was on the whole gender-friendly.[10]

The industry grew up around three major centres, Bangalore in Karnataka, Mumbai/Pune in Maharashtra, and Delhi. Bangalore was the site of major public sector corporations in defence and telecommunications. Mumbai and Pune were the traditional locations of the private sector, largely foreign owned firms established in the late 1940s to the early 1950s. Delhi became important from the 1960s when it emerged as the most concentrated centre of small-scale industry in the country, which in the electronics sector was involved in making radios, components for radios and later black and white televisions. Although television broadcasts were initiated in 1959, television manufacturing in India began only in 1973.

Early Liberalization

Until the 1970s, electronics policy in India favoured self-reliance in technology and production and capital imports were actively discouraged. Manufacture of certain electronic products was either restricted to the public sector or to small firms. Production techniques had a large manual labour content, and industrial capacities had to be approved based on estimated demand over the next five years.[11] Until the 1980s, imports were permitted only to fulfil requirements of the state for defence and telecommunications, and electronics was considered to be the most protected of all industries. But a series of new policies from the early 1980s onwards brought about revisions in the tariff structure to reduce the cost of imported components and aimed for a progressive reduction of the high import duties on electronic products, purportedly to encourage producers to become more internationally competitive.[12] In 1982, a policy decision was taken to introduce colour television, which required import of colour picture tubes and semi-conductors required for assembly.[13] Following this, the Indian industry continued to remain dominated by labour-intensive assembly in consumer electronics, especially that of television sets, but with higher import content, all catering to the domestic market. From being the most protected sector, electronics became one of the first industries to open up. In a sense, the policy changes in electronics typified the manner in which the government and industry sought to deal with the industrial slowing-down of the preceding fifteen years by focussing on manufacture of products catering to the middle classes in whose hands purchasing power was concentrated. Nevertheless, since it was one of the expanding industries of the time where women tended to be preferred, the period saw the entry of significant numbers of women in electronics employment, although their share of employment in the industry as a whole remained quite low. By the early 1990s, women's employment share of electronics employment stood at a little less than 15 per cent.[14]

The 'Reforms' Decade: Slowing of Growth in Manufacture

In the 1990s, in line with the 1991 new industrial policy approach to integration of the Indian economy with globalization processes, and following GATT '94, the high customs tariff on all electronics and IT products were slashed heavily and quantitative restrictions were removed. Foreign equity participation was liberalized, and by 1996, foreign subsidiaries with 100 per cent equity were allowed, barring strategic industries like defence. This opened the doors to some of the major multi-national producers in the field of consumer electronics, who soon became major players in the Indian market. The new policy regime instituted in 1991 entailed no reservation for public sector enterprises and by the end of the 1990s, with the exception of aerospace and defence electronics, the electronics industry had been fully delicensed. All components, raw materials and capital goods were freely importable.

Thus the stated focus of attention in the eighth five year plan (1992–1997) was on production at internationally competitive scales, encouraging export-orientated production, technology development, manpower development, rural industrialization and application of electronics in key socio-economic sectors. The plan envisaged that the opening of the economy would lead to restructuring of the entire electronics industry, including 'closure of a number of sub-economic units', consolidation and amalgamations of units and increased tie-ups with foreign firms to provide a 'sound base' for sustained development of the industry.[15] Again the ninth five year plan outlined a principal strategy of 'Export and Productivity led growth of Electronics and Information Technology'.[16]

In 1997, the Government of India hurriedly and without any public debate, signed on the Information Technology Agreement (ITA-1) of WTO (see section on the elctronics industry in the WTO for details of ITA) with a commitment to bring down customs tariff rates of IT products to 0 per cent by 2005. In fact, the government initiated a much faster process of tariff reduction than was required under the agreement. Several representations from electronics manufacturers' associations to the government indicated that the manner of reduction of import duties during the transition to the 0 per cent duty regime was having an adverse impact on Indian manufacturing.[17] On the one hand, reductions in import duties on computers and peripheral products ensured that the few Indian manufacturers of computers started closing shop, with some becoming sales agents for multi-national corporations. At the same time, duties on components were brought down drastically while higher duties remained on raw materials required for manufacture of electronic components, skewing the whole process against local production supply even for the relatively protected (from imports) consumer electronics which had not been incorporated within the ITA. Imported components thus tended to be cheaper than locally manufactured components, particularly for the expanding multinational producers who could import from their parent or subsidiary concerns located in other countries at reduced rates. The rate of growth of the electronics industry dropped sharply in the 'reforms' decade in comparison to the high growth rates of the 1980s, and India's share in world production of electronics hardware actually fell from 0.55 per cent in 1995-1996 to 0.48 per cent in 2000-2001.[18] The grim situation in Indian electronics manufacturing at the end of the 1990s was reflected even in official documents. Thus, the report of the Working Group on Information Technology Sector for the Tenth Five Year Plan (2002-2007) noted that the country's manufacturing sector in electronics was in danger of becoming extinct.[19]

Slower Growth of Employment: Decline in Public and Small-Scale Sector Share

Declining rates of growth in manufacturing in the 1990s reflected in the slowing down of growth of employment in the electronics manufacturing industry. Table 3.1 gives the sectoral distribution of employment in the electronics industry of India. Between 1981 and 1990, some 155,000 new jobs were generated in the sector, of which 29,500 were in the public sector, 35,500 in the organized private sector and 89,000 in the small-scale industries. But between 1990 and 1999, the generation of new jobs was reduced to almost one-half of this, with the public sector witnessing an absolute loss of over 15,000 jobs between 1990 and 1997. A brief recovery in public sector employment in 1998 began to taper off within the next year and still fell short of the peak of 1990. At the same time, the small-scale sector, which had led the growth pattern of employment in the electronics industry in the 1980s by providing an additional 89,000 jobs between 1981 and 1990, was able to add considerably less than one-half that number across the 'reforms' decade. Only the large organized sector seemed to be expanding, adding on an average of 5,000 employees per year across the 1990s in comparison with less than 4,000 per year in the preceding decade. Such a growth of large private sector operations was perhaps also due to some new multi-national entrants who set up manufacturing facilities in India across the 1990s.

Table 3.1 Employment in electronics by sector* over all of India

	1981	1990	1997	1998	1999
Public Sector					
- Central Public	67,000	83,000	70,000	78,000	78,000
- State Public	4,500	18,000	16,000	20,000	19,000
Organized Private Sector	27,500	63,000	95,000	100,000	108,000
Small-scale sector	31,000	120,000	164,000	157,000	160,000
Total	130,000	285,000	345,000	355,000	365,000

Source *Electronics Directory 1999.*

*Unfortunately sex disaggregated figures of employment were not available in any of the reports of the Department of Electronics.

The commanding position of public sector employment in electronics established in the earlier period, when 'self-reliance' was the object of controls and protections, had of course begun to decline during the first phase of liberalization in the 1980s. The share of public sector employment which was 55 per cent in 1981 had dropped to a little over 35 per cent by 1990, its addition of 29,500 new jobs across the decade being less than one-third of the 124,500 additional jobs in the private sector. With cutbacks in the public sector in the 1990s and a net reduction in its employment by 4,000, its share dropped further to reach 27 per cent of total employment in electronics by 1999. In fact, between 1990 and 1997, some 15,000 jobs were reduced in the public sector, and from all reports a substantial number of the semi-skilled women workers exited in this period. Among the additions that were made in the following two years, the proportions of high-skilled workers, who were generally men, was substantially increased.

At the other end, employment in the small-scale sector, whose share had risen from a little less than 24 per cent in 1981 to reach 42 per cent by 1990, continued to rise to over 47 per cent by 1997 and then suddenly saw an absolute drop in 1998. Even after a mild increase in absolute numbers in the following year, the sector saw a net loss of 4,000 jobs between 1997 and 1999, and its share in employment continued to decline and stood at a little less than 44 per cent in 1999. Small-scale industries had become the largest employers since the mid-1980s. Ancillary or component manufacture in the small-scale sector had started growing around the consumer electronics industry of the pre-liberalization period; however, with the liberalization of import controls and then the massive tariff cuts on components in the 1990s, local component manufacture became progressively constricted. The share of components in the country's electronics production declined from 23 per cent in 1981 to around 20 per cent in 1991 and further dropped to 18 per cent by 2001 despite fairly rapid increases in consumer electronics manufacture.

At another level, with the loosening of import controls on capital goods for the sector, the labour-intensive assembly manufacture of consumer electronics products from largely imported components that had acquired a significant presence in the small-scale sector, required little investment in plant and machinery. Its expansion was premised on a boom in sales of consumer electronic goods, particularly colour televisions for the expanding middle classes. Such a trajectory, of course, lent itself to fly-by-night industries (entailing fly-by-night employment opportunities) requiring little more than 'screwdriver technology', although a few became large enough to become household brand names. With concentration and consolidation at one end, and then the entry of multi-national producers on a fairly large scale by the second half of the 1990s, many of such small-scale assemblers were weeded out by the end of the decade and the process is still continuing. All this was reflected in the absolute reduction of employment in small-scale industry towards the end of the 1990s.

Concentration and Increasing Weight of the Organized Private Sector Including MNCs

Concentration of production in the hands of a few companies and regions has marked the intensification of the liberalization rocess in electronics. In 1999, of the seventy-one public sector units, 625 units in organized private sector, and more than 2,800 units in the small-scale sector, roughly totalling 3,500, the top hundred units accounted for about 63 per cent of the total production, and the next hundred units for about 10 per cent. Thus, some 6 per cent of the units accounted for about 73 per cent of production.[20] Two-thirds of the overall increases in electronics employment between 1992 and 1999 were concentrated in just four states, Karnataka, Maharashtra, Uttar Pradesh and Gujarat. The top companies now include a significant presence of multi-national corporations, who, in the 1990s, have invested relatively more strongly in electronics than in other sectors in India. Foreign Direct Investment in the two categories of Electronics and Electrical Equipment, and Computers rose from about 15 per cent of total FDI inflow in 1992-1993 to 27 per cent in 2000-2001.[21] At the same time, some of the major private sector Indian companies have started investing abroad, one even going so far as to shift its manufacturing establishments outside the country.[22]

It is the organized private sector, consisting of a handful of Indian companies and the new MNC entrants, who are the ones who have gained most in the era of liberalization and globalization, increasing their share in total electronics production from 31 per cent in 1981 to over 42 per cent in 1999. Their share of employment, on the other hand, was just less than 30 per cent indicative of the relatively greater capital intensive and relatively less employment generating potential of the organized private sector particularly in comparison to small scale. Thus, the restructuring of the Indian electronics industry has, in essence, been more favourable to concentration in the private organized sector primarily at the cost of the public sector, but also perhaps in a less apparent manner to the detriment of employment in the many small-scale units.

Whither Export-Led Growth?

Despite the policy direction of export-led growth for the electronics industry, the facts indicate that exports have remained relatively insignificant for Indian electronics manufacturing units whose composition characteristics have been more geared to the domestic market.

Consumer electronics is the sub-sector where distinct and palpable growth in manufacturing has taken place, basically catering to the domestic market, with an increasingly strong presence of multi-national producers and contributing very little of its output for exports. Consumer electronics increased its share in India's electronics manufacture from close to 28 per cent in 1994 to 38 per cent by 2001, falling off slightly to 35 per cent by 2004. 95 per cent of consumer electronics production was for the domestic market in 2004, while its share in the country's electronics exports dropped from 21 per cent in 1997-1998 to just 5 per cent in 2003-2004 See Table 3.2 for a display of the share of different sectors in production and exports. Clearly the domestic market has been the prime driver for expansion of the consumer electronics manufacturing, no doubt due to the fact that the home market still remains somewhat protected with a higher import tariff rate since consumer electronics is yet to find its way into the 0 per cent duty regime of the ITA. That the expansion of production for the domestic market itself rests on an insecure base has become increasingly clear in the last two or three years; even the few large players in this segment seem to be facing problems as the limited markets have reached saturation point. Some of the Indian companies who are clearly losing market share to multi-national producers have already started closing down units. And even some of the multi-national companies seem to be following the same pathway.

Component production, which was earlier driven by the expansion of consumer electronics but which is not similarly protected, faced stagnation and even periods of absolute falls in production terms.[23] Clearly the uninterrupted growth of consumer electronics was not fueling domestic demand for components. In fact, local manufacture for the domestic market-oriented consumer electronics industry has been increasing its imports not only for components which have no manufacturing base in the country, but also for those components which were earlier sourced locally, due to the duty regime instituted under the ITA making imported components cheaper in comparison to local manufactures.[24] Attempts to meet such a situation by focusing on exports is reflected in the rising share of exports in component production which reached 49 per cent in 2004, but as can be seen in the case of export of computers and of perhaps even communications and broadcasting equipment, there is an inbuilt volatility with a tendency towards slumps in production and exports following the export highs. In the case of instrumentation and strategic production, the base of production and demand was always provided by the public sector (including for defence purposes), and the recent surge in exports remains of a relatively low order.

Table 3.2: Electronics production by sub-sector and share of exports

Sector	1996–97	1998–99	2000–01	2003-04
Consumer Electronics				
Production (U.S.$ Mln.)	1830.99	2216.87	2543.48	3374.02
Exports (percentage)	21%	9%	6%	5%
Comm. and Broadcasting Equip.				
Production (U.S.$ Mln.)	845.07	1060.24	1239.13	1187.56
Exports (percentage)	11%	6%	10%	3%
Instrumentation and Strategic				
Production (U.S.$ Mln.)	1239.44	1108.43	1195.65	1964.48
Exports (percentage)	4%	4%	9%	17%
Electronic Components				
Production (U.S.$ Mln.)	1042.25	1204.82	1195.65	1687.01
Exports (percentage)	17%	18%	37%	49%
Computer Hardware				
Production (U.S.$ Mln.)	771.83	554.22	739.13	1509.43
Exports (percentage)	49%	13%	37%	21%
Total				
Production (US$ Mln.)	5729.58	6144.58	6673.91	9722.53
Exports (percentage)	15%	10%	16%	18%

Data sources: Statistical Year Book of Indian IT and Electronics Industry-2000-2001 and www.mit.gov.in/dbid/eproduction.asp and www.mit.gov.in/dbid/eexport.asp for 2003-2004 Export percentages calculated and rounded off.

The envisaged exports providing the engine to growth has clearly not manifested itself in electronics manufacturing. What has, in fact, taken place as a consequence of the pursuit of globalization policies is a level of destruction of local manufacturers, particularly in the small-scale sector. Some of the effects of the immanent collapse of small-scale industries on women's earnings and conditions of work are discussed through the findings of our field survey in the Delhi region. A look at global events and trends in the electronics industry provides some insights into the reasons why export-led growth rates are perhaps not as promising as expected.

GLOBAL DRIVERS OF THE ELECTRONICS INDUSTRY

Early Domination by Transnational Corporations

Unlike the simpler and more dispersed form of labour-intensive technologies involved in garment manufacture, electronics production involves complex technological and organizational capabilities, combined with capital intensive production-related scale economies. More importantly, a greater presence of transnational corporations (TNCs) can be seen in electronics production than in clothing. Nineteen of the top hundred TNCs identified by UNCTAD are involved in electronics production.[25]

The domination of TNCs whose home base is located in the advanced capitalist countries and their establishment of cross-border production links in countries of the Asia Pacific rim, where significantly lower wage rates prevailed, was an early feature of the industry. Such relocation (of production) was, in fact, an instrument of intra-Northern TNC rivalry. Accordingly, the TNCs did not press their governments to impose trade restraints on imports of electronics components or assembled products, since they largely represented intra-firm transactions. Super 807 type provisions were introduced under pressure from TNCs to prevent trade duties being levied on intra-firm trade and on trade between parent and sub-contractor.[26] Thus trade in electronics equipment increased to supersede clothing exports from developing countries, not only without much opposition from manufacturers or MFA type restraints, but rather precisely due to TNC pressures for greater openness of trade in this area.

And yet the facts show that some two-thirds to three-fourths of the assets, employment and sales of most MNCs, and an overwhelming percentage of their best-compensated and highest-skilled jobs, are still in a home base. Further, almost 60-90 per cent of the range of assets of the world's top fifty MNCs of all national origins, which might be expected to be the most non-national ones, are located within the home country. Equally significant, almost all MNC firms still explicitly exercise control from their home country Thus it has been argued that TNC or MNC domination of the electronics industry has not been an equalizing developmental force, but rather a method of concentrated surplus appropriation and domination by corporate interests located in the advanced economies.[27]

The Electronics Industry in the WTO

A significant development affecting the electronics industry in the present era was the coming into force of the ITA, which emerged as a Ministerial Declaration on Trade in Information Technology Products made at Singapore in 1996. At the time it was proposed and signed only by the United States, members of the European Community and a few other European countries, Japan, Canada, Australia and Republic of Korea Hong Kong, Chinese Taipei and Indonesia. Since these countries did not cover the stipulated 90 per cent of world trade (they together constituted 83 per cent), it was only in 1997, when eleven other countries (including India) notified acceptance, that the ITA came into force. Under the ITA, all products listed in the Declaration had to be reduced to a zero tariff level, and all other duties and charges (ODCs) must be bound at zero. The product coverage of the ITA includes practically all electronic items except for a few such as the television.[28]

An aspect of the ITA, which some commentators consider as important as its terms, was the manner of its negotiation. In its essentials, the agreement was not negotiated in the traditional way where each nation offers to disarm a bit if the others will disarm a bit more. Rather, it was based on an initial common position arrived at between the European Community and the United States. Given the dominance of U.S. corporations in electronics, the interests of U.S. transnational producers in the dismantling of market entry barriers across the globe could be understood; however, the same could not be said of European producers whose own protections were being dismantled under the agreement. Arguing that in Europe and in the United States, policy at the sector level, especially trade policy, is strongly reflective of organized interests, with both producers and big, organized users—as distinct from consumers, they conclude that the 'new transatlantic axis' behind the ITA was driven at the European end by the major banking interests. They highlight the role of financial institutions (as major users of IT products) in promotion and growth of the U.S. dominated IT industry.[29]

Zonal Concentration and Hierarchies in Production

According to an ILO report, sources of low-cost manufacturing in electronics shifted over the years from the United States to Japan to the newly industrializing economies (NIEs) of Asia. Korea and Taiwan were the low-cost sources of labour in the 1970s, to be replaced in the early 1980s by Singapore and Malaysia and in the late 1980s and 1990s by China and other less-developed countries of Asia. More than 80 per cent of world electronics production is located therefore in the four zones of United States, Japan, Western Europe and the Asia Pacific, with China making a strong additional pole in the last decade. See Table 3.3 for a description of the zonewise distribution of production and market of the electronics industry.

Table 3.3: Global zone-wise production and market distribution of the electronics industry

Country/region	Share in Production (%)		Share in Market (%)	
	1998	2002	1998	2002
United States	30.1	25.6	35.8	38.8
Western Europe	21.5	18.6	25.2	22.1
Japan	18.3	18.6	13.6	16.2
China	4.9	8.9	4.4	6.2
Asia Pacific*	13.1	15.4	—	—
Rest of the World	12.2	13	21.0**	16.2**
Total (US$ billion)	1078	1248	1065	1253

*Only South Korea, Singapore, Taiwan and Malaysia from Asia Pacific have been counted here. ** Inclusive here of Asia Pacific

Source: Krishna Kumar, *Electronics Outlook*.

At the same time, the concentration of firms in almost all sub-sectors of electronics industries has grown. In the computer industry, the top ten firms earn over 50 per cent of the world revenues and the top twenty account for approximately 70 per cent of the earnings. It is evident that many of the top firms have held their position for many years. The computer industry is also dominated by two countries, the United States and Japan. The consumer electronics industry is also highly concentrated. The market share of the top five television producers is greater than 75 per cent although the geographical distribution of the key consumer electronics companies is somewhat different from that of the computer industry.[30] In the telecommunications industry, the top ten firms control more than 75 per cent of the market for telecommunications.[31] Such concentration has been additionally spurred by a spate of mergers and acquisitions in all sub-sectors of electronics.[32]

Such virtual monopolies are perhaps not always visible as from the mid-eighties very different kind of international production networks have evolved, becoming 'emblematic of globalization', in which cross-border, inter-firm (rather than intra-firm) relationships have grown tending to blur the easy identity of nations and firms. Increasingly commentators are pointing to elements of control or domination of international production networks through non-equity methods.[33] In such a background, production and asset-based data of individual TNCs is perhaps an insufficient indicator of the scale of control exercised by individual corporations. But almost all commentators have pointed to a hierarchy of production that favours control over widespread production networks in developing countries by lead companies located in the developed countries.

The following have been identified as the chief features of such hierarchies:

(*i*) The lead position that product introduction centres (PICs) in developed countries play in prototyping and in the ramp-up of new product lines towards volume manufacturing. This implies inequality in the distribution of engineering capacities and the access of plants in low-cost locations to advanced engineering know-how within the global production system. It also implies a greater relative significance of skilled labour in strategic plants in developed economies;

(*ii*) The location of specialized products with high diversity in manufacturing requirements and low volumes (low volume/high mix) in developed countries as opposed to standardized mass production (high volume/low mix) in low-cost locations.

(*iii*) The concentration of specialized units in the design and manufacturing of critical components in developed countries.[34]

Several of these lead firms, initially in the United States and later in Europe have now divested themselves of mass manufacturing responsibilities increasingly turning to defining marketing and brand name control areas as their focus of activity along with retaining product definition capacities. Some scholars affirm that 'the epicenter of the global electronics industry has shifted to R&D and other forms of intangible investment directed at the enhancement of speed of response to changes in technology and markets'.[35]

International Contract Manufacturing and Unequal Working Conditions

Such a shift in the emphasis of lead firms has been made possible by the emergence of a new model of outsourced manufacturing that has emerged as the centre-piece of globalized production networks: Contract Manufacturing (CM) or Electronics Manufacturing Services (EMS). The leading players of the industry were, most of them, former sub-assembly companies, having developed into major transnational corporations themselves. The five major players in whose hands international contract manufacturing is concentrated are all of North American origin.[36] In 1996, the leading contract manufacturer had about ten locations worldwide, today there are more than fifty. Contract manufacturing companies have built a presence in every region in the triad of the capitalist world economy, combining operations in the lead economies with mass manufacturing in developing countries of the respective regions. For North America, Mexico has emerged as the prime low-cost location, for Asia, Malaysia and China (the latter already hosting the largest number of CM-plants around the world), and for

Europe, Hungary, Poland, Czech Republic and Romania.[37] Contract manufacturing is an industry in which size matters, that is, the big players dominate through sheer size. They must also have the cash flow, close association with lead product defining companies, and be able to buy in bulk in order to secure lower prices. Since 1996, in India, contract manufacturing was propagated as the area where entry by Indian manufacturers could grow and enhance exports; however, the few units that did manage one or two outsourced orders as contract manufacturers had to close down operations when the order expired, since they were unable to get any fresh orders.[38] It is quite widely accepted that in contract manufacturing, smaller firms are disadvantaged by size and cash shortage. In fact, outsourced contract manufacturing on a global scale has been moving towards acquisition, consolidation, concentration and centralization. The top ten global companies have seen annual growth rates topping 60 per cent. Since the whole system seems to be premised on tight controls on intellectual property by global firms located in the developed world with monopolistic market shares, control over globalized contract manufacturing is also likely to remain there.

Further, contract manufacturing is part of a more general system of interlinked industry segments with relatively autonomous norms of productions; a continuous fragmentation and centralization that have become defining features of the industry. Studies have shown that such network-centric production, which is based on a highly political process of inter-company relationships based on systems of trust and tight controls on intellectual property rights, leans towards distribution of low end and limited technology-based production in developing countries and a permanent creation of unequal working conditions both at a global and a local level.[39]

WOMEN'S EMPLOYMENT IN ELECTRONICS MANUFACTURE IN INDIA

Mixed and Uneven Trends

Unfortunately, reliable in-depth data on women's employment in the electronics industry in India is perhaps even harder to find than for garments, since the Department of Electronics does not provide any sex-disaggregated information on employment in the industry. Given the fact that electronics manufactures include several industry groups, aggregated trends in women's employment in the industry are also difficult to establish from National Sample Survey data due to problems in comparability across rounds. For example, of the five electronics industry groups netted in the 1993-1994 and 1999-2000 NSS rounds, only three are common.

In these comparable common groups,[40] women's share in principal status employment seems to have risen from 12 per cent to 22 per cent between 1993-1994 and 1999-2000, with the estimated number of women employed more than doubling from 22,260 in 1993-1994 to 52,436 in 1999-2000, and close to 49 per cent of the interim additional employment being of women. Shockingly, by 2004, the numbers of women workers in these segments of the electronics industry had obviously been reduced to statistical insignificance and not even one woman per thousand appeared in the employment survey of that year. At the same time the number of male workers in these segments were reduced by almost two thirds from 188,067 in 1999-2000 to 67,723 by 2004. Overall in the 1999-2000 NSS round, women workers in all electronics industry groups that were netted, numbered 65,545 in comparison to 313,445 male workers (see Figure 3.1), and women's share in electronics employment stood at 17 per cent.[41] By 2004, although the proportion of women increased to 24 per cent, their numbers had shrunk by close to 36 per cent to less than what prevailed a decade before, in 1993-1994. In fact, a striking revelation is that the combined male and female employment in electronics manufacture has been practically halved within the four years between 1999-2000 and 2004 (i.e., 47 per cent of the jobs had evaporated), indicative of the scale of deindustrialization. Further, despite the increased share of women in the industry, obviously electronics manufacture in India is not as feminized as is commonly thought. In fact, the shrinking numbers indicate that a significant number of women have been losing jobs in the post-liberalization decade, and in a situation of deindustrialization, any opportunities for expansion of women's employment in the sector are actually closing down.

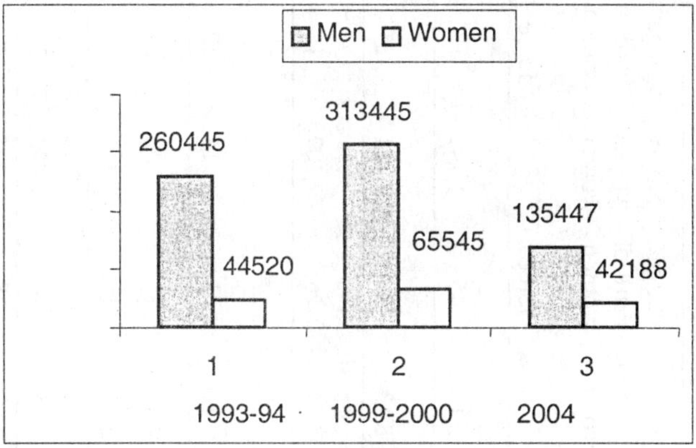

Figure 3.1 Workers in all electronics industry groups (NSS)

A comparison between the NSS data which cover organized and unorganized manufacturing and organized sector data in the Annual Survey of Industries for the year 1999-2000 showed that women workers had a mere 12 per cent share in unorganized sector employment in electronics as compared to 29 per cent in the organized sector. Obviously, the organized sector of the industry was more prone to hiring women than the unorganized segments and accounted for one-half (50 per cent) of all women workers in India's electronics industry that year. By 2004, the organized sector accounted for 51 per cent of women workers, and although women's share in the unorganized sector doubled to 24 per cent, in real terms the number of women employed in electronics manufacture was reduced by 23,357, of which half (11,629) were from the unorganized sector. In absolute terms, the losses of jobs in the organized sector were a little more at 11, 728, and the share of female employment in the organized sector of electronics manufacture fell from 29 per cent in 1999-2000 to 24 per cent in 2002-2003.

For the organized sector, sex-disaggregated figures for workers at three-digit levels of industrial classification are available from 1998-1999 to 2002-2003 from the Annual Survey of Industries. Even a cursory examination of the ASI data shows that apart from manufacture

Table 3.4: Directly employed women workers (All India) from ASI, 1998–99 and 1999–2000.

National Industrial Classification three digit	1998-1999		1999-2000		2002-2003	
	No. of women workers	%age share of women in work force	No. of women workers	%age share of women in work force	No. of women workers	%age share of women in work force
NIC 300 Manufacture of office, accounting and computing machinery	711	15	3,168	45	1,297	17
NIC 321, Manufacture of electronic valves, tubes, other electronic components	8,330	23	8,434	34	7,484	25
NIC 322, Manufacture of TV, radio transmitters and apparatus for line telephony telegraphy	3,473	11	4,441	26	2,209	18
NIC 323, Manufacture of TV, radio receivers, sound or video recording or reproducing apparatus and associated goods	11,697	43	7,110	31	4,714	30
NIC 331, Manufacture of medical appliances and instruments for measuring. checking, testing, navigation except optical instruments	3,261	14	3,930	15	2,840	11
NIC 332, Manufacture of optical instruments and photographic equipment	390	16	555	16	1,090	27
NIC 333, Manufacture of watches and clocks	5,750	38	5,698	38	3,094	32
All the above	33,612	24	33,336	29	21,638	24

of office, accounting and computing machinery (NIC 300) and of optical instruments and photographic equipment (NIC 332), where a few hundred jobs for women have been added, in every other segment of electronics manufacture, the number of jobs for women and their share in employment have both declined. The most marked decline is visible in the television and radio segment (NIC 322, and 323), where more than half the jobs for women (54 per cent) seem to have vanished in the five-year period between 1998-1999 and 2002-2003. Table 3.4 gives the distribution of directly employed women as per the Annual Survey of Industries.

For the electronics industry as a whole, in this most recent period (Table 3.4) it appears that the total number of women workers was reduced by more than a third. For a more comprehensive account of the the trends in electronics employment across liberalization era, it is useful to also look at the information on the organized sector available in the fourth and fifth rounds of Occupational Wage Surveys (OWS) by the Labour Bureau for the preceding period (i.e., for 1987 and 1995-1996), although the system of classification of the segments is different, making exact comparison with ASI data impossible; however, some idea of the trends in women's employment that took place between 1987 and 1995-1996 for three product groups which broadly cover the electronics industry do provide a useful reference point for comparison with the ASI data of a later date. OWS employment figures are given in Table 3.5.

As per the estimates of the occupational wage surveys, a 48 per cent increase in the number of women workers over 1987 brought the percentage of women workers in the electronics industries to 39 per cent by 1995-1996 in contrast to a decrease in the numbers of male workers by 22 per cent in the same period. Going by the ASI figures for the later period, it seems that such increases in women's share have been reversed from the latter half of the 1990s.

At a broad level, the overall trend in organized sector electronics showed a marginal rise in the numbers of women workers combined with a much more substantial increase in their share in employment, from 25 per cent in 1987 to 39 per cent in 1995-1996. At the same time, there was an absolute fall in numbers of male workers till the mid-1990s, which could indicate a degree of replacement of male jobs by female jobs having taken place, or a classic case of feminization; however, the latter half of the decade witnessed a slow expansion of women's jobs while men's jobs rose steeply till 1999-1998 and then started falling almost as sharply in a rather wildly fluctuating pattern. This time the fall in male employment did not mean any replacement by women since women's employment was also falling, although at a slower pace.

Table 3.5: Estimates of women's employment in electronics from Occupational Wage Surveys

Industry	1987		1995-1996	
	Estimated number of workers	% share of women in total work force	Estimated number of workers	% share of women in total work force
Manufacture of Television sets and Teleprinters	14,490	27 (24)	26,821	37 (42)
Manufacture of Electronic Computers, Components, Control Instrumentation, Accessories and parts	30,083	17 (32)	18,329	61 (47)
Manufacture of Watches and Clocks	18,769	37 (44)	15,262	31 (11)
All the Above	63,342	25 (100)	60,412	39 (100)

Source: Occupational Wage Surveys
Figures in parentheses refer to percentage distribution of women workers among the different segments

Although the gap between men and women was widest in 1998-1999, even in 2002-2003 the gap can be seen to be considerably wider than what prevailed in 1987. Figure 3.2 gives a pictorial representation of these employment trends. This trend of a wider gap in the latter half of the 1990s is not explained by changes in product profiles or production systems away from areas where women are traditionally employed. The same trend makes its appearance in even those segments where women had already reached critical mass levels.

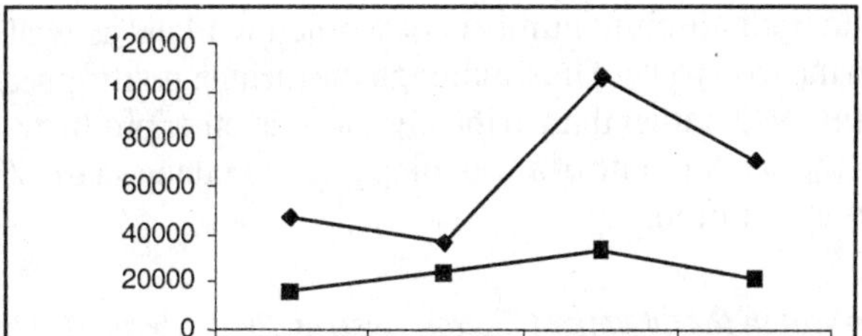

	1987	1995-96	1998-99	2002-2003
Men	47506	36851	106438	70349
Women	15836	23561	33612	21638

Figure 3.2 Employment trends in organized sector electronics manufacturing

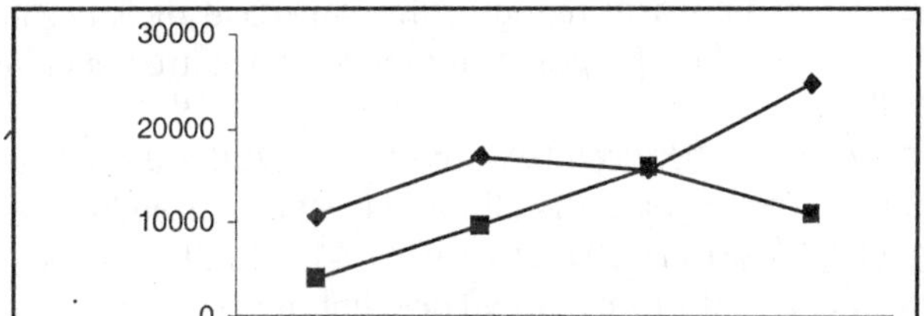

	1987	1995-96	1998-99	2002-03
Men	10578	16897	15505	24906
Women	3912	9924	15825	10843

Figure 3.3 Employment trends in television assembly

For example, the data provides some evidence of a relative concentration of women workers in what could broadly be termed the television segment of the electronics industry. Figure 3.3 gives a representation of the situation in the television assembly segment. This segment, which had witnessed a fairly substantial increase in both numbers and proportions of women workers, accounted for some 35 per cent of the women workers in the industry as a whole in 1998-1999, with women's share within the segment also having increased from 27 per cent in 1987 to 43 per cent in 1998-1999. Then suddenly, within one year, that is, between 1998-1999and 1999-2000 there was a drop in both absolute numbers of women workers as well as their share in the workforce. Thus, although the turning point appears at the end of the 1990s rather than in the middle as in other product/ industry groups, the net outcome of a widening gap and falling share of women workers is common.

Employment in the Organized Sector: Insecure, Volatile and Uneven

Despite marked fluctuations in share, the all-India trends in terms of the numbers of women workers in organized sector electronics manufacture yet appear to move at a sedate pace. But a closer look at the state-wise data reveals the generalized instability reflected even in periods of increases in women's employment, which remains hidden in consolidated countrywide figures. In Table 3.6, the ASI figures include data relating to the manufacture of medical appliances, optical instruments and photographic equipment, which are not covered in the OWS.

As may be seen, between 1987 and 1995-1996 the absolute number of women in the sector at the all-India level increased by over 7,000 and again by close to 10,000 between 1995-1996 and 1999-2000. What is interesting is that more than 90 per cent of the additional jobs for women between 1987 and 1995-1996were concentrated in the state of Maharashtra where women's employment more than trebled, coinciding with a 46 per cent loss of jobs for the male workers in the state. But between 1995-1996 and 1999-2000 (when at an all India level women's jobs were still showing an increase), many of the additional jobs for women workers in Maharashtra seem to have evaporated, while a threefold increase took place in men's jobs. By 2002-2003, the absolute number of women workers in Maharashtra's electronics industry were actually less than in 1987. Figure 3.4 gives a picture of the situation in Maharashtra.

Table 3.6: Workers in the organized sector in the top electronics producing states.

State	Women Workers				Male Workers			
	1987	1995 1996*	1999-2000	2002-03	1987	1995-1996*	1999-2000	2002-03
Maharashtra	3,260	9,923	8,155	3,910	9,909	5,350	14,237	12,174
Karnataka	1,272	5,711	5,881	5,557	3,972	4,450	9,897	11,315
Uttar Pradesh	1,996	2,132	2,655	2,440	5,050	5,156	9,359	12,338
Delhi	777	572	761	278	1,740	3,098	2,739	2,526
Andhra Pradesh	963	-	1,003	499	5,367	-	4,115	5,016
Tamilnadu	1,148	-	3,690	2,579	3,585	-	7,358	6,655
Gujarat	214	178	2,570	1,520	1,876	722	3,882	4,362
Residual (Other states)	6,400	4,871	8,621	4,855	14,665	18,248	31,542	15,963
Total	16,030	23,387	33,336	21,638	46,164	37,024	83,129	70,349
% of total workers	26	39	29	24	74	61	71	76

Note: In the occupational wage surveys, states with major concentration of the industries are given individually, while other states are covered as residual.

*Andhra Pradesh and Tamilnadu partially included with Karnataka and partially in residual for this column. Similarly the Delhi figure applies to television and teleprinters only. Other product groups in Delhi are incorporated in residual.

Source: For 1987 and 1995-96 Occupational Wage Survey (Fourth Round), Report on Four Engineering Industries, 1987, vol 4, Labour Bureau, Government of India; Occupational Wage Survey (Fifth Round) Report on ten Engineering Industries, 1995–1996, Labour Bureau, Government of India; For 1999-2000 and 2002-2003—Annual Survey of Industries.

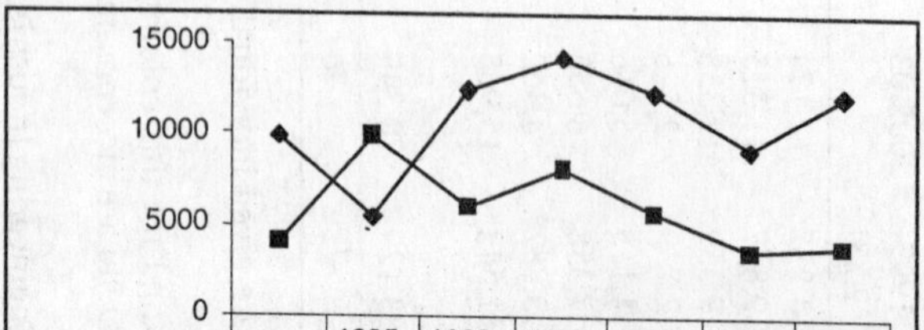

	1987	1995-1996	1998-1999	1999-2000	2000-2001	2001-2002	2002-2003
Men	9909	5350	12471	14237	12,274	9090	12174
Women	4007	9929	5939	8155	5751	3544	3910

Figure 3.4. Employment trends in the electronics industry in Maharashtra

This phenomenon of sharp swings and volatility of employment for both men and women in the electronics industry is not confined to Maharashtra. In Karnataka, as depicted in Figure 3.5, women's jobs jumped from 5,711 in 1995-1996 to 9,861 by 1998-1999, the same period when women were losing their jobs in droves in Maharashtra. Then in the space of just one year, 40 per cent of women's jobs disappeared and they were reduced to 5,881 in 1999-2000. This time, they were obviously not being replaced since almost an equal number of men lost their jobs along with the women.

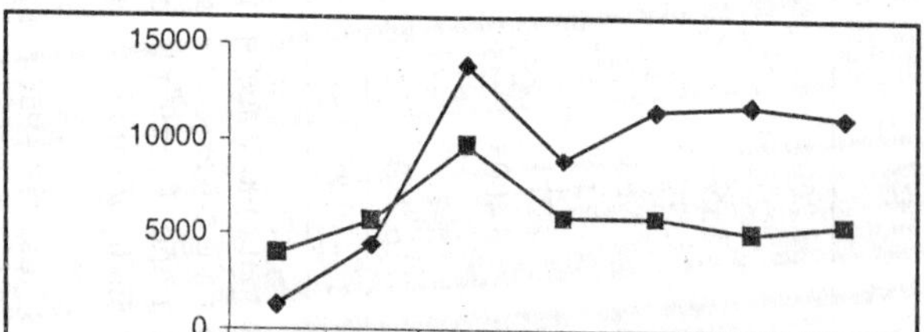

	1987	1995-1996	1998-1999	1999-2000	2000-2001	2001-2002	2002-2003
Men	1272	4450	13785	8887	11468	11777	11315
Women	3972	5711	9661	5881	5931	5168	5557

Figure 3.5 Employment trends in Karnataka

Maharashtra and Karnataka represent one end of the spectrum of patterns of women's employment in electronics, although similar fluctuations have made their appearance in several other states including Tamilnadu, Gujarat, Andhra Pradesh and even Punjab. Swings, volatility and instability in employment seem to have become the principal characteristics of all segments of the electronics industry in these states with rapid increases in the number of women workers or their share in overall employment generally being followed by drastic falls.

At another end of the spectrum are states such as Uttar Pradesh which has emerged as the top electronics producing state in the country but where women workers have stagnated in numbers, their share of employment falling from about 22 per cent in 1987 to 16 per cent in 2002-2003. Figure 3.6 gives a graphical representation of the trends in Uttar Pradesh from 1987 to 2000.

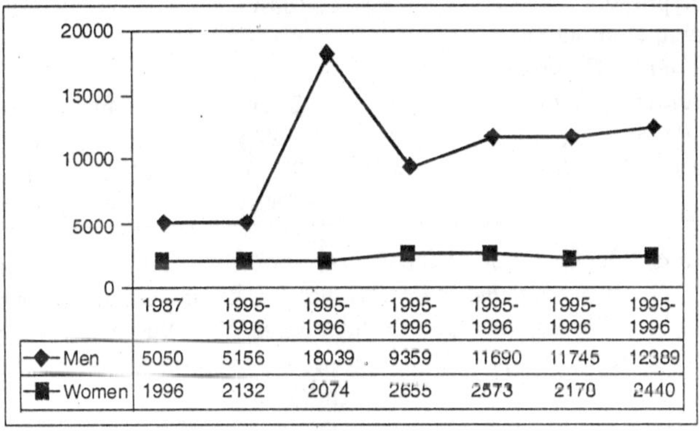

	1987	1995-1996	1995-1996	1995-1996	1995-1996	1995-1996	1995-1996
Men	5050	5156	18039	9359	11690	11745	12389
Women	1996	2132	2074	2655	2573	2170	2440

Figure 3.6 Employment trends in Uttar Pradesh

Across all states and including their several fluctuating specificities, however, the broad tendency for a widening of the gap between male and female workers, that is, a fall in the relative share of women in electronics manufacturing employment seems to have been the final consequence of the overall instability in the sector.

Persistent Wage Inequalities

Unlike in the garment industry where the entry of women was effected as part of a de-skilling process, in electronics it is precisely women's 'natural skills' or dexterity that are considered to make them suitable for the industry. One might think that since women are therefore more in demand their wage rates should be higher. And yet, electronics is no exception to the pervasive and universal phenomena of lower wage rates for women.

Table 3.7: Average daily minimum wage rates in electronics industries (from 1987 to 1995–1996)

Industry	Average Daily Minimum Wage Rates (Rs) 1987		1995–1996	
	Men	Women	Men	Women
Television Sets and Teleprinters	28.63	22.97 (80%)	63.27	49.49 (78%)
Electronic Computers, Components, Control Instruments, Accessories and Parts	39.7	29.34 (74%)	61.49	35.41 (58%)
Watches and Clocks	31.78	27.99 (88%)	66.78	59.33 (59%)

Source: Occupational Wage Survey (Fourth Round), *Report on Four Engineering Industries, !987*, vol 4, Labour Bureau, Government of India; vol 4 and Occupational Wage Survey (OWS) (Fifth Round) *Report on Ten Engineering Industries, 1995-1996*, Labour Bureau, Government of India.

At a preliminary level, wage rate data at the lower end of the wages (minimum wage rates) show that the gap between male and female wages has increased during the globalization decade. Table 3.7 presents data from the Occupational Wage Survey on the differentials in average minimum wage rates of men and women in 1987 and in the years 1995-1996. The gap appears to have widened most in electronic computers, components, and so on, where the difference between male and female wages has increased from 26 per cent to 42 per cent at the lower end of the wage scale. At the higher end the increases in male-female wage differential is even sharper from 26 per cent to 55 per cent. Maximum wage rates in the industry are given in Table 3.8. Perhaps this is the explanation for the fact that the proportions of women workers in this segment showed the maximum increase from 17 per cent in 1987 to 61 per cent in 1995. In other words, once again we see the connection between wage inequality or wage discrimination against women and availability of employment for them. It points to the fact that inequalities become further institutionalized by purely market-determined systems of wage fixation.

Table 3.8: Average daily maximum wage rates in electronics industries (from 1987 to 1995-1996)

Industry	Average Daily Maximum Wage Rates (Rs)			
	1987		1995–1996	
	Men	Women	Men	Women
Television Sets and Teleprinters	44.76	33.77 (75%)	82.16	65.78 (80%)
Electronic Computers, Components, Control Instruments, Accessories and Parts	63	46.55 (74%)	101.82	45.33 (45%)
Watches and Clocks	51.72	45.24 (87%)	93.91	89.21 (95%)

In television and teleprinter manufacturing on the other hand, the wage gap has only marginally increased at the lower end while at the higher end it has actually narrowed. Yet in the same period, there was a threefold increase in the number of women workers in this segment and an increase in share from 27 per cent to 37 per cent. What did change was the composition of the workers. In 1987, the OWS delineation of occupations did not include the category of assembler although possibly assemblers were categorized as TV fitters who constituted about 22 per cent of all workers and of whom 45 per cent were women. In contrast, by 1995-1996, assemblers constituted 53 per cent of the workers of whom 63 per cent were women.

Thus the several processes associated with globalization, namely, increased foreign investment combined with lifting of import restrictions, de-licensing and de-reservation for the small-scale sector have had a significant impact on the employment in the electronics sector. Among other implications has been a general slowing down of growth in manufacturing leading to a slowing down of employment growth and finally negative growth. If some jobs initially grew due to foreign investment and large employers in the organized sector, many others were lost due to increased import penetration and the cornering of the home market by a few major players at the cost of several smaller units. The most adverse effects on women's employment can be seen in their declining share and falls in total employment in several states. At the other end, their gains in employment share and absolute employment in some concentrations is accompanied by a widening gap between their wage shares.

FIELD SURVEY

Widespread Closure of Electronics Factories in the 1990s

As has been mentioned in an earlier section, Delhi had emerged as an important electronics manufacturing centre, particularly for small-scale consumer electronics in the pre-liberalization era. Through the 1980s too, a number of units were established in several industrial areas, where a significant proportion of the workers were women. During our field survey in 2002-2003, however, it was found that several of these units had closed down while a few had relocated mostly in the neighbouring township of Noida.[42] In fact, most of the units which were known as high employers of women had closed down, including a number that were covered by a similar field study conducted in 1994-1995.[43] According to DOE, there were 373 units in Delhi in 1999 of which 345 were small-scale and employment in the industry was 37,000. The number of women in most of them, however, were almost negligible while the organized sector figure of 761 women workers in 1999-2000 are almost all concentrated in one unit.[44]

On the other hand, Noida, Uttar Pradesh, the neighbouring industrial township whose development has essentially been as an outgrowth of Delhi, has become one of the most important centres of electronics production, outstripping Delhi in the 1990s and is second now only to Bangalore in Karnataka. Such production, however, is concentrated in only a few units as there are just 78 units in Noida in comparison to the 334 units in Bangalore and 373 in Delhi.[45]

Of the sixty women workers covered by the field survey, although more than one-half (thirty-four) lived in Delhi, less than one-fourth (fourteen) were working in factories located in Delhi. The others were all located in factories in Noida. Nevertheless, as evident from Figure 4.6, despite rapid growth in production, women's employment in the electronics industry in Uttar Pradesh too appears like a worm at the bottom of the employment graph and has remained more or less stagnant. This is despite the fact that from the latter half of the 1990s, Noida has seen the entry of important MNC-owned manufacturing units who have succeeded in establishing themselves as major players in India's market for consumer electronics.[46] Declining opportunities for employment of women in electronics in both Delhi and Noida is further evidenced by the fact that some 3 per cent of the surveyed garment workers had been formerly employed in the electronics industry.

A Younger Workforce with Educated and Unmarried Members

A striking aspect of the profile of electronics workers that emerged from the field survey is the larger presence of young and/or unmarried workers in comparison to the garment industry. While more than one-half (55 per cent) of the workers were in the age group 18-25, 45 per cent were unmarried, and a surprisingly high 8 per cent were separated. Table 3.9 gives a quantitative measure of these emergent trends and Figure 3.7 gives a pictorial representation of the same.

Table 3.9: Emerging trends in age and marital status of women workers

Marital status	Age of women workers						
	18-20	21-25	26-30	32-35	40-42	All ages	%
Unmarried	9	14	4	-		27	45
Married	1	8	8	8	3	28	47
Separated		1	3	1		5	8
All	10	23	15	9	3	60	100
%	17	38	25	15	5	100	

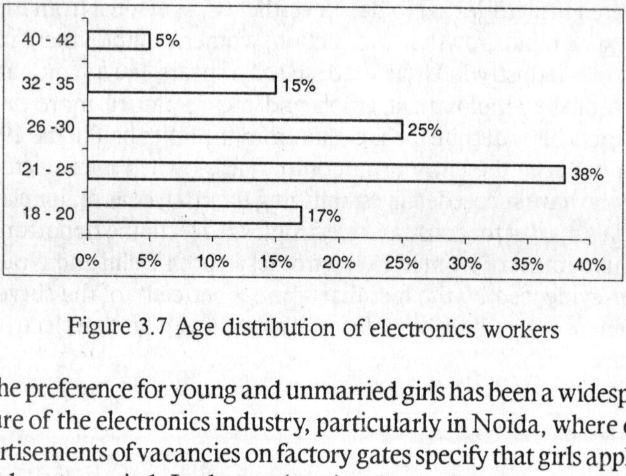

Figure 3.7 Age distribution of electronics workers

The preference for young and unmarried girls has been a widespread feature of the electronics industry, particularly in Noida, where often advertisements of vacancies on factory gates specify that girls applying must be unmarried. In these advertisements, the same condition of course does not apply to boys or men.

Most of the twenty-seven unmarried workers were either born in Delhi or had spent the better part of their childhood in the city. Only three of the unmarried workers were direct migrants and all were living with their brothers who had either preceded or accompanied them in search of work. Of course, it is natural for unmarried girls to be staying with their families, and equally natural for most of them to be from locally settled families; however, an earlier survey done by the CWDS in Noida in 1997 had pointed to a significant presence of single migrant women in the electronics factories of the region who were staying in groups independent of families.[47] Practically all of them were from the southern state of Kerala. After an extensive search, it was found that only a few of these women who had been surveyed in 1997 were to be found in the area in 2002-2003; of these women, only one or two had continued working in electronics. Among those that remained, a few had married and settled here, but the majority had returned home (or perhaps gone elsewhere), since their companies had closed down or their working conditions had deteriorated.

In the 1997 survey, it had been found that at least one of the prestigious auto-electronics firms established in the late 1980s (which had expanded into several units in the early 1990s) had actually recruited girls from Kerala as a conscious strategy. It was also a firm where most of the labour laws used to be implemented other than, of course, the required statutory provision of a crèche and even that was provided following an agitation by the workers and the formation of a union; however, in the several units that the firm has in the area even today, according to its workers, recruitment patterns have changed and the practice of employing workers for seven months and then giving a break of service, or in other words permanent casualization, has been institutionalized. Unmarried women workers recruited from Kerala had earlier been provided some security of service, including leave facilities which allowed them to visit their homes once in three years. They are obviously unable to cope with the new situation and have stopped coming. Similarly, where the earlier study had cited the story of a padre from Kerala having brought some twenty-five unmarried girls from his village to Noida around 1994-1995 when it seemed that industry was expanding on some scale and work opportunities were to be found in the area. Almost all of them had left Noida by 2003 since many of the units where they had found work (which most of the time was without minimum wages or other legal entitlements) had closed down. Clearly, even the limited opportunities that had drawn these young unmarried women workers to Noida had dried up over the last few years. Manufacturing industry and in particular the electronics industry is no longer drawing single women migrants to either Delhi or its neighbouring industrial township of Noida as was quite distinctly the case just a few years ago.

Among the unmarried women workers in the present survey, around two-fifths were in the age group 22 to 29 years, which is higher than the average age at which girls get married in the social groupings to which these girls belonged. In itself, this could perhaps be considered a sign of social advance but at least some of them for whom the prospect of their marriage appeared increasingly remote were unhappy (some actually broke down and cried during interviews). In a few cases it was clear that, since they were important earners for their natal family, marriage had become a difficult proposition as their families would find it difficult to manage without their income. In at least a couple of cases they belonged to depressed castes and their education and work had given them a certain upward mobility for which there was little scope for finding compatibility within their traditional community; neither would they generally be accepted as brides in other communities (although there was one instance of a girl who had married an upper-caste coworker). In all, the continued unmarried state of many workers is perhaps indicative of some social changes at the margins being engendered by both education and employment patterns in such industries, but its very marginality in the overall community and societal conditions houses possibilities of emotional difficulty and personal isolation for women. Figure 3.8 gives a chart depicting the fractions of women of different marital status working in the electronics industry in the Delhi-Noida region.

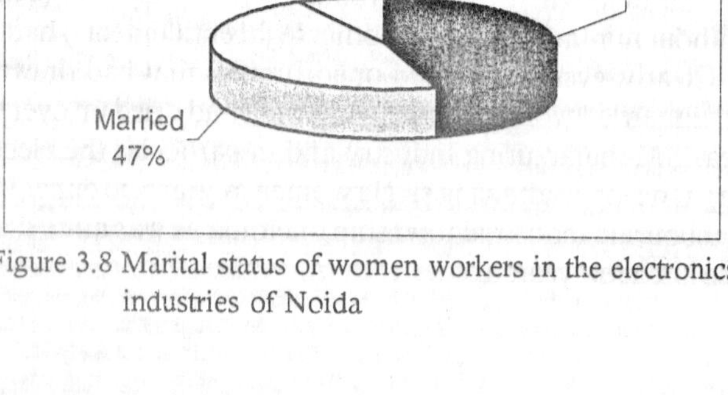

Figure 3.8 Marital status of women workers in the electronics industries of Noida

Even as, in some of the older units, the proportions of married women have increased, generally speaking this was made possible by the fact that in these units, which had ridden the crest of the boom in the industry during the 1980s and early 1990s, workers had tended to get organized, if only in bursts. Even if Unions were broken and their leaders thrown out (the mortality of factories in Noida is perhaps equally if not more than matched by the mortality of Unions), some benefits and stability of service had to be given to workers when the industry was in an expansionary phase, if only to wean them away from their dismissed leaders.[48] In these older units, formal sector rights had thus been largely acquired, which allowed some space for women to continue in service even after marriage. Not surprisingly, six of the eight workers in the highest wage group (Rs 3,300 to 3,900) had such histories. And yet, even these workers reported that the proportions of women were falling in their units as their companies were no longer in an expansionary mode, and any vacancies that came up tended to be filled by men.

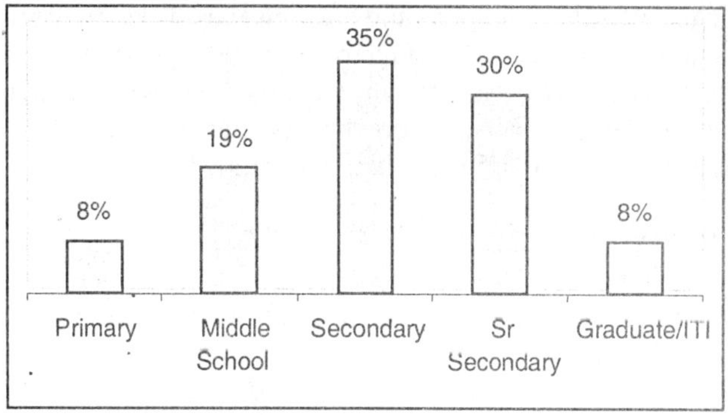

Figure 3.9 Education levels among women workers in Delhi-Noida electronics industry

Close to three-quarters (73 per cent) of the surveyed women workers in electronics were at least educated up to secondary school in comparison to the figure of less than one-third (32 per cent) among garment workers. And none were illiterate. One of the workers told us that she had been recruited from her school in the mid-1990s, indicating perhaps that young girls were not yet spontaneously available in the local market for industrial labour, and also showing a preference in the industry for girls fresh from school. An earlier survey of women workers in garments and electronics conducted in the 1980s (in the state of Maharashtra) had also noted that education up to the high school level was more or less a precondition for getting a job in the electronics industry.[49] This obviously has remained the case at least for the more organized segments of the industry in Delhi and Noida. Figure 3.9 shows the distribution of education levels among women workers in the electronics industry in Delhi-Noida

The 1980s study in Maharashtra, quoted above, had noted that differing educational levels did not get reflected in different levels of earning in the electronics industry, and what distinguished electronics workers was that they received well above minimum wages. Wage rates in electronics amounted then to at least one and a half times the average wage of garment workers, and over 60 per cent of them were earning double that and more. As we shall see, by 2003, the more privileged working conditions and higher wages of electronics workers are no longer the case, and in fact the average wage of the electronics workers has fallen to below minimum wage levels while their average wages are a mere 5 per cent more than garment workers even as their levels of education continue to be significantly higher.

New Restrictions and Restraints on Women's Employment in Electronics

Over three-fifths of the surveyed women workers were working in processes for the manufacture of television, audio and video consumer products, while one-tenth were working on complex component assembly. Close to one-sixth of them were involved in the manufacture of watches and clocks, while another one-sixth were involved in manufacture of simple engineering parts components required for electronics manufacture. These findings are depicted in Figure 3.10.

The size of the workforce in the factories in which they were working ranged from 12 to 2,000, although this largest firm was spread across several buildings. Of the two largest factories, one was in auto electronics in collaboration with a multi-national, while the other was an Indian brand manufacturer of audio and video cassettes and televisions. Among the smaller units, components and watches and clocks were dominant although some were also involved in television assembly on a sub-contracted basis. Multinational companies and established Indian brands dominated the group of factories employing workforces in the range of 250 to 880, although one or two in this group were also sub-contractors.

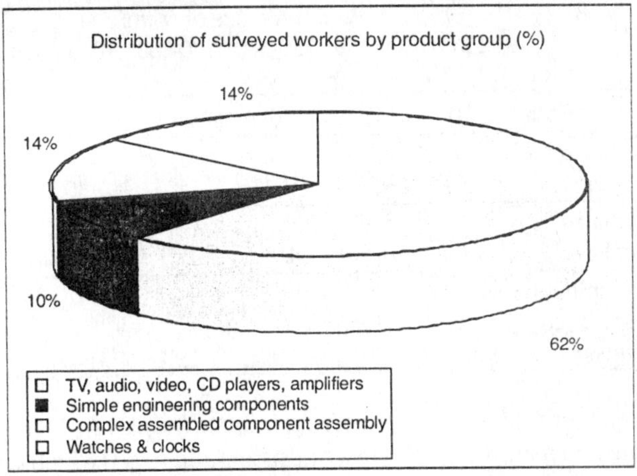

Figure 3.10 Distribution of surveyed workers over different product groups

As may be seen from Table 3.10, estimates of employment in these factories exceeded 8,000 of which women constituted 49 per cent. These of course are workers' estimates, which although no less reliable than official estimates, tend to be somewhat more than the actual, particularly in units where the numbers exceed hundred. Our own estimate based on whatever could be gathered from other sources would be that these units employed in all perhaps 5,000-6,000 workers and the number of women workers who were represented would be at best around 2,500. Further, it is highly improbable that the total number of women workers in the full range of electronics manufacturing and types of units in the entire region exceeds 10,000 at present. From our own observations, it was clear that in some of the largest factories and particularly in new units involved in industrial electronics and even products such as floppy diskettes the production workforce is entirely male. Similarly in the proliferating small-scale unorganized computer assembly (which generally also includes servicing), the workers are required to be quite mobile and are almost entirely male.[50]

Table 3.10 Gender specific estimates of employment in electronics factories

	Workforce size of factories					
	12-60	100-150	250-300	500-880	1000-2000	All factories
No. of factories	10	7	6	4	2	29
Estimated No. of workers	291	930	1725	2580	3000	8526
Estimated % of women	51%	29%	46%	48%	58%	49%
% Distribution of surveyed workers	35%	27%	18%	16%	4%	100%

Even for the large grey market assembling (largely from imported or smuggled parts) of CD players, transistors and so on (which are then stamped and passed off as well known brand names), such assembly and related small engineering work is concentrated in workshops in densely populated working class districts close to Delhi's principal electronics goods market (opposite the Red Fort). Young, unmarried, girls are generally socially restrained from working in such workshops, while wives and mothers are not preferred, especially since young and more easily adaptable unemployed boys are available in large numbers. In our view, even in the electronics industry so famed for its preference for women workers, recent developments are moving in the direction of restricting and restraining further entry of women workers. In some cases it might be due to the types of technology involved in the newer segments of the industry where the 'nimble fingers' attributed to women workers are not so necessary. An equally important reason lies in the social nature of the new patterns of organization of production in the unorganized segment, which prefers young boys to girls. Finally, it is also due to the closure of the expansionary phase of many of the earlier units which did tend to employ women in some numbers, including full-scale closure of several units, and the tendency to replace women by men, even where they remain operational. The limited recruitment in the new multi-national firms, has been insufficient to offset this process, although as we shall see the distribution of women workers seems to be narrowing down to the expanding but relatively less employment spreading MNC segment.

Increasing MNC Domination of Female Employment

Of the twenty-nine factories in which the surveyed workers were working, six were MNCs, seven were Indian branded products while ten were unbranded products or those doing job work for a range of brands. Another six were called vendors by the workers; they were actually sub-contracting units tied to one or other of the major brand manufacturers and they worked exclusively for only one product manufacturer, generally an MNC. Of the estimated total number of women workers working in the twenty-nine factories (over 4,000 according to the workers), it seems that around two-thirds are now concentrated in the MNCs, with perhaps another 2 per cent in MNC vendors. Such a high concentration in MNCs as appears in our survey is largely because of one extremely large unit in auto electrical and electronic assembly, which alone accounts for more than one-third of female workforce of all the twenty-nine units covered by the survey.[51] But even if we remove this one large employer from the reckoning, close to one-half of the female workforce in the industry were still found to be located in MNCs.

At first glance, as Table 3.11 shows, the high share of MNCs in female employment in electronics manufacturing might appear to confirm the general perception that the entry of MNCs or foreign direct investment has an expansionary effect on women's employment; however, given the fact that from 1987 and 1999-2000, women's employment in organized sector electronics in Uttar Pradesh increased from 1,966 to a mere 2,655, and then declined to 2440 in 2002-2003 that is, a mere 484 jobs have been added over a fifteen year period, their entry does not appear to have greatly enhanced opportunities for women.[52] In fact, along with the expansion of the MNCs in Noida, many women seem to have been displaced or reduced in number and

Table 3.11 Distribution of units employing women by nature of ownership over different product groups

	Distribution of units by nature of ownership and other characteristics					Estimated women workers in estimated workforce by product group (%)	Estimated share of product among industry's workers (%)
Product group	MNC	Indian brand	Vendors	Unbranded	All types of factories		
Television, audio, video and other consumer products	3	4	6	2	15	44	45
Electronic components, PCB, computer motherboard	1	2	-	6	9	21	4
Watches and Clocks	1	1	-	2	4	50	18
Auto electronics	1	-	-	-	1	75	33
All products	6	7	6	10	29	50	100
Estimated share of women in workforce by type of factory (%)	59	38	19	56	50		
Estimated distribution of women workers by type of factory (%)	66	18	3	13	100		

proportion in the unbranded as well as the Indian brand manufacturers as quite evident from the closure of units in Delhi as well as in similar reports from workers from Noida. We found that even the units that had been relocated from Delhi to Noida were employing workers in far smaller numbers than earlier.

Closures now seem to be affecting the MNC segment as well. One of the most prestigious and state-of-the-art MNC factories was moving towards closure during the course of the survey. Even as one of its workers with six years of service in this factory filled our questionnaire, the management was closing up most of its departments, retrenching most of its 'permanent' workers, selling off the factory premises, while retaining only some fresh trainees temporarily in the one department still functioning. This particular factory used to employ some 680 women out of a workforce of 880 workers and had established itself only in 1996. It seems it is now outsourcing a vastly reduced range and quantity of its manufacturing requirements and has announced relocation to another state, although it is likely that there too it will be outsourcing a substantial part of its operations. A few of the workers who have been thrown out of their jobs are now being offered casual employment in their old company's outsourcing unit at vastly reduced wages (their earlier wages were among the highest in the industry). Similarly, in the MNC units established in an earlier phase (that is, factories between eight and twelve years old), workers reported that the numbers of workers were declining and again some departments had been closed down over the last few years.

Persistence of Low Wages Despite Hi tech Production and Demand for Skill

As discussed earlier, electronics workers were far better paid than garment workers in the 1980s; however, by now it is clear that there is little difference in the average earnings between the two sectors. In fact, well over three-fifths of the workers were not receiving even minimum wages. This was true across the board, including in the MNCs, which many might find surprising since it is generally believed that MNCs provide high quality employment. Of course the worst paid were the workers in the unbranded and vendor factories where the average wages were around one-half of the official minimum wages. The Indian branded factories have the best record as far as minimum wages are concerned, with more than four-fifths of the workers in these units being permanent, and most receiving more than the official minimum wage. In contrast, only one-half of the workers from the MNC units were receiving minimum wages.

One of the methods of evading minimum wages in the case of the MNCs was to, at all times, keep a large batch of trainees in their production workforce who did not have to be paid minimum wages (such a method has been reported in a detailed study of a white goods MNC in Chennai as well).[53] Another was to keep a permanent force of casual workers. Most of the casual workers in the MNCs had service tenures of over three years but were still casual and were being denied the minimum wages. The high proportion of MNC workers earning less than the minimum wage in our sample is probably larger than what actually exists since newly permanent workers in the two major companies that now dominate the Indian market, which had both set up manufacturing facilities within the last five years, were too afraid to talk to us. Nevertheless, from discussions with two workers in these two units who did respond to our questionnaire, it was clear that a substantial use of casual or trainee workers for actual production work was a distinctive feature in all the MNCs. See Table 3.12 for figures on the fractions of casual, contract and permanent workers in different types of company and their corresponding wage rates.

Table 3.12 Distribution and monthly wage rates of casual contract and permanent workers by type of company

Type of company	Casual		Contract		Permanent		All workers	
	No.	Avg. wage (Rs)	No.	Avg. wage (Rs)	No.	Avg. wage (Rs)	No.	Avg. wage (Rs)
MNC	5	1,950	-	-	5	2,850	10	2,400
Indian Brand	4	1,760	-	-	18	2,822	22	2,547
Vendor	5	1,457	-	-	3	2,162	8	2,021
Unbranded	9	1,457	2	1,500	9	1,387	20	1,425
All factories	23	1,725	2	1,500	35	2,326	60	2,082

The use of contract workers does not seem to be as widespread in electronics (at least among women workers) as in garments. Only two of the workers were contract workers and both were working in the unbranded segment of the industry. The proportion of casual workers was, however, very high (close to two-fifths), and clearly most marked in the vendor and MNC segment (close to two-thirds in the former and one-half in the latter). In the unbranded segment the proportions of those declaring themselves as casual workers (here including contract workers) were again more than one-half, although actually many of those who declared themselves permanent did so not on the basis of any legal entitlements and were in a sense also casual. And in a strange inversion, statedly 'permanent' workers were, on average, earning less than the workers declaring themselves casual (see Table 3.12).

Universal Squeeze on Wages: MNCs Lead the Way in Extending Hours of Work

A remarkable feature of the electronics industry's approach to its women workers is reflected in Table 3.13. While 57 per cent of the workers had some social security entitlements in the form of provident fund and health insurance, only 25 per cent were receiving minimum wages. None of the workers in the vendor and unbranded segments had minimum wages while one-half of the MNC workers were being denied minimum wages, although all the MNC workers and three-quarters of those working for vendors seemed to be getting health insurance and provident fund. Similarly, where 45 per cent of the Indian brand workers were deprived of minimum wages, a much larger proportion had access to some social and health insurance, while in the unbranded segment (largely unorganized sector) none had minimum wages and only 10 per cent had access to health and provident fund entitlements.

Equally important, however, is the pattern of labour time exploitation that appeared in the survey. From Table 3.14 it is apparent that the MNCs lead the way in extending the hours of work, with 90 per cent of their workers working on an average some 10 to 11 hours a day, and only one worker working the normal eight hour day. Further workers from the newer and larger MNC players, reported that they

Table 3.13 Legal entitlements of workers in different types of company (Percentages of the total number of employees)

Labour rights	MNC	Vendor	Indian Brand	Unbranded	All factories
Minimum Wage	5 (50%)	-	10 (45%)	-	15 (25%)
ESI (health insurance)	10 (100%)	6 (75%)	16 (73%)	2 (10%)	34 (57%)
Provident Fund	10 (100%)	6 (75%)	16 (73%)	2 (10%)	34 (57%)
Uniform	2 (20%)	1 (13%)	2 (9%)	- -	5 (8%)

normally had to work on the weekly off days as well and on an average received one off day in four to six weeks. This was confirmed through several visits to their homes on Sundays (their weekly off day) only to find that they had been called to work. At the other extreme, although still better than the MNCs, some two fifths of the workers in the unbranded unorganized segment were working extra hours.

Table 3.14 Work hours in companies of different types.

Daily work hours	MNC	Vendor	Indian	Unbranded	All factories*
10 – 11 hrs	9	2	-	5	16 (27%)
9 – 9.5	-	5	9	3	17 (28%)
8 hrs	1	1	13	12	27 (45%)
Workers provided with company transport	8	4	10	-	22 (37%)

*Figures in parenthesis represent percentages of all surveyed women workers.

Overall, more than one-quarter of the workers were working extended hours ranging from 10 to 11 hours a day, with another 28 per cent working 9 to 9.5 hours, or in other words, some 55 per cent of the workers were working more than the regular eight hours a day.

Finally, although the public sector in electronics manufacturing has no presence in Delhi and Noida, there are two public sector units in the neighbouring Ghaziabad. There could be no greater contrast between the wages, conditions of work, and facilities available to the workers in these units in comparison to the workers in the private sector. On an average, the salaries of public sector production workers was at least three times what was available in these new and highly modernized factories being set up through foreign direct investment, even though it was clear that most of the women were concentrated in the semi-skilled categories of workers and the new recruitment favoured more skilled engineering graduates or diploma holders and the proportions of women were coming down. In contrast to the workers in the private sector, the average public sector woman worker was at least in her mid- or late-thirties indicative of some stagnation in recruitment. Where the expansion of the public sector, had clearly opened opportunities for high quality employment to women workers of an earlier generation, under the new dispensation of increasing priority to private and foreign-direct-investment-driven growth in the electronics industry, not only have such opportunities been curtailed but even in the private sector there does not seem to have been much expansion of employment while wages and working conditions are increasingly becoming more exploitative, and ridden with discontinuities.

SUMMING UP THE ISSUES

Electronics, was one of the first industries to open up to the liberalization process in India from the 1980s. The loosening of import restrictions in this first phase had led to a certain kind of expansion of low-investment assembly which initially drew significant numbers of women workers into the industry. But with the deepening of the liberalization process across the 1990s, and the large-scale entry of multi-national corporations, such opportunities for women workers are increasingly facing closure. Employment in the industry has tended to swing wildly almost from year to year, as has also the gender composition of the workforce, indicating a high level of instability, volatility in the industry and large-scale displacement of workers.

The export thrust of government policy has failed to materialize and the result of the entry of multi-national producers has only led to displacements in local industry. Evidence of widespread closures emerged in the field survey, along with the introduction of employment patterns which institutionalize casualization. Although the workforce in electronics is predominantly young with a large proportion of unmarried women, over the last few years closures and casualization have reversed the earlier process of immigration of single-women workers into the electronics industry of the Delhi region. Liberalization of imports has also led to the proliferation of unorganized small workshop-based assembling in the computer industry, which demand a high level of mobility of workers and where women are clearly not preferred. On the other hand, the older Indian branded product factories are no longer expanding, their workforces are shrinking in numbers and a trend of replacing women workers by male workers is noticeable.

Within such patterns of otherwise closing opportunities, multi-national corporations have emerged as the largest employers of women workers in general at the cost of workers in the older local units. Even MNCs are unstable employers, evidenced in incidents of closure and downsizing within MNCs over the past few years. Employment practices in MNCs, particularly those that have risen to dominance in Indian markets, are marked by extended working hours, use of trainees for production work and even denial of minimum wages to many workers. Average wages in this hi-tech industry with a more educated workforce are practically converging with the average wages of less-educated garment workers in contrast to the 1980s when electronics employment, which generally demanded at least high school education, paid far better wages. Clearly foreign direct investment in the electronics industry has not led to either expanded employment or improved quality of employment, particularly when one compares its role with that played by the public sector in the electronics industry during the pre-liberalization era.

NOTES

1 UNDP, Human Development Report 1999: 57.
2 The Department of Electronics has now been brought under the Ministry of Information Technology by the Government of India too.
3 D. Ernst, From Partial to Systemic Globalization: International Production Networks in the Electronics Industry, BRIE, Working Paper 98, 1997.
4 Although the largest part of the increased share of the developing countries in world exports of manufactures (from 17 per cent in 1990 to 27 per cent in 2000) was accounted for by exports of office and telecom equipment from just a few countries, electronics manufactures also accounted for a very large share of manufactured exports from a wider range of developing countries.
5 For over a decade, worldwide market data shows the break-up of sector outputs as–EDP 42 per cen; Communication 24 per cent, Indûstrial 18 per cent; Consumer 12 per cent, Strategic 6 per cent. Source: B. Wadia, From Roots to Fruits, *Electronics Outlook*, June 2002.
6 Source: WTO Trade Statistics. It should be noted that the effects of the slowdown began to be felt well before the events of 11 September 2001.
7 D. Elson, Appraising recent developments in the world market for nimble fingers, in Amrita Chhachhi and Renee Pittin, eds., *Confronting State, Capital and Patriarchy* (London: Macmillan, 1996): 35-55.
8 Specialized public sector electronics firms were ECIL and BEL, while BHEL was the major large engineering undertaking.
9 Public sector concerns under state governments included Keltron in Kerala and Uptron in Uttar Pradesh.
10 N. Banerjee, Something old, something new, in Swasti Mitter and Sheila Rowbottom, eds., *Women Encounter Technology* (New York: Routledge, 1995).
11 Government of India, Department of Electronics, Data Bank and Information Division, *Guide to Electronics Industry in India*, 1999, hereafter called *Electronics Directory*, 1999.
12 Government of India, Department of Electronics, *Integrated Policy Measures in Electronics*, 1985.
13 *Electronics Directory*, 1999.

14 Based on NSSO *Employment and Unemployment in India, 1993-1994* distribution of principal usual status employment by industry group in manufacture of apparatus for TV and radio transmission (NIC 365), TV receivers (NIC 366), electronic valves, tubes (NIC 368), radiographic x ray (NIC 369) and watches and clocks (NIC 382).

15 Government of India, Planning Commission, *Eighth Five Year Plan (1992–1997)* vol 2.

16 Government of India, Department of Electronics, *Ninth Five Year Plan (1997–2002) Electronics Industry.*

17 The three major associations of electronics manufacturers, ELCINA, MAIT and, CETMA had, in fact, given a joint representation to the government in this regard.

18 *Statistical Year Book of Indian IT and Electronics Industry, 2000-2001*, Electronics and Computer Software Export Promotion Council.

19 Govt. of India, Planning Commission, *Report of the Working Group on Information Technology Sector for the Tenth Five Year Plan* (Part II), Electronics Information & Planning, IPAG, Ministry of Information Technology Jan 2002 .

20 Of the top 100 units, about 25 are in the small scale sector. Electronics Directory, 1999.

21 Government of India, Planning Commission, 2002. *Foreign Investment in India.*

22 For example, Ajanta clocks, considered to be the largest clock manufacturer in the world has shifted most of its manufacturing establishment to China, while Samtel and Videocon (both major Indian players in the domestic consumer electronics sector) have recently invested in manufacturing units in Germany.

23 Data Source: Electronics and Computer Software Export Promotion Council (ESC), New Delhi *Statistical Year Book of Indian IT and Electronics Industry 2000-2001.*

24 See R. Rastogi, Electronics and information technology production trends in 2001, In *Electronics Information and Planning*, IPAG, Ministry of Information Technology March–April, 2002.

25 See list of top 100 TNCs in UNCTAD, World Investment Report 2002.

26 S. Joekes, Trade-related employment for women in industry and Services in developing countries.

27 M. Borrus, Left for dead: Asian production networks and the revival of US electronics in Barry Naughton, ed., *The China Circle: Economics and Technology in the PRC, Taiwan and Hong Kong* (Washington D.C. Brookings Institution Press, 1997).

28 The ITA covers five main categories of products: computers (including printers, scanners, monitors, hard-disks drives, power supplies and so on.), telecommunications products (including telephone sets, fax machines, modems, pagers and the like), semi-conductors (including chips and wafers), semi-conductor manufacturing equipment, software (for example, diskettes and CD ROMs) and scientific instruments. Attempts were made to bring even consumer electronics within the scope of the ITA in what is known as ITA-II which, however, did not go through.

29 M. Borrus and S. Cohen, Why now? A new transatlantic initiative in information technology, *BRIE Working Paper 119*, 1998 http://brie.berkeley.edu/publications/WP119.pdf

30 Of the thirteen major consumer electronics' manufacturers in 1991, eight were Japanese companies, one was from the Netherlands (Philips), one from France (Thomson), one from Finland (Nokia), and two from the Republic of Korea (Samsung and Goldstar) while Whirlpool and Electrolux are the largest firms in the household appliances or ' white goods' sector in the United States and Europe, respectively.

31 In terms of origin, firms in the telecommunications industry are geographically dispersed, with half the firms being of European origin.

32 ILO, Impact of flexible labour market arrangements on the machinery electrical and electronic industries, 1998. http://www.ilo.org/public/english/dialogue/sector/techmeet/tmmei98/tmmeir1.htm

33 Dieter Ernst, Michael Borrus, D. Ernst and S. Haggard, eds., *International Production Networks in Asia. Rivalry or Riches?* (London: Routledge, 2000).

34 B. Lüthje, IT and the changing social division of labor: the case of electronics contract manufacturing, in William H. Dutton, Brian Kahin, Ramon O'Callaghan and Andrew W. Wyckoff, eds., *Transforming Enterprise: The Economic and Social Implications of Information Technology*, MIT Press, 2004):. 335-358

35 D. Ernst From partial to systemic globalization: international production networks in the electronics industry, April 1997 http://brie.berkeley.edu/publications/WP%2098.pdf

36 The major contract manufacturers are Solectron, Flextronics, SCI, Celestica and Jabil Circuits. Scholars have noted that most of these names are unfamiliar even to many insiders, since CM-providers do not post their brand name on any product. The *Los Angeles Times*, therefore, called the EMS-industry a system of stealth manufacturing; Lüthje, IT and the changing social division of labor.

37 Ibid.

38 In 1996, a study was commissioned by the Department of Electronics, Government of India, and conducted by the management consultants, Arthur D. Little. It had emphasized contract manufacturing as a key success factor for Indian hardware exporters. Taking the cue, almost half-a-dozen companies, had created contract manufacturing outfits on a reasonably large scale. Riding on a two-year confirmed order for manufacturing components, the largest of these companies Altos basked in the limelight for a couple of years, but the expiry of the contract without any new orders led to collapse. K. Thiagarajan, Hardware: An experiment in globalisation, *The Hindu Business Line,* May 5, 2002. The article points out that wafer-thin margins are the order of the day, and scale manufacturing a prerequisite. With a few other countries such as China already dominating this area, it is unlikely that Indian firms would be able to enter so late in the day.

39 B. Luthje, The Detroit of the new economy: the changing workplace, manufacturing workers and the labor movement in Silicon Valley, *Journal Assoc. History and Computing* 5, 2 (Sept 2002).

40 The comparable common groups are *(a)* manufacture of electronic valves, tubes, other electronic components; *(b)* manufacture of TV, radio transmitters and apparatus for line telephony telegraphy; and *(c)* manufacture of TV, radio receivers, sound or video recording or reproducing apparatus and associated goods

41 If all the five industry groups are clubbed together regardless of comparability, women's share in employment shows a much smaller increase from 15 per cent in 1993–1994 to 17 per cent in 1999–2000, in absolute numbers, from 44,520 to 65,545.

42 Among the major units that were found to be closed in Delhi were Beltek, Mayapuri, Calcom, Wazirpur and Okhla, In Okhla at least three units of Onida, Weston, Bestavision and other such companies we found along with several smaller sub-contracting units. An exception was Continental Device in Naraina; even there, the workforce has been reduced.

43 Mimeo, study conducted by Amrita Chhachi under Project: Women Workers and Organisational Strategies of the Institute of Social Studies, The Hague and FREA (India).

44 Continental Device located in Naraina employed more than 700 women workers.

45 Source: R. Rastogi, Indian electronics industry: geographical spread, *Electronics Information and Planning,* Sept 2000.

46 LG Electronics, Samsung and Timex.

47 J. Ranadive and I. Mazumdar, The effect of an urban environment upon the lives of women: a case study of women industrial workers in Noida, CWDS (mimco), 1998.

48 The story of such a process has been outlined in the CWDS mimeo (1998). See also Indrani Mazumdar and Indu Agnihotri, Labour in Times of closure, in U. Kalpagam, ed., *Labour and Poverty in Uttar Pradesh* (Delhi, Segment Books, 2003) for a description of the situation of trade unions in Noida.

49 Kumud Pore, *Women at Work – A Secondary Line of Operation*, in Nirmala Banerjee, ed., *Indian Women in a Changing Industrial Scenario* (Delhi Sage, 1991).

50 A recent survey conducted by the Centre for Education and Communications, New Delhi, which took into account this large unorganized computer assembly sector, has also confirmed this observation.

51 This factory is actually a joint partnership between an Indian (37 per cent) and a Japanese MNC (holding the rest of the shares.)

52 Of the six MNC units covered in the survey, only two could be said to have come up after 2000, which together employed some 700 women.

53 See M. Vanamala, Informalisation and feminisation of a formal sector Industry: A Case Study. *Economic and Political Weekly*, 2001-06-30:2378-2389.

FOUR

Lengthening Shadows: The Closing Walls of Home-Based Work

A striking feature in the landscape of the working class areas of India's capital city over the last 15 years has been the visible increase in numbers of women, children and even men who are engaged in piece-rated wage work in the home-based sector. Several working class localities, particularly some *jhuggi bastis*, have begun to take on the appearance of vast and sprawling manufactories. The spread of such home-based work had already come to the attention of the women's movement and its mass organizations in the city in the 1980s, during the interregnum before the formal introduction of the policies of integration with the global economy in 1991.

By the 1990s, however, issues related to home-based work came even more to the fore as women's organizations grappled with the reality that enhanced economic need was driving ever- increasing numbers of women into such work, and this included activists of the movement. No longer was tradition-based social confinement in the home the only barrier that had to be broken to organize women into movements to fight for their rights. Economic confinement through home-based work was emerging as a material buttress for the social confinement of women. Such a link between organizational development of the movement and the overall economic and social trends and experiences of masses of poor women, in a sense reflects the broadening and deepening of mass contact achieved by the second wave women's organizations and movements. More important, it calls attention to the necessity of addressing the social dimensions and not just the economic aspect and the implications of the spread of home-based work among women.

ELEMENTS OF THE DISCOURSES ON HOME-BASED WORK

Since the 1970s there has been the opening of debates on the concept and role of the 'informal sector', particularly in relation to women and work in developing countries. Faced with the empirical reality that large segments of the working population in several developing countries and even larger proportions of women workers are involved in economic activities that fall outside the given official statistical and legal definitions of formal or organized production and distribution structures, the use of the term 'informal sector' to encompass all such activities has acquired universal currency. A plethora of literature has emerged around this concept of the informal sector that increasingly informs policies of governments, international agencies and even women's organizations. The concept has absorbed within itself the experience of a lack of clear definition or record and the invisibility of not only several aspects of women's economic activity but also major contingents of women workers such as home-based workers. Despite the fairly universal usage of the informal sector as a term of description, there are several questions and divergences on the ascribed or prescribed role for the informal sector and even its definition. Such questions are of some significance to current approaches to women in home-based work, particularly in the context of globalization.

The Concept of the Informal Sector: A Contested Terrain

Although the term 'informal economy' was first coined by anthropologist Keith Hart in 1971 to describe urban employment outside organized labour activities in the city of Accra in Ghana, the concept of the informal sector was given currency by the ILO following the report of its employment mission to Kenya in 1972.[1] According to Hart, self-employment was the most significant feature of the informal economy, and a distinction was drawn by him between 'activities classified as formal wage-earning employment, and informal self-employment'.[2] According to the report of the ILO's Kenya mission, 'informal activities are the way of doing things, characterized by:

(a) ease of entry; *(b)* reliance on indigenous resources; *(c)* family ownership of enterprises; *(d)* small scale of operation; *(e)* labour-intensive and adapted technology; *(f)* skills acquired outside the formal school system; and *(g)* unregulated and competitive markets.'[3]

Others approached the informal sector in terms of relations and conditions of employment rather than enterprise. Jan Breman, for example, identified three classes in the informal sector: *(a)* a petty bourgeoisie including owners of mini-workshops, self-employed artisans, small traders and shopkeepers, brokers and agents such as moneylenders, labour contractors and intermediaries who collect and deliver piece work; *(b)* the sub-proletariat, which subsumes the largest segment of informal workers, including labourers in the service of small workshops and the reserve army of labourers who are recruited and dismissed by large enterprises; *(c)* itinerant semi-artisans who offer their services and (paltry) tools for hire at morning markets, day labourers, home workers, vendors and other types of of labourers in open air. He argued that the fluidity in the transition between different social classes, as well as shifts in the proportional distribution among them, that occur over time under the influence of contraction or expansion of the economy mitigate against a division (between the informal and formal) which is unduly rigid or static.[4]

Initial representations of the informal sector by the ILO were located solely within the urban milieu, and the definition was based on the nature of the organization of economic activity or enterprise.[5] Since then, at one level, there has emerged a widespread use of the term to encompass rural areas, loosely inclusive of agriculture for developing countries. At another level, attempts have been made to broaden the definition by incorporating and focusing on conditions of work or relations of employment as a category of distinction between formal and informal sectors (no formal working contract, irregularity of employment, hours of work, uncertain earnings, and so on, being seen as distinguishing characteristics of the informal sector).[6] At yet another level, questions have been raised regarding the validity of a rigid distinction between the formal and informal sectors, given the evidence of sub-contracting from the formal to the informal sectors, and especially with large-scale contractualization and casualization (informalization) of the workforce within the formal sector becoming a global phenomenon. As the ILO itself admitted, 'Despite three decades of work, the informal sector is still a topic which elicits diverging views, sometimes passionately so, about how to define it, how to measure and to classify it, and especially about how to respond to it'.[7]

Nevertheless, in spite of the analytical vagueness of the concept of the informal sector, debates and discussions on poverty eradication or development have increasingly used the concept (interchangeably in India with the older term of unorganized sector) as a reference point and target area in the formulation of several new policy approaches. More recently, the term 'informal sector' is being replaced by 'informal economy'. The report of the 2002 session of the International Labour Conference, for example, held that the term 'informal sector' had been found to be inadequate if not misleading in reflecting the 'dynamic, heterogeneous and complex aspects of a phenomenon which is not, in fact, a "sector" in the sense of a specific industry group or economic activity.'[8] Breaking with its earlier focus on the urban informal sector, the ILO seems to be now using the term 'informal economy' to encompass the expanding and increasingly diverse group of workers and enterprises in both rural and urban areas operating informally.

The substitution of economy for sector, however, has been essentially an expansion and elaboration of detail and of recognition of interconnection with the formal or organized sector, rather than a significant change in the analytical discourse around the informal sector. At the core of the analytic behind the concept of informality, and as it has established itself in common discourse, has been a questioning of the more dominant paradigms of development and modernization that had been adopted in many of the decolonizing nations. Differing and, in truth, diametrically opposite points of view underlie such questioning. Such polar oppositions are often covered up amidst the range of descriptive literature that has developed around the concept of the informal sector/economy, and these perhaps need greater attention.

Earlier, in the decolonizing third world, the unorganized sector was generally viewed as reflective of the lack of sufficient economic advance, characterized by petty production. It was assumed that over time it would become transformed into organized modern production and formalized through economic, social and political development.[9]

A central pillar of much of this earlier development literature was the emphasis on land reform or revolution in agrarian relations (resolution of the agrarian question) as the key to industrialization and economic development. Experience has shown that on the one hand this process was constricted or partial in India. In the absence of thorough-going land reforms, generally, expansion of commoditized agricultural output (for example, through the green revolution) took place without the redistribution of agricultural surpluses or expansion of domestic demand (home market) on a scale sufficient for sustained industrialization.[10] Consequently, as the initial spurt of industrialization (largely enabled by state investment and intervention) foundered, a qualitatively new situation emerged as disproportionately large masses of immiserized and unemployed peasants crowded into urban centres but were unable to be absorbed into state-recognized industrial employment. Entering on the periphery of a declining formal industrial economy, this ever-expanding reserve of surplus labour eked out its subsistence in multiple ways in a netherworld of unregistered manufacturing, petty trade or services. Such was the context in which the concept of the informal sector was born, its initial focus being the poorer sections of the urban people and later extended to include the rural populace.

Following the rise of neo-liberal ideology and practice of globalization, and the drive to deregulate and 'flexibilize' both the organization of production and the employment relations established in the formal sector (including the largely formalized economies of the developed capitalist countries), the terms of debate on the informal sector were significantly altered. Increasingly in the era of globalization, the informal sector (which is characterized by lack of regulation), began to be viewed more positively as, first of all, a 'catchment reservoir' for jobseekers unable to be absorbed in formal sector employment in sufficient quantities and who would otherwise be unemployed. More and more began to be written about the informal sector as a source of job creation, flexibility, adaptability, ingenuity, enterprise and, sometimes, even efficiency. Such an approach fitted neatly into the pressures of the ideologues and institutions promoting neo-liberal policies towards dismantling of the nation state–based regulations to give primacy to purely market-based regulation. Indicative of the interests involved, within the ILO itself, during the debate on the informal sector in 1991, representatives of employers or the owners of capital openly stated that the informal sector is a reaffirmation of market forces against the state which has made legitimate activities illegal.[11] Some ten years later, a World Bank Discussion paper on the Informal Sector aiming at 'A Synthesis across Space and Time' takes 'as a starting point the importance of the informal sector as an engine of economic growth and job creation'.[12]

Others of the same ilk have concentrated their fire on the wage and social protection differentials between formal-sector workers and informal-sector workers, arguing that the low wages and income of the latter were due to the high wages and protections offered to the former. In other words, curtailment of formal-sector workers' rights (presented as labour market rigidities and distortions) would enable informal-sector workers to get a better deal. These arguments have been forcefully countered at one level, on the basis of empirical studies (in India) of the degraded conditions of work and income in the informal sector, and the fact that large-scale displacement of workers from the formal sector has only led to a continuation and expansion of such degraded conditions of work.

Among the casualties of the altered terms of debate were, of course, issues related to land reform or 'the resolution of the agrarian question', which no longer have their earlier prominence in discourse. In much of the rhetoric surrounding the informal sector, rural workers including agricultural workers are often used to pad the numbers, although such an umbrella generally hides and obfuscates the real nature of the differences in production and employment relations much more than it reveals. Another casualty has been the role of the state in directly generating employment. On the one hand, the public sector as archetypical of formal-sector employment, has come under severe attack. On the other, anti-poverty programmes and policies have in general effected a shift to a new focus supporting micro-enterprise, thrift and credit groups and the like, in other words, away from labour and employment to the promotion of private enterprise as the foremost area of state intervention.[13] But the principal casualty has been the surrender of any vision of a labour policy of the nation state towards mitigation (if not eradication) of exploitation of labour by capital that marked at least the political mobilizational rhetoric of an earlier era (although much less in practice). As we shall see, such dominant discourses on the informal sector and the changing paradigms of development thinking have had much influence on the present official perspectives towards home-based women workers in India.

Approaches to Home-based Workers: Shramshakti and the ILO Convention

An important area of tension within the concept of the informal sector is the respective weight given to self-employment or wage labour within the sector. The tension remains even after the change in nomenclature to informal economy. This is of special relevance to home-based women workers. In India, the issue was discussed at the time of the constitution of the National Commission on Self-Employed Women in 1987. As the name of the commission suggests, its initial brief was to conduct a 'comprehensive examination and study of self-employed women workers.' But after an initial debate within the commission, its terms of reference were modified to 'also cover all unprotected women labourers in the country and extend to women in the informal sector.'[14]

Specifically in relation home-based workers, the report of the commission, *Shramshakti* (1988) made a distinction between piece-rate wage work and own account work, classifying them as two separate categories of home-based workers. The need for such a distinction was made explicit in the chapter on legislative protection, which stated that 'the nature of legislative protection that is needed for these two categories of workers is not the same. The piece-rated workers need better rates of wages, better implementation of labour laws; on the other hand, the own account workers need remedies that generally lie beyond the scope of labour laws, such as better facilities and arrangements for purchase of raw material, for marketing, for credit, for storage, for work, and place, for better prices and for protection against the harassment from public authorities.'[15]

At an empirical level, the commission's report stated that piece-rated wage work was predominant among home-based workers in manufacturing, and even own account workers were increasingly becoming piece-rate workers. It drew attention to sub-contracting (including formal-sector sub-contracting) into the home-based sector as a means of transferring investment costs on to the worker producers, and highlighted the harsh, exploitative and insecure conditions of work among piece-rate workers. Accordingly, for piece-rated home-based workers, legislative protection was advocated through a new law covering wages, safety, welfare and working conditions, which were to be implemented by and through the constitution of a tripartite board consisting of representatives from the three parties involved, that is, workers, employers and the government. For own account workers, a framework of policies of active support by the government in terms of facilities (provision of cheap raw material, easy terms of credit, marketing support and the like) and removal of administrative obstructions and restrictions on the practice of trades was proposed.

Since the publication of the *Shramshakti* report, while several target-based support programmes (however inadequate) have been introduced for own account workers, the recommendation on legislation for piece-rated workers has languished in obscurity. This is despite the fact that in 1996, India became a signatory to the ILO Convention on Home Work where home workers are defined as *(a)* those working at home or premises other than the workplace of the employer, resulting in a product or service specified by the employer, for remuneration; and *(b)* those working for employers who either directly or through intermediaries give out home work in pursuance of their own business activity.[16] In clear terms the ILO Convention is directed at the wage workers who, as *Shramshakti* and several other later surveys show, constitute the majority of women home-based workers and since its adoption, home worker is more often used to refer to wage workers in the home-based sector..

A Reversal in Perspective in the Era of 'Economic Reforms'

It might therefore seem surprising that in the Discussion Paper on Home-Based Workers prepared by the Ministry of Labour (2000) that was prepared 'pursuant to the adoption of the ILO Convention', and a Draft National Policy on Home Work (that is doing the rounds within the Ministry of Labour and is yet to be finalized), the distinction between the two categories of own account work and piece-rated wage work have been subsumed in a common policy framework that is primarily directed at own account workers. Thus, the Discussion Paper states that home-based workers are 'workers within the confines of their respective homes and could be termed "self-employed" as well. In many of these cases, either the head of the family or a member of the family does the work himself/herself with the help of other members of the family. It is a collective self-employment effort, and, strictly speaking, there is neither an employee nor an employer. In fact, all these home-based workers are workers, materials managers, production managers, finance managers, personnel managers, marketing managers and chief executives of their businesses all rolled into one'[17] Accordingly, the paper states, 'the basic criteria to include HBW [home-based workers] for the purpose of national policy framework are: location of workplace irrespective of linkages with formal or informal sectors; low level of income; unprotected nature in terms of basic security coverage'.[18]

In a strange inversion of the above definitional ambiguity, the same paper lists the 'advantages of home-based work for the *economy*' [italics ours] as: *(a)* no overhead costs, as these costs are borne by the workers *(b)* the fact that workers subsidize the costs of raw materials; *(c)* that workers form a dispensable pool for employers; *(d)* that unionization is difficult because workers work in isolation and hence employers can pay them very low wages; *(e)* that employers do not provide them with social security; and *(f)* that piece rates ensure that workers bear responsibility for quantity and quality of output, which saves the cost of supervision for the employer.[19]

In other words, the criteria for evolving a policy subsumes wage work and own account work into a single category. At the same time, the focus is on piece-rated home-based wage work when listing the advantages for the economy. The interests of the economy and those of employers of home-based wage workers (in paying low wages, treating the workers as dispensable and profiting by transferring their own costs on to workers) are thus clubbed together. Further, the few words on the 'disadvantages' of home-based work that appear in the last paragraph of the section entitled 'Advantages of Home Based Work' in the paper (the low wages, long hours of work, concealed army of unpaid assistants and child labour and lack of social security), appear more in the form of an afterthought rather than a central issue to be addressed.

The ambiguity in the definition of home-based workers in the two documents just discussed was transformed into a mere technicality by the Second National Commission on Labour (NCL). In its 2002 report, the Commission stated, 'Technically, it is important to note that there are both wage-employed and self-employed among the home-based workers. These two groups of home-based workers *may* need different measures for protection and welfare'(italics ours).[20] And further, in its conclusions and recommendations, the commission stated, 'Home-based workers fall within a grey area between employed workers and self-employed workers'.[21] From the definitive practical distinctions in *Shramshakti*, the NCL regressed to a less definite and greyer distinction. This is notwithstanding the elaboration of the distinctions between the two categories of workers that was made in the NCL report itself while discussing the ILO convention. The reversal and regression in perspective was completed in the NCL report through the shelving of the Shramshakti proposal for a separate law for piece-rate home workers. Recommendations of the NCL were confined to bringing piece-rate home workers within the coverage of the Minimum Wage Act and other existing labour laws to be dealt with by the already inadequate prevailing structures and premises of labour law enforcement.

To comprehend the extent of the reversal, one has only to refer to the *Shramshakti* report which stated, 'In deciding on the nature of legislative protection that must be given to home-based piece rated workers, the question naturally arose as to whether the same result could be achieved by making suitable amendments to existing labour laws. After earnest consideration, we came to the conclusion that the best way of helping the home-based workers would be to have a new law specific to the needs of home-based workers as this would give them greater visibility. The vexatious question of employer–employee relationship tests can be avoided altogether and a new method for fixing responsibility by looking at control over the production process and ultimate product can be introduced'.[22]

Why *Shramshakti's* recommendations are important and necessary have to be understood in terms of the principles and practices of the established labour laws (including the Minimum Wages Act). As is known, the generalized framework of labour law is premised on a relationship between employer and employee, since historically such laws themselves emerged from the development of expressed conflicts between collectives of wage workers on one side and the owners of capital (the employers) on the other. Physical inspection of premises and/or written records, registers, and so on, are the conventional methods of proof of the employer–employee relationship under existing labour laws. For piece-rated home-based workers, the employer–employee relationship is difficult to identify and legally prove in the absence of either the work premises being owned by the employer or of written work contracts, rendering the existing forms of inspection inadequate. Additionally, and, perhaps more important, the principal employer is often camouflaged or hidden by intermediate contractors. Taking account of these difficulties, Shramshakti had recommended the enactment of a separate new law for home-based workers designed to avoid 'the vexatious question of employer–employee relationship tests' that are operational prerequisites under all other existing labour laws. As has been mentioned earlier, the proposed law for home-based workers was also to define employers by a new method, that is, by looking at control over the production process and the ultimate product. Thus the term 'employers' was extended to include contractors and where the workers were working for a 'principal employer' they were to be considered to be directly in the employment of the principal employer.[23] It was this depth of understanding of the real situation of piece-rate home workers and the inability of the prevailing laws to address their problems that was done away with in the NCL recommendations.

The shelving of proposals for a separate legislation for piece-rated home-based workers seems to be clearly a consequence of the general approach to labour and labour law that characterizes the liberalized and globalization-oriented policies of 'economic reforms' in India. The terms of reference of the second National Commission on Labour were thus directed at 'rationalisation of existing laws in relation to labour and to suggest an umbrella legislation for ensuring minimum level of protection to the workers of the unorganised sector'. The basis of rationalization of labour laws were defined as 'the emerging economic environment . . . requiring response in terms of change in methods, terms and conditions of work in industry, trade and services, globalisation of the economy, liberalisation of trade and industry and emphasis on international competitiveness'.[24] Also, the minimum of labour protection and welfare measures were to be examined in a manner that was conducive to flexible labour market and adjustment necessary for furthering economic growth. It is from within such an overall perspective that the commission was also entrusted with the task of evolving an umbrella legislation for unorganized workers.

The ability of the umbrella concept to actually address the issues of the diverse contingents of unorganized workers (including very large industry segments) remains a matter of dispute which we do not enter into here. Nevertheless, it must be pointed out that from the indicative Bill for unorganized workers appended to the NCL report up to the most recent draft bill prepared by the National Commission for Enterprises in the Unorganized Sector, home-based workers have been included in the definition of workers to be covered by the umbrella legislation as a subset of the self-employed.[25] But the crucial question of the definition of employers by a new method, as proposed in 1988, has been done away with, to the detriment of the interests of piece-rate home workers who remain the most neglected section of home-based workers. Thus the relations of employment that give rise to severe and excessive exploitation of not only piece-rate home workers but also several other contingents of unorganized workers, are not given due recognition in the Bill.[26] Under such conditions, it would seem that the recognition of all workers in the unorganized sector given as the first objective of the indicative Bill is more a detailing of forms of labour rather than a recognition of the exploitation that is concealed by the informal relations of employment and production that govern the lives of the majority of unorganized workers.

The Promotion of Home-based Work: Promoting Marginality and Patriarchy

Some idea of the direction of official thinking regarding a more long term policy towards home-based workers, may be found in the Draft National Policy document, which approaches home-based work primarily as an avenue of income generation for workers. To this, it is said, the home-based sector 'lends itself as a large segment of the informal sector which works within the discipline of the market without imposing the extra responsibility of formal employment'.[27] Organization of home-based workers is stated to be 'the foremost issue' in 'harnessing this vast labour force'.[28] And further, 'There is need for an apex level body which could take up the cause of such workers in promoting certain strategic interests such as procurement of raw materials, [and] ensuring fair wages, mobilize resources for further investment, explore markets in design development and quality improvement and seek export opportunities . . . appropriate technologies . . . research and development . . . to identify new technologies'.[29] Such organizational initiatives are to be supported 'by conscious efforts of Government', and 'it shall be the deliberate policy of the Government, therefore to enable the worker to manage his own resources and eventually to own them. In this way, a basis can be created for long-term sustainability of home-based enterprises'.[30]

Thus, the evolving official approach to home-based work is, first of all, laudatory in terms of the discipline that is established by the market without requiring formal employment. The second aspect is the *promotion* of home-based work with an emphasis on own account work. Flowing from such a perspective, ensuring fair wages is clearly a minor function of the much touted need for organization of home-based workers. The primary function and purpose of organization is viewed as to be directed towards facilitating supply of credit, basic goods and raw materials, designs and techniques for home-based production at the one end and marketing of the products at the other end.

The fact that this promotional approach to home-based work accompanies an overall set of policies of liberalization, active promotion of private large capital accumulation and opening of the economy to the forces of global competition (rendering any remnants of the earlier reservation for small-scale industry irrelevant) is so self-contradictory as to beggar the imagination. The grounds on which a national policy can conceive of millions of petty home-based producers being able to compete with national and global technology-based mass production and realize sufficient or increasing income is beyond comprehension. At best, a few groups of craft workers might be able to periodically make an appearance in high-priced market niches, and that too for uncertain periods according to the vagaries of fashion (which are in any case largely moulded by the marketing techniques of major corporate companies bent on maximizing their own profits).

As we have seen in earlier chapters, the driving characteristics of the global and national economy have made for a squeeze on manufacturing and incomes of workers even in large scale organized production. In such a context, the promotion of home-based work can only be viewed as a policy of perpetuation of large numbers of home workers at a marginal level of existence. Similarly, the proposed functions of the organization of workers seem to be directed towards maintaining a channel of organization for the purposes of political control. Such a mode of organization of home-based workers, unlike the trade union organizations in other sectors, would be unlikely to challenge the central power correlations being established through macro-policies tailored to the path of globalization. Seen in this context, it is no surprise that among the proposals in the Draft National Policy, it is suggested that in consideration of the fact that women constitute the bulk of home-based workers the organization of home-based workers could form 'nodal points' for an activist family welfare and population control programme that could be periodically monitored by the State Family Welfare and Population Control Organisation.[31] In other words, far from being representative organizations of workers, the form of organization of home-based workers that this particular draft sought to promote is merely in the form of a government policy delivery agency.

The unquestioning acceptance of inequalities within the patriarchal family that marks the promotional approach to home-based work for women is further reflected most clearly in the Discussion Paper of the Ministry of Labour. It states, 'The system of home work is sometimes advantageous to them [women] because while doing their routine work at home, they do the job and supplement the incomes of their families. The raw materials are generally collected from the employers/contractors by the men folk of the household and finished goods are also delivered to the contractors/employers by them. The women have flexibility in working as there are no fixed hours of work and they do not have to move out of their houses. The situation is, however, different in the case of single women or households where women are the sole or main income earning members. In such cases, sometimes, the women home workers are exposed to different forms of labour exploitation'.[32]

In other words, home work is viewed as advantageous for women within the patriarchal family, where their social confinement within the house and family becomes implicitly supported by promotion of home-based work for women. Further, their low and highly exploitative wage rates cease to become a principal concern, since the women's earnings are explicitly defined here as only supplementary.[33] And finally, the labour exploitation of the women home workers by employers is reduced to a problem for those women who lack any male members in their families.

It must be said that the advocacy of changeover from wage work to own account work as the solution for the problems of home-based workers is not new. For example, the 1988 *Shramshakti* report stated, 'The future of home-based workers largely depends on the government's industrialization policy and its recognition as regular work. Piece-rate workers should be encouraged to do their own account work as regular work by providing them a package of incentives such as low-interest loans, cheap raw material, and marketing. The package should also give help in providing work place and space to market their products'. Such an approach might have some relevance for traditional artisans or craft-based workers for whom the combination of primitive accumulation of capital by the moneylender and merchant trader has led to large-scale transformation of own account workers into disguised wage workers. It fails, however, to take note of the changing characteristics of home-based work, particularly in urban areas where home workers are increasingly located in a labour-intensive part process of modern mass manufacture rather than being producers of an individual salable commodity.

EMPIRICAL REALITIES: FIELD SURVEY OF HOME-BASED WORKERS IN DELHI

The field survey of home-based women workers covered seventeen working class colonies or *bastis* located in seven of the nine districts in Delhi.[34] It was a survey of the poorer sections of working class women and its findings are therefore not related to the other new forms of home work that have emerged among middle class women, particularly in the context of the spread of information technologies. Almost all the women workers were engaged in manufacturing activities producing a wide range of products. The 150 women workers surveyed were found to be engaged in the production of sixty-nine distinct products.

Home-based work among women was found to be most densely concentrated in the *jhuggi bastis*, with 49 per cent of the surveyed workers living and working there. *Jhuggi* clusters tend to grow near and around industrial and commercial centres, which allows for closer links with the larger production and marketing institutions. In contrast, the more planned resettlement colonies have been located in the periphery of the city with less easy access to such centres, while the unauthorized working class colonies are generally scattered even further beyond. Regular colonies are more dominated by middle class residences, even though the regular areas covered by the survey were established initially (in the 1950s and 1960s) as workers' colonies. It is the increasingly middle class character of these colonies which accounts for the low proportions of home-based workers there, despite being located in more strategic areas than either resettlement or unauthorized colonies.

Table 4.1 Distribution of home-based workers by broad industry division and type of settlement

Industry Division	*Jhuggies*		Resettlement Colonies		Unauthorized Colonies		Regular Colonies	
	No.	%	No.	%	No.	%	No.	%
Textiles	24	46	15	29	6	12	7	13
Engineering	10	43	7	30	2	9	4	18
Chemical	13	59	5	23	4	18	-	-
Paper Products	5	42	2	17	4	33	1	8
Leather Products	6	100	-	-	-	-	-	-
Others	15	43	11	31	6	17	3	9
All	73	49	40	27	22	15	15	10

In Table 4.1, home-based work products have been classified by broad industry division and the distribution of the workers by type of settlement is given. It may be observed that all industry divisions appear in greater concentration among *jhuggi* dwellers. This is in contrast to factory workers among whom *jhuggi* dwellers constitute a much smaller proportion.

Depressed and Subhuman Incomes and Wage Rates

Of the 150 home-based women workers surveyed, only 10 per cent were self-employed, that is, they worked on their own account. All others (90 per cent) were unquestionably wage workers working on piece rates. Confirming the well-known position that home workers are the most poorly paid workers, the average monthly household income from home-based work in Delhi was found to be roughly around one-fifth (less than 22 per cent) of the legal minimum wage for an individual worker in Delhi. Among these workers, such an income included the labour of not just the woman, since in 65 per cent of the households more than one member of the family was also working in the same trade, most of them minor girls. Where the average monthly income of the family from home-based work was found to be Rs 577 per month, the average monthly wage per individual was Rs 306, which amounted to roughly one-tenth (11 per cent) of the minimum wage.[35] Shocking as such averages are, the wages and income of the majority of workers were even worse than the above figures suggest since the monthly individual wages of 67 per cent of the workers and the household income from home-based work of 38 per cent was found to be Rs 250 and below. The survey data on this aspect is presented in Table 4.2.

Only 37 per cent of the home-based workers were able to access work regularly (that is, for about twenty days in a month round the year). 56 per cent of the workers said that the work was irregularly available while just 6 per cent stated that it was clearly, seasonal. Irregular availability of work was thus one of the reasons for low monthly incomes; however, the overall average individual hourly wage was found to be Rs 2.13, which would work out to a monthly wage of Rs 443 for an eight-hour working day, twenty-six days a month.[36]

Thus we can see, even if work is regular and regular working hours established, the wage earned by home-based workers at the prevailing rates would still be less than one-fifth (17 per cent) of the statutory minimum wage. A comparison with market-determined wages of garment and electronics factory workers, as revealed in the preceding two case studies, shows that the average monthly wage rates of home-based workers (assuming work is available throughout the month) is less than one-third of the lowest rung of women factory workers.[37]

Table 4.2: Monthly household incomes and individual wages/ income from home-based work

Monthly household income from home-based work (Rs)	No. and percentage of surveyed workers		Monthly wages/ income of individual workers (Rs)	No. and percentage of home-based workers	
	No.	%		No.	%
100 – 250	57	38	50 – 250	100	67
300 – 400	24	16	275 – 400	21	14
450 – 550	24	16	450 – 600	18	12
600 – 800	12	8	750 – 1,200	9	6
1,000 – 1,500	30	20	1,400 – 2,000	2	1
2,000 – 5,000	3	2			
All income groups	150	100	All wage income groups	150	100

Products, Labour Processes, and Labour Time

The products of home-based work recorded in the survey initially presented a bewildering range. As mentioned earlier, the 150 workers surveyed were involved in the production of some sixty-nine different items. Very few of the women were traditional craft workers although some of the products might be seen in the market as craft based. Only twelve women (8 per cent) could be said to be involved in forms of labour handed down by community tradition. They included two potters (of the caste of kumhars), one shoemaker (belonging to the chamar [Ravidas] caste), four involved in reeling or weaving (one belonging to the Koli caste, three to the Ansari caste) and five doing *zardozi* work (traditional gold embroidery all practiced by Muslims, but from different sub-communities).

The overwhelming majority (92 per cent) had thus acquired the skills or lack of skills necessary for home-based work through exposure to the industry, commerce and labour market of modern metropolitan Delhi. As such, it would be erroneous to locate home-based work in Delhi as an outgrowth of traditional craft sectors of the economy and society. Table 4.3 describes the labour process by broad industry divisions with the numbers and proportions of women working in each process. Along with the hourly wage rate, the earnings out of a day's labour have also been given. The day's labour here refers to periods when work is available and the required labour time includes time put in by other family members.

As might be expected, textile products constituted the largest industrial segment, employing some 35 per cent of the home-based workers, while engineering and chemical industries together employed another 30 per cent. What might be surprising initially is the low proportion of employment in leather goods (just 4 per cent of the workers). Among the principal items in the other unclassified industries, the sticker bindis and imitation jewellery trades stand out as significant employers of home-based workers in Delhi. In fact, bindi pasting is probably more significant than the proportions in this survey suggest, since, in an attempt to capture the widest possible range of products and workers, collection of repetitive information from the visibly numerous bindi pasters was avoided in the final stages of data collection. The description of the labour process makes apparent the fact that, in most cases, the workers are working at a part of a chain of production that extends only partially into the domain of home-based work.

Extended hours of work among home-based workers is a well-known feature, which as can be seen from Table 4.3 was confirmed by the Delhi survey. Of course, in many cases, the extreme hours contain the labour time put in by other family members. Nevertheless, the combination of pittance wage rates, irregular availability of work and dire economic necessity create conditions for exploitative and excessive hours of labour whenever work is available. Close to 20 per cent of the workers reported that they alone put in a minimum of 10 hours of labour in a day for their home-based product—of these workers, about 40 per cent were working 12 hours and more (including two who worked

Table 4.3 Labour process, number of workers and earnings by broad industry division

	Labour Process in Textiles	No. of surveyed women workers	%	Average wage per individual per hour	Average household earnings for a day's labour (required labour time in man hours)
1	Hand embroidery with silk or silver thread on readymade garments, kurta pieces and plain cloth, sequin embroidery on readymade garments; traditional *zardozi* (gold embroidery) on large rectangular wooden frame (*karchop*); stitching other add ons—patchwork, chains, and the like on garments, napkins, cushion covers and so on.	52	35	2.23	26.00 (12 h)
2	Stitching using sewing machine or by hand	15	10	4.25	30.55 (7 h)
3	Reeling with *charkha*; weaving of fancy net scarves or stoles[38]; knitting (with hand needles or machine); traditional specialized hand weaving of gold borders for dupattas on horizontally fixed iron rods	9	6	1.92	19.33 (10 h)
4	Cutting squares from old sequin-worked saris and sticking on buckram for making Gujarati-style cushion covers.	2	1	2.40	60.00 (25 h)

Table 4.3 (*continued*)

Labour Process in Engineering (including electricals)	No. of surveyed women workers	%	Average wage per individual per hour	Average household earnings for a day's labour (required labour time in man hours)
	23	15	1.91	33.00 (17 h)
1 Fixing wires on electric irons, inserting wires in bulb chains and fuse wire case chains.	6	4	2.40	28.50 (!2 h)
2 Hammering to flatten metal eyelets (rivets) on polythene carry bags or cardboard, or to insert metal piece in slot of inverter part	6	4	2.71	47.00 (17 h)
3 Simple fitting together of metal parts with fingers (sewing machine bobbins), assembling screws on cycle reflectors, fixing and tightening screws on voltage stabilizer board with a screw driver; greasing and fitting metal auto-parts together.	7	5	1.23	37.00 (30 h)
4 Operating machines—using a micrometer to measure thickness of metal washers and then sorting them; shaping aluminium buttons by operating the lever on the button-making machine; making bottle brushes by fixing plastic bristles on an iron rod using a machine.	3	2	1.56	26.66 (17 h)

Table 4.3 (*continued*)

Labour Process in Chemical Products	No. of surveyed women workers	%	Average wage per individual per hour	Average household earnings for a day's labour (required labour time in man hours)
	22	15	1.76	21.51 (12 h)
1 Cutting out straps for rubber slippers (moulded on sheets of rubber) with scissors and then snipping off extra edges; cutting off rubber stuck on 2-inch or 8-inch long metal pieces (of old car window frames) with scissors and knife; cutting out small rolls from rubber moulds (for auto-parts); peeling plastic insulation from old and used electric wires with a knife and separating plastic shreds and metal wire.	9	6	2.20	29.20 (13 h)
2 Direct handling of toxic chemicals: packing naphthalene balls in small polythene packets and sealing with heated metal plate; rolling agarbattis.	6	4	1.35	31.50 (23 h)
3 Sticking labels on plastic toys and crayons; painting black eye pupils on plastic moulds of eyes for dolls; tying up plastic net into scrubbers and packing and sealing them in polythene packets.	7	5	2.10	10.10 (5 h)

Table 4.3 (*continued*)

Labour Process in Paper Products	No. of surveyed women workers	%	Average wage per individual per hour	Average household earnings for a day's labour (required labour time in man hours)
	12	8	2.44	29.10 (12 h)
1 Simple folding of envelopes or book pages; cutting, folding and sticking of paper packets; cutting cardboard for mirror backs with a slicer, inserting spiral binding for diaries and pads.	4	3	3.92	55.50 (14 h)
2 Patterned work—cutting of decorative paper chains, making paper flowers, decorating files.	8	5	1.45	20.50 (14 h)

Table 4.3 (*continued*)

Labour Process in Leather Products	No. of surveyed women workers	%	Average wage per individual per hour	Average household earnings for a day's labour (required labour time in man hours)
Leather Products	6	4	1.97	39.80 (20 h)
1 Footwear: stitching sneaker shoes by hand with a needle and shoe stand; stitching designs on slipper straps.	4	3	2.43	53.33 (22 h)
2 Sticking leather patches on padding material for jackets or bags.	2	1	1.27	19.50 (15 h)

Table 4.3 (*continued*)

Labour Process in other Miscellaneous Products	No. of surveyed women workers	%	Average wage per individual per hour	Average household earnings for a day's labour (required labour time in man hours)
	35	23	2.23	36.00 (16 h)
1 Imitation Jewellery—picking up or threading different types of minute beads on a wire according to given designs for bracelets, necklets and so on; implanting of stones on bangles; threading beads according to a design with needle and thread for necklaces.	16	11	2.06	33.40 (16 h)
2 Bindis, pasting velvet sticker bindis by hand on cellophane packing; sticking minute decorative stars and small beads on bindis according to given designs using Fevicol with the help of a small sliver of wood and pasting the bindis on packets.	11	7	1.47	17.60 (12 h)
3 Assembling nail polish brushes; pasting holograms on small aluminium-foil gutka packets; making crude clay pottery without using a wheel (diwali mandirs, toys, pots and so on.); decorating hairclips with needlework.	8	5	2.76	64.10 (23 h)

up to 16 hours a day). Another 24 per cent worked between 8 to 9.5 hours. Thus at least 44 per cent of the workers were working full-time whenever they could access work. A further 17 per cent worked 6 to 7 hours in a day, and the average number of individual hours for a day's work among all the workers worked out to 6.5 hours.

Predominance of Market Determined Employment Contracts Among Home-based Workers

Of the home-based workers, 46 per cent were involved in part processes outsourced by factories located in Delhi; 30 per cent were linked through contractors to traders in the principal wholesale markets of the city which are distribution centres for a wide range of markets across the country, while another 20 per cent were linked to the local retail markets through shopkeepers, local tradesmen or on their own account. The relation between product sources and wage rates is shown in Table 4.4.

Table 4.4 Distribution of home-based workers by source or destination of their products and wages/income

Home-based work linkages	No. of women workers	%	Average monthly individual wage (Rs)	Average monthly house-hold income (Rs)	Average individual hourly wage (Rs)
Factories	68	45	294	602	1.30
Principal wholesale markets	45	30	276	575	3.42
Local market shopkeepers or vendors	15	10	229	457	1.94
Own account sale	15	10	515	804	1.50
Through contractors to export merchants	7	5	286	382	2.50

As may be seen, factories and wholesale trade centres in Delhi are the principal institutions linked with the spread of home-based work in the city. Together they are the source or destination of the products of 75 per cent of the workers and could be viewed as the principal employers. While this raises several possibilities for regulatory mechanisms, the problem as is generally known lies in the role of contractors mediating the relationship between factory owners or wholesale traders and the women working in the home-based sector.

An interesting and revealing find of the survey was that the overwhelming majority of the home-based workers had only a commercial relationship with the contractor. Unlike the perception that family-based social connections generally mediate the relationship between the home-based woman worker and the labour market, only ten women (7 per cent) had any kinship relationship with the contractors, while another nineteen (13 per cent) reported that the contractors were neighbours or acquaintances. Thus, 70 per cent of the women (after excluding the 10 per cent of own account workers) had no relationship with the contractors other than as suppliers of work orders and wages. In many cases, women reported that the contractors came to their houses initially as strangers (some from outside the colonies) and asked if they were willing to work. In other cases, the women had found out how to access work from other neighbourhood home-based workers.

Transfer of Fixed Costs of Tools and Space onto Home-based Workers

Among the women surveyed, seventy-nine (53 per cent) reported that the tools required for their work were provided by themselves. Such worker-supplied tools included scissors, knives/blades, screw drivers, pliers, hammer and anvil, needles, brushes, small wooden sticks and so on. Traditional tools included *charkha*, *karchop* (wooden frames for *zardozi*), while machines included sewing machines and knitting machines. A smaller proportion (23 per cent) said that their residence was also used to store raw material and product. While on average the space required for work was about 12 square feet, it could go up to 100 square feet which would be practically a whole room, particularly when storage space was involved. Although only one worker reported frequent rejections (for *zardozi* work), over one-third of the women experienced occasional rejection of their product. In most cases, they had to redo the work, and in any case were not paid for extra labour time put in.

Occupational Health Hazards and Uncounted Cost of Suffering

An overwhelming majority (87 per cent) said they felt extremely strained and tired out by the work; thirty-three (22 per cent) complained of eye strain, often accompanied by headaches and body ache. This was most common in cases of fine embroidery work, bindi decoration, or imitation jewellery where concentrated peering at minute parts (mostly in dingy and windowless quarters) as well as bending over in a fixed position for long hours were involved; fifty-five (37 per cent) said work resulted in a permanent state of body ache and nineteen (13 per cent) said that their work led to cuts, blisters and/or swelling in their fingers and hands—cuts were caused while peeling wires (their toes would also get cut) as well as while fixing electric wires on irons and screws on voltage stabilizers. Blisters and swelling of the fingers was common among those cutting rubber (slipper straps, insulation for auto parts and car window panes).

An extreme case of body distortion was seen in the case of forty-year-old Najma working on the *charkha* reeling silver thread. Her body was permanently bent and she was unable to stand because her ankles too had become fixed in a twisted position. She had been suffering from tuberculosis of the bone yet had to continue to work.

In the case of the women directly handling chemicals, the houses of those who were packing napthalene balls were found to be reeking of the fumes to which they said they and their children had become accustomed. Similarly, the pungent chemicals of *agarbatti* masala was being handled by children as young as 5 years.

Workers Perceptions on the Social Confinement of Women in Home-based Work

An overwhelming majority (87 per cent) of the workers had never worked outside the home, more than half (53 per cent) stated that they could only work at home due to social and ideological restrictions by family or community (see Table 4.5). Of the workers surveyed, 26 per cent had children of 5 years and below, but surprisingly, only 6 per cent gave this as the reason for not working outside.

Table 4.5 Home-based workers without outside work experience, distributed by age group

Age group	No. who had never worked outside the home	% in each age group	No. of home-based workers confined to the home owing to ideological restrictions by age group	% in each age group
5 – 18	23	88	17	65
19 – 25	29	91	15	47
26 – 30	24	83	13	45
32 – 35	20	95	14	67
36 – 45	20	77	12	46
48 – 68	14	88	9	56
All ages	130	87	80	53

Just 13 per cent of the home-based workers had had some experience of working outside the home. Half of them left their earlier jobs as a result of closures, relocation, dismissal (in two cases the reason was illness and unavailability of leave) or unavailability of work—a by now all too familiar story. Among the reasons given by those who could be said to have voluntarily given up employment outside their homes were marriage, family problems, entry into own account home-based work as a joint venture with husband and so on, again, surprisingly, only two women said that their decision was because of children.

The low proportions of women who stated that children were their reason for working at home and not outside should, perhaps, not cloud the fact that the compulsions of childcare has been a real deterrent for many workers. This is evidenced by the fact that about 74 per cent of the workers were mothers, of whom a substantial proportion had children below 5 years of age although a large number (57 per cent of the mothers) had at least one child of 15 years and above. What is of note is that in their own perceptions among the factors restraining them from working outside, the most important factor was social restriction.

Apart from those who felt that social restrictions prevented them from working outside, the workers offered a variety of reasons. A few (5 per cent) gave lack of knowledge as the reason, another 5 per cent said that there had been no need to work earlier, while 2 per cent said it was because they had shifted residence and were unable to commute to work (this was in unauthorized colonies on the outskirts). A few of course were girls who were obviously too young to work outside. Among the workers, 6 per cent were 15 years old and below, although only one-third of them (three out of nine) were studying in schools. Of all the workers, only two gave the fact that they were still studying as the reason for not working outside, one was in class ten (age 18) and the other in college (age 22).

Blurred Contours in the Sexual Division of Labour

Among the women, fifty (33 per cent) reported that their particular work was not done exclusively by women and men were also working like the women as home-based workers.[39] Bindi-pasting, specialized weaving of dupatta borders, painting pupils on doll's eyes, pasting leather patches on padded sheets, fitting together sewing machine bobbins, labelling wax crayons or plastic toys, threading fuse wire, making bottle brushes, measuring metal washer thickness, making bulb chains and rolling of agarbattis, were the processes that were reported as being done exclusively by women.[40] Men were found to be working in all other processes although not across all areas: for example, in Seelampur[41], where women reported that home-based embroidery work was being done by men as well; in Karampura[42] it was found to be exclusively women's work. There seems to be some difference along community lines as well. In comparison with 50 per cent of the Muslim women, only 25 per cent of the Hindu women said that men were also employed. Such interpretations of data should not be overextended and can only be viewed as clues or hints of a degree of complexity and variability in the intertwining of social and economic factors in determining the sexual division of labour in home-based work for a mega city like Delhi. At a general level, perhaps all that can be said is that its contours are getting somewhat blurred, particularly in the face of overall declining 'decent employment' opportunities for men as well as women, which creates conditions for their acceptance of low-paid home-based work.

In the majority of cases where men were also performing the same tasks as women in the home-based sector, their piece rates were the same as women; however, eight women reported that men's wage rates were higher. Of these women, four were embroiderers out of whom one was linked to an export factory, while the other three were doing *zardozi*. While the export worker could only state a general impression that men were paid more, in the case of *zardozi* there was a difference in the functions performed by men who did what they called *aari* work with a thicker and longer needle while the women did the fine-needle embroidery. But as seventeen-year-old Ayesha explained, 'we put in more labour but are paid less'.

In the case of the other two operations with wage rate differentials (peeling plastic insulation off from used electric wires and embroidering of leather straps), the difference between men and women could be attributed to the fact that the men were working on time rates. They were being called home-based workers by the women because their residence doubled as a small workshop. This only emphasizes the fact that piece rates form a key instrument in keeping down women workers' wages.

Home-Based Work: Primary Earnings for Many

Around one-third (34 per cent) of the women reported that the entire household income was from home-based work. They included the 10 per cent who were widowed, separated or divorced, one-fourth of the married women whose husbands were unemployed and a similar one-fourth of the unmarried girls whose fathers were either not alive, unemployed or, as in some cases, had deserted the family. Only 5 per cent of the women reported that their husbands were also employed in the same home-based activity.

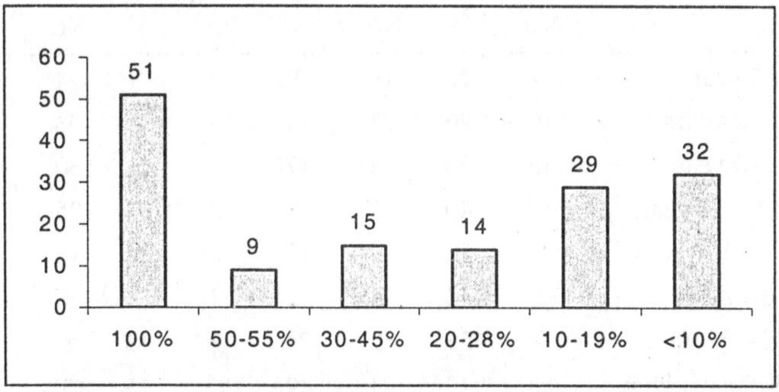

Figure 4.1 Distribution of surveyed workers by the share of home-based work in household income

From Figure 4.1 it becomes clear that for 34 per cent of the workers, home-based work was the only source of income for the household, while for 6 per cent it was at least equal if not more than any other source.

Under Globalization : Widespread Decline in Incomes

More than one-third of the workers (35 per cent) said that their nominal household income from home-based work had declined over the years, while close to one-half (49 per cent) had stagnated indicating a clear decline in real income for the majority (62 per cent) of the households. Some 16 per cent had been working for less than a year, and another 25 per cent for over a year but less than two years. Although 44 per cent of those who had been working the same trade for over 3 years[43] showed decreased income, even among those who had worked from 1 to 2 years, over one-fourth reported that their incomes had declined. Data supporting these arguments are presented in Table 4.6.

Table 4.6: Changes in income from home-based work in recent years

Years of work in a trade	Deceased nominal income		Unchanging or stagnating income		Increased nominal income		Total	
	No.	%	No.	%	No.	%	No.	%
< 1 year	3	13	19	79	2	8	24	16
1 – 2 years	10	26	28	74	-	-	38	25
3 – 5 years	15	50	14	47	1	3	30	20
5.5 – 10 years	10	40	7	28	8	32	25	17
11 – 15 years	8	50	2	12	6	38	16	11
16 – 20 years	4	44	2	22	3	34	9	6
22 – 50 years	3	38	2	24	3	38	8	5
Total workers	53	35	74	49	23	15	150	100

Among the principal reasons for the decline in income was a decline in the availability of work. Over two-thirds of those showing declining incomes reported increasingly irregular availability of work. For the remaining one-third, declining income was linked to either falling piece rates or reduction in the number of family members working. Loss of employment or increasing underemployment has thus affected home-based workers, too. It would seem that the low wages and 'flexible' employment contracts that characterize home-based work are not a viable way of escaping the deep developmental crisis in the system.

Of the women surveyed, 17 percent said there had been a fall in their actual nominal piece rates; 25 per cent had seen increases in rates, while 58 per cent had the same rates. Two thirds of those reporting falling piece rates were doing embroidery work of all kinds. It may be recalled that this is the work process employing the largest contingent of women in home-based work (17 per cent). Declining piece rates in embroidery could be seen in all areas across the city and included work done for exports as well as for the domestic market. Other items showing decreases in piece rates included hammering rivets, cutting rubber rolls for auto parts, sticking leather patches for manufacture of bags/jackets and traditional own account pottery products. Table 4.7 lists the results of the survey regarding changes in piece rates.

Table 4.7: Changes in piece rates and household income for home-based workers

Changes in Piece Rate	Changes in Monthly Household Income from home-based Work							
	Increased		Decreased		Same		All	
	No.	%	No.	%	No.	%	No.	%
Increased	16	42	9	24	13	34	38	25
Decreased	3	12	16	64	6	24	25	17
Same	4	5	28	32	55	63	87	58
All the above	23	15	53	35	74	49	150	100

To get a better idea of the scale of stagnation and decline in wage rates, we looked separately at workers who had been working a trade for at least 5 years and more. Among them 33 per cent reported stagnation while 18 per cent reported a decline in piece rates, together constituting 51 per cent. The items where rates had been stagnant for 5 years and more included agarbatti, bindis, bobbins, doll's eyes, tailoring, peeling electric wire, reeling, rubber slipper straps and shoe-making.

Even among the twenty-three workers who said that their piece rates had shown increase, a little over one-third had actually seen declines in their household income. In about one-half of these cases, the decline could be attributed to less availability of the work, which was increasingly irregular. In the remaining cases, it was owing to reduction in number of family members working (moving out of daughters after marriage, and so on.)

Declining Work Availability and Piece Rates in Garment Exports

Only twenty workers (13 per cent of home-based workers) were involved in export industries consisting of two items: garments and imitation jewellery. While the garment export workers were linked to factories and more dispersed across the city, in the case of imitation jewellery, the entire manufacturing process seemed to be located in the home-based sector through contractors who supplied the product to merchant exporters. The making of imitation jewellery for export was concentrated in a few *jhuggi bastis*, but with a far greater density of the workforce than was seen for garment exports.

Table 4. 8: Wage rates and household income of home-based work for export products (in rupees)

Export Product	Export-oriented No. of home-based workers	Export workers among home-based workers in similar trades (%)	Average hourly wage	Average income for a day's labour (required labour time in man hours)	Export-oriented workers' wage rates on legal minimum wage (%)*
Garments	12	29	3.33	24.83 (7.5 h)	26
Imitation jewellery	8	50	5.08	32.70 (6 h)	40
All	20	25	3.95	27.80 (7 h)	31

*Assuming availability of work for 8 hours a day and 26 days a month.

In many areas, workers who were earlier involved in outsourced work from garment export factories, particularly thread-cutting or button-hole stitching, said that such work was no longer available. Of the twelve home-based outworkers of garment export factories located by the survey, eight were doing hand embroidery including sequin work, while the remaining four were involved in part-stitching processes. In only one area was there a regular supply of embroidery work for garment exports, which was all traced to a single supplier. And even that supplier informed us that the amount of work coming in was far less. Where earlier it was distributed among 200 women, at the time of the survey the number of workers had been reduced to less than 100. In all other areas, work was available only irregularly. Two-thirds of the garment export workers who were all relatively new to the industry, with service periods ranging from 6 months to 3 years, reported that piece rates had remained the same. But every worker who had been in the trade for more than 3 years reported a reduction in the piece rates and all of them were doing embroidery work. Table 4.8 gives the present status of wage rates and household income related to home-based work in export products.

At one level it might seem that export industries' wage rates per hour are somewhat better than the rates in the domestic-market oriented industries; however, export industries are no exception to the rule that home-based workers' wage rates are far below the minimum wage rates (26 per cent of the minimum wage in the case of garment workers and 40 per cent for imitation jewellery) and less than one-half the market determined wages of the lowest rung of unskilled contract workers in the factory sector. In the context of declining availability of work and decrease in piece rates in the principal export industry of the city—garments—the links between home-based work and garment exports are becoming far more tenuous than is perhaps described in the internationalized literature on home-based work.

Product Focus: Outline Architecture of Bindi Manufacture

An analysis of the items where work is regularly available showed that bindi pasting was the most regularly available work across the city, although it seems to have become most concentrated in the resettlement colonies of two districts of northeast and northwest Delhi. Like most of the commodities and labour processes covered in the survey, bindi pasting has been a part of home-based work in Delhi for over 15 years.[44] The tenure of bindi workers ranged from 1 to 16 years and most of them said that the work was regular.[45] Earlier we have mentioned that the proportions of bindi workers among home-based women workers in Delhi is higher than our sample suggests, and going by the large concentrations in some areas, we would estimate their numbers in the city to be well above 20,000.[46]

According to traders in the bindi business, the bindi trade has an annual turnover of Rs 1000 crore. The traditional cultural requirement of wearing a bindi by women in many communities[47] has provided for a widespread and continued level of market demand. In the pre-industrial era, sindoor and kumkum for bindis were made at home using turmeric and alum or other similar commonly available colouring agents; however, such domestic forms of bindi making for direct consumption in the home gave way to mass manufacture (initially of powdered or liquefied bindis) a long time ago. So far back that most people do not even remember a pre-industrial form of bindi making.[48] About 25-30 years ago, sticker bindis entered the market and, according to one bindi manufacturer cum trader, these readymade sticker bindis have rapidly overtaken powder-based or liquefied bindi products to become a member of what they now call the fast-moving consumer goods (FMCG) sector.[49] As tradition merged with fashion, readymade sticker bindis, generally made of synthetic velvet, started acquiring decorative embellishments of beads and stones and came to be known as fancy bindis. Such bindis have even made a small entry in the country's export basket, although they are basically manufactured to cater to the home market whose increasing size may be attributed to the continued status of bindis as a cultural necessity.

Gender-Based Hierarchy of the Labour Process

Ready-made bindi manufacturing and trade is overwhelmingly located in the unregistered, unorganized or informal sector.[50] This is despite the fact that the velvet from which bindis are cut is manufactured in the machinery-based modern textile factory sector,[51] and cutting too is similarly mechanized in some (very few) bindi factories. Hand tools for cutting are the norm in workshop style *karkhanas* employing anything between just one individual own account worker to four or five hired workers plus owner worker. Where the few factory owners have their own wholesale trade outlets, the workshop *karkhanas* are involved in only production for supplying wholesale traders.

Within the chain of manufacturing, the pasting of the cut bindis on cellophane and paper packaging is done only by hand and almost completely outsourced to the home-based sector both from the factories as well as the workshop *karkhanas*. Whereas the workforce in the factory sector of the industry (inclusive of the small *karkhanas*) is entirely male (at least in Delhi), everywhere the home-based hand task of pasting is done by women. The wages of factory or *karkhana* workers are usually time rated and their daily earnings are higher than those of the women. The contractors' (*thekedars* who are also own account workers) incomes derive from their own labour as well as the women's and is of course the highest within the labouring community of the bindi industry. Thus, the characteristic method of production of sticker bindis is highly labour intensive and contains a sequence of production that leads from the factory to the workshop *karkhana* to the homes of women. Such a process has inevitably shaped a gender-based hierarchy of labour processes.

The Domination of Traders and Dispersed Production by Worker Thekedars

The bindi merchant traders in Delhi, some of whom shifted to bindi trading as preferable and more profitable than a range of manufacturing industries in which they were earlier involved, are overwhelmingly from the Punjabi community (mostly of partition refugee origin). From the mid-1980s, the number of wholesale traders dealing almost exclusively in bindis have proliferated, and the principal wholesale market of Delhi provides testimony to this. Where ten years ago, in some of the *galis* of Sadar Bazaar, there would be one dealer in bindis, today you can find several. Estimates of the number of bindi traders in Sadar ranges from 300 to 1000. A few of the initial lot of bindi traders (who entered the business in the mid-1980s or early 1990s) tried their hand midway at factory-based manufacturing, only to close down within a few years.[52] It is the wholesale traders in the bindi industry who are able to profit the most since in such a small and low priced commodity, only a scale of volume in trade can yield any reasonable returns.

As some of the relatively larger bindi factories (with workforces ranging from 40 to 200) closed down, several of their erstwhile male workers took to bindi manufacturing independently. These worker *thekedars* take orders from wholesale traders, invest their own labour (alongside their male *karkhana* worker employees) in first applying gum (with a screen or brush) onto velvet sheets covered with thin paper, then cutting out the bindi dots or other stylized shapes with metal hand tools. They then distribute the pasting work among home-based women workers with instructions on the arrangement or display of the bindis. In some cases, since the packets tend to get grubby in the women's homes, the *thekedars* give them old packets (so that the frame of display is clear) and then themselves transfer the cellophane on which the bindis are pasted on to fresh new packets in their *karkhanas* before packing them into boxes to take to the traders. The women peel the paper off the gum with nails or teeth and paste the bindis on the cellophane according to the given arrangement instructions. Their piece rates are fixed per gross, that is, 144 packets, each packet containing from eight to fifteen bindis.

As a matter of course, the *thekedars* buy all the raw material themselves, with wholesale bindi traders providing them only with brand name printed packets. Occasionally *thekedars* might deal directly with petty local retailers or hawkers and print their own brand name, but this is relatively rare, the quantities required being insufficient to be other than purely subsidiary. In some cases worker *thekedars* operate from their homes, but mostly they work from what they call *karkhanas,* which are usually little more than small 10 feet by 10 feet rooms where two or three of them work together. These *karkhanas* are to be found in precisely those areas where female labour for pasting work is readily available, that is, the heart of working class residential areas (mostly resettlement colonies), and the women generally collect their work from *karkhanas* located in their own or adjacent *galis* or blocks.[53] Interestingly, the overwhelming majority of these worker *thekedars* seem to hail from a few specific districts (Siwan or Araria in Bihar or Ballia in eastern Uttar Pradesh), part of Delhi's evergrowing migrant working class. According to them, bindi making is widespread in the rural areas of their home districts catering to markets in Kolkata, Benares or Patna.

Kinship or other social ties originating in their village backgrounds often provide a basis for the forging of apprentice/partnerships among male *thekedars* and even labour supply within the *karkhanas*. But the relationships between the *thekedars* and the women workers are almost never kinship-based. For example, not one of the bindi pasters in our survey belonged to the same districts or communities as the *thekedars* for whom they worked. On the other hand, in five out of seven *karkhanas* that were visited and even between different *karkhana* owners, kinship and village-based connections among the male workers were evident.

Declining Returns From Bindi Manufacture

Despite the overall growth of the sticker bindi trade and the obviously expanded market a common refrain from all the worker *thekedars* was that their earnings had fallen sharply, particularly in the last four or five years. As of today, their incomes after deducting all costs range from Rs 2,000 to 6,000 per month. In the perception of most of those with longer stints in the trade and who had at one time even been able to accumulate some investible capital,[54] the decline was attributed to the phenomenal growth in the number of workshop manufacturers. According to them, the enhanced competition among the producers had led to a lowering of the price of their product bringing down their own profit margins to subsistence level. Among the younger and newer entrants, the prevailing view was that the few relatively large-scale producers, were able to corner a greater share of the market while keeping their prices low leading to loss of competitiveness of the smaller producers. In depth interviews with several such worker *thekedars* in three different areas revealed the same story.

Several traders too complained of declining returns with the expansion of supply outstripping the growth in demand. They were highly critical of the small producers (on whom they otherwise depended for their own supplies having failed as manufacturers) for having proliferated and expanded production so much. Even more were they critical of the attempts of some of these producers to set up streetside shops in the wholesale trade area with cheaper wares. But it was left to one of the own account worker *thekedars* to say that the decline in demand relative to supply was 'a question of the whole economy. Only when people are able to fulfil food and drink requirements can they buy other things'.[55]

The Limitations of Skill and Innovation

As sequin-decorated bindis (fancy bindis) have been popularized, many of the male worker *thekedars* who specialize in decorative bindis (mostly Muslim) have become informal designers, getting orders from traders after showing them sample designs. It would seem that their ideas and inclinations have grown out of the aesthetic traditions of glass bindi (tikuli) makers which were at one time located in their home districts.

Increasingly, varied and innovative designs are brought to the market by these workers in a desperate bid to try and overcome saturation in the market. While design samples are made in the *karkhanas* by men and a part of the production may also be carried out there, the bulk of the sequin-embossing work for mass production is now done by the home-based women workers.

Women's labour has become even more onerous with the addition of sequin sticking to their already established labour process of pasting. Incorporating new technologies, some varieties of bindis have moved away from their velvet base to computer generated sheets with readymade shaped bindis already stuck on them. In such cases, bindi-pasting work is not required and the women cut out small squares with ten or twelve already arranged and pasted bindis from the sheets and paste the squares on branded packets. However, the actual bindi-pasting work is generally replaced by sequin-embossing work, which almost everyone finds much more difficult, requiring greater concentration, placing greater strain on the eyes and involving a higher level of fine manual dexterity. Naturally, the piece rates for embossed bindis is higher than only pasting, and varies according to complexity of design; however, it makes little difference to the earnings of the women since the labour time involved in embossing is far greater per piece than in just pasting.

This was said explicitly by thirty-nine-year-old Omwati from Nand Nagri (resettlement colony in northeast Delhi) who has been pasting bindis for over 16 years. In the beginning, she started alone by pasting simple bindis. Now she and her three daughters (aged 17–21, all having dropped out of school after class four) together emboss and paste the bindis. After putting in anything from 8 to 16 hours of work each, they manage to earn on average Rs 40 a day. This represents an increase from Omwati's initial earnings of around Rs 5 to Rs 7 a day when she first started the work, but as she said, this increase is 'because we are all labouring much more to earn more as we need more'. The rates for embossed bindis vary from Rs. 15 to Rs 30 per gross (144 packets), but it makes no difference to their daily income, as the bindis with higher rates also involve more labour time.

While Omwati represented the average situation of bindi workers, Nirmal Devi of Jahangirpuri (the easternmost resettlement colony of northwest Delhi), also working on sequin-embossed bindis together with her two daughters and two nieces, earned somewhat more: her daily income from bindi work ranging from Rs 60 to Rs 80. The piece rate for four levels of embossment plus pasting on foil, sticking of foil on packet, then making 48 packs of six packets each was Rs 60. This would be the equivalent of Rs 30 per gross, the highest end of the bindi piece rate. Nirmala Devi and her family (whose living quarters were considerably better than Omwati's and whose daughters are in high school) are obviously also more productive since their hours of work ranged from 4 to 8 hours. Their rather above-average piece rates, however, were also somewhat special as their *thekedar*, who basically focused on *karkhana*-level production, had recently entered the business and only employed this one family for outsourced home-based work. Between the time of the survey and the writing of this report, that particular *thekedar's* business had folded up, he has vacated his rented *karkhana* premises and moved elsewhere. Nirmal Devi and her daughters who said that bindi pasting was no longer so widely available in their area, have shifted to making cushion covers (item listed in textile products in Table 4.3).

On the other side, fifty-year-old Meena Devi from Mangolpuri (resettlement colony at the western extreme of northwest Delhi), who just pastes simple bindis of varying sizes at the rate of Rs 3 to Rs 5 per gross (packets) for the larger bindis and Rs 7 to Rs 10 per gross for the smaller ones, had a different complaint. Earlier the rates were lower, for example, Rs 3 where now it is Rs 5, and Rs 7 where now it is Rs 10. But whereas earlier a *thekedar* who lived at walking distance from her home used to bring the work, she now has to pay for transport to go herself to Punjabi Bagh (about 7 km from her house) to fetch the work from the factory. Meena also has three daughters working alongside, of similar age to Omwati's. Together, the four of them earn around Rs 24 a day, with each putting in from 4 to 6 hours of labour time. The lower number of working hours is because unlike Omwati's daughters, Meena's are also going to school and one of them even beyond. As may be seen, there is little difference in earnings between the embossed bindis where the women's labour might be seen as adding greater value and the lower value addition simple pasting work. Where the individual hourly wage in the case of Omwati's sequin-embossed bindis was Rs

1.25, it was Rs 1.20 for Meena's simple bindi pasting. In other words, for a regular eight-hour day, 26 days a month sequin-embossed bindis fetched an individual wage of Rs 260 in comparison to Rs 250 for plain bindi pasting.

Product Focus: Imitation Jewellery for Export

A comparison between workers with longer tenures and those having a shorter period of service revealed the probability that the emergence of imitation jewellery as a significant commodity in the home-based women workers' product basket is a relatively new phenomenon. Only one worker making some specialized bone jewellery in the Jama Masjid area had a history of 10 years in the same industry and is probably somewhat unique. None of the other workers had been in the trade for more than 4 years, and more than half of them had started within a two-year period.[56] The expansion of the production of imitation jewellery to levels requiring more workers than were available in the already established workshop systems, has been driven at one level by an increase in exports. However, such expansion has been of insufficient order to provide regular work to the larger pool of labour required for such production. Thus over the last 5 years a part of the manufacturing tasks, particularly the beading work (which requires no machines), has been transferred at piece rates to women in their homes.

Although a relatively small export item constituting just 1.7 per cent of India's handicrafts export basket, imitation jewellery exports have grown from Rs 19.05 crores in 1992–1993 to Rs 117.53 crores in 2001–2002.[57] The Export Promotion Council for Handicrafts has Delhi listed as a craft concentration area for imitation jewellery.[58] Over 74 per cent of the exported imitation jewellery goes to the developed countries, but the overall scale of exports are clearly not of significant magnitude. Like the increasingly demand-constrained bindi industry, the manufacture of imitation jewellery for exports follows a similar pattern of dispersion of production from workshop to the home, with merchant exporters at the top of the pyramid. But unlike in bindi manufacture, some male workers can also be found in the home-based sector of imitation jewellery. Also, unlike bindis, imitation jewellery is more concentrated in just a few *jhuggi bastis* close to the walled city of Old Delhi which has emerged as the hub of manufacture.

Manufacture of Imitation Jewellery and Role of Migrant Labour

The present form of manufacture of imitation jewellery might be seen as having some continuity with the craft traditions among the Muslim communities of mediaeval Delhi linked to concentrations of village-based production centres in northern India. According to manufacturers who have been in the business for 20 to 25 years, while traders in imitation jewellery in Delhi may belong to other communities, the manufacturers are almost exclusively Muslim. But what is of note is the fact that the workforce in present day manufacturing workshops has clearly been carved out from migrants from rural areas not linked to the traditional centres of production supplying Delhi in an earlier era. The district of Katihar in Bihar seems to have emerged as the principal source of the supply of labour in the scores of imitation jewellery workshops that have proliferated particularly in the Turkman Gate area of the old city.[59] The spread of a part of manufacturing into the home and the employment of principally women has largely been effected through these very migrant workers (of whom many actually acquired their skills as child workers in Delhi's workshops) as they set out to establish themselves as independent manufacturers. Such expansion of the industry being relatively recent, the youth of these worker *thekedars* is quite marked, their ages ranging from about eighteen to thirty years and rarely more than that. Their incomes after deducting costs range between Rs 30,000 to 50,000 a year (averaging 2,500 to a little over 4,000 per month). Older and more established manufacturers clearly no longer want to bear costs of labour when earnings are not high; instead, more of them seem to be becoming merchants without any production responsibilities.

Again similar to the social architecture of the bindi industry, community connections are visible among the male workshop workers and the new breed of worker *thekedars*, but completely absent in their relationship with the home-based women workers. For example, in the large *jhuggi basti* that lies along the river Yamuna opposite the eastern ramparts of the Lal Quila, large numbers of the women home-based workers involved in bead-work for these young Bihari *thekedars*, are Bengali migrants. An estimated 1,500 imitation jewellery home workers were found in this area alone of whom 80 per cent are women.[60]

The Continuum of Informality Between Workshop and Home

The task of the home workers is essentially threading beads on wire (often beads of variable colours, sizes and proportions) according to design specifications. The beads may be of plastic (occasionally glass) or silver- and gold-coloured metal. These are then checked and finished by the workshop workers by sometimes just attaching fastenings or alternately transforming the beaded wires into bracelets or more stylized necklaces through wire attachments. In another *basti* close to the *jhuggi* cluster near Lal Quila, the women home-workers may, in addition be bending the wires with pliers to make eyelets for facilitation of such attachments. In such cases, beading work is of just a few beads for earrings or hanging attachments to necklaces.

Hourly wage rates of these home workers vary from Rs 3 to Rs 6 according to their individual speed of work. Such a wage rate may be seen to be higher than in most other forms of home-work and may account for the fact that a few men also work alongside the women (but not in all areas). Such hourly wage rates are also more or less equivalent to the wage rates of the time-rated workers in the workshop who are paid around Rs 1,000 per month. The difference between them lies in the fact that unlike the home-workers, the workshop boys are paid even when orders are low or absent. As a result, although their wages are far lower than the legal minimum wage (37 per cent), their monthly income is more than double the average monthly income of the home workers, which was Rs 400.

Merchant Exporters as the Principal Beneficiaries

From the above, it is clear that the freely available supply of concentrated and extremely cheap female labour in the *jhuggi bastis* has fed the expansion of the export of imitation jewellery from Delhi.

And yet, quite in contrast to the hovels in which the workers perform their labour, stand the air-conditioned pristine ambience of the show rooms of exporters. Of course, even among them there are gradations with the lower-end wholesalers located in the crowded bazaars of Chandni Chowk who cater to local as well as export markets. Nevertheless, as in bindis, it is the merchant interests that reap the maximum gains.

SOME CONSIDERATIONS FOR POLICY

Conceptual advances in relation to home-based workers made by the National Commission of Self-Employed Women and women in the Informal Sector in 1988, which stressed the need for a separate law for piece-rated home-workers, have been reversed in recent policy documents. Official documents of the post-liberalization era all tend to ignore or underplay the exploitative aspects of home-based work. Instead the value of market discipline is stressed in relation to home-based work, sometimes supporting the patriarchal underpinning of women's confinement to the home within an inherently promotional approach to this form of work. And yet, it is precisely the high levels of exploitation of home-workers along with the declining availability of even such work that need to be highlighted in the ongoing discussions for a national policy for home-based workers.

The empirical findings of the field survey in Delhi reveal the dominant linkages of home-based manufacturing with small-scale factories and wholesale markets servicing primarily domestic markets. The nature of the production process, which is manual labour intensive, is driven by excessive labour supplies that makes such manual labour cheaper than any mechanical or technological input. It makes for greater competition among workers relative to demand for their goods, and has led to phenomenally low and below subsistence wage rates and harsh conditions of work. In the era of globalization, even nominal piece rates have declined in some products—most significantly in embroidery which is the labour process employing close to one-fifth of all home-workers. The principal beneficiaries from home-based work being volume traders and merchants, there is obviously a need to focus on them as employers and bind them into contributing for institutional welfare for these workers whose labour has been contributing to their accumulation of wealth.

NOTES

1 To quote, 'The problem with employment is that the statistics are incomplete, omitting a range of wage earners and self-employed persons, male as well as female, in what we term the informal sector'. Report of the Kenya Employment Mission (1972) quoted in P. E. Bangasser (2000), The ILO and the informal sector: an institutional history. *ILO Employment Paper 2000/9.*
In 1991, the Director General of the ILO in his report to the 78th session of the International Labour Conference (*The Dilemma of the Informal Sector*), considered that the concept of the informal sector was the ILO's most distinctive contribution to development thinking.

2 K.Hart, Informal income opportunities and urban employment in Ghana, in R. Jolly, E. De Kadt, H. Singer and F. Wilson, eds, *Third World Employment: Problems and Strategy* (Harmondsworth: Penguin, 1973):

3 Report of the ILO Kenya Employment Mission quoted in Bangasser, ILO and the informal sector.

4 J. Breman, The informal sector of India's economy: the state of art and the art of state, in Oshikawa Fumiko, ed., *South Asia under Economic Reforms*, JCAS Symposium Series no.6, Osaka, 1999.

5 The conceptual definition of the informal sector adopted by the Fifth International Conference of Labour Statisticians, 1993 is as follows: 'The informal sector may be broadly characterized as consisting of units engaged in the production of goods or services with the primary objective of generating employment and incomes to the persons concerned. These units typically operate at a low level of organization, with little or no division between labour and capital as factors of production and on a small scale. Labour relations—where they exist—are based mostly on casual employment, kinship or personal and social relations rather than contractual arrangements with formal guarantees'.

6 See Aanchal Kapur, ed., *Working Women's Rights in India: Issues and Strategies* (New Delhi: ILO, 1999). For an account of some of the debates, see J. Breman, *Footloose Labour* (Cambridge: Cambridge University Press, 1996).

7 Bangasser, ILO and the informal sector.

8 ILO, Geneva, Decent work and the informal economy, *Report VI*, 90th Session, International Labour Conference, 2002.

9 Of course, the Gandhian perspective was somewhat different. Although elements of this approach could be seen in government policy of support to handicraft based cooperatives, the central thrust of policy was of industrialization through development of modern industry.

10 See U. Patnaik, India's agricultural development in the light of historical experience, in T. J. Byres, ed, *The State, Development Planning and Liberalisation in India* (New Delhi: Oxford 1996).

11 Conclusions of a seminar of the International Organisation of Employers quoted by a representative at the 78th session of the International Labour Conference. Source: Reply of the Director General, ILO to the discussion on his report, Annex II, Bangasser, ILO and the informal sector.

12 N. H. Blunch, S. Canagarajah, D. Raju, The informal sector revisited: A synthesis across space and time. *Social Protection Discussion Paper, Social Protection Unit, World Bank*, July 2001.

13 Recently, the need for the state to provide employment has resurfaced in the context of unprecedented levels of agrarian distress and led to the enactment of the National Rural Employment Guarantee Act, 2005.

14 Appendix II, *Shramshakti*, Report of the National Commission on Self-Employed Women and Women in the Informal Sector, 1988.

15 *Shramshakti*, p. 115.

16 The Convention on Home Work was passed in 1996. India, although a signatory, has yet to ratify it, since then it would become legally binding.

17 Ministry of Labour, Discussion Paper on Home-based Workers, para 8, Ministry of Labour, Government of India, 2000.

18 Ibid: para 9.

19 Ibid:para 13.

20 Ministry of Labour, *Report of the National Commission on Labour*, vol 1 part 1, chapter 7, para 7.45, Ministry of Labour, Government of India, 2002.

21 Ibid.

22 Shramshakti (1988): 116.

23 Ibid: 115–117.

24 From the Press statement of Labour Secretary at the time of Constitution of the NCL.

25 See Report of the National Commission on Labour, vol I, Part-I, Unorganised Sector Workers (Employment and Welfare) Bill, 2002;. 766 (I) – (xii) and NCEUS draft bill available on http: / / www. nceus. org
26 Throughout the debate on the unorganized sector bill, Central Trade Unions have been pressing for a separate law for agricultural workers, who as the largest category of workers also face very specific problems and forms of exploitation.
27 Draft National Policy on Home Based Work (Unpublished), (2000), para 12.
28 Ibid: para 13.
29 Ibid: para 17.
30 Ibid: para 19.
31 Demography and Population Control, *Draft National Policy,* para 46.
32 Ministry of Labour, Discussion Paper on Home-based workers, para 15.
33 Treating women's wages as supplementary was the basis on which unequal wages were incorporated even within the statutory minimum wage notifications until as late as the 1970s. It was only after the enactment of the Equal Remuneration Act, 1976, that such a practice was abandoned (although it still persists in indirect ways). The revival of the supplementary wage argument again in 2000 is both ominous and regressive.
34 The field survey did not cover the districts of New Delhi and North Delhi.
35 The legal minimum wage for unskilled workers at the time of the survey was Rs 2,668 (U.S. $56) per month.
36 Industrial wages are generally calculated for 26 days, with extra days entitling the worker to overtime wages.
37 See Tables 3.6 and 4.12 for average wages for garment and electronics workers.
38 Interestingly the weave for the non-traditional item of the scarves or stoles was similar to the net weave for fishing nets, and the women workers doing it belonged to a caste of fisherfolk (*machherey*). Obviously, this was an exceptional case where skills acquired from community tradition were being used for making a non-traditional product.
39 In most cases, they were not referring to male members of their own family, but to their observation of other households in their area.
40 Such reports of work being done only by women must be taken to reflect only the characteristics in the immediate locality.
41 Seelampur, located in the district of northeast Delhi is one of the few areas with a large concentration of Muslims. Although it is a hotchpotch

of resettlement colony, *jhuggi basti* and regularized unauthorized colonies, our survey was largely concentrated in the *jhuggi basti*.

42 Karampura, located in west Delhi was one of the older workers' colonies catering initially to the textile workers of Swatantra Bharat Mills and DCM Silk. As the textile mills declined and mostly closed down, only a few of the erstwhile textile workers remain in the colony, and it has over the years acquired more middle-class characteristics.

43 Thirty-nine workers out of the eighty-eight had worked in the same trade for more than 3 years.

44 Forty-one of the surveyed workers (27 per cent) had been working the same trade for 10 years and more. On the basis of a separate analysis of those workers with 10 years and more in a particular trade, it could be seen that most of the products and labour processes have been a part of the home-based sector in Delhi for over 10 years. Although the composition of the actual product basket has some new items, such as inverter parts, voltage stabilizers or fuse wire chains, cutting off rubber from car window frame pieces for recycling (where earlier it was predominantly cycle tyres) and so on, the nature of the work has remained roughly the same.

45 Here tenure is not necessarily with any particular contractor but refers to duration in the occupation or trade.

46 The estimate of 20,000 bindi pasters is a conservative estimate. According to some contractors involved in bindi manufacture, the numbers exceed 50,000.

47 Either red (sindoor) bindis in several parts of north and eastern India, or maroon bindis (kumkum) in the southern parts of the country. Not wearing a bindi is considered a sign of widowhood in most Hindu communities.

48 In some parts, kumkum is still made at home. Industrial production of powder or liquid bindi is in the small-scale industry sector under cosmetics requiring licenses from the Drugs department and covered by regulations for Drugs and Cosmetics.

49 Velvet sticker bindis appeared in the market about 25 years ago and according to one of the large manufacturers in Delhi, sticker bindis constitute 60 per cent of the bindi market.

50 Reportedly, there is only one organized sector company involved in sticker bindi manufacture located in the western region of India.

51 From all accounts, it seems that the velvet used in bindis was initially imported and used for making bags or shoes. Some velvet manufacturing factories have since been established (only one in Delhi),

but even now a significant part of the velvet used in bindi manufacture is still imported.

52 Source: Interviews with traders

53 Such collection from the *karkhanas* is generally done by the older matrons in the family—mothers or mothers-in-law, although with the establishment of fairly regular relations with individual *thekedars*, more and more younger girls can be seen going to collect work.

54 For example a worker *thekedar* who came to Delhi in 1982 was able to directly retail his bindis for Rs 100 when cost of production was Rs 25, and able to save around Rs 400 per month. Together, he and his brother accumulated enough to buy the 25 square yard house where his karkhana is now located in the resettlement colony of Nand Nagri as well as a small stall in Sadar Bazaar. Today he is unable to generate any profit over and above the consumption needs of his family.

55 Statement recorded in interview with Shivji, a forty-year-old worker *thekedar* for 10 years in Delhi.

56 Similarly in paper products, only paper packet making seems to have a longer history although clearly declining in numbers Until some years ago, the making of paper packets from newspapers or old printed pages employed a substantial number of women. On the other hand the decorative and stationery items seem to be relatively new.

57 Source: Export Promotion Council for Handicrafts

58 Other areas of craft concentration for imitation jewellery included Moradabad and Sambhal in western UP and Jaipur in Rajasthan.

59 Every *thekedar* involved in distributing home work in imitation jewellery that we met was from Katihar, and some of the local manufacturers also confirmed that the workers were largely from Bihar. A few of those who were more discerning also mentioned Katihar.

60 Estimates of the number of home workers in imitation jewellery are based on interviews with a cross-section of home workers and *thekedars* operating in the area and visual impressions. The uncertain fate of jhuggi manufacturing bases became clear when in 2005 the basti near Lal Qila was demolished leading to displacement of the workers from their occupation.

FIVE

Neither Mental nor Manual Labour: The Service Factories of the 'New Economy'

The expansion and growing importance of services has been a much marked feature of globalization. In fact, when identifying 'what's really new' about globalization, UNDPs Human Development Report of 1999 placed the growing 'global markets in services—banking, insurance, transport' at the top of its list. Various theories have emerged, arguing that in this period the service sector has acquired a new and dynamic identity as a result of the development of the so-called 'knowledge economy'. A more historical perspective on the subject tells us that many of the industrialized countries were already service dominated in terms of employment by the mid-twentieth century.[1]

Under globalization, however, there has clearly been a relatively sharper tilt towards the service sector in terms of employment as well as contribution to GDP. Some have attributed this phenomenon to being caused by some fundamental 'structural change' in the workings of capitalism being brought about by Information and Communications Technology (ICT). Although not central to the argument regarding such a perceived socially transformatory character of ICT, gender tends to figure prominently in the discourses around it. A growing body of literature is in circulation as to how the growth of ICT offers new opportunities to women, particularly in developing countries, through enabling access to wider markets if they are small entrepreneurs, but more importantly through the possibilities of their employment in IT-enabled services.[2] In this chapter, we conduct an initial investigation of some of the recent global features of the service economy at a point of its intersection with ICT and interaction with the processes of globalization. In the context of the Indian experience, we look at the overall characteristics and trends in women's employment at an all India level to arrive at a perspective on the role, scale and significance of service sector employment. And finally, we present the findings of a survey of women workers in the IT-enabled service sector in the Delhi–Gurgaon–Noida region. But first, let us refer to history in order to understand the underlying processes behind the growth of services in the developed industrialized countries in comparison with developing countries such as India and their concrete socio-economic contexts as mediators of the role, status and conditions of women's employment in services.

A LONGER VIEW ON WOMEN IN 'WHITE-COLLARED' SERVICES

The rise of 'an economy of services and other tertiary occupations', providing 'a wider range of jobs for women, [and] the rise of a consumer economy' making women 'the central target for the capitalist market' made its appearance, according to historian Eric Hobsbawm, in the early years of the twentieth century.[3] He argued that 'structural transformations and technology [at the time] altered and greatly increased the scope for women's employment as wage earners' through the rise of new service occupations as distinct from 'nineteenth century industrialization—using the word in its widest sense—which tended to extrude women, and particularly married women, from the economy officially defined as such'.[4] Thus, according to him 'From the end of the nineteenth century onwards, office work and shops and certain kinds of services, for example, telephone exchanges and caring professions, were powerfully feminized, and these tertiary occupations expanded and swelled at the (relative and eventually absolute) expense of both primary and secondary ones, that is to say, agriculture and industry. In fact, this rise of the tertiary sector was one of the most striking tendencies of the twentieth century.'[5]

Such a description of course primarily refers to the industrialized capitalist world of Europe and the United States. The phenomenon of the rise of the service economy there has to be, first of all, located in the enormous expansion of agricultural and industrial surpluses available to support such tertiarization, which in turn was based on great increases in labour productivity in the commodity producing sector effected by industrialization; however, the precise contours, causes, and manner of expansion of services including the tendency of concentration of women in service sector employment are based on a larger complex of social and economic factors.

The historical roots of the concentration of women in the service sector lay in the fairly universal pattern of change in women's lives effected by the process of capitalist industrialization itself, which had engendered a new form of economic dependency of women on wage-earning male breadwinners. Behind it lay the erosion of the economics of 'common family labour' in agriculture and then even 'family manufacture' in proto-industries (cottage industries and the 'putting out' system for sale in wider markets). Large-scale industry, which separated the household from the place of work, left women in general and married women in particular confined to kitchen work and child rearing, with at best a supplementary role in the family's wage or non-wage income.[6] If in the course of industrial development, young unmarried girls and children were an important source of cheap and easily browbeaten labour in textile factories, the workforce of large-scale, more capital-intensive and somewhat better-paid industries, particularly the engineering industries, were exclusively male. It was the socialized supplementary status of women's employment (as daughters or wives), which translated into what economists now call a lower 'reservation wage' for women, as well as to the practice of their exclusion from several forms of industrial employment. But even in the industrialized world, the male breadwinner's 'family wage' was rarely sufficient to fully support the family, and increasing numbers of women had to also work for income. Thus in western capitalist countries, when from the early part of the twentieth century, newer tertiary services emerged, such as shop assistants, local government (including schools), and an expanded number of lower grade commercial and business clerks, they became employments with concentrations of women.[7] Clearly, a special concentration of women in particular segments of what came to be known as white-collared services (but characteristically low-paid and subaltern) has a century-long history in the developed world.

How and why such tertiary occupations grew so significantly, is inextricably linked to the advent of monopoly capital, beginning around the end of the nineteenth century.[8] On the one hand, concentration of capital led to an enormously increased size and scale of production (often vertically integrated from production of raw materials to transportation to institutions for raising of capital or extending credit) entailing a vast apparatus of production process management and including the management of finance. On the other, combined with centralization of capital and growth of monopolies, it led to the quick exhaustion of the extant markets compelling a more expansionist approach to the market. One of the means of widening the market was bringing into its ambit several aspects of life that were earlier located in the interpersonal sphere outside the market. This in turn meant an enhanced 'sales effort' directed at *inducing* as well as *raising the intensity of* demand to levels where prices could be maintained at profitable levels, requiring organization of services on an unprecedented scale in sales (including advertising and retailing) and transportation. From financial management and accounting to production logistics to marketing, an entire apparatus of 'white collared' services grew, which were otherwise considered unproductive as they in themselves could not add to the value of commodities.[9] Such an apparatus required a large staff, which was soon drawn into a pattern of organization of labour (its division and sub-division) similar to the actual production process. Growing out of what is known as 'scientific management' in the organization of production or 'Taylorism',[10] what developed was fractionalization and routinization of clerical and sales work into a series of subaltern functions that now had to be performed by a new mass of labour quite distinct from the handful of clerks of an earlier stage of capitalism.[11] This transformation of the category of clerical work from an integral part of the upper echelons of the production management hierarchy to a subaltern status even lower than blue collared manual work was expressed in the change in their relative pay scales, which sank below even unskilled non-farm labourers.[12] An inseparable part of such subalternization was the increasing employment of women, whose recruitment was made easier since it did not lead (in most places) to displacement of already employed men. A similar fractionalization and routinization of work took place at the retailing end, where too, monopolies increasingly established their dominance, and where again women were employed (for the less mobile and more routine functions) in large numbers at low rates of pay.

The other important force behind tertiarization was the enhanced role of the state inherent in the age of modern imperialism, whose emergence meant an enhanced role for imperialist states, as aggressive agents of their national capital interests; however, through the two world wars, interspersed with the Great Depression in the 1930s, it had become clear that 'monopoly capitalism tends to generate a greater economic surplus than it can absorb. As a result, it becomes increasingly vulnerable to disorders in its overall functioning, in the form of stagnation and/or severe depression, marked by unemployment and idle plant capacity'.[13] Such disorders having been generally diagnosed as being due to a shortage in 'effective demand', states undertook a broader role in management of their respective economies to fill the demand gap through increases in government spending.[14] One of the methods of such increased activity of the state was the provision of several services by government on an expanded scale, which included not just basic infrastructural services and education, but health and several other social support services in the form of the welfare state.[15] The expansion of government services, while contributing to the social and political coordination required to prevent major conflicts or breakdown of the system, also provided a whole range of service employments that absorbed much of the labour surplus that could no longer be absorbed by an increasingly capital intensive industry.

A Different Trajectory in the Developing World

If this has been the characteristic history of the developed countries, in the ex-colonial world the trajectory has been somewhat different. (This is notwithstanding the fact that it shares many common characteristics in terms of the changes in the economic role of women effected by the growing penetration of capitalism breaking up aspects of earlier social relations.) Modern imperialism that dominated relations between industrialized countries and the more backward areas of the world (where capitalist industrialization had not taken place independently), drained the latter of a substantial part of their surpluses that might otherwise have provided initial sources of primitive accumulation of capital and prepared the ground for internal industrialization. Already such areas were largely under some form of colonial control, having been plundered and impoverished by colonial looters (which, incidentally and to a not insignificant extent, facilitated the industrialization of the capitalist core countries). The inclusion of major pre-capitalist economies of the colonies, such as India, in the world capitalist market had led to deindustrialization (destruction of local crafts) and initial depopulation of several mediaeval towns (usually centres of handloom industry) through displacement of labour by manufactured imports from the industrializing centres. The ground was thus laid for acute pressure of surplus population in agriculture and mass poverty, which became the defining feature of such economies. Despite integration into the world market as producers of primary commodities and later some industrial manufactures associated with local primary products (that is, the shift of certain activities or processes from the metropolis to the underdeveloped country), any internal industrialization on the basis of such export earnings was of necessity severely limited. First, because a virtually continuous process of drain of wealth from the backward countries to the advanced capitalist ones, meant that capital available for investment was limited.[16] Second, because of a slow growth of the home market, which remained confined to a thin strata of society, the limited industrialization that did take place (such as jute, textiles) adopted high productivity technology similar to that of the metropolis. They absorbed a relatively small section of the surplus population, leaving vast masses of people in perpetual poverty and underemployment and providing little demand stimulus for wider industralization. Imperialist domination itself had thus moulded several initial differences between the occupational patterns of the imperialist core countries and their formal or informal colonies. Although among and even within the former colonies, significant differences existed and their societies are not entirely repetitive, a common feature was the retarded form of industrialization that was itself the consequence of the domination by the imperialism of the more industrialized nations. This was reflected in the continuing domination of agriculture in occupational distribution, which, in India at least, has persisted through the century.

As such, the growth and characteristic features of the white-collared service sector employment in the colonies did not emanate from the demands of an expanding industry and associated expansion of commerce in the context of an all encompassing industrial revolution.[17]

Rather, as in India for example, office type service employment grew primarily around the structures and demands of an imperial and later, an independent government—namely, through the growth of a salaried bureaucracy. Also, such white collared service drew from only specific strata of a predominantly agrarian society, that is, from the upper castes, whose high status in the continuing social hierarchies (sometimes despite impoverishment) hinged on their distance from manual work (considered polluting). For these castes, white-collared employment, even as they were subordinate to colonial authority (and often subject to white racism), remained the preferable economic option. Such upper castes were already characterized by that particular form of patriarchy which denied outside labour or employment to women, often forming a part of the practice of seclusion. If the sweepers and sanitary service workers that were needed by the establishment and development of the major cities of the British Raj, were recruited from the 'untouchable' castes in the rural areas (both near and far), the white-collared government service employees were inevitably male and belonged to the upper castes. It was this section that gave initial numerical body to what is generally referred to as the middle class.

We have not come across any documented history of how in India women entered forms of what may be broadly termed 'office employment', but from oral reports it seems that Anglo Indian girls (who were not bound by social seclusion) were the first to be employed in some services such as the telephone exchanges. During World War II, given the pressures of inflation and with the introduction of examination-based recruitment, some educated upper caste women, who by earlier tradition had been prevented from taking such employment, began to enter the expanded staff requirement in government service. At this time, in almost all regions, in commercial institutions such as banks officers as well as clerical staff continued to be almost totally male. The relatively greater mass entry of women into these segments of white-collared service as well as the teaching profession was far greater in the period following independence and was based on their expanded presence in middle class-dominated higher education. There can be little doubt that independence, with its constitutional mandate for equality, and government policy itself opened the doors for education and services employment of middle class women, even as it largely bypassed poorer and more socially deprived women in industry and agriculture.[18] Thus, the 1974 Report of the Committee on the Status of Women in India noted, 'Unlike the situation in non-agricultural occupations and organised industry, the services and professions have provided greater opportunities to women in the post-independence period. Earlier, both in the public and private sectors, women's participation was practically confined to health and education, though the World War II period ushered in a small but significant entry of women into clerical and secretarial occupations. Other services and professions were the monopolies of the urban educated middle class, whose views about women's employment were extremely restrictive'.[19]

As such, white-collared services have drawn only a small section of women into their fold. And although within the service or office employment hierarchies the trend in women's employment tended to follow the worldwide pattern of their clustering at the lower clerical levels, the share of women in even these segments have certainly not been of the scale witnessed in the developed capitalist countries. Under conditions of retarded industrialization, the government continued to be principal employer of white-collared service workers and the combined weight of government and private white-collared services could not absorb the surplus labour even from among the relatively small strata of people with access to education. It was perhaps for this reason that they have remained largely male dominated. And even the more subaltern categories of service employment never sank as low in the framework of the Indian social hierarchy as in the West, which meant also that they remained the preserve of a relatively more socially privileged section of the male and female labour force.

ELEMENTS OF CURRENT CONJUNCTURE: SERVICES AND THE NEW ECONOMY

Despite the differences outlined above, under globalization, the increasing weight of services within national economies has not been confined to the developed world alone. It has emerged within developing countries as well. In India, at the time of writing, the share of services in GDP and employment stood at 52 per cent and 25 per cent, respectively. Some commentators have begun to view this expansion of services, relative to both agriculture and manufacturing as a positive feature and indicative of 'maturity' of an economy. For them, the yardstick of judgement of maturity is the prevailing internal characteristics of the 'high income' advanced capitalist economies. It is assumed that if in these countries, services now account for more than two-thirds of GDP and, as in the case of the United States, above three-fourths of employment, processes that have led to a somewhat similarly enhanced share of services in the GDP (although considerably less in employment) of developing countries may be viewed as following the same trajectory. Such an argument now bases itself on the view that taking advantage of information technology-based service expansion, developing countries can skip over the process of historical transition from agrarian to industrial to service-dominated economies that characterized the history of the developed capitalist world. According to such commentators, 'IT allows leapfrogging which can help countries skip generations of technology and stages of growth and place them directly in a service dominated economy'.[20] These perspectives tie in with the views of the 'new economy' theories that originated in the United States in the latter half of the 1990s, but which in one form or the other quickly became part of common discourse across the globalizing world.

'New economy' theories emerged in the context of the long boom of the 1990s in the United States, which was seen as being 'due to a favourable interaction between increased global competition, labour market flexibility and the technological dynamism of the information and communication technology (ICT) sector'.[21] According to its theorists, the development of a 'new economy' based on ICT and globalization of trade, marked a structural break with the earlier experience that a capitalist economy cannot for long sustain strong growth, low joblessness *and* low or no inflation. Further, the technological dynamism of ICT, was seen by them to have generated an economy where 'knowledge is more important to economic success than money or machinery'.[22] Characteristic of the euphoria of the protagonists of the new economy is the following statement, made in 1997, 'We have entered a period of sustained growth that could eventually double the world's economy every dozen years and bring increasing prosperity for—quite literally—billions of people on the planet. We are riding the early waves of a 25-year run of a greatly expanding economy that will do much to solve seemingly intractable problems like poverty and to ease tensions throughout the world'.[23] However, as became clear when the long boom came to an end in 2001 (and particularly when technology stocks crashed), the boom itself was based less on any intrinsic qualities of the new technology-based service products, and more on the speculative expansion of financial assets. As is now widely accepted, 'the financial buoyancy of the 1990s, triggered by the process of financial liberalization worldwide, had embedded in it a major role for speculation, rendering suspect the productive implications of such growth'.[24]

Nevertheless, within the portals of the Organisation for Economic Co-operation and Development (OECD), the 'new economy' was still being theorized and elaborated upon, into a message for the developing countries.[25] The ground reality behind such theorization is a hollowing out of the manufacturing sector in many of the advanced capitalist countries, and particularly in the United States which has been 'the principal home of the new economy'. What such theorization fails to take into account is the fact that although such a process has led to large-scale imports of commodities, the relative decline in manufacturing in the United States, even where based on relocation to other countries, has not meant any decline in the surplus commanded by U.S. companies, which has in fact risen through an acceleration in expansion of U.S. MNC operations. In practice this means that a major share of the value that is embodied in these commodities is appropriated by U.S. based companies. A significant portion of imports are thus based on the expanded capacities of MNCs to extract surpluses from around the globe and from which a share of profits may be realized within their home country.[26] As clear from the preceding case studies of readymade garments and electronics, even where outsourcing is the norm, monopolistic market control and imperialist global domination may achieve a similar result.

Second, it fails to take into account the all-important role and nature of internationalized finance that, according to one analysis, allows for maintaining high levels of economic activity and employment only in certain specific conditions: they are 'either if [the country] is so decisively the financial centre of the world that the sheer expansion of its financial sector which must necessarily occur in the era of globalized finance is enough to generate high employment; or if its currency is so decisively the lynchpin of the entire system that everyone has confidence in its value'.[27] It is extremely doubtful that the record of high economic growth in the U.S.A. of the 1990s could have been maintained without the maintenance of high levels of inflow of capital by virtue of the favoured role of its currency and its central role as a powerhouse of global finance. In general, greater servicization of the developed economies has remained premised on their greater command over huge material surpluses and much of the value embodied in them as well as the principal markets, albeit unevenly spread between countries even within the developed world. In this, as we shall see, ICT has been only an added tool in exercising such command.

The situation for developing countries is, however, quite different. Far from being able to overcome limitations on their economic potential, ICT-based services in developing countries are being almost completely limited to becoming mere suppliers of cheap and subaltern labour for global monopolies established by the corporate bosses of metropolitan countries. The view that is propagated regarding the 'leapfrogging' developmental role of IT in developing countries is thus inherently flawed on the count that it fails to take into account the role of imperialism, not only in IT service expansion but also in the integrated spheres of other sectors of the world economy. Even more importantly, as we shall see from the structure of employment in India, ICT-based service expansion has had little influence on the dominant employment patterns (even within the service sector). The reasons and character of service sector expansion in India are clearly more reflective of the deep-rooted crisis that afflicts industrial development and the agrarian social order for which the hype around IT can hardly offer a solution. Nor can the demand stimulus to the economy that is expected from increased income and the resulting increase in spending of and by the extremely small strata of ICT-based service employees (relative to the mass of workers in the service sector as well as other sectors), be other than limited.

But before we enter the main features of the service sector of India, or the limited macro-transformatory role of IT services and the actual contours of the women's employment and labour in this sector, first, an overview of the global features of trade in services.

Expansion of Global Trade in Services

On a trajectory similar to merchandise trade, trade in commercial services has vastly expanded in the era of globalization. World exports of commercial services, as may be seen from Figure 5.1, rose significantly from 1985, and according to UNCTAD's E-commerce and Development Report of 2002, between 1990 and 2000, world trade in services grew at an annual average rate of 6.6 per cent, which almost equals the rate for merchandise trade (6.8 per cent).[28]

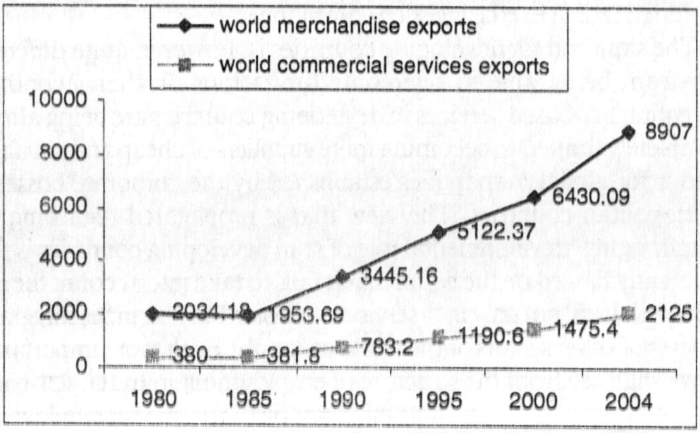

Figure 5.1 World exports of merchandise and commercial services 1980-2004 (in billion U.S. dollars)

According to WTO data sources, of the three categories within commercial services—travel, transportation, and other services—it is the last category of other services, whose exports have been expanding the fastest: its share of world service exports increased from about 38 per cent in 1990 to 45 per cent by 2001 and 48 per cent in 2003.[29]

A more disaggregated breakup of service export shares for the year 2000 is available in UNCTAD's E-Commerce and Development Report 2002, see Figure 5.2. It reveals that within such other services, it is the other business services sector that dominates, exceeding transportation by over U.S.$7 billion, and by itself accounting for over 22 per cent of all commercial services exports.

The UNCTAD report additionally concluded that in the decade 1990-2000, all exports services defined as 'dynamic services', that is, with exports experiencing above-average growth over a certain period, can also be defined as E-services, that is, computer-related services. Thus ICT has been an important factor driving the expansion of international trade in services.

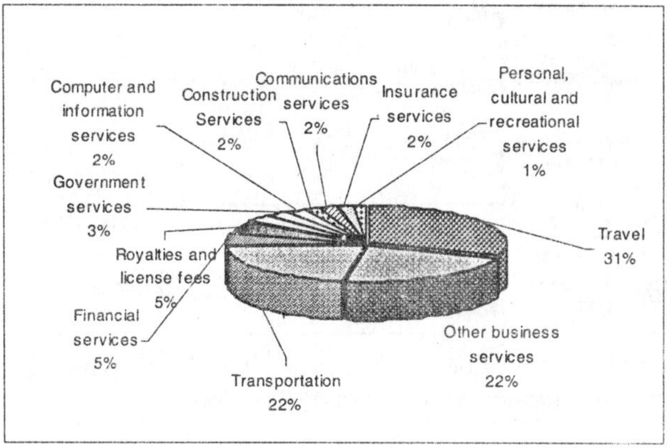

Figure 5.2 Distribution of world exports in services in the year 2000 by major categories. Data source: UNCTAD, 2002.

The Domination of Service Exports by Developed Countries

The domination by the developed countries in service exports in all categories is apparent from Figure 5.3. Taken together, the share of developed countries accounted for close to 80 percent of world service exports in 2000.

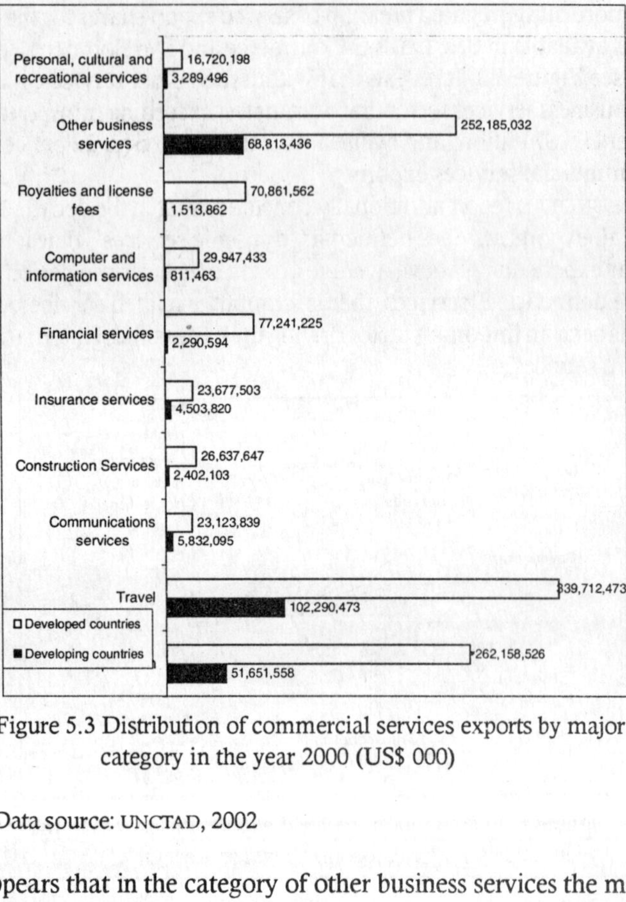

Figure 5.3 Distribution of commercial services exports by major category in the year 2000 (US$ 000)

Data source: UNCTAD, 2002

It appears that in the category of other business services the market share of developing countries stood at 21.4 per cent, second only (in both volume and market share) to travel (which includes foreign tourists' consumption expenditures).[30] However, although the average growth rate of other business service exports from developing countries was 9.4 per cent between 1990 and 2000 in comparison to 5.3 per cent from developed countries, growth rates actually turned negative in the latter half of the decade (1995-2000) for developing countries while those for developed countries remained positive, albeit slower. In computer and information services, the average growth rate of exports of developing countries for the decade 1990-2000 was significantly higher at 58.4 per cent as compared to 31.1 per cent for the developed countries, and although it had clearly slowed down to 45.3 per cent in the latter half of the decade (1995-2000), it remained higher than the developed countries' growth rate of 25.3 per cent. It is difficult to discern the precise contours of such service exports and the relations concealed in them from the available data. Nevertheless, the domination by the developed countries remains visible in the fact that in not even one segment of service exports was the market share of developed countries less than 76 per cent.[31] In computer and information-related service exports, the share of the developed countries was in fact over 97 per cent, while in other business services, it was close to 79 per cent.[32] The domination of production and consumption of service exports by the developed capitalist economies and particularly the United States, has been a particular feature of globalization.

Trade in services and its liberalization was specifically introduced in the Uruguay round leading to the General Agreement on Trade in Services (GATS). At the core of the discussions on GATS was the pressure to privatize services hitherto delivered by the state in several countries, and largely this has been the issue on which most controversy has been generated. While greater heat has been generated (in developing countries) regarding privatization in the health and education sectors, the telecommunications sector was one of the prime areas where pressures for privatization were greatest. Tele-communications have a crucial role to play in the expansion of cross-border trade in services, particularly in what has come to be popularly known as the Information Economy, which has itself been an enabler of the expansion of trade in the category of other business services.

Technology and the Development of the Cross-Border Information Economy

The rise of cross-border 'information economy' based on the digital convergence of information and communication technologies is widely perceived to have bridged the gap between communication and distance on a global scale. Three developments underlie the technological origins of the digital phenomenon: rapid advances in computing power, followed by exponential increases in telecommunications capacity and, finally, the union of the two—networking.[33] Through user-friendly innovations such as the creation of the World Wide Web, the Internet became widely accessible in the early 1990s.[34] It soon acquired central importance in global commercial operations, particularly for finance capital, which, as an investor as well as a major user of ICT, had a special role to play in its promotion and diffusion.[35] Additionally, telecommunication or data networks have created conditions for other new forms of cross-border delivery of services. With the development of the Internet, the submarine fibre-optic cable and the communications satellite, not just atoms but bits can be traded across oceans in rapidly increasing volumes. Customer support, medical analysis, technical work, computer programming, form-filling and claims-processing—all these jobs can now move around the globe. The digital revolution has enabled many services to be provided by workers located in a country different from the one in which the service is actually delivered. However, as one commentator has pointed out, 'The ICT revolution comes wrapped in a package "Made in the USA". It proclaims the US model of capitalism, complete with flexible labour markets, a low tax regime, venture capital, a competitive internal market, continual corporate reengineering, property rights and patent protection.'[36]

Emergence of ICT-Based Call Centres as Service Factories

Among the new services that have developed out of the ICT technologies, call centres are perhaps the most significant in terms of employment. Call centres emerged about 25 to 30 years ago, then forming an insignificant source of employment in the west; however, since the early 1990s, they have expanded dramatically to become elements of a multi-billion-dollar industry. Call centre employment has grown rapidly in several countries and, according to the ILO (2001), their number exceeds fifteen million worldwide.[37] In the UK, workers in call centres alone are more than those in the car, steel and coal industries put together. Similarly, in the United States, several of the thirty fastest-growing occupations were found in the very rapidly expanding computer and data processing services industry.[38]

Although not so much an industry in their own right, call centres have been developed within other industries to lower costs. Telecommunications, banking, insurance, government departments, tourism and retailing have been the principal drivers of the call centre industry, as part of their major restructuring to shift transactions away from the office counter towards semi- and fully automated telephone and computerized environments.[39] Of course, such restructuring also meant a reduction in the numbers of office-counter workers and the replacement of tasks performed by several workers by those involving fewer workers.

Call centres are places where business is conducted over the phone by those whom some commentators call 'computer telephonists', who are usually called agents rather than telephone operators. They are places where workers wearing headphones sit at desks with a personal computer in front of them and speak to customers using information transmitted to their computer screens, that is, through computer telephony integration. Call centres provide remote customer communication for the companies that use them. Depending on the business in which they happen to operate, call centre workers may be selling anything from kitchenware to life insurance, taking orders for airline, cinema or other tickets, helping panicked computer owners, giving complex financial advice or otherwise talking to customers. The technology of automated call distribution switching allows incoming calls to be sent out in orderly queues to waiting operators. Similarly, computer telephony integration allows customers' records to be called up on screen as their calls are answered. What distinguishes call centre services from the traditional telephone operations is this high degree of integration of the telephoning and information functions. The telephone operator no longer transfers a call to a specialist. Transnational corporations have taken advantage of new communication technologies and the lowering costs of telephone calls to make their call centres not just centralized places for processing transactions servicing one country but several.[40]

Unlike the earlier assumption that ICT technologies would tend to lead to far greater openings for working from home, all over the world call centres tend to bring together a lot of people in one workplace. Generally they have seven-day, twenty-four-hour shift-working 'which is more akin to manufacturing than to a traditional day-work arrangement for white-collar staff'.[41] One characteristic that is mentioned by all observers is the very high degree of monitoring in call centres. Technology allows managers to monitor calls for quality and length. According to some commentators, call centre workforces are the most closely supervised ever.[42] 'Working conditions of call-centre staff are based on a maximising of monitoring . . . What [they] most resemble are factories effectively industrialising white collar staff'.[43] Managers not only listen in on calls without the operator knowing, but also generate daily detailed reports of their performance, measuring how many calls they take, the average time on a call and how long they have been available to take them. Despite objective limitations on how many calls can be handled in one day, constant pressure is mounted on employees to lift productivity. Often they have quotas of hundreds of calls per shift. Call centre workers must turn up exactly on time, must be constantly attentive and conscious of what the customer is saying, while at the same time they must be recording the call through notes on a computer and simultaneously resolving the inquiry. This same process repeats itself every 5 to 10 minutes, every hour, every day.[44]

Another universally observed phenomenon is that labour turnover in call centres is usually high. Labour turnover rates of up to more than 30 per cent a year have been reported in UK call centres. In Belgium the rate is said to be in the region of 20 per cent to 30 per cent. In Germany, call centre staff tend to leave their employers after one to two years. An average stay of 18 months is considered typical of the industry in Ireland. This period of 18 months seems to be the maximum a call centre worker can go before 'burning out'.[45] The typical call centre worker is under 30 years of age, with a high-proportion of workers being casual and part-time.

Growth of Business Process Outsourcing and 'Offshoring' of ICT Services

Despite the obviously degraded characteristics of call centre employment, in an era of otherwise jobless growth, call centres have clearly emerged as a significant avenue of mass employment in the developed countries. It must be remembered that they emerged and grew at a time when cost-cutting including government cutbacks were hitting white-collared clerical jobs, while manufacturing jobs were also vanishing through increases in capital intensity or migration to low-wage countries. In the face of shrinking avenues of employment in such segments, call centres were able to absorb fresh entrants into the labour force who would otherwise perhaps have been unable to find employment.

The expansion of the call centre industry in the developed world was also linked to outsourcing in the service sector, that is, contracting out of some back office processes by core companies to service contractors, what is often referred to as Business Process Outsourcing (BPO). Such outsourcing (particularly of government services through privatization) contributed to the tilt towards such service provision as a source of profit, and therefore of investment. In general, from the late 1970s through the 1980s, major outsourcing of white-collared services did not follow an offshore trajectory in developed countries. The development of call centre type service industries were therefore among the key new technology-based service segments seen to be generating new forms of white-collared employment in the core capitalist economies. While no doubt having contributed to degradation of work and restricted collective bargaining by workers vis-à-vis core companies, outsourcing within the developed countries was an issue confined to the embattled and weakened unions there, as long as it was seen to be generating some employment.

From the mid-nineties, however, a growing trend of 'offshoring' appeared, initiated by multinational financial majors seeking to cut costs by moving their labour-intensive processes out of high-wage to lower wage areas.[46] At this point, India, with a sizable pool of English-educated graduates and technical personnel emerged as a preferred destination for US- and UK-based corporations. Middle-class educated Indian workers could be hired here at wages well below wage rates for far less educated workers in the metropolitan core countries. Offshoring, which was seen to reduce costs by 40 per cent to 50 per cent, soon became attractive to a wider range of companies in developed countries, not all of whom were multinationals, and included government service providers. Outsourcing and offshoring began to combine and a number of Indian companies, including software corporates, entered the BPO field considerably aided by the Indian government's policy of no taxation on IT export earnings. Even western multinational BPO companies began to locate some of their operations in India. Not surprisingly, the trend of 'offshoring' of such work to India has led to widespread opposition and resistance in the United States and United Kingdom. Unlike outsourcing within their own countries in the earlier phase, BPO offshoring, at a time of rising unemployment, was perceived as white-collared jobs being taken away from workers in these core countries by workers in foreign countries. Unemployment-driven xenophobia could be seen to override the earlier popular acceptance of outsourcing. The argument that increasing profits must rule supreme over all else was accepable, as long as outsourcing was within their countries. If in the sphere of software services, offshoring seemed to be eroding high end 'techie' jobs of the American and British middle class, offshoring of call centre type work threatened to close avenues of a form of mass employment. Where outsourcing and offshoring combined, the resistance became the greatest, no longer confined to unionized workers, and acquired explosive political overtones.[47]

Indian IT Service Exports and 'Offsite' Delivery

From the 1970s till the 1990s, service exports other than travel or transportation from India and including IT services, was mostly in the form of migration of personnel to the location where the service was provided for 'onsite' delivery of services. This was 'epitomized by the migration of skilled technicians, doctors and nurses to the United Stats [and later software service personnel] and of semi-skilled and unskilled workers, including carpenters, masons, chauffeurs and housemaids to the Gulf countries from India. Benefits to the home country [India] came in the form of remittances of hard currency earnings by these migrants to their families'.[48] Such income was of course limited by restrictive immigration laws and practices of particularly the industrialized countries which were, as far as IT services were concerned, the principal sources of demand. This changed with the digital revolution, following which increasingly cross-border service exports in the IT sector began to be delivered by workers located within

India. The dramatic rise in exports of software and IT-related services from India, which grew from U.S. $485 million in 1993-1994 to U.S $9.5 billion in 2002–2003, was largely owing to the increase in such 'offsite' exports. Exports of IT services lifted the share of service exports in total Indian exports from 8.9 per cent in the 1980s to 14.6 per cent in the 1990s, and raised the share of the category of 'miscellaneous services' within service exports from 43.7 per cent in 1991 to 75.1 per cent in 2001.[49] As noted by the Reserve Bank of India, because of 'offshoring by both existing and new customers...[and] driven by drastic cost-cutting measures undertaken by corporates in the industrial countries, mainly the US' the 'onsite-offsite ratio of software and services exports is currently 43:57 [in 2003] compared with a ratio of 80:20 a few years ago'.[50]

The rapid expansion of IT service exports, in terms of revenue has led to euphoric statements emerging from the industry as well as official circles regarding the possibilities of India emerging as an 'IT superpower'. However, in 2002-2003, 89 per cent of India's IT service exports were destined for North America and Western Europe, indicative more of India's dependent status rather than superpower status. Table 5.1 shows the shares of different countries in IT services spending and India's market share.

Table 5.1 IT services spending: regional shares, 2002-2003

	IT services spending (billion U.S. $)	India's exports (million U.S. $)	India's market share (%)	Relative depen-dence ratio*	Share in India's exports
North America	171.1	6,685	3.92	1.4	67.7
Western Europe	109.6	2,103	1.92	0.7	21.3
Japan	34.9	193	0.55	0.2	2.0
Latin America and rest of world	17.5	583	3.33	1.2	5.9
Asia Pacific	16.0	311	1.94	0.7	3.2
Total	349.1	9,875	2.82		100

*Relative dependence measures the region's share in Indian exports vis-à-vis the region's share in world IT services spending.

Source: IDC, NASSCOM

Although it was in the area of software services that India made an initial niche for itself in 'international markets', from the latter half of the 1990s, the rate of growth in India's exports has been far greater in what is called IT enabled services, whose share in IT service exports rose from 14 per cent in 1999–2000 to close to 25 per cent in 2002-2003. Thus according to the RBI, from the mid-1990s, the 'IT enabled services (ITES) and the Business Process Outsourcing (BPO) segment have emerged as the main drivers of growth'.[51]

ITES-BPO involves processes that can be enabled with information technology such as customer care (database marketing, web sales/marketing), back-office finance (billing services, accounting transactions, financial analysis), human resource hiring, payment services and other administrative services. Within ITES, the most rapidly growing segment and single largest component in terms of both revenue and employment is that of call centre services. Call centre employment (designated customer care service) expanded from some 8,600 in 1999-2000 to 65,000 in 2002-2003 and reached 95,000 in 2003-2004. Table 5.2 illustrates this growth by giving the figures, sourced from NASSCOM, corresponding to different service lines.

Table 5.2 ITES-BPO growth by service lines.

Service lines	Employment		
	2001-02	2002-03	2003-04
Customer Care	30,000	65,000	95,000
Finance	15,000	24,000	40,000
HR	1,500	2,100	3,500
Payment Service	7,000	11,000	21,000
Administration	14,000	25,000	40,000
Content Development	39,000	44,000	46,000
Total	106,500	171,100	245,000

Source: NASSCOM

Unlike software services, call centre work does not involve a high level of skill or technical expertise. Nor is there a shortage of call centre labour in the developed countries as is generally talked about in relation to software; however, despite ICT-based technological rationalization of the labour time involved in individual transactions, call centre services are still labour-intensive in process, as is typically the norm for most services. Profitability therefore is most crucially dependent on the level of wages. It is wage levels that thus drive the direction of offshoring and the reasons why India has become one of the preferred destinations become apparent from a comparison of wages in different countries. India's call centre wages are less than one-fifth of those in the United States a little over one-fourth of those in the United Kingdom and one-third of those in New Zealand. Table 5.3 gives the average call centre wages in different countries.

Table 5.3 Average call centre wages in different countries

Country	Call Centre wages (1998) (U.S. $ per annum)
Japan (Tokyo)	32,000
United States	26,000
Hong Kong	24,000
Singapore	22,000
Ireland	20,000
United Kingdom	19,000
Australia	17,000
New Zealand	15,000
India*	5,000

*The wage rate for India given here is based on international perceptions and is higher than what is revealed from our primary survey.[52]

Nevertheless, at the time of writing, the wages of call centre workers in India in the export segment were still somewhat higher than the average forms of clerical labour within India and considerably higher than manufacturing or agricultural labour. The rapid expansion of this new form of employment combined with the relatively higher earnings, has provided the ground for a much more positive inclination towards call centres among the Indian middle classes. If the IT industry representatives such as National Association of Software Service Companies (NASSCOM) and the Indian government have been busy projecting IT service exports as a great achievement of the Indian corporate sector (and an important component of the 'India Shining' campaign in the 2004 elections), sections of the salaried middle class have been no less backward in welcoming offshoring of IT services to India as an employment opportunity, particularly for women. Academic circles too have been affected: witness the thesis on IT service-driven economy leapfrogging into advanced stages of development mentioned earlier. As we shall see from the findings of the primary survey of call centre workers, all is not as rosy as propagated. But more importantly, a macro-view of the nature of service sector growth in India, particularly in the 1990s, and the dominant characteristics of service sector growth in women's employment belies all the hype around the transformatory developmental role of IT services for both the economy and for women's empowerment.

A PERSPECTIVE APPROACH TO WOMEN'S EMPLOYMENT IN THE SERVICE SECTOR IN INDIA

At the risk of what might be considered a digression, we enter the arena of analysis of the role of the service sector in India, with reference to the continuing dominance of agriculture in the workforce distribution. Figure 5.4 gives a graphical representation of such continuity across 1993-1994 to 2004. Despite signs of relative decline over the five decades since independence and at a slightly faster rate between 1980 to 2000, agriculture continues to be the source of employment of three out of every five of India's workers and three out of every four of the country's women workers. Applying the ratios of the last major round of the NSSO's employment survey in 1999-2000 to the census population estimates had revealed that agriculture, employed well over 237 million workers that year, of whom over 92 million were women. According to the ratios of the most recent 'moderately large' NSS Employment Unemployment Survey, in 2004 agriculture employed well over 248 million workers constituting 57 per cent of the workforce and indications that the pace of decline of agriculture in employment might even be slowing down.[53] Of those employed in agriculture, 40 per cent are women, numbering over 100 million, and constituting 73 per cent of the female workforce in 2004. Any discussion on the nature of development in India which seeks to eliminate particularly the peasantry and agricultural labour from view and fails to incorporate their important location in determining the characteristics of India's economy and society, is thus clearly off the mark and even more so as far as women are concerned. Just as much as developmental roles of either industry or services cannot be analysed or properly understood when detached from developments in agrarian India, so also the features and potential of employment in the respective sectors cannot be identified without reference to the single largest employment category—agriculture.

(a)

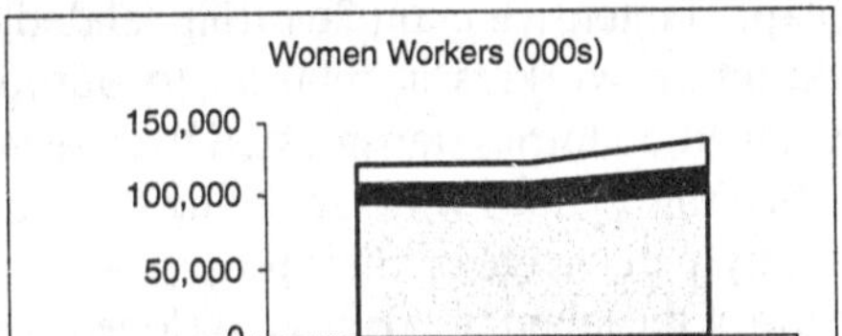

	1993-1994	1999-2000	2004
Services	13,869	15,873	18,844
Industry	13,668	14,953	17,476
Agriculture	94,065	92,212	100,252

(b)

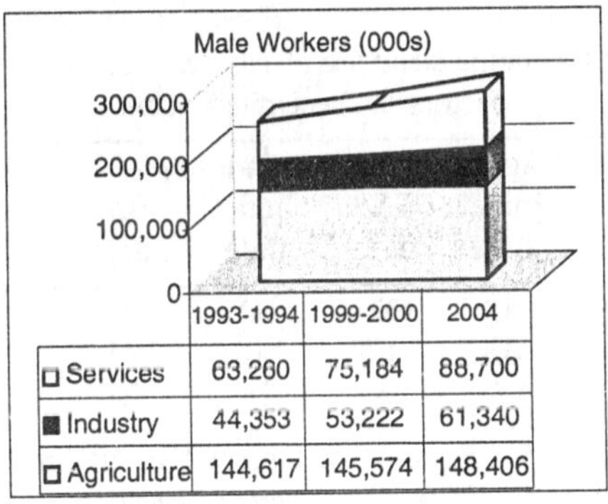

	1993-1994	1999-2000	2004
Services	63,260	75,184	88,700
Industry	44,353	53,222	61,340
Agriculture	144,617	145,574	148,406

Figure 5.4 Gender-wise distribution of employment (principal+ subsidiary) by sector (Figures in inset table in thousands)

Note: In these charts agriculture includes forestry and fishing. Mining, quarrying and construction have been included in Industry. Figures in inset data tables are in thousands.

A COMPARATIVE DEVELOPMENT OVERVIEW

In the developed industrial countries, the process of transformation to service domination due to industrialization has already been discussed at some length. What perhaps needs to be emphasized here is that it was accompanied by a dramatic decline in number of workers in agriculture there due to the spurt in capital-intensive productivity per head of agriculturists engendered by large-scale industrialization. Just as increases in capital-intensive manufacturing tended to reduce the number of production workers in relation to output, so also in agriculture developed countries transformed themselves into major producers of agricultural goods while reducing their actual farming population to a tiny percentage of their people. An example of the changing structure of the labour force in a developed country is given in, Table 5.4 for the United States. The figures refer to the share in total labour force at the beginning and end of the range mentioned in the first column. It may be seen that from employing 51 per cent of the labour force in 1870, by 1990 only 3 per cent of the labour force in the United States was engaged in agriculture.

Table 5.4 Changing structure of labour force by three major sectors in the United States

United States	Agriculture %		Industry %		Services %	
	Initial date	End date	Initial date	End date	Initial date	End date
1870 - 1910	51	32	30	41	19	27
1910 - 1950	32	12	41	45	27	43
1960 - 1990	7	3	36	28	57	69

Source for Tables 5.4, 5.5 and 5.6: Terence J. Byres, *Structural Change, the Agrarian Question and the Possible Impact of Globalization.*

Moving away from the early industrializers or core metropolitan countries to East Asia—if we take Taiwan and South Korea as the much heralded instances of fast-track economic transformation in the developing world—here too the pattern of development accords an important position to industrialization as the prime driver of development and related expansion of employment in services. And here too, their development is marked by dramatic falls in the share of agriculture in employment. In South Korea, agricultural employment fell from from 66 per cent in 1960 to 17 per cent in 1991, while in Taiwan it fell from 56 per cent in 1952 to a mere 9 per cent in 1998. Table 5.5 gives the relevant data for South Korea and Taiwan. In all, it appears that expansion of industrial employment to critical mass levels provides an essential precondition for any major shift in the structure of the labour force away from agriculture.[54]

Table 5.5 Changing structure of the labour force by major sectors in South Korea and Taiwan

Country and Dates	Agriculture % Initial date	End date	Industry % Initial date	End date	Services % Initial date	End date
South Korea						
1960-1980	66	37	9	27	25	36
1980-1991	37	17	27	35	36	48
Taiwan						
1952-1970	56	37	17	28	25	35
1970-1985	37	17	28	42	35	41
1985-1998	17	9	42	38	41	53

The fact that industrialization in both South Korea and Taiwan took place in close interconnection with Japan and the United States has led many in India to assume that greater co-ordination with imperialist countries offers opportunities for external market-driven industrialization. But what is perhaps less understood or ignored regarding the fundamentals of the industrialization process in South Korea and Taiwan is that after 1945 (when they were relieved of their colonial masters), in each case landlordism was destroyed by a land reform programme. As noted by a historian of agrarian development, 'There can be no doubt that in both cases this agrarian structure... [described as] a multiplicity of small peasant proprietors-throughout the 1950s and 1960s, delivered a productive, fast growing agriculture that was an essential source of accumulation in industry, and that the respective states were effectively, pervasively and ruthlessly central to this process'.[55]

In contrast, in India, the crux of the developmental crisis lay in the lack of land reform in agriculture as mentioned in Chapter Four and any decline in employment in agriculture has been at a much slower pace.[56] Over the first four decades since independence, state aid to private investment in agriculture through irrigation, provision of subsidized fertilisers, introduction of new high-yielding crop varieties (the green revolution) and state procurement at a 'remunerative' floor price had ensured a secular growth rate of food-grain production at a little higher than the population growth rate; however, an unreformed agrarian structure meant that agriculture had little 'internal dynamism'. On the one hand, in conditions of widespread poverty and insecure conditions of tenure, the majority of cultivators had neither the means nor the incentive to invest in land. On the other, as has been convincingly argued, 'given the high returns obtained by the rural rich from their participation in the interlinked markets for land lease at rack rates of rent, for lending at usurious rates of interest, and for access to labour at low costs, they too had no incentive to invest in land'.[57] Thus, developments in agrarian India, remained characterized by far greater social stagnation, and agriculture has continued to retain the major part of the labour force within its fold, often living and working in pauperized conditions. At the same time, industrial expansion remained constrained by lack of sufficient expansion of purchasing power or demand in the agrarian hinterland and industry's share of the labour force in India has yet to reach even 20 per cent. Table 5.6 gives India's labour force distribution across different sectors.

Table 5.6 Changing structure of the labour force by major sectors in India by major sectors

India	Agriculture %		Industry %		Services %	
	Initial date	End date	Initial date	End date	Initial date	End date
1881 - 1950	74	76	15	12	11	12
1950 - 1960	76	74	12	11	12	15
1960 - 1980	74	70	11	13	15	17
1980 - 1990	70	64	13	16	17	20
1990 – 2000*	64	60	16	17	20	23
2000 - 2004	60	57	17	18	20	25

*Figures for 2000 and 2004 added from the results of NSS 55th and 60th rounds. (1999-2000 and 2004).

Post-Liberalization Convulsions in the Agricultural Heartland of India

Within such a broad context, it is important to note the changes that appear in the 1990s or the first decade of liberalization and greater integration with the world economy. Through the 1990s, characterized by a drastic decline in real public investment in agriculture (as part of neo-liberal reforms), there was a decline in the rate of growth of output for every single one of the major crop categories.[58] At the same time, the number of cultivators dropped steeply, by over 6.5 million between 1994-1995 and 1999-2000, while those of agricultural labourers increased by over 5 million, both signs of pauperization and loss of land by the peasantry. Between 2000 and 2004 however, with the deepening of agrarian crisis (as peasants bearing the burden of increasing costs of inputs and declining rates of return on agriculture were additionally disturbed by extreme volatilities and sharp falls in the prices of several crops), wage employment in agriculture seems to have become more scarce and the number of agricultural labourers fell steeply by almost 10 million.[59] Table 5.7 provides the details of number of cultivators and agricultural labourers across three employment surveys by the NSSO.

Table 5.7 Cultivators and agricultural labourers (1993-1994 to 2004)

Year	Cultivators (000s)			Agricultural labourers (000s)		
	Women	Men	Combined	Women	Men	Combined
1993-94	41,269	80,195	121,464	37,688	52,196	89,884
1999-2000	37,793	77,202	114,995	38,844	55,879	94,723
2004	46,770	85,133	131,903	35,700	49,447	85,147

A startling feature of the period between 2000 and 2004 is that, the number of cultivators appear to have risen substantially. Significantly, the number of additional women declaring themselves cultivators between 2000 and 2004 was over 53 per cent of the net increase in cultivators, bringing the share of women among the class of cultivators to an all time high of 35 per cent in 2004. It appears that as more layers of the peasantry (i.e., including the middle and perhaps even a section of the rich peasantry) have fallen victim to the agrarian crisis, the known trend of women being left to bear the burden of subsistence or rather below subsistence agriculture has become enhanced.[60] Additionally, one of the features of the crowding of more workers into cultivation at a time of deceleration of its annual growth rates (from 4 per cent in the 1980s to the present 2 per cent) could be a reflection of a process of substituting unpaid family labour for hired workers in peasant families. Supporting evidence for such an analysis may be found in the fact that the most substantial increases in the WPR for rural women between 1999-2000 and 2004 have been in the older age groups among whom those aged 45-49 have registered the sharpest increase (See Table 5.8). In the latter half of the 1990's, an absolute fall in the number of women cultivators had been accompanied not only by a marked increase in casualization of, particularly, female labour in agriculture, but also a slowing down of the rate of growth of real wages for female casual labour in agriculture, for the period from 1993-1994 to 1999-2000 in comparison to the period from 1983 to 1993-1994.[61] By 2004, even such casual employment in agriculture was becoming scarce. From all accounts therefore, it seems that escalating agrarian distress and its reflected convulsions in employment patterns in agriculture is the major factor in pushing larger numbers of workers—including especially women—into low-paid service sector employment as well as into low-paid manufacturing. Between 1993-1994 and 1999-2000, when women were obviously being driven out of agriculture, it was the lowpaid piece rated beedi industry that showed the single largest increase in women's employment in the manufacturing sector. In the service sector across the same period the single largest increase was in self-employed retail trade. By 2004, in beedi manufacture, there appears to have been a fall in numbers, a slowing down of employment expansion for women in retail trade, and a movement back into agriculture. In such a context, the picture acquires a bleakness, which is missing from the literature extolling the virtues of service driven growth.

Relatively Low Levels of Women's Employment in the Service Sector

Three aspects have been borne in mind while looking at the role of the service sector in women's employment and social advance in India. The first is the actual changes in the distribution of women workers across all the major sectors. Within such changes, the characteristics and nature of their employment in services have to be culled out in order to arrive at an understanding of the causative factors, conditions and consequences of the tilt towards services in the female labour force composition across the last decade. The second is an understanding of the specific factors determining variations in the work participation rate of women in this period. For such purposes available macro-statistics provide us with some clues, but cannot adequately capture the impact of real social differentials. The third is the position of women's employment relative to men and recent changes effected therein.

At the outset it must be noted that the share of services in women's employment is considerably lower than that of men. While for the entire workforce, the share of service sector employment was 25 per cent in 2004, the share of services in women's employment was just 14 per cent.

Table 5.7 compares women's employment in different sectors, across periods between 1961 and 2000.

Table 5.7 Structure of the female labour force in India by major sectors (1961-2004)

India (women)	Agriculture	Industry	Services
1961	86	8	6
1977-78*	79	10	11
1983*	78	11	11
1987-88*	74	14	12
1993 – 1994	78	11	11
1999 – 2000	75	12	13
2004	73	13	14

*Services here excludes construction

* Figures from 1961 to 1987-1988 cited in Byres, *Structural Change, the Agrarian Question and the Possible Impact of Globalization*. The category of services here excludes construction.

In other words, as regards women's employment, the tilt towards services is not of such significant magnitude as is commonly perceived. In fact, even as far as overall (combined male and female) employment is concerned, the slow increases of services in terms of employment share (from 15 per cent in 1960 to the present 25 per cent) provides a sharp reality check on the hype about the country leapfrogging into a service dominated economy. The widening gap between services as the leader of India's growth pattern (now accounting for some 52 per cent of its GDP) and its low share of employment, is indicative of mounting inequality and perhaps more of a cause for concern than celebration.

Further, as far as women are concerned, not only do services account for only 14 per cent of the female workforce (in comparison to 30 per cent of male workers), but also, women's share of total service sector employment at 18 per cent, is lower than their share in manufacturing employment (28 per cent), while it is still in the sectors of agriculture, forestry and fishing that women have the most significant share of 40 per cent of employment. It becomes clear therefore that the growth of services in terms of contribution to GDP has remained of little relevance in either leveling inequalities in terms of employment shares of men and women or in determining the occupations of the overwhelming majority of India's women workers.

Rising Unemployment and Declining Options

Of singular importance is the fact that the process of liberalization in India has been marked by lowered work participation rates among women in both rural and urban areas. This is no doubt a consequence of the disruptions and volatilities in employment patterns that have marked the advance of neo-liberal policies. For example, in the 1990s, that is between 1993-1994 and 1999-2000, female employment in agriculture fell by more than 2.3 million of whom some 30 per cent seemed to have been replaced by men who actually increased their numbers in the sector. The reduction in absolute number of women workers in agriculture across those years was clearly not offset by expanding employment for them in either services or manufacturing, and the work participation rate of rural women declined steeply from 328 women workers per thousand women in 1993-1994 to an all time low of 299 in 1999-2000 with the number of women workers in rural India actually having fallen in absolute terms by over 185,000 in that period. Although between 1999-2000 and 2004, rural women's WPR again rose to 315, it still remained lower than in any of the preceding major rounds of the NSS across three decades (i.e., apart from 1999-2000), and much of the increase was in the subsidiary status category of workers. In relation to principal status employment, WPR continued to fall (from 234 in 1993-1994 to 231 in 1999-2000 to 228 in 2004). The replacement of women by men in agricultural employment of the latter half of the 1990s seems however, to have been reversed between 2000 and 2004 during which more than 8 million women were added to the workforce in agriculture in comparison to the increase of a little less than 3 million men in agricultural employment. Nevertheless, despite such increased shares of women, clearly crisis ridden agriculture (and its reducing share of GDP [at present around 20 per cent]) is not in a position to provide for the growing employment and income needs of women. It is the absence of other opportunities for employment diversification including in services that would also probably account for more women and perhaps even men declaring themselves as cultivators in 2004. Reports from field activists and almost every micro-survey in rural areas have all pointed to the expressed and increasing need for employment among women (for example in *Womenspeak*) and it is the inadequate growth of such employment that is reflected in the lowered work participation rates of women in rural India as well as what appears from the data to be a regressive overcrowding into agriculture.

On the other hand, in urban India where the number of women workers has consistently expanded, by some 1.6 million in the latter half of the 1990s and more than double that number in the following four years, yet the urban female WPR too dropped from 155 per thousand in 1993-1994 to 139 per thousand in 1999-2000, and its enhancement to 150 per thousand by 2004 still remained lower than at the beginning of the preceding decade. Further, despite common perceptions to the contrary, the share of women in urban employment has not increased, having stagnated at around 21 per cent between 1993-1994 and 2004. What is remarkable in urban areas is that in all age cohorts above 15 it was lower in 2004 in comparison to 1993-1994 with the solitary exception of the 35-39 age group. The steepest decline is visible for the age group of 30-34, which fell from 301 per thousand in 1993-1994 to 235 per thousand in 1999-2000, with the improved rate of 259 in 2004 still 40 points less than ten years before. In general, lowered female WPR in urban areas is most visible among the age groups between 20 and 49, which is precisely the age group where employment needs, abilities and therefore rates are the maximum. A drop in WPR in this age group is clearly an indication of increasing numbers of potential or even previously employed women workers unable to find employment. Table 5.8 illustrates the distribution of female worker population (principal + subsidiary status) by age across rural and urban India.

Table 5.8: Age specific Female Worker Population Ratios by Rural-Urban Residence

Age-Group	Rural			Urban		
	1993-94	1999-2000	2004	1993-94	1999-2000	2004
5-9	14	7	4	5	2	2
10-14	141	96	77	45	36	26
15-19	364	304	301	123	105	114
20-24	456	409	409	180	155	160
25-29	525	491	497	224	194	218
30-34	585	555	572	301	235	259
35-39	608	579	630	301	285	307
40-44	606	586	619	320	283	299
45-49	594	566	663	317	267	281
50-54	542	515	542	286	262	230
55-59	467	450	478	226	207	195
60+	241	218	244	113	94	83
All	328	299	315	155	139	150

Data Source: NSS Employment Unemployment Surveys, 50th, 55th and 60th rounds.

Across the reform years, in both urban and rural India growing unemployment among women, both as a proportion of the female population as well as relative to men has emerged as the most significant feature rather than the opening of new avenues for better employment. This accounts for the lowered WPR for women, and is also reflected in the increased unemployment rate (current daily status)[57] which rose from 5.6 per cent in 1993-1994 to 9.3 per cent in 2004 for rural women and from 10.5 per cent to 11.7 per cent for urban women across the same period.[62] The corresponding increases for rural men were from 5.6 per cent to 9 per cent and for urban men from 6.7 per cent to 8.1 per cent. Further, a longstanding measure of women's underemployment in India that many commentators have noted is the substantially greater proportions of subsidiary status workers in the female workforce.[63] Traditionalists would, of course, view this as a matter of 'choice' for women otherwise engaged in dutiful domesticity of the non-economic variety, that is, in activities not defined as economic. Others, like us, view it as reflective of constraints (both economic and social in nature) on women's employment and income opportunities. In 2004, the proportion of women workers who were solely subsidiary status workers was 28 per cent in rural areas and 19 per cent in urban. In comparison, the proportions of male workers who were solely subsidiary status were 3 per cent in rural areas and 2 per cent in urban. In fact the absolute number of subsidiary status women workers increased by over 9 million between 1999-2000 and 2004, a period during which the number of principal status women workers rose by just a little over 4 million. In other words the greater part of even what appears as relatively larger increases in the numbers of women workers in recent years is actually a reflection of enhanced levels of unemployment or underemployment among them.

Significance of the Pattern of Absolute Losses Followed by Increases in Some Sectors

We have already referred to the changes in employment patterns in agriculture—the loss of employment in the sector in the latter half of the 1990s followed by a crowding back into agricultural employment visible in the 2004 employment data. Turning to other sectors and segments by industrial classification, it appears that between 1993-1994 and 1999-2000 absolute losses in women's employment also took place in mining and quarrying by 191,000, in public administration and defence by 91,000, in electricity, gas and water by 14,000 and in personal services by some 497,000. By 2004, however, although losses continued in public administration, in the other sectors, i.e., in mining

Table 5.9 Industrial Distribution of Workforce in thousands: All India (1993-1994 to 2004)

Categories of Industrial Classification	1993-94			1999-2000			2004		
	All workers (in '000s)	Female workers (in '000s)	Female share (%)	All workers (in '000s)	Female workers (in '000s)	Female share (%)	All workers (in '000s)	Female workers (in ('000s)	All workers (%)
Agriculture, forestry, fishing	238,682	94,065	39.41	237,786	92,212	38.77	248,658	100,252	40.31
Mining and Quarrying	2,676	580	21.67	2,263	389	17.18	2,922	487	16.67
Construction	12,127	1,648	13.58	17,618	2,057	11.67	24,830	2,783	11.21
Transport, storage, communications	10,757	329	3.05	14,757	446	3.02	17,974	469	2.61
Finance,insurance, real esate, business services	3,653	433	11.85	4,924	474	9.62	7,259	798	10.99

Table 5.9 (*continued*)

Categories of Industrial Classification	1993-94			1999-2000			2004		
	All workers (in '000s)	Female workers (in '000s)	Female share (%)	All workers (in '000s)	Female workers (in '000s)	Female share (%)	All workers (in '000s)	Female workers (in ('000s)	All workers (%)
Manufacturing + repair services (of which)	43,218	11,500	26.6	48,296	12,510	25.9	51,232	14,205	27.73
Food products	4,843	1,353	27.93	5,409	1,317	24.34	5,596	1,393	24.89
Beverages and tobacco	4,410	3,019	68.46	4,925	3,676	74.64	4,891	3,292	67.31
Textiles and products	10,335	3,624	35.07	10,480	3,479	33.20	10,055	3,758	37.77
Wood products and furniture	4,295	1,129	26.29	5,367	1,147	21.37	5,864	1,071	18.26
Leather, fur and products	730	87	11.92	1,081	114	10.55	830	87	10.48
Non-metallic mineral products	3,134	798	25,46	3,484	900	25.83	6,072	1,268	20.88
Metal products and parts	1,638	35	2.14	2,276	180	7.91	3,816	87	2.28
Electricity, gas, water	1,394	52	3.7	1,048	38	3.62	1,285	66	5.14

Table 5.9 (*continued*)

Categories of Industrial Classification	1993-94			1999-2000			2004		
	All workers (in '000s)	Female workers (in '000s)	Female share (%)	All workers (in '000s)	Female workers (in '000s)	Female share (%)	All workers (in '000s)	Female workers (in ('000s)	All workers (%)
Trade, hotels, restaurants (of which)	28,459	3,919	13.77	37,128	5,253	14.14	46,009	5,595	12.16
Retail Trade	21,384	3,122	14.59	28,887	4,228	14.6	33,202	4,496	13.54
Hotels, restaurants	3,436	556	16.18	4,600	834	18.13	5,971	983	16.47
Community, social, personal services (of which)	32,866	9,136	27.79	33,200	9,662	29.1	35,017	11,916	34.03
Public admn + Defence	10,349	1,248	12.05	10,589	1,157	10.92	9,124	1,130	12.30
Education + research	6,513	2,322	35.65	8,554	3,290	38.46	10,283	4,457	43.35

Table 5.9 (*continued*)

Categories of Industrial Classification	1993-94			1999-2000			2004		
	All workers (in '000s)	Female workers (in '000s)	Female share (%)	All workers (in '000s)	Female workers (in '000s)	Female share (%)	All workers (in '000s)	Female workers (in ('000s)	All workers (%)
Medical and health	1,966	624	31.73	2,522	853	33.8	3,628	1,354	37.33
Community services	1,125	173	15.37	1,055	199	18.86	2,674	339	12.67
Personal services	10,654	4,422	41.5	9,429	3,925	41.6	9,308	4,636	49.81
All service sector categories including construction	89,256	15,517	17.38	108,675	17,930	16.49	132,374	21,628	16.24
All service sector categories excluding construction	77,129	13,869	17.98	91,057	15,873	17.43	107,544	18,844	17.52
Total Workers	373,832	121,602	32.52	397,018	123,038	30.99	435,160	136,714	31.42

*Major categories given in roman letters and their subcategories placed below in italics.

Note: The figures in the table are for usual status principal + subsidiary status workers (UPSS).

and quarrying, electricity, water and gas, and in personal services, the absolute falls in women's employment were reversed. Table 5.9 shows the changes in employment figures by industrial classification from 1993-1994 to 2004.

Such losses in the 1990s are at one level, perhaps indicative of a widespread tendency for women to lose jobs at a higher rate both when men's jobs are also lost and also when increases in male employment follow a low growth pattern. In the case of mining, women's losses of employment between 1993-1994 and 1999-2000, although disproportionately higher than men's, reflected an aspect of the overall job loss in the sector at the time by some 363,000.[64] Across the same period, the loss of a much smaller number of women's jobs in electricity, gas and water were more or less proportionate to their extremely small share in the sector where again there was an overall loss of 346,000 jobs;however, in public administration and defence, women lost jobs even though the overall number of employed increased by 240,000 in the latter half of the 1990s. Thereafter although women's jobs in public administration continued to decline, albeit at a slower pace, but this time (i.e., across the four years between 2000 and 2004) women were not alone in their losses and the 27,000 women who lost their jobs were a small fraction compared to the 1.4 million men who lost their jobs in public administration and defence.

On the other hand, in mining and quarrying, an addition of 659,000 jobs between 2000 and 2004, of which 98,000 were women's jobs, appears as almost exclusively an expansion of the hazardous, lowpaid and highly exploitative unorganized segment since in mining and quarrying, between 2000 and 2003 both the public sector and organized private sector saw a loss of 79,000 and 15,000 jobs respectively. Similarly, the inclusion of an additional 28,000 women workers out of the 237,000 increased jobs in electricity, water and gas between 2000 and 2004 (amounting to a net increase of 14,000 jobs for women from 1993-1994) is once again reflective of privatization and a concomitant growth of an unorganized segment, since the public sector shed 33,000 workers and the organized private sector added only 9000 jobs between 2000 and 2003.[65] Thus, it seems that the loss of jobs in the 1990s in the three sectors of (i) public administration; (ii) mining and quarrying; and (iii) electricity, gas and water are part of the process of loss of better quality employment primarily in the public sector, but also in the private organized sector. This then is paving the way for expansion, albeit of an extremely limited quantity, of poor quality, insecure and highly exploitative unorganized sector employment for both men and women. Although such a phenomenon is a well known outcome of the neo-liberal agenda and part of the micro-experience of workers on the ground, its reflection in the macro-statistics on employment need also to be highlighted. The statistics also provide clear indication that the positive arithmetic of expansion of new forms of service sector employments such as in IT enabled services virtually gets cancelled out by the negative employment trends in segments such as public administration.

Increase in Menial Women Servants and Declining Independent Workers in Personal Services

The absolute decline in women's employment in personal services (which includes household domestic servants) in the latter half of the 1990s (see Table 5.9), accompanied by a marginal decrease in their share of the workforce in personal services appeared to be initially somewhat more puzzling. It ran counter to all micro-impressions of an expanding number of women domestic servants to the extent that studies had pointed to female migration for domestic work being an important factor in bringing about 'changes in the gender balance of the migratory stream.'[66] Nevertheless, at least one commentator had hailed the decline in personal services as a 'positive development', on the grounds that 'this segment has been traditionally a low-productivity-low income-per-worker sector.'[67] It appears however, that such optimism was misplaced at least as far as women are concerned, since the 2004 data shows that although the decline in total employment in personal services has continued, women's employment in this sub-sector is increasing. A look at employment data in terms of occupation of the workers given in Table 5.9 *(a)* reveals that even in the 1990s, women's employment in menial services such as maids, cooks, sweepers, cleaners, etc. was increasing and continued to increase in the following four years [see subcategory 51-54 in Table 5.9 *(a)*]. It would seem that the most convincing explanation for the reduction in personal services in the 1990s might be found in a loss of employment by independent service providers such as launderers (perhaps traditional *dhobins*) and other such, although such a decline does not appear even in the occupational data. The decline in launderers and pressers was possibly masked in the occupational data for 1999-2000 because of expansion in the numbers of beauticians and hairdressers. Going by the occupational figures for 2004, however, it appears that even beauticians and hairdressers might now be facing problems, since the numbers in the occupational sub-category 55-56 [see Table 5.9 *(a)*] dropped to even less than what prevailed in 1993-1994.

A closer look at somewhat more disaggregated data by industrial classification revealed the interesting fact that even between 1993-1994 and 1999-2000, in the principal status category of personal services, the numbers of women had continued to increase by over 77,000 in urban areas and by over 72,000 in rural areas. Although at an all India level this was not a substantial increase, it makes clear that reduction of women workers in personal services was therefore entirely concentrated in the subsidiary status category and perhaps indicative of the tendency towards consolidation of the position of menial domestic service as regular work for women rather than any reduced importance. This is confirmed by the occupational data where the numbers of women being counted as maids, sweepers and so on have maintained an upward trajectory throughout. (It may be noted that maids, cooks, sweepers and so on appear to be more in the occupational figures than the numbers recorded in personal services by industrial classification because such occupations would be spread over institutions located in other industrial categories as well).

What is of note is that, between 1993-1994 and 1999-2000, while the numbers of male principal status workers in personal services declined (by well over 536,000) in urban areas, in rural areas their numbers increased substantially. Thus, in the latter half of the 1990s women increased their share of principal status personal services sharply in urban areas from 41 per cent to 49 per cent, maintaining the trend towards feminization of personal services. In contrast, in rural areas their share declined marginally from 31 per cent to 30 per cent indicating perhaps the closing of even such limited (and often socially degraded) employment opportunities for women in rural areas. By

Table 5.9(a) Employment of women in different occupations from 1993-1994 to 2004 (in 000s)

National Classification of Occupation	1993-94		1999-2000		2004	
	Principal status	Principal and subsidiary status	Principal status	Principal and subsidiary status	Principal status	Principal and subsidiary status
Div 0-1, Professional, technical and related workers (of which)	3,220	3,644	3,792	4,187	4,585	5,074
08 Nursing, and other medical and health technicians	347	382	576	625	530	548
15 Teachers	2,100	2,273	2,816	2,993	3,471	3,908
Div 2, Administrative, executive and managerial workers	1,031	1,285	1,585	1,932	1,773	2,272
Div 3, Clerical and related workers	1,292	1,318	1,534	1,544	2,172	2,199
Div 4, Sales (of which)	2,833	3,542	2,964	3,542	3,313	4,233
40, Merchants and shopkeepers, wholesale and retail trade	1,992	2,518	1,891	2,339	1,995	2,692
Rest of Div 4, technical salesmen, commercial travellers, shop assistants, insurance, real estate, moneylenders, and other sales workers	841	1,024	1,073	1,203	1,318	1,541

Table 5.9(a) (*continued*) (in 000s)

National Classification of Occupation	1993-94		1999-2000		2004	
	Principal status	Principal and subsidiary status	Principal status	Principal and subsidiary status	Principal status	Principal and subsidiary status
Div 5, Service workers (of which)	3,755	4,252	5,043	5,521	6,031	6,747
51-54, Housekeepers, stewards, cooks, waiters, maids, sweepers, cleaners, etc.	2,603	2,932	3,311	3,504	4,712	5,152
55-56, Launderers, pressers, hair dressers, beauticians and related workers	813	886	1,107	1,279	721	881
Div 6, Farmers, fishermen, hunters, loggers and related workers (of which)	67,659	93,863	69,149	91,542	71,720	99,929
61, Cultivators	28,034	41,269	28,051	37,793	33,470	46,770
63, Agricultural labourers	33,440	37,688	34,824	38,844	30,856	35,700
64, Plantation labourers and related workers	1,137	1,147	1,221	1,240	895	938
Rest of Div 6, Forestry workers, hunters, fishermen, other farm workers and related workers	5,045	13,759	5,047	13,542	6,400	16,521

Table 5.9(a) (*continued*) (in 000s)

National Classification of Occupation	1993-94		1999-2000		2004	
	Principal status	Principal and subsidiary status	Principal status	Principal and subsidiary status	Principal status	Principal and subsidiary status
Div 7, 8, 9, Production and related workers (of which)	11,665	13,698	12,089	14,874	12,696	16,258
75, Spinners, weavers, knitters and related workers	1,967	2,674	1,700	2,206	1,358	1,637
77, Food and beverage processors	549	747	722	918	619	768
79, Tailors, dress makers, sewers and related workers	1,208	1,944	1,409	2,017	1,903	3,168
80-89, Makers of leather goods, carpenters, stone cutters, blacksmiths, fitters, assemblers, plumbers, jewellery and precious metal workers, glass formers, potters and related workers	637	868	754	823	743	937
95, Bricklayers and other construction workers	855	955	1,170	1,079	1,587	1,768
All workers	88,005	121,602	96,367	123,038	100,763	136,714

2004, however, male employment in personal services can be seen to have dropped further in urban areas and also in rural India. A similar fall of principal status employment also took place for women workers in rural personal services, confirming the view that even such avenues of employment seem to be shrinking in rural India. Once again, the occupational figures for 2004 indicate that it is the shrinking of opportunities for women are being experienced by the category of independent service providers. Perhaps they too are being driven into the expanding numbers of employer dependent menial servants who till today constitute the single largest service occupation for women in India, which is why by 2004 women accounted for close to 50 per cent of the employment in personal services.

Increasing Marginalization of Women Workers in Construction and Manufacturing

In the employment data by industrial classification, there appears to be a steady, although not substantial increase in the numbers of women workers in both manufacturing and construction between 1993-1994 and 2004. In overall terms employment in construction seems to have grown phenomenally, having doubled its numbers across the decade; however, women's share in such increases have been at the lower margins and in the industry as such, the share of women workers has consistently declined. This is especially true of the more mechanized segment. Even casual observation of the major construction being undertaken in the larger cities of the country indicate that women are not being employed by the large firms involved in the construction of flyovers, expressways and so on. As a result, in urban areas women's share of the additional employment in construction from 1993-1994 to 2004 amounted to a paltry 6 per cent (in fact between 1999-2000 and 2004 it was still lower at less than 4 per cent). Even in rural areas, women's share in the expanded employment in construction across the whole decade was a low 8 per cent. For women, the net result of the nature of expansion in construction employment has therefore been a greater level of marginalization with their share falling from around 14 per cent in 1993-1994 to a little over 11 per cent in 2004.

In manufacturing on the other hand, the share of women's employment shows a marginal increase, from a little less than 27 per cent to a little less than 28 per cent across the decade. And yet, even what appears as an increase in share is almost entirely accounted for by an increase in the share of solely subsidiary status women workers in manufacturing. In principal status employment the share of women workers actually declined from 24 per cent to 22 per cent across the decade, while the share of subsidiary status workers among women workers in manufacturing rose substantially from 15 per cent in 1993-1994 to 22 per cent in 2004. Since, as explained before, increasing levels of subsidiary status employment might equally express growing unemployment along with underemployment, it appears that marginalization of women workers is a common feature in both construction and manufacturing.

Further, within manufacturing, what is of note is that between 1993-1994 and 1999-2000, 60 per cent of the additional jobs for women were concentrated in the sub-sector of beverages and tobacco, most of which were in low-paid beedi manufacturing. By 2004, even beedi manufacturing, otherwise the most clearly female dominated industry, seemed to be rejecting women. A similar rejection, although to a lesser degree, could also be seen in wood and metal products, while it was in textiles and textile products from which at least some sections of men seemed to be moving out, where the numbers of women seemed to be increasing. Withal the ups and downs and minor redistribution of workers within manufacturing, what is clear is that the sector as a whole has remained stagnant in terms of share of total employment at a little less than 12 per cent across the decade, and is unable to absorb the labour surpluses, male and female, in both rural and urban India.

Declining Share of Women's Employment in Trade, Transport and Finance

It is in such a context that the largest increase in employment between 1993-1994 and 2004 was in the major category of trade, hotels and restaurants, where the numbers of workers increased by over 17 million across the decade of which well over 11 million were concentrated in retail trade alone. In general, wholesale and retail trade (i.e., after excluding hotels and restaurants) increased their share in overall non-agricultural employment from less than 19 per cent in 1993-1994 to over 21 per cent in 2004 in contrast to manufacturing whose share was reduced from 32 per cent to 27 per cent. For women the expansion of wholesale trade seems to have had a displacing influence with the number of women workers being practically halved from an already low 241,000 in 1993-1994 to 116,000 in 2004. In the increasingly crowded sub-sector of retail trade however, women more or less maintained their share of a little less than 15 per cent of the employment in the 1990s which tapered somewhat to 14 per cent by 2004. In absolute terms the numbers of women workers in retail trade increased by over 1.3 million across the full decade. From the occupational data, it appears that most of such increases are spread over the supportive functions of gathering, production, or processing for retail trade or among the itinerant vendors. This is why the number of women workers in the category of merchants, shopkeepers, and so on, did not register any significant increase. As noted in the NSSO's report on employment in the informal sector, four fifths of all non-agricultural workers engaged in wholesale or retail trade and also hotels and restaurants in 1999-2000 belonged to the informal sector alone—a clear indication of the insecure and poor quality of the employment in the one sector that has shown the most remarkable growth in employment terms.[68] It therefore seems that although gross value added (GVA) in the major sector of wholesale and retail trade and including hotels and restaurants did increase in the 1990s, it is unlikely that the gains so made are evenly distributed. While no doubt the increased GVA is indicative of a relative increase in the volume and value of commodities commanded by particularly the large merchants, traders, and even perhaps that segment of the growing large scale retailers (where the dividing line between wholesale and retail trade becomes blurred), it is the petty retail segment whose expansion is driven by the growing scarcity of wage employment in agriculture as well as manufacturing. And it is in the expanded segment of petty retailing, where the overwhelming majority of women workers in trade have become concentrated.

The larger volume of commodities being traded by merchants is also reflected in the expansion of employment in transport, storage and communications, particularly in the segment of land transport, where the bulk of the increase is both urban and male oriented. As such, the additional 140,000 jobs for women in the whole sector accounted for even less than 2 per cent of the overall additions to employment in the sector. Similarly, even in finance, insurance, real estate and business services whose growing importance is a universal feature of globalization, the insignificant increase of jobs for women constituted just 10 per cent of the increases in overall employment in the sector. Clearly, women workers have not been the beneficiaries of expansion in wholesale trade, transport and finance, since all three display a downward trend in female share of employment. Even in communications, which would include some of the IT enabled services, women's share of employment has declined indicating once again that there are losses in other sub-segments within the broader rubric of communications.

Overall, taking all service sector categories together, the share of women in the increased employment between 1993-1994 and 2004 was a little over 16 per cent. If one includes construction in services, then their share was a little over 14 per cent. Whichever way it is viewed, the net conclusion remains that the expansion of service sector employment has contributed little towards leveling the gender imbalance in terms of access to employment even within the more mass employing service industries.

Some Increases in Employment for Educated Women

The notable exceptions to the general trend of persistently low shares for women in employment in service industries are education, medical and health services where women's absolute employment as well as their share of employment in the sectors has increased in substantial terms. The increase of over 2 million women's jobs in education, accounting for over 61 per cent of total additional employment in education, is perhaps of the greatest significance, especially with education increasing its share of female service sector employment from 18 per cent in 1993-1994 to 21 per cent in 1999-2000 to 24 per cent in 2004. On a smaller scale, the addition of 730,000 jobs for women in medical and health services accounted for 44 per cent of the additional employment in this sub-sector, bringing up the share of health and medical services from around 4 per cent of women's service sector employment in 1993-1994 to 7 per cent in 2004.

Since in both education and medical services the expansion of women's employment has gone hand in hand with an expanded presence of the private sector, it lends some credence to the argument that under liberalization some employment opportunities have opened up for sections of educated women; however, in the absence of information regarding the conditions of work and wages among these sections, a stamp of unqualified approval is perhaps unwarranted. This is particularly so in a context where over 47 per cent of urban women workers in education and 37 per cent in rural areas were found to be working in the informal sector in 1999-2000. Anyone who is familiar with the proliferating teaching shops in urban areas would know that at least in a sizable number of them women workers including teachers are paid less than the statutory minimum wage for unskilled workers and often even below the market wages for industrial workers. In the subsector of health and medical services, the consistent increases in numbers of women workers is partially explained by female domination in nursing, but in fact nurses constituted only 40 per cent of women workers in the subsector and actually registered a decline in absolute numbers between 1999-2000 and 2004. Obviously the known expansion in the number of women doctors at one end, and perhaps sweepers at the other end, were able to ensure that the number of women workers continued to increase in the subsector. More importantly, despite the increase in share of education and health from 2 per cent to 4 per cent of the total female workforce, the proportions are obviously too small to be other than at the margins of aggregate female employment.

Running alongside the increasing numbers and proportions of women in the higher services such as education and health, the class of women professional, technical and related workers increased their numbers fairly significantly across the decade as per the occupational data. Nevertheless, going by the same occupational figures, it is quite clear that the bulk of India's women workers, that is, more than 91 per cent are clearly concentrated in forms of manual work in agriculture and industry as well as services. Further, the decline in the aggregate (rural + urban) work participation rate for women by 15 points (from 283 per thousand in 1993-1994 to 268 in 2004) and the fact that 26 per cent of women workers are confined to solely subsidiary status employment, are both testimony to the fact that overall women's employment has been placed under severe pressure in absolute as well as relative terms. In such a context, discourses and arguments that privilege some increases in service-sector employment of sections of educated women while ignoring the compulsions and trajectories governing the employment or unemployment, of the majority are not only misleading but display a class bias detrimental to the interests of the majority of women.

Finally, it remains to be pointed out that even within the service sector, the base of employment remains concentrated in manual labour oriented petty retail trade, personal services, and construction, which together constitute 54 per cent of women's employment in services and 50 per cent of total employment in services (and if one adds transport in which a sizable pool of manual labour is involved, it would be around 64 per cent of total employment in services). The increased role of services in both men's and women's employment thus carries within it a far greater load of manual service activity based in the low-end marginalized and poor-income sectors than the far smaller weight of segments such as IT services. Such a process of servicization can hardly be touted as indicative of a developmental leap. Further, all such developments have to be located in the broader context in which the vast reservoirs of labour surplus are being pushed around and crowded into the low end segments, some in retail trade, some in construction, and some in agriculture, all of which provides evidence of the low distributional potential of the growth of the more high end white collared services of which call centres are a part.

PRIMARY SURVEY OF WOMEN WORKERS IN CALL CENTRES

The first company that started offshore call centre operations in the Delhi region was the US owned multinational finance company, GE Capital. GE Capital established a large unit in Gurgaon (on the border of Delhi) in 1996, for provision of various back-office services for its own operations across the world, marking the beginning of the call centre industry in and around Delhi or the National Capital Region (NCR). They offered salaries for call centre work that were a quarter of what was paid to less qualified workers in the United States, but would be considered relatively attractive for student graduates in India. Students who were truly fluent in English were obviously preferred and the company drew graduates with private school backgrounds, initially from the somewhat westernized upper middle class, who could easily flow into the cultural requirements for servicing American customers; however, given the fact that the company was shifting operations to India on a large scale, requiring recruitment of over 5,000 employees within the space of a few years, its labour requirement could not be met by the local upper middle class alone. Neither was the thin segment of those who would undertake such work only for pocket money sufficient as a source of labour supply.

And so recruitment for the Gurgaon unit of GE Capital was also undertaken in several other towns across the country. A larger pool of young graduates whose employment needs were of a more essential nature, and who therefore included less affluent layers of the middle class, also entered the industry. Since the form of work was completely new and as no local training institutions existed, initially workers were sent to the United States for training by the company.[69] As a result, in these initial years, early entrants and quick learners would rapidly advance their careers into becoming team leaders and trainers, which spread the word that there were possibilities of rapid career advance in this field. Following the company's reported success in cutting costs by some 40 per cent to 50 per cent through offshoring major aspects of their business processing and back-office operations to India, other such multinational finance companies began operations in similar fashion. Such units, called 'captive' units since they service only their own operations, despite being small in number, employed around 15,000 in the Delhi-Gurgaon-Noida region in 2003.[70] Their establishment was followed in quick succession by several Indian IT-enabled BPO service companies (also known as vendors) who sought outsourced back-office business from American and British companies. For these activities, venture capital funding was sometimes raised within the United States through cross-border collaborative partnerships. Numbering over forty by 2003, Indian owned IT-enabled BPO service providers employed roughly another 30,000 in the region. Apart from the Indian companies, foreign-owned MNC contract service providers, or multinational BPO companies, have entered the region and employed another 5,000. Captive MNC units, Indian-owned BPO units and foreign-owned BPO units together had over 50,000 employees in the NCR and accounted for close to one-third of the employment all over India in IT-enabled services in 2003.[71] According to company reports, women constituted between 35 per cent and 40 per cent of their workforce.

Our primary survey of women working in such units, primarily in call centre functions, conducted from November 2002 to July 2003, covered a sample of fifty employees, working in thirteen units. Twenty-five of them were working in Indian-owned BPOs, thirteen in MNC captive units and twelve in MNC BPOs. Not surprisingly, given the newness of the industry, two-thirds of the workers had been employed in this form of work for less than two years, a little less than one-half had been engaged for less than a year and only one had worked for five years in full.

Nature of Work

These workers were delivering live telephony-based or e-mail based services to customers of a variety of businesses located primarily in the United States and the United Kingdom. Since the time difference between India and these countries amounts to close to twelve hours, call centre workers here have to work primarily at night. Only one employee was working on a regular day shift. All others were working during or into the night. The beginning of their shifts varied from any time between 3 p.m. in the afternoon to 2 a.m. in the middle of the night. Accordingly, their shifts ended at times varying from midnight to 10 a.m. or 11 a.m. on the next day. Twenty-two of the fifty surveyed workers worked on extended shifts, eleven for nine-hour shifts, nine in shifts ranging from nine-and-a-half to ten hours, one for twelve hours and one for fourteen hours. Although, according to Indian labour laws, employing women for night work is still technically banned, the government has allowed it in the IT industry through a special dispensation (1998).

Since most of the processes are voice-based, the first requirement demanded of the workers at the time of recruitment was the ability to speak English in the accents of the country to which the service is being provided. Thus, graduate level knowledge of English was not a sufficient precondition for employment. Such knowledge had to necessarily include what is termed a 'neutral accent', that is, the absence of any marked influence of Indian languages on the pronunciation of English. In fact, any applicant with a non-neutral accent is rejected outright at the recruiting stage. The *first* training task of all the call centre workers surveyed involved learning to speak with either *American* or *British* accents. Additionally, they were made to memorize some general features and cultural signage of the concerned country. Generally some minimal typing skills and basic computer knowledge are also required, although these could be acquired during training also. Most of them (60 per cent) had to *change* their names and were given *English names* for their actual call centre operations.

At a broad level, the concrete functions (called processes) performed were making outbound calls (mainly sales talk including announcements of special facilities, or for collections of dues and so on), and receiving and replying to inbound calls or queries from customers. More than half of the workers (54 per cent) were involved in processes for banking, finance and insurance companies, 10 per cent for telecommunications, close to another 10 per cent for transport industries and the remaining 26 per cent were involved in marketing and customer services for miscellaneous manufactured products.

The specific nature of the processes that the call centre workers had to undertake varied on the basis of the company and product of the purchaser of services. While in most cases it was fairly simple, as in the case of billing, collections, or provision of account details to credit card or bank account holders, in some processes more complex operations may be required.

An example of a somewhat more complex operation was reported by an employee from a multinational service company, working on a process for a mobile phone company in the United States. Training for this particular process took around three weeks. After training she was put to work with telephone headphones and microphone in front of a computer terminal. Customers in the United States would call after buying a phone and ask how to make it operational. The worker had to first ask for the details of the type of phone and the code numbers displayed on the phone itself and the name, address and payment details (credit card number) of the customer. These would have to be typed into the computerized database of the phone company. Credit card rating had to be ascertained from another database, and a password for the customer's account would then be agreed upon and typed in. Following this the code numbers required to activate the phone would appear on the computer screen and had to be read out to the customer, who could then punch them into the mobile and activate the phone. Similarly, if a customer called to change any details (such as an address), the changes would have to be typed into the customer's account in the database. Customers would call in with several different types of queries, which had to be answered by the call centre worker as per the given company's policy. For example, in the case of the mobile phone company, if a customer called in to report theft of the phone, account details, including the customer's particular password, had to be asked for and typed in to access the account on the computer. Instructions would then have to be fed in and sent to the company's technical office computer so that the connection could be jammed. An example of a different type of query was when a lady called to say that her phone had been disconnected because she had been unable to pay her bills because of a period of unemployment. With a new job, her salary would be available after 3 weeks and could she avail her connection on promise of payment then? The call centre worker of course had to say no.

While in the above example, the worker was expected to actually personally interact, in most processes, workers were not allowed to deviate from a given script. In such cases, they typed in the customer's queries as they came in and read out the reply that would appear on the screen. Such a practice of reading from a given script was also the norm for outbound calls and required less process training. On the other hand, it was reported that there are also other services such as computer troubleshooting which involved more intelligent application. Such technical processes are, however, less significant in terms of number of employees, require much higher qualifications than the average call centre worker's and are generally not handled by women. None of the surveyed workers were involved in such a process. As might be expected, workers in almost all processes reported that frequently customers would be abusive both for inbound call work as well as outbound. While new workers tended to get shocked and intimidated by such abuse, older hands became inured.

Constant Monitoring to Intensify the Labour Process

While it is difficult to see the form of work as little more than a new form of clerical work, the workers are given the designation of customer care *executives*. This is similar to the current practice of private and foreign banks in India, where several forms of clerical posts are given the designation of officer or 'junior executive'. In the case of banks, such a designation has an important function of excluding such employees from the category of workman covered by the various judicial awards for bank employees which grew out of powerful union organization.[72] In the case of call centres, which have no history of trade union organization here, it is probably designed to vest the job with higher status to make it attractive for aspirants from a higher layer of the middle class than that section which has traditionally supplied clerical staff.

Outbound calling was of course, continuous, but the experience of the workers dealing with inbound calls too was that calls came in continuously without break. While for both outbound and inbound calls their interaction has to be kept to a minute or so in order to field larger numbers of calls, even the longer operations, such as the one described above, were expected to not exceed three minutes. Across the board, the productivity of a call centre worker is determined by the number of calls she manages to handle while maintaining appropriate 'quality' levels. As the reduction of labour costs is the prime driver of the expansion of the industry, *acute* pressure is exercised on each individual worker to deal with more and more calls every day or rather night.

Generally, the call centre workers function in groups known as teams having ten to fifteen members with a supervisor designated as team leader. Monitoring and supervision is a *constant* activity. Workers reported that their supervisors and managers would listen in on their calls while the number of calls were recorded by the computer and constantly checked. Such close monitoring would result in several workers being repeatedly and frequently humiliated and harassed, particularly to push up the number of their calls. A common management practice was a *public* display of the daily output of each worker on charts along with their individual ratings and remarks. Two tea breaks of 15 minutes and one lunch break of half-an-hour was the norm, with strict regulation of the time spent, which is recorded on the computer where the worker logs in after each break. One worker reported that in her unit, if a worker logs in even a few seconds late, she is accorded a deficit point in her daily or weekly chart and warned. Deficit points are similarly awarded for shortfalls in terms of productivity. Some workers complained that productivity targets were awarded individually and even the relatively faster and 'efficient' workers were pushed into even faster work by being given increasing targets. If these higher than average targets were not met, she would be given deficit points even though her individual productivity level remained higher than others. Such deficit points had great coercive power, since the accumulation of more than three could even lead to termination of employment, while the system of display of ratings on public charts generated both individual competitive pressure and a constant fear of humiliation in front of co-workers.

The *premium* placed on productivity through intensification of the individual labour process is evidenced from the close monitoring and supervision systems that are a universal hallmark of the call centre industry. Where individual rewards and incentives are used to spur labour intensification, it was reported that those who are not able to process calls quickly tend to be fired within a short while. Such pressures were being exercised even as several of the units were still functioning below capacity, that is, all their established call centre 'seats' or 'stations' may not be occupied or in use.

Formal but Insecure Employment Relations

Although the hand of the labour law enforcement machinery had not as yet touched call centres, generally employment conditions followed the legal norms of the organized sector. Around three-fourths of the surveyed workers reported that they had 'permanent' jobs (although through renewable employment contracts), as well as provident fund benefits. In the BPO units, the few who were casual or temporary were mostly employed for a specific process, leaving the employers with the option of dropping them if that particular contract came to an end or was withdrawn. But even the 'permanent' employees in BPO units were sometimes sent on furlough if the contract for the process they were working on was withdrawn. Redeployment in another process is not guaranteed and cases were reported when 'permanent' employees had been asked to leave where redeployment did not take place within a month.

Well over one-half of the surveyed workers were covered by medical insurance, and over two-thirds received bonus, albeit the latter being mostly linked to individual output and productivity. While service conditions included formal earned and casual leave entitlements, leave appeared to be a somewhat vexed issue as permission was not always easy to obtain. Several workers reported that prior permission had to be obtained for even casual leave. Table 5.10 gives the percentages of workers of different categories obtaining benefits in addition to their salaries.

All the workers save one reported that cab transport is provided by the company from their doorstep to workplace and back. In fact these jeep cabs, each ferrying some eight to ten call centre workers, have become a noticeable feature on the roads of Delhi. While such transport provision is clearly a compulsion of the odd timings of work when no public transport is generally available, and is a legal necessity for employers of women for night work, it has played a role in making the job possible and even attractive for many. Such transport has enabled several college and university students to enter the industry while pursuing their studies, but as reported by some workers, combining fulltime call centre work with study was extremely difficult and soon a choice had to be made between the two.

Veneer of Glamour

Lunch and tea/coffee was provided to employees by the management in all the units covered by the survey. Particularly in the larger and more prominent units (both MNC as well as Indian-owned), such catering came from upmarket hotels or restaurant chains. An attractive ambience in the cafeterias and in-house facilities for recreation (gyms,

Table 5.10 Percentages of workers receiving various benefits by contract status

Employment contract	Workers		PF		Medical benefit		Leave (EL/CL)		Bonus	
	No.	%	No.	%	No.	%	No.	%	No.	%
Permanent	38	76	38	100	25	66	31	86	28	74
Temporary	6	12	1	17	2	33	3	50	3	50
Casual	6	12	1	17	2	33	4	67	3	50
All workers	50	100	40	80	29	58	38	76	34	68

lounges with television and music facilities as well as computer facilities for private use) was generally provided by the managements of all the call centres. Such facilities have gone a long way in making employment in call centres appear glamorous, or what one commentator describes as the 'Portrayal of "work as fun" and "workplace as yet another campus"' in the industry.[73]

Nevertheless, several workers had already felt the weight of stagnation, as the early experiences of quick promotions and career advance have tapered off. This tapering off was most marked in the MNC that had established the first call centre in the region. One of the methods adopted by workers of trying to escape such stagnation was to shift to another company. At least 20 per cent of the workers surveyed by us who were at the time of the survey working in other companies, had worked for some time in this first company. They had left that company and entered the second batch consisting of the newer captive or the large corporatized service providers (Indian and foreign), because of what one worker called 'the oppressive atmosphere and stagnation' in their earlier company. Yet even in the Indian-owned and other multinational BPOs, employees obviously burn out quickly. At least five of the surveyed workers have left their jobs shortly after the survey, confirming newspaper reports that employee turnover in Indian call centres is quite high. Of course, according to a report commissioned by the industry's association Nasscom, the employee turnover in India is still lower than the international average.

Trends in Call Centre Wages and Comparison with Other White Collared Service Sectors

The salaries of the surveyed workers ranged from Rs 5,000 to Rs 20,000 per month, but there appeared to be no uniformity in starting salaries. Generally, in the units that were established in the first phase, that is, 1996 to 2000, starting salaries stood between Rs 7,500 and 8,000. But in the later batch of units, while a few seem to have maintained the mid-1990s entry wages, others (including some large software majors), have started engaging new employees at Rs 5,000 per month. Even the higher-end entry wages given above, are reported to be lower than what was paid to the first batches of employees recruited in the early 1990s and who had been sent to the United States for training before the fullscale establishment of the first unit in Gurgaon. These first recruits of the U.S. owned MNC, generally with the same graduate qualifications, started on monthly salaries of at least Rs 12,000,[74] however, the starting wages of the same company were Rs 8,000 according to our survey. Thus, along with the *expansion* of the industry, despite its short history of less than ten years here, a *downward* movement of the wages of call centre operatives had already made an appearance. With rapid expansion of actual exports, the number of units and investments have also expanded rapidly, not all of whom have been able to find sufficient custom. Unutilized capacities have led to an already observed tendency to lower the price of call centre services. Companies anticipating high profit margins inevitably move towards lowering of wages. Corporate propaganda generally assumes that small companies dogged by lack of expertise (referred to as 'reckless startups') alone are the ones 'who are responsible for irrational pricing behaviours'.[75] Our survey, however, shows that even some premier corporates (with presumably rational pricing behaviours) are among the units paying the lowest wages. Table 5.11 illustrates salary trends in call centres.

Although most of the workers with monthly salaries between Rs 5,000 and Rs 10,000, were simple call centre operators, one of them had the designation of a technical support engineer with a salary of Rs 9,500. (She had a graduate degree in Mathematics, had been trained in hardware maintenance within the company which was one of the first Indian-owned BPO service providers), and was the only worker in our survey who was working a day shift. Of the five who earned a salary of Rs 15,000, three were in supervisory posts. Among the other two, one had advanced computer skills, and had earlier been a faculty member of a computer educational institute in eastern India, while the other performed e-mail tasks as well as voice-based interaction. The lone worker who had a salary of 20.000 (the highest in our sample) gave her designation as a credit card analyst in a major multinational banking corporation and had been working in the company for three years.

Table 5.11 Salary trends in call centres

Salary range	Surveyed Workers No.	%	No. of workers by duration of work experience 2½ to 5 yrs	1 to 2 yrs	Less than 1 yr
5,000 – 8,500	17	34	1	5	11
9,000 – 10,000	17	34	2	6	9
11,000 – 14,000	10	20	1	8	1
15,000	5	10	2	3	-
20,000	1	2	1	-	-
All	50	100	7	22	21

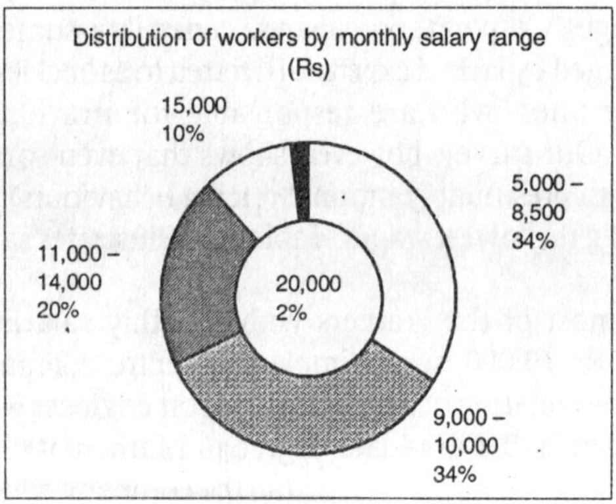

Figure 5.5(*a*): Distribution of workers by monthly salary range

The average monthly wage worked out to around Rs 10,200 although the majority of the workers (68 per cent) were earning salaries ranging from Rs 5,000 to Rs 10,000 [See Figure 5.5(*a*)]. Among them, close to three-fifths (20), were beginners, with less than a year's work experience [See Figure 5.5(*b*)]. Of the remaining 14 in the Rs 5,000-10,000 salary range, three had been working for above two years, while eleven had been working for between one and two years.

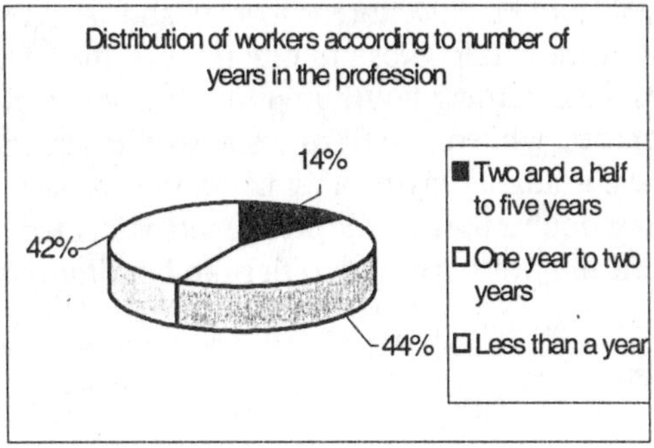

Figure 5.5(*b*): Distribution of workers according to the number of years in the profession

In comparison, the starting salary of what is designated 'lower division clerk' in the government or public sector banks requiring graduate qualifications (but not necessarily private schooling), stood at around Rs 6,500. In the few premier private corporate offices, where recruitment tends to be more exclusive and generally requires secretarial diplomas or degrees, clerical and secretarial salaries may be higher and roughly equivalent to the call centre wages revealed by the survey. In most of the private sector, however, starting salaries for clerical work tend to be much lower and generally vary between Rs 2,000 and Rs 5,000. While the starting wages of the surveyed call centre workers were at least double clerical wages in private sector offices in Delhi, one-fifth of them were earning less or equal to a 'lower division clerk' in government service. Most of them, including those in supervisory posts, had salaries roughly equivalent to trained secretaries in some premier corporate offices.

Among other professional occupations with a similar or even higher qualification base, central government grades for primary school teachers start at over Rs 8,500, and for the more technically trained sections such as nurses, at Rs 10,000. But for both school teachers and nurses, private sector wages (apart from the relatively smaller number of institutions following government grades) generally tend to vary between Rs 2,000 and Rs 5,000 for the former, and between Rs 3,000 and Rs 6,000 for the latter. Close to one-third of the surveyed call centre workers were earning less than primary school teachers with government grades, while three-fifths were earning less than nurses with government grades. On the other hand, the average call centre wage was at least double the average private sector for clerks, teachers and nurses in the majority of private offices and institutions in Delhi.

Workers' Profiles

The youthful character of the call centre workforce was evident from the fact that all the workers fell within a 19-to-30 age group, with more than three-fourths being not more than 25 years old. While around 16 per cent were below 21 years, 64 per cent were between 21 and 25 years old. The average age of the workers stood at 23 years, which is quite distinctly less than that of call centre workers in the United States and the United Kingdom.[76] Given the age profile, quite naturally, an overwhelming majority of workers (92 per cent) turned out to be unmarried. The few in our sample who were married, had no children. Although some workers did report that there were a few widowed or separated women in their units—particularly at the level of team leaders—none were netted in our survey. Of the eight workers in the age group 27 to 30 years, only one had been in the industry for less than a year; the other seven had all been working for over two years, with the solitary 30-year-old having been in the industry for 5 years.

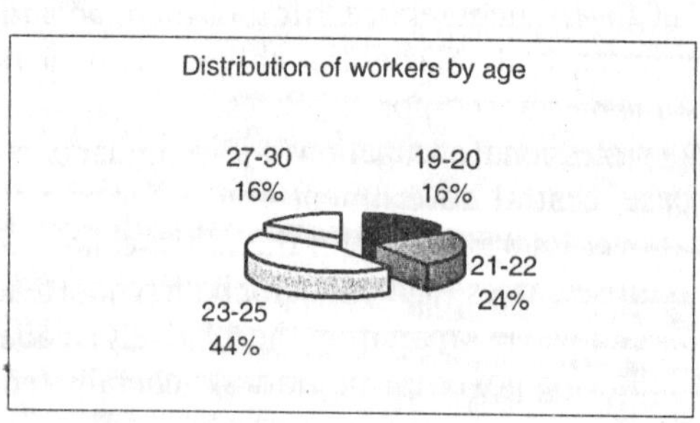

Figure 5.6(*a*): Distribution of call centre workers by age

It seems quite clear that the young are preferred and 25 years is the usual age limit at the time of recruitment. What is interesting is that in the slightly older age cohort (between 27 and 30 years) too, the majority (six out of eight), were unmarried. It would seem that as yet call centre jobs have not drawn many married women, and employers themselves prefer to hire unmarried women. Figure 5.6(*a*) gives the distribution of call centre workers by age and Figure 5.6(*b*) gives the distribution by educational qualifications.

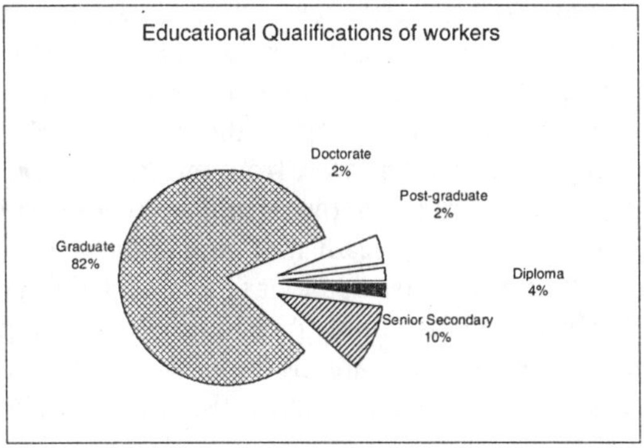

Figure 5.6(*b*): Distribution of workers according to educational qualifications

The educational qualifications asked for in the call centre industry is generally a graduation degree, and the overwhelming majority (more than four-fifths) of the workers were graduates, although two had post-graduate degrees one of whom had a PhD. Another two held professional diplomas (both in hotel management). The remaining four had only senior secondary level qualifications, although all of them said that they were registered for graduation.

As the prime requirement for service is verbal fluency in English, it should come as no surprise that an overwhelming 96 per cent of the workers had had private schooling, the other 4 per cent having studied in special English medium central government schools established for children of government servants and armed forces. English medium school education is sustained primarily by private school education, and therefore has an inbuilt degree of larger investment in acquiring the 'skill' of fluency in English. Thus, it is not just the certificate or degree qualification that is demanded, but also a more expensive or privileged institutional and class background narrowing access to call centre employment to a relatively small section of the middle class that has had access to and paid for private schooling.

Social and Economic Background

An investigation into the social background of the surveyed workers revealed some striking features and characteristics. First, all the workers had urban backgrounds. Although two of them gave their origins as rural, both of them had spent most of their lives in urban areas.[77] Almost half, that is, 48 percent, were from metropolitan cities, while the others were from a range of towns and smaller cities in various parts of the country. Second, the fathers of most of the workers belonged to the salaried or professional middle class, and a little over one fourth were from the business community [See Figure 5.7(*a*)]. While half of their mothers were housewives, among the working mothers, the single largest occupation was of school teachers [See Figure 5.7(*b*)].[78]

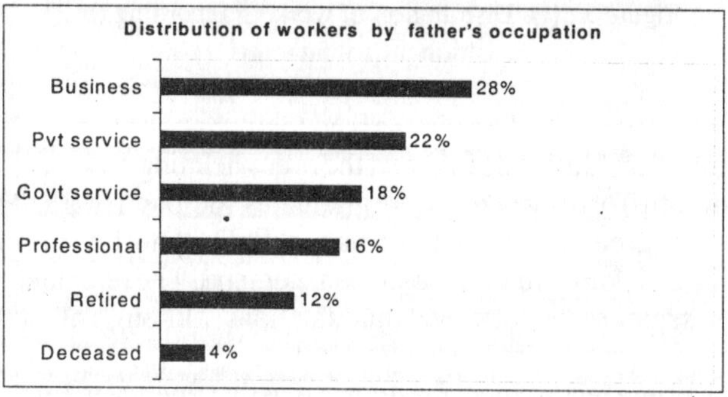

Figure 5.7(*a*) Distribution of Workers by Father's Occupation

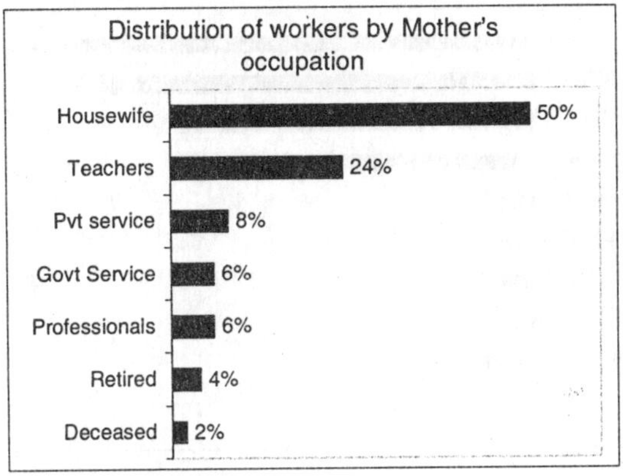

Figure 5.7(*b*) Distribution of Workers by Mother's Occupation

Third, although most of them came from college or university educated families, with just 7 percent of the fathers and 24 per cent of the mothers having educational qualifications of only school level, top elite education and occupations were few and far between. The educational qualifications of the parents of the workers are presented in Figure 5.8(*a*) and 5.8(*b*).

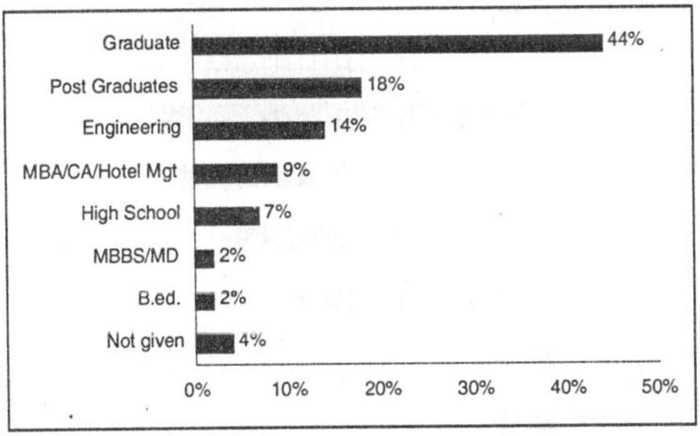

Figure 5.8(*a*) Distribution of workers by father's education

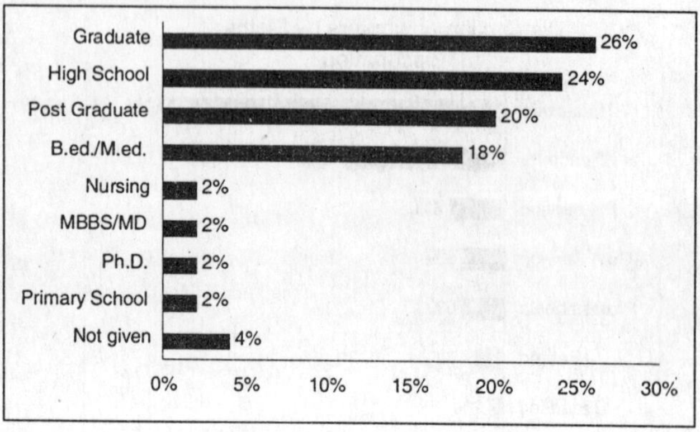

Figure 5.8(b) Distribution of workers by mother's education

Fourth, although many of the workers were either unable or unwilling to provide the incomes of their parents, apparently, only a few of them come from the wealthier sections of the middle class. Figure 5.9 shows the percentage proportions of 35 of the workers who did provide such details. As may be seen the parents of the majority (54 per cent) have incomes ranging from Rs 7,500 to Rs 15,000 per month. For many then, call centre wages would be greater than what their parents were earning.

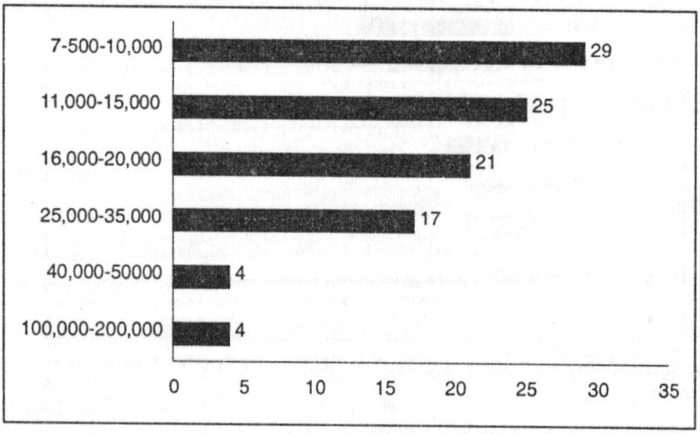

Fgure 5.9 Distribution of workers by monthly parental incomes

The fact that the majority of the call centre workers belonged to the middle rungs of the middle class is further underscored by the fact that few also came from families with property based incomes for which all except one worker did provide details. Parents of most of them (78 per cent) owned only their own residential house or no property at all, while 12 per cent came from families owning some agricultural land (Fig 5.10). However, the consumer durables owned by them was indicative of a relatively higher consumption category, in line with the style of living that has acquired a wider base among the urban middle classes under liberalization (Fig 5.11).

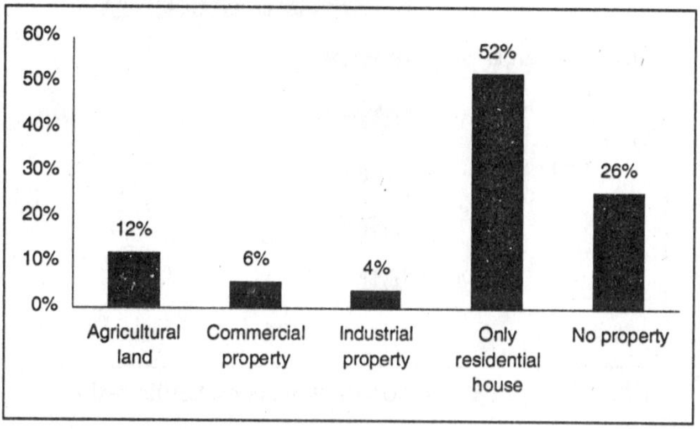

Fig 5.10. Property assets of parents of workers

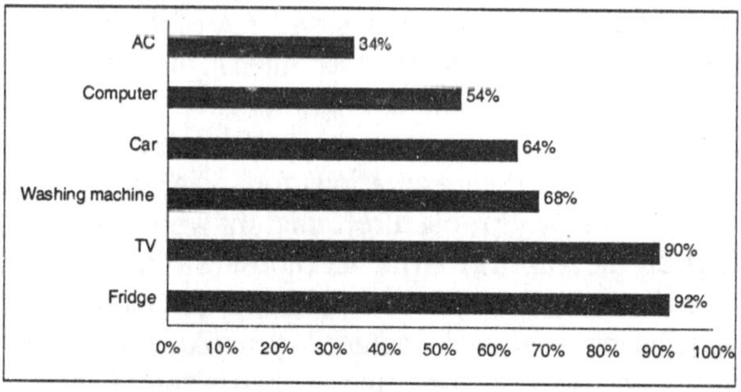

Figure 5.11 Consumer durables owned by parents

Significant Presence of Single Women Migrants in Call centre Workforce

A surprising finding of the survey was that the majority of the workers were not of local origin (here 'local' includes Delhi, Noida, Gurgaon), that is, their families were not living or working in the Delhi region (see Fig 5.12). Some 64 per cent of the workers came from outside Delhi, of which about half had come to Delhi initially as students in the three central government universities located here.

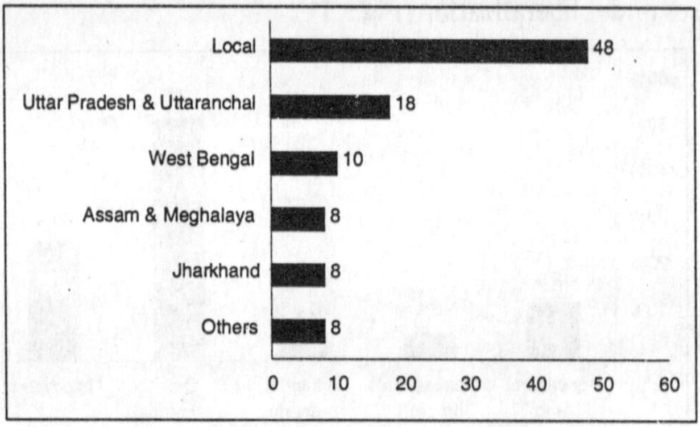

Figure 5.12 Distribution of workers by family residence

But the other half, that is, around 32 per cent of all workers had not even been college students in Delhi, and had come here directly for employment in the call centre industry. A few of the workers reported that they had been interviewed and recruited in their home state. While most of the workers including migrants gave 'money' and 'wider experience' as the reasons for taking to call centre employment, a few actually articulated their aspirations for social independence. For example, for one 24-year-old direct migrant who came and took the job at age 22, the reason given for her choosing to become a call centre worker was because the job 'was in Delhi, far away from home—wanted to be independent.' Another 24 year old, who had entered the industry a few months ago wrote that she had 'wanted to be in a different stream, get into the Indian Army, but couldn't. Didn't want to stay in the same place', and 'circumstance' led her to take the first job away from home to come her way.

The convergence on the metropolis of such young girls with independent aspirations and individual motivations is a social phenomenon that has obviously acquired some impetus from the emergence of the call centre employment. It is evident that even our small sample of 21 direct migrants hailed from as many as 16 towns and cities dispersed over 9 states of India. According to a rough estimate, there would be anywhere between 4,000 to 7,000 young and unmarried women migrants who have come to the region to work in call centres alone. Although not statistically significant in terms of the overall population, the numbers acquire somewhat greater importance in the context of the fact only 46,628 women were recorded as having migrated to Delhi for any kind of employment in 1991.[79]

A relatively greater freedom from family based social restrictions among the migrant call centre workers is also a special feature. Only two of the migrants among the surveyed workers were residing with family relations, the others mostly living independently in rented accommodation along with other similarly young and single working women, while a few were staying in hostels. Thus call centres have obviously brought in a new stream of educated, young and single female migrants into metropolitan Delhi with aspirations for a degree of social and economic independence.

The presence of young single women migrants in Delhi was earlier somewhat confined to the profession of nursing, and nurses were largely drawn from one state, Kerala. To a much lesser extent, from the late 1980s, similarly young and single migrant women could also be found among factory workers in the region, again largely from the state of Kerala.[80] Studies on domestic servants in Delhi, who have increasingly become feminized, have also pointed to female led immigration for domestic service. Among them the proportions of married women are perhaps greater, and they come from a wider range of regions than nurses.[81] Among the more middle class occupations, employment based single women migrants may also be found among teachers and in government service, but generally not in significant proportions. Across all categories of such single migrants, some of course would return to their native regions, but many have no doubt become embedded in the social fabric of the city.[82] Of course, the overwhelming majority of women migrants to Delhi, come as social attachments to their menfolk and remain in the status of economic dependents.[83]

Another discovery was the fact that while expectedly the mother tongue of more than half (28) was Hindi, surprisingly Bengalis outnumbered the Punjabis in our survey sample,[84] and while around three fifths were Hindus, again a surprisingly large proportion were Christian (13). Not one of the workers was Muslim. Such proportions cannot and ought not to be taken as representative. Nevertheless, it is not unreasonable to infer that while the proportions of Christians in call centres are significantly higher than their share in the population, Muslim girls are not generally entering call centre work.

Table 5.12 Distribution of workers by their mother tongue

Mother tongue	No.	Hindu	Christian	Sikh	Other faiths
Hindi	28	19	8	-	1
Bengali	8	7	1	-	-
Punjabi	6	3	-	3	..
Malayalam	2	-	2	-	-
Others	6	3	2	-	1
All languages	50	32	13	3	2

Impact of Call Centre Work on Health: The Issue of Night Work

Despite the youth of the workers, and despite the fact that most had not been working for very long, more than half the workers (56 per cent) were already experiencing health disorders due to the nature and pressures of their form of work as well as the timings. Close to one third were suffering from sleep disorders, one fifth had digestive problems, mostly hyper-acidity, while a quarter complained of headaches, backaches or general bodyache. Such disorders were not necessarily mutually exclusive.

What perhaps marks out the prevalence of such health disorders among call centre workers from the disorders experienced by workers in other industries is not only the fact that they are appearing amongst such a youthful workforce, but also that they highlight the ill effects of night work on health. This is an issue which has not received the attention it deserves in the several layers of debate and discussion on the issue of night work for women that has come to the forefront under globalization. In general, there appears to be an ascendance of the view that there should be no ban on night work for women on the grounds that it prevents women from gaining equal access to employment opportunities, particularly those forms of employment that have received a growth impetus from globalization. If the experience of call centre workers in India could be taken as an indicator, it appears that night work does cause health problems whose long term implications are still to be fully played out. What can at this point be said is that among other things, the adverse impact of night work on the health of call centre workers in India has contributed to the relatively high turnover or early burnout in an employment category that is otherwise projected as privileged and of high quality.

SOME ISSUES OF CURRENT DEBATE

The rapid growth of software and IT enabled services in India has led to an illusion that the country can jump stages of development and arrive at a higher stage. Opening of employment of avenues for women in call centres is viewed by many as being along such a trajectory. However, data show that the employment of women is still concentrated in agriculture, and low end manual labour in services accounts for the lion's share of women's service sector employment. The proportions of both men and women employed in IT and related services is too small to have much influence on the overall employment patterns and on development in such a large economy as India.

Within the export oriented IT services, which have seen the maximum growth impetus, an over dependence on outsourcing or offshoring from western countries has led to it being dominated by night work and employees have to undergo a degree of cultural degradation to affect accents of the countries where service are being delivered. The worldwide trend in call centres has been of extreme pressure on productivity and maximization of monitoring—all enabled by technology. This same was observed in the primary survey of call centres workers in Delhi. However, the share of women in call centre employment is less than in western countries—probably, because, of night work. Nevertheless, call centres have drawn in a section of new young unmarried middle class women who come mostly from other urban areas to metros such as Delhi and who live independently of their families. Their aspirations for social independence seem to be finding some social space through the expansion and availability of call centre employment.

At another level, despite the perception that call centres pay high salaries with several promotional avenues, the study has pointed to a distinct trend of stagnation among many, while their salaries, although higher than most private sector services, seem to be showing a tendency to decline. The combination of night work and high productivity demands also seem to have adverse effects of the health of even a class of workers who otherwise have more privileged backgrounds and social and economic status than the majority of Indian women workers who are concentrated in forms of manual labour even in services. Such features of call centre work foreground the possibilities of the emergence of organization among Indian call centre workers in the coming years. Recently, at the instance of some central trade unions putting forward the view that call centres should be covered by factory legislation and should not be exempted from labour laws, a debate has begun regarding these aspects. In response to the trade union view, call centre employers' groups argue that their employees are so well taken care of that they do not want to associate with unions. As of now, there can be little doubt that the manner of supervision and close monitoring combined with social and lifestyle incentives at call centres have so far held back any process of independent collective organization by workers, even as individual reactions against oppressive practices have already made their appearance.

Further, the rape and murder of a night working woman employee of the back office of Hewlett Packard at Bangalore in December, 2005 has reintroduced the issue of security concerns for women undertaking night work in the call centre industry, an issue that has begun to exercise the minds of many of the call centre employees themselves and is now being taken up by the National Commission for Women (NCW). In response to the NCW's expressed concern regarding the security of women call centre workers, the view of the larger call centre employers has so far been that putting in place and stepping up of security protocols at the company level would be sufficient to deal with such security problems associated with night work. Nevertheless, the security issue is likely to keep cropping up, particularly since the transport arrangements are universally outsourced by call centres to transport companies where informal, impermanent and unregulated employer employee relations dominate. So far, call centre employers have been able to maintain a privileged position vis-à-vis all forms of regulation by government agencies on the grounds that employment is being generated. While there can be little doubt that some employment has been generated, employment statistics indicate that it is not of sufficient magnitude to warrant the extraordinary privileges (including tax exemption) that they have so far obtained. At the same time it remains to be seen as to how long call centre employees themselves will give greater importance to their apparent social status over the multilayered subordination and degradation to which they are subjected.

NOTES

1 By 1948, for example, services accounted for 48 per cent of private gross product in the United States and 56.5 per cent of full time employment. Source: C. P. Chandrashekhar, Services and the New Capitalism, in J. Ghosh and C. P.Chandrasekhar, eds., *Work and Well-Being in the Age of Finance* (New Delhi: Tulika, 2003).

2 See UNCTAD E-Commerce and Development Report, 2002 and 2003. http://www.unctad.org/Templates/Page.asp?intItemID=2641&lang=1.

3 E. Hobsbawm, The new woman. In *The Age of Empire*, 1875-1914 (New York: Vintage, 1987).

4 Ibid. Among the structural changes of the time referred to by Hobsbawm (in the context of economic concentration as capitalism entered a new stage, the tendency towards monopoly or oligopoly and the emergence of international rivalries of economies) were the advent of modern corporate organizations transforming large enterprises from shop floor to office and the emerging of a system of accountancy, with salaried executives, serving bankers, or shareholders replacing the individual managing capitalist.

5 E. Hobsbawm, *The Age of Extremes* (New York: Vintage, 1996):310.

6 In the United States the supplementary role in some places also took the form of producing for several basic consumption necessities of the

family (apart from the kitchen and child rearing) through vegetable gardens, food processing, sewing and tailoring and livestock rearing (R. M. Tyron, *Household Manufactures in the United States: 1640-1860* , quoted in H. Braverman *Labor and Monopoly Capital: The Degradation of Work in the Twentieth Century* (New York: Monthly Review Press, 1974). This was to change as industrial capital appropriated all such functions extending the commodity form to food in its semi-prepared or even fully prepared forms and as Braverman noted 'the urban rings close around the worker, and around the farmer driven from the land, and confine them within circumstances that preclude the above self-provisioning practices of the home'.

7 Just as in a preceding period more women became domestic servants. See Hobsbawm, *Age of Empire.*

8 The analysis that follows is mainly drawn from Harry Braverman's seminal work, *Labor and Monopoly Capital.*

9 As such, while they did not create the value necessary for the accumulation of capital, and their cost was drawn out of existing or potential revenue even as it was transferred to the consumer in terms of prices. Nevertheless, particularly the sales service effort was essential for the realization of surplus value embodied in the materially produced commodities.

10 'Scientific management' is associated with Frederick Taylor.

11 Braverman, *Labor and Monopoly Capital*, quoting Sidney Pollard's, *The Genesis of Modern Management*, informs us that the large-scale entrepreneur began with very limited clerical or administative staff. The Arkwrights, for example, employed only three clerks to look after 1,063 workers, nearly all of whom were paid by complicated piece rates. The small number of clerks who existed in the earlier stage of capitalism were often honoured employees, and as undeniable members of the middle class often became partner in the business.

12 For example, the *lower* grades of British clerks in the period 1850 to 1880 were paid salaries equivalent to only a small elite section of the industrial working class, a 'highly select super-aristocracy', while in the United States, in 1900, clerical employees of steam railroads and in manufacturing establishments had average annual earnings equivalent to twice that of manual workers in these industries. In contrast, by 1971, the median usual weekly earnings of full-time clerical workers in the United States was U.S. $115, compared to U.S. $117 for non–farm

labourers, U.S. $120 for operatives and U.S. $167 for craftsmen and foremen; Braverman, *Labor and Monopoly Capital*.

13 Braverman, *Labor and Monopoly Capital*, following on the analysis of P. A. Baran and P. M. Sweezy, *Monopoly Capital: An Essay on the American Economic and Social Order* (New York: Monthly Review Press, 1966).

14 Such a prescriptive analysis of the capitalist economy is associated with John Maynard Keynes.

15 In the case of the United States, Baran and Sweezy showed that government spending rose from 7.4 per cent of GNP in 1903 to 28.8 per cent in 1961, with the big leap from 9.8 per cent to 19.2 per cent taking place between 1929 and 1939.

16 'The chief mechanisms of this drain are unequal exchange in trade relations, transfer of profits, interest and dividend payments on account of foreign capital, and different kinds of unrequited exports made by the backward countries. In this last category, outflow on account of colonial administration, for example, India's payment of "Home Charges" to Britain before 1947, and other similar items are included'. Prabhat Patnaik, Political economy of underdevelopment, in *Whatever Happened to Imperialism* (New Delhi: Tulika, 1995).

17 The differences become clear from the structure of the labour force in the mid-twentieth century. Its distribution in agriculture, industry and services, respectively, were 32:41:27 in the United States (1950), 5:57:38 in the United Kingdom (1951), 20:47:33 in France (1951). As may be seen, in all the above, industry was dominant. In comparison, the ratio was 76:12:12 in India (1950), 84:7:9 in China (1952), 75:8:17 in Indonesia (1960), 86:5:9 in Kenya (1960) and 52:15:33 in Brazil (1960), which not only show the low proportion of labour in industry, but also the overwhelming weight of agriculture. What is striking is that in the developing world, services were equal if not greater in weight than industry, clearly indicating a different foundation for service sector employment. Data source: Tables 1,2,3 and 4 in T. J. Byres, Structural change, the agrarian question and the possible impact of globalization, in Ghosh and Chandrashekhar, eds., *Work and Well Being*.

18 For example, in the commercial or financial services such as banks and insurance, a critical mass to women's employment was achieved only after nationalization, and was to a great extent facilitated by it. In 1999, more than 90 per cent of women working in banks were employed in public sector banks. This is notwithstanding their low share, of less

than 14 per cent, in total bank employment. Source: Unpublished ILO sponsored study, *Equal Remuneration in India,* 2000.

19 Government of India, Ministry of Education and Social Welfare Report of the Committee on the Status of Women in India, *Towards Equality*, 1974.

20 J. Unni and U.Rani, Globalisation, information technology and service sector in India, *Indian Journal of Labour Economics* 43, 4, 2000.

21 A. Kleinecht and C.W. M. Naastepad, Much a ado about nothing? Growth, productivity and employment in the OECD's new economy. In Ghosh and Chandrashekhar, eds. *Work and Well-Being.* which provides a critical assessment of new economy theories.

22 Cox and Alm *The New Paradigm* quoted in C. P. Chandrashekhar, Services and the new capitalism in Ghosh and Chandrashekhar, eds., *Work and Well Being.*

23 Peter Schwartz and Peter Leyden, 1997, *The Long Boom: A History of the Future, 1980-2020,* www.wired.com/wired/archive/5.07/longboom_pr.html.

24 Chandrashekhar, Services and the new capitalism.

25 See for example, P. Sauve, 2000, *Trade Policy Implications of the New Economy: Preliminary Thoughts,* OECD Trade Directorate, Document TD/TC: 13, 5.

26 Arguments here drawn from Chandrashekhar, Services and the new capitalism. Despite relocation of manufacturing capacity or services by US MNCs to other countries, as mentioned by C.P. Chandrashekhar, 'evidence shows that acceleration in expansion of MNC operations has been as true of the parent firms as of their MOFAS [U.S. majority owned foreign affiliates]. This is true of both gross product and of employment . . . whether relocation occurred or not, the parents of US multinationals were making a significant and persisting contribution to overall US economic activity'.

27 P. Patnaik, Imperialism and diffusion of development, *The Retreat to Unfreedom*, p.79.

28 UNCTAD, E-Commerce and Development Report, 2002. http://www.unctad.org/Templates/Page.asp?intItemID=2641&lang=1.

29 Other services are defined in the WTO technical notes as including *(i)* communication services (telecommunications, postal and courier services); *(ii)* construction services; *(iii)* insurance services; *(iv)* financial services; *(v)* computer and information services (including news agency services); *(vi)* royalties and licence fees covering payments and receipts for the use of intangible non-financial assets and proprietary rights, such as patents, copyrights, trademarks, industrial processes and

franchises; *(vii)* other business services comprising trade-related services, operational leasing (rentals) and miscellaneous business, professional and technical services such as legal, accounting, management consulting, public relations services, advertising, market research and public opinion polling, research and development services, architectural, engineering and other technical services, agricultural, mining and on-site processing and *(viii)* personal, cultural and recreational services including audio-visual services.

30 Where travel constitutes a little less than 35% of developing countries' service exports, other business services accounts for over 23% followed by transportation accounting for another 18%. For developed countries too other business services accounted for 22% of their service exports.

31 The sub-sector with the lowest market share for developed countries (i.e., 76.9 per cent) was travel, probably owing to tourists from Northern countries coming to Southern countries. In other sub-sectors of service trade, the market share of the developed world was generally 80 per cent and above.

32 In comparison, developed countries accounted for some 64 per centof merchandise exports.

33 ILO, *Life at Work in the Information Economy*, World Employment Report 2001 (Geneva: ILO, 2001).

34 UNDP, *Human Development Report*, 1999.

35 Many of the innovations in IT came about through venture capital investment in small firms. This was also backed by financial majors since through the development of ICT, finance capital was now able to operate more easily in capital markets across the globe and in real time.

36 J. Story, The ICT revolution background paper for the ILO World Employment Report, 2001. He points out that geographically, about 75 per cent of ecommerce takes place in one country alone, that is, the United States, and successive technologies, such as semiconductors and the internet, were launched by the United States.

37 In the United States, estimates of the number of workers now vary from 2 to 7 million, working in 70,000 call centres. In the United Kingdom there are 1.6 to 2 million workers. Companies in Germany employ 65,000 and in Australia the numbers have reached 60,000. The current expansion rate is 20-30 per cent internationally, adding hundreds of thousands of workers each year. Website of World Socialist Workers, *Telephone call centres expand worldwide*, by a correspondent, 9 December 1998.

38 ILO, Geneva, *World Employment Report 2001,* Life at work in the Information Economy, and J. Somavia, *Exploring the High Road to*

Technology and Globalization (Opening Ceremony, Conference on Emerging Global Electronic Distance Learning, Tampere, 9-12 August 1999 (ILO, 1999).

39 The financial savings to businesses are clear. One study of US banks found that it costs between US $2.50 and US $3 to process a transaction within a branch. Alternatively, transactions within a call centre cost between US $175 and US $2 and Internet transactions as little as 25 cents. The finance industry has become one of the most pronounced in shifting from public offices to call centres. In the United States, the top twenty banks operate an average of twenty-three call centres each.

40 Such developments are not limited to the English-speaking world. French companies are looking to African francophone countries, such as Mauritius and Morocco, as suitable destinations for call centres. Latin America provides an obvious location for Spanish companies looking to move offshore, while even German-language call centres have been established in lower-cost locations in developing countries.

41 A. Bibby author of *Organizing in Financial Call Centres* and on whose website the information given below can be accessed. He lists the following: The German Postal Workers' Union (DPG) points out that the working environment of all too many call centres can be described in the following terms—no discussion with colleagues except during rest breaks; monotonous, low-skill work; bad microclimatic conditions and open-plan offices with bad acoustics and lighting; unergonomic workstations (cramped posture ad so on). Many of the U.S. telecommunications workers who suffer from repetitive strain injuries (RSI) work in call centres, shows a recent study by the Communications Workers of America (CWA) and the University of Wisconsin. 'When you have jobs that are very tightly controlled, where you have to complete a call every 18 to 22 seconds and you have limitations on breaks, then you have effects that contribute to motion-repetitive injuries', observes the CWA.

'Eighty-eight per cent of German call centres work round the clock. And a survey of 33 British centres found that staff were also subjected to productivity targets including piecework quotas. This, too, reminds one of manufacturing practices. Call centres have a 'modernistic image, but the work is not that different from the secretarial pool of 15 years ago', notes Chris Hudson, organizing officer at Ireland's Communications Workers' Union (CWU)'. (quoted from Bibby)

42 Bibby, quoting a UK research group.

43 Bibby quoting from the journal of the Communication Workers' Union (CWU) of the United Kingdom, which has members in a number of British Telecom call centres.

44 When it comes to taking breaks, these are also monitored, from the time each operator logs off to the time they log back in again. Rules require them to be logged in and taking calls for a specified number of hours in a day. This prevents too many toilet and coffee breaks. And if they want to have a discussion with their co-workers, they have to watch out because the supervisors are quick to send instant messages via computer to anyone 'caught' being logged out or unavailable to take calls for more than a few minutes.

45 The Communication Workers' Union of the United Kingdom quoted by Research Officer, Communications International, E. Sussex Trends in telecommunication work, Mimeo, July 1998.

46 Initially, the Caribbean islands such as Jamaica and Barbados had led the development of 'offshore' working from developed to developing countries. The transfer of data processing and data inputting there dates back to the 1970s, when such work typically consisted of routine administrative work such as processing airline ticket stubs and credit card applications, and remained on a limited scale.

47 In 2004, the US President George Bush signed an Omnibus Appropriations Bill (Jan 2004) containing the Thomas–Voinovich amendment forbidding certain segments of the government from using foreign companies when outsourcing some government work, while at least thirteen bills seeking to ban offshore outsourcing (in one way or another) were wending their way through various state legislatures in the United States. Despite financial circles continuing to favour offshoring, popular pressures against offshore outsourcing had also been gaining ground. Under such pressures, the state of Indiana had actually cancelled a signed contract with an Indian company for processing of pensions. In the United Kingdom, although the government had given a statement saying it would not oppose offshore outsourcing, unions of call centre workers were becoming increasingly vociferous in their opposition.

48 C.P. Chandrashekhar, The diffusion of information technology: The Indian experience, *Social Scientist*, 31, 7-8 (July-Aug 2003).

49 Source: Reserve Bank of India, Report on Currency and Finance, 2002-2003. Service exports are categorized by the RBI under the heads of *(i)* Travel, *(ii)* Transportation, *(iii)* Insurance, *(iv)* Government and *(v)*

Miscellaneous. The category Miscellaneous includes communication, construction, finance, software, news agency, royalties, copyright, licence fees, management, advertising, office maintenance and exhibitions.

50 Reserve Bank of India, *Report on Currency and Finance,* 2002-2003, p 139.

51 Ibid.

52 Compiled from U.K. and Australian studies by Unions. The Communications Workers of America (CWA) has pitched the Indian call centre wage rate at US $720, which is way below actual wages.

53 Although we have used the 2004 NSS Employment survey data since it provides the most recent trends, an important caveat that needs to be borne in mind is that the 2004 survey was neither as large as the major rounds of 1993-1994 or 1999-2000 nor exactly comparable with them in terms of survey duration.

54 The critical importance of growth of industrial employment rather than services in making the qualitative leap away from domination of employment by agriculture may be confirmed by the data on more than 100 countries provided by Byres, Structural change, the agrarian problem and possible impact of globalization, in Ghosh and Chandrashekhar, eds, *Work and Well-being.*

55 Ibid. Byres goes on to elaborate 'In South Korea, the "flow of marketed food surplus, savings and people out of agriculture has been a substantial factor in industrialization"; the inter-sectoral terms of trade, through deliberate state policy, favoured industry throughout the 1950s and 1960s; and taxation of agriculture was heavy. In Taiwan, perhaps even more effectively, agriculture gave industrial capital a labour force, surplus of foreign exchange and an important source of demand; the terms of trade were significantly unfavourable to peasants; and there were heavy land taxes. Central to this particular form of agrarian transition was an "agriculture thoroughly embraced by the state." Landlords were not part of this transition. But their place was taken by the state . . . agrarian transition [in Korea and Taiwan] took place after 1945, with a marked absence of capitalist production relations in agriculture (that is of the capitalist farmer/wage labour relation). We cannot understand the dramatic structural transformations of these two countries . . . without reference to their agrarian roots.'

56 While the size of the Indian labour force might be an important factor here, its size alone should also preclude facile prognosis of middle class 'servicization' as the route to development.

57 Chandrashekhar, Behind the agrarian crisis of the 1990s, *People's Democracy* 4 Jan 2004.

58 In at least five states which together account for more than half the population, i.e., Andhra Pradesh, Bihar, Gujarat, Orissa and Uttar Pradesh, growth during the 1990s was clearly below the rate of growth of rural population. That this was accompanied by an accumulation of huge 'surplus' food-grain stocks with government agencies is evidence of growing hunger caused by lack of even minimal purchasing power in the hands of many with a real and serious decline in food consumption by large sections of particularly the rural poor.

59 K. Sundaram, Employment and poverty in the 1990s, further results from NSS 55th round employment-unemployment survey, 1999-2000, *EPW*, 35, 32 (11 Aug 2001).

60 Over the past few years, the enveloping spread of the agrarian crisis has been brought into national focus by the spate of suicides by farmers in several states.

61 For details of the slowing down of the growth in wages of female casual labour in agriculture, see Sundaram, Employment and poverty in the 1990s.

62 The unemployment rate is defined as the percentage of person-days unemployed of total person-days in the labour force which includes both the employed and the unemployed.

63 According to the NSSO, a person categorized as 'worker' engaged for a relatively longer time in the year preceding survey is categorized as a principal usual status worker. A person categorized as a non-worker who pursued some economic activity in a subsidiary capacity in the year preceding, is called a subsidiary status worker. Non-workers are defined as unemployed or out of the labour force, the latter being defined as engaged in non-economic activities for a relatively longer time of the preceding year)

64 Women accounted for over 46 per cent of job losses in mining between 1993-94 and 1999-2000, while their share in employment was around 22 per cent in 1993-1994.

65 Figures for public sector and organized private sector employment taken from Tables 3.1 and 3.2 in the *Economic Survey*, 2005-2006.

66 N. Neetha, *Migration, Social Networking and Employment: A Study of Domestic Workers in Delhi*, NLI Research Studies Series No. 037/2002 (Noida: V. V. Giri National Labour Institute, 2002).

67 Sundaram, Employment and poverty in the 1990s.

68 See NSSO, Report No. 460(55/10/3), *Non-Agricultural Workers in the Informal Sector Based on Employment-Unemployment Survey 1999-2000.*

69 In GE Capital, such a practice of sending recruits abroad for training continued even after the establishment of large-scale operations, but has tapered off in recent years. One of the surveyed workers reported that she had been in one batch that was sent to the U.S., but the whole batch was sent back within days as the U.S. employees refused to allow the training.

70 GE Capital alone employs over 10,000 in its Gurgaon unit and close to another 8,000–10,000 in other parts of the country.

71 The weight of the captive units has since increased owing to acquisitions of large vendor units by MNCs including at least one that at the time of the survey was an independent vendor. According to Nasscom, at an all India level, captive units accounted for 65 per cent to 70 per cent of the 210,000 call centre seats in 2004.

72 I. Mazumdar, R. S. Misra and A. Kapur, *Equal Remuneration in India, Law and Practice on Gender Based Wage Differentials with Special Reference to the Banking Sector* (New Delhi: ILO, 2000).

73 Babu P. Ramesh, Cyber Coolies in BPO: Insecurities and Vulnerabilities of Non-Standard Work, *EPW,* 39, 5 (Jan 31-6 Feb 2004).
Babu P. Remesh, Insecurities and vulnerabilities of non-standard work: A case study of business process outsourcing, V.V. Giri National Labour Institute, Mimeo.

74 As reported by Siddhartha Mukherjee, partner in Calibre Human Resources Ltd, a Delhi-based placement agency.

75 General manager of a multi-national BPO company quoted in the *Businessworld* article: The BPO status report, *Businessworld,* 4 August, 2003. The same article reported that in most startup BPO companies, capacity utilization was 'less than one (of three shifts)'. Quoting the CEO of an Indian company, the report went on to say, 'Desperate-for-work companies are offering to undertake [call centre] services at an unviable U.S. $8 per hour'. The multi-national's general manager is further reported to have said, 'The problem is that everybody is trying to compete on price'.

76 The average age of call centre workers is twenty-seven in the United Kingdom.

77 One of them had been educated in Muscat where her father worked in the tourism industry, and the other in Delhi where her father was a journalist.

78 The mother of only one worker was a college lecturer.

79 *A Portrait of Population, Delhi* (New Delhi: Directorate of Census Operations, 2001). According to the 1991 census (as yet the latest migration statistics available), 3 per cent of female migrants gave employment as the reason for migration, 41 per cent gave marriage, 48 per cent family moved 4 per cent for other 4 per cent for other less than 1 per cent for education less than 0.5 per cent for business.

80 This was confirmed in a survey of factory workers in Noida. CWDS mimeo, 1998.

81 See N. Neetha, *Migration, Social Networking and Employment: A study of Domestic Workers in Delhi*, NLI Research Studies Series, No. 037/2002.

82 A quite common feature among single women factory workers was the use of their earnings in Delhi for accumulation of dowry.

83 According to census 1991, 90 per cent of female migrants into Delhi had given marriage or family movement as their reason for migration, and less than 1 per cent gave education as the reason.

84 Since Delhi is the major metropolitan city in the North Indian Hindi speaking heartland, it is not surprising that Hindi speakers were the majority. However, the low proportions of Punjabis is surprising because since independence, Punjabis have been traditionally far greater in the population, and particularly in the middle class.

Conclusion

The sectoral studies have highlighted some features of the impact of globalization on women workers in the given sectors at an all-India level; however, the more detailed primary surveys which were exclusively conducted in the Delhi area must also be viewed in the context of the specific characteristics of the region. There are some special features to the social context of Delhi and its neighbourhood, which if ignored, would not only tend to give an incomplete picture but also perhaps hide aspects of variation and difference in the social conditions in which women workers live and work in the country as a whole. Before presenting the conclusions of the more generalized sectoral studies when taken together, we present below some of the social specificities of the context of the primary surveys.

PRIMARY SURVEYS: FEATURES OF LOCAL RELEVANCE

At the outset, it must be made clear that the primary survey was conducted in the capital city of Delhi, which has been taken as the main indicative unit. The urbanized areas of Noida and Gurgaon that were the part of the survey's universe, share fundamental characteristics in common with Delhi, not least because both grew as spatial, economic and social outgrowths of the capital city, rather than out of the dominant social and economic characteristics and formations of their respective states of Uttar Pradesh and Haryana. Markers of some differences would be the absence of large-scale industries in Delhi, since from the early 1960s they were debarred under the city's Master Plan. In that sense a distinguishing feature of both Noida and Gurgaon is the presence of a few fairly large-scale industries, and including the new major motor vehicle factories that have been set up. Nevertheless, the employment in such large scale capital intensive factories are unlikely to be more than 25,000 in all, with unorganized type workers in garments, leather products, electricals work, auto parts, and so on, being numerically far more dominant. Medium- and small-scale factories, similar to those in Delhi, dominate industrial employment in both Gurgaon and Noida.

Noida was established as a satellite industrial township of Delhi in the 1970s, its early years being clearly dominated by Delhi-style small-scale industries, with the medium- and larger-sized industries developing later. Gurgaon, on the other hand, was initially a locus for the large-scale Maruti car factory, with its emergence as an important centre of garment manufacture and Delhi-style smaller industries taking place later. Of course, the number of medium-sized and, to a lesser degree, even some large-scale industries, is greater in both Noida and Gurgaon than in Delhi but the dominant regional characteristics and regional origins of indigenous capital and labour flows are the same and the local culture is similar too. A substantial portion of capital invested in Noida and Gurgaon have origins in the commercial and industrial activity of Delhi, and their similarities and connections extend to the profile of the distribution of products being made in the industrial sector. Many of the region's industrialists own units in Delhi and Noida or Delhi and Gurgaon, and sometimes in all three, often having their head offices within the precincts of the capital city itself. Across the board, the garments industry leads in industrial employment followed by electricals and so on, while commercial distribution networks for the region as a whole generally work through the wholesale node within Delhi. Further, workers resident in Delhi may be working in Noida or Gurgaon and to a lesser extent those residing in Noida or Gurgaon may be working in Delhi (the latter is more prominent among the middle class), while the features of working class residence and regional and social origins of workers living in the satellite townships also share common characteristics with Delhi. Women in particular share the broad social, cultural and even civic context in common along with its internal forms of relationships and differentials. According to the 2001 census, the work participation rate (WPR) among women in Noida (urban) was 10.4 per cent in comparison to 50.45 per cent among men, while in Gurgaon (urban) female WPR was slightly higher, at 12.18 per cent in comparison to 49.86 per cent among men.[1] Such variations may be seen among the nine districts within the political state boundaries of Delhi as well. For example, the smallest district within Delhi, showed a female WPR of more than 15 per cent, while other substantially larger districts ranged between 9 per cent and 11 per cent (as per Census 2001). In terms of population, these areas of Noida and Gurgaon would be roughly equivalent to a *tehsil* in any of the larger districts of Delhi. As such NSS and other more detailed state level data that is available for Delhi, would broadly reflect the characteristics of the composite economy and society of the whole contiguous urban organism that radiates from Delhi including into Noida and Gurgaon.

Low Female Work Participation Rates in Delhi

The first and perhaps most significant aspect of the social context in which women live and work in Delhi, is the extremely small proportion of those who work for income. Delhi has perhaps one of the lowest female work participation rates in comparison to other states, even as male work participation rates in Delhi are similar to the all India rates. Table C.1 shows the comparison between male and female WPRs at all-India levels and within Delhi. If according to the census, female WPR in Delhi was 6.84 per cent in 1981, 7.36 per cent in 1991 and 9.15 per cent in 2001; in the NSS data, which is generally considered to be better in capturing female employment, the absolute and relatively low work participation rates among women are equally obvious.

Table C.1 Comparison of male and female WPR between all India and Delhi (in percentage terms)

Year	Rounds	Male		Female	
		All India	Delhi	All India	Delhi
1987-88	43rd	53.0	54.4	28.0	9
1993-94	50th	54.4	54.3	28.3	10.2
1999-00	55th	52.7	52.8	25.4	10.5
2004*	60th	54.1	53.9	26.8	7.5

Source: Different rounds of Employment Survey: NSSO
*Although the 2004 figures have been given here, it requires mention that the 60th round was based on a smaller sample and may not be fully comparable.

It might be argued that higher work participation rates for women would appear at an all-India level because of much larger proportions of rural women being included in the total count. Rural women's work participation rates are generally three to four times higher than in urban areas, particularly because of their greater presence in agriculture. But even in comparison to other major cities, Delhi compares poorly in terms of female work participation rates. This is despite the capital city and its surroundings having emerged as a significant concentration of small-scale industry, a long time centre of the two industries that generally have greater intensity of female employment, and containing a vast network of administrative and service organizations, where women could, in theory, find employment opportunities. Table C.2 gives the values of WPR in major class 1 cities of India available for 1999-2000.

Table C.2 : Usual status WPR in major class 1 cities of India[2]

	Male	Female
Chennai	76.4	26
Bangalore	74.7	23.2
Ahmedabad	77.7	20.4
Varanasi	75.8	20
Calcutta	78	18.7
Mumbai	75.3	17.4
Kanpur	69.9	15.4
Lucknow	77.2	14.9
Delhi	52.8	10.5

Source: 55/468;Employment & unemployment situation
In major towns and cities in India, NSSO 1999-2000

This low work participation rate of women in Delhi is accompanied by an additional feature, a relatively low share of women in the population. While in general, the trend over the past 50 years, was for an increasing sex ratio in Delhi (the sex ratio rose from 768 females per thousand males in 1951 to 827 females per thousand males in 1991), the decade 1991-2001 has, reversed the process and the sex ratio dropped from 827 females per thousand males in 1991 to 821 females per thousand males in 2001.[3] But even if we leave aside such a reversal, Delhi (and also Bombay), ranks amongst the lowest out of the 35 million plus cities in the country in terms of sex ratio, with only four of these cities having sex ratios lower than Delhi. In comparison, all the major cities located in southern India, have sex ratios well above 900 (see appendix). These regional differences in urban sex ratios and women's work participation rates is a fact whose reasons require greater study, since no single generalization as yet fits all the facts. It is possible however, that low work participation rates and perhaps low sex ratios are more the norm where long distance migration into cities is more marked. This in turn might be linked to the nature of the agrarian order from where migrants are drawn.

High Concentration of Migrant Workers

In its population growth, Delhi is known to have outpaced all million plus cities in India. From 1951 to 1991, it continued to maintain a decennial growth of over 50 per cent, although growth rate dropped to 47.02 per cent across 1991-2001. In 2001, the population of Delhi stood at over 13.78 million (urban Gurgaon and Noida housed populations of 370,000 and 450,000 respectively).[4]

Migrant workers have been coming to the capital city in ever swelling waves (445,000 in 1951-1961; 525,000 in 1961-1971; over 1.2 million in 1971-1981; over 1.9 million in 1981-1991; and 2.2 million between 1991 and 2001).[5] Increasing proportions of women in Delhi, until 1991, represented the settling down process through which male migrant workers brought in their families to become an intrinsic part of the people of the capital city. Migrant streams to Delhi have been dominated by workers coming from the rural hinterland of northern India. The proportion of migrants from northern India, rose from 49.5 per cent in 1951 to 80 per cent in 1991, with Uttar Pradesh alone accounting for from around 26 per cent of all migrants in 1951 to close to 50 per cent in 1991.[6] In the 1990s, growth rates of immigration from Bihar, of course, far outpaced Uttar Pradesh, bringing down the proportions of migrants from Uttar Pradesh to 45 per cent, while the number of migrants from Bihar to Delhi surpassed that of Haryana for the first time.[7]

The Economic Foundations of the Capital City

Unlike Mumbai and Calcutta which grew largely on account of their industrial development, Delhi emerged first as an administrative city. Nevertheless, taking off from its location as a commercial and trade centre with access to an expanding internal and external market, industry grew rapidly. As the capital city, Delhi housed a vast apparatus of several central government offices providing an initial growth and size to the middle class and the city's internal market for goods and retail services. It is one of the largest grain markets of Asia, and the wholesale centre for the whole of northern India and even beyond, of some twenty-seven manufactured products. Industrial development in Delhi has been dominated by numerous small units since the setting up of large-scale and heavy industries in Delhi was ruled out by the Master Plan for Delhi, and by the end of the 1960s, Delhi had 'emerged as the single biggest centre of concentration of small scale industries in the country'.[8] It is this concentration of industry, commerce and government that served to draw in millions of migrants from far flung areas to the capital for here they could find some form of employment. In 1998, the city's industrial units numbered 126,220 in 1996, employing some 1.2 million people, while the number of trading enterprises were 268,000, employing close to 700,000 people.[9] If the sea of industrial units with small numbers of workers that eluded registration with the Factories' Inspectorate accustomed migrant workers towards the acceptance of the domination of unregulated, non-formal or informal employer–employee relations in industry, the relatively traditionally more closed social circuit of trading intermediaries benefited immensely from the small and unorganized manufacturers, and themselves utilized the services of a vast irregular army of 'coolies' and transport workers, not recorded as their own workers. The sheer spread and magnitude of numbers which enfolded the capital's workers and the ever flowing in stream into the ranks of the job seekers, have determined the conditions of not only their work, but also of their organization and consciousness. This was not an environment which favoured easy entry of women into the labour market.

AN OVERVIEW OF WOMEN WORKERS IN THE CAPITAL CITY

Categories of Women Workers

According to NSS employment data for 1999-2000, of around 700,000 women workers in Delhi in 1999-2000, less than one-third were self-employed.[10] Of these, roughly 450,000 were regular and salaried women workers. Among such regular workers, a little over one-quarter were in the organized sector, of which three-quarters were in the public sector, or in other words, some 13 per cent of all women workers in Delhi worked for the government, and another 5 per cent in the private segment of the organized sector, the remaining 82 per cent being located in the unorganized sector. Two-thirds of the organized sector women workers were concentrated in community, social and personal services (probably predominantly the somewhat better-paid among teachers, nurses and government servants, and including the low-paid *anganwadi* workers) and only 7 per cent in manufacturing.[11] In contrast, more than one-quarter (26 per cent) of women workers in the unorganized sector could be found in manufacturing. The proportion of community, social and personal services among women workers in the unorganized sector looked to be considerably less than in the organized sector, although this segment (which includes the single largest category of women's employment in Delhi, that is, domestic servants), still employed over 56 per cent of women workers in Delhi's unorganized sector.[12] Table C.3 gives the category-wise status of the workforce in Delhi.

Table C. 3: Category-wise usual status (PS+SS) of workforce in Delhi

		Self Employment		Reg & Salaried		Casual	
year	rounds	Male	Female	Male	Female	Male	Female
1987-88	43rd	38.2	30	58.1	66.7	3.7	3.3
1993-94	50th	44.4	25	45.5	57.3	10.1	17.7
1999-00	55th	43.5	31.3	54	64.6	2.6	4.1
2004	60th	44.8	18.4	51.1	73.7	4.7	7.9

Source: 43/1, 50/409, 55/455—Different rounds of Employment Survey: NSSO

Overall in Delhi, it appears that close to three-fifths of women workers worked in community, social and personal services, a little over one-fifth in manufacturing followed by one-tenth in trade, hotels and restaurants. Despite Delhi being a centre of small-scale manufacture, it is clearly services that dominates the employment pattern, although within the broad category of services, women's employment is overwhelmingly dominated by menial domestic service. Table C.4 gives a distribution of employees by industry type.

Table C.4 Distribution of urban employees by industry type

Industrial Classification	Urban Male			Urban Female		
	1987-1988	1993-1994	1999-2000	1987-1988	1993-1994	1999-2000
Agriculture	0.9	1.1	0.8	2.4	2.5	6.8
Manufacturing	27.9	26.2	24.8	16.2	10.1	21.8
Electricity, gas, etc	3.5	0.8	0.3	0.2	-	0.8
Construction	6.1	11.2	6.2	2.9	6.3	0.9
Wholesale, retail trade, hotels, restaurants	23.2	23.8	31.7	11.6	13	9.7
Transport,storage, communications	8.4	7.5	7.6	2.6	1.3	1.4
Community, social and personal services	28.7	39.1	28.6	62.1	66.8	58.6

The distribution of women's employment between community, social and personal services, manufacturing, and wholesale, retail trade, hotels and restaurants, however, while clearly evidencing a continuing dominance of the first category, did not display much stability in any segment across the 1990s. The share of community, social and personal services peaked in 1993-1994 and then rapidly fell in the latter half of the 1990s, while the share of manufacturing dipped sharply in the early half of the 1990s and then rose in the latter half. Agriculture, otherwise peripheral to the urban economy, doubled its share of female employment between 1993-1994 and 1999-2000. Such fluctuations tie in with the general experience of increased volatility and impermanence that characterizes the employment scenario in the current era. A particular feature that can be noted even in casual observation is the sharp reduction in the employment of women in construction, with large mechanized companies, including MNCs now dominating the construction sector in Delhi, that clearly do not employ women. Such a trend is reflected in the reduction of construction workers to less than 1 per cent of women working in Delhi.

Changing Relations of Women and Work Among Migrant Worker Communities

The principal areas where the working classes of Delhi live are the shanty clusters (*jhuggi bastis*), the resettlement colonies (where in several waves, *jhuggi* dwellers were resettled), the designated slum areas, as also the several unauthorized colonies (of which some have been regularized) which stretch across the erstwhile rural belt around the periphery of the city. According to official figures, some 15 per cent of the population of Delhi lives in *jhuggies*, over 19 per cent in designated slum areas, close to 13 per cent in resettlement colonies, over 6 per cent in urban villages, over 5 per cent in unauthorized colonies and 13 per cent in regularized unauthorized colonies, in all accounting for 58 per cent of the total population of the city.[13]

The transition of migrant workers towards more permanent settlement in the city has generally been through the *jhuggis* which tended to come up around centres of commerce, industry and construction sites, but have over the years been compressed into more inhospitable terrains along drains and the railway lines. In these rough schools, migrant workers of Delhi learnt the arts of survival in the metropolis. Social networks reaching out from the rural hinterland combine with more marketized relationships with the commerce and industry of the capital, and urban style government and politics; a combination out of which many distinctive characteristics of the social consciousness of workers in Delhi has been shaped. The crowded yet exposed nature of life in the *jhuggies* made the practices of segregation, exclusion based on 'pollution', and the graded seclusion of women, that marks the traditions of caste-ordered social hierarchies, virtually impossible to maintain, while the changed context of urban life and work and the externalization of most forms of work for income out of the household, altered the socially inherited divisions of labour between men and women in the economic sphere. Whereas in the case of some upper-caste women, traditionally disallowed from working outside their homes (even in their own fields), perhaps with a little education, the city provided a break with past seclusion, and the possibilities of looking for employment. On the other hand, for several women from communities where work for income both within and outside their rural households was traditional for women, the urban context led to their 'housewifization'. But in general, the city has engendered the male breadwinner norm, and reinforced forms of socially controlling women within the domestic sphere as practiced by the dominant upper castes. Such practices of confinement (increasingly social rather than physical) have spread to other communities seeking to change their low social status by adopting upper-caste social norms in relation to women. Added to this broad social tendency to confine women to the domestic sphere are the real and actual difficulties of looking after homes in conditions where civic amenities are inadequate (such as water having to be collected at specific times and there are long queues), with family bases being more nucleated requiring wives (and often daughters) to stay at home to look after children, and so on. The process of emergence of women into the sphere of paid work has therefore had to traverse through several social and logistical constrictions. It is from such a social context that the women workers covered by the primary surveys have emerged as workers in the sectors covered by the preceding chapters.

In the 1990s, when larger numbers of women could otherwise be seen entering the labour market, beautification and commercialization drives at the instance of both administration and the courts have induced large-scale disruptions in the hitherto established modes of settlement in several parts of the city. Such disruptions have particularly affected *jhuggi* dwellers, the targets of demolition in the centres of the city for resettlement in peripheries at great distance from their earlier places of work, and increasing difficulty in accessing their places of work becoming the norm. This in turn has introduced new levels of uncertainty and insecurity at their new places of residence where generally basic civic amenities remain long denied resulting in an enhancement of the unpaid labour of women in the domestic sphere and a drawing back from paid forms of employment among many women. It is possible that some of these processes may have been reflected in the rather surprising fall in the work participation rates among women in Delhi between 1999-2000 and 2004, although the 2004 data must be approached with a degree of caution since the sample size is smaller.

Aspects of the Social Composition of Women Workers in the Surveyed Sectors

Despite the growing awareness that social aspects such as caste and community origins get linked into the operation of even the urban labour market in several ways, this is an area where the relationship between the micro- and macro-picture is always difficult to establish partly because the macro-data available are inadequate. Government employment data by sector does not provide us with details of the caste and community composition of workers; however, some features of these aspects may be gleaned from our four primary surveys taken in combination. It was found that the largest concentrations of scheduled caste and Muslim women among these workers were employed as home-based workers. In the case of scheduled caste women, the implication is a clear tendency for the more socially oppressed sections to predominate in the lowest echelons of the employment hierarchy. At the same time, considerably high proportions of young and more educated scheduled caste girls in the relatively higher-status electronics industry also illustrates a degree of upward mobility due to education. The more widespread garment export industry seems to also have drawn in greater numbers of scheduled caste women in Delhi, although in the newer and larger units at Gurgaon and Noida, the proportions of scheduled caste women are distinctly lower. Table C.5 gives the distribution of surveyed workers by caste and community.

The large proportions of Muslim women in home-based work and their negligible presence in other sectors, is perhaps more linked to the practice of social confinement of Muslim women.

In general, it is quite clear that apart from home-based workers, in almost all other sectors upper caste women tend to predominate, which at one level might be a reflection of the population composition of the city, but perhaps also indicates a relatively greater facility for mobility

Table C.5: Percentage distribution of surveyed workers by caste and community in each sector

Industry	Upper-caste Hindus	Backward caste Hindus	Scheduled Caste Hindus	Muslim	Others (Sikh, Christian, Buddhist)
Garment exports	53	19	25	2	1
Electronics	64	1	34	-	1
Home-based	22	5	41	32	-
IT-enabled services	60	2	2	-	36
All workers	44	10	30	12	4

among those upper-caste women who have been able to (perhaps compelled to) emerge out from the traditions of social seclusion. As regards the small proportions of women from the intermediate backward castes among these workers, while again this feature is perhaps reflective of a lower proportion of such women in the general city population, such a phenomenon might also be indicative of a stronger pressure towards greater seclusion with less of mitigation through education and other elements of wider social intercourse for these particular segments of society in comparison to the upper castes. All these can only be taken as preliminary sketches of possible issues and trends that are a part of the social context that influences the lives of women workers in Delhi. More definitive analysis of course requires greater study of the complex of interactions between caste and community hierarchies and economic developments, including the changes taking place in personal and social life, and the influence exerted by such factors on women and work. It requires investigations of greater social depth and covering a larger social canvas than has been possible in this brief foray.

GLOBALIZATION AND WOMEN WORKERS IN INDIA: THE ISSUES, EXPERIENCES AND QUESTIONS

Common to all the sectoral studies as well as the analysis of macro data on employment, was the finding that the globalization decade in India has been marked by an extreme volatility in employment. Such volatility is generalized across all sectors, and includes both the organized and unorganized sectors within its ambit. Within manufacturing, such volatility appears even in the export oriented garment industry in the form of what appears statistically as a redistribution of workers, with some increased numbers of women workers entering de-skilled and consolidated production units as tailors, while others are losing employment through closures and decimation of the fabricating units. In actuality, such statistics mask the increasing levels of unemployment among garment workers, as not only older and unskilled workers but also younger and more skilled women tailor operators are now constantly thrown out of work with contractualization of their employment increasingly becoming the norm. Workers displaced by the changing profile of the garment industry, are facing greater difficulty than earlier in finding avenues for re-employment in the garment industry. In electronics, the volatility in employment appears quite graphically at a statistical level as well, while among the chronically underemployed home-based workers, there appears to have been a drastic reduction in the availability of work. The general results of such volatility have been an extreme and continuous pressure on the wages and incomes of the majority of women workers in the manufacturing sector, in many cases to levels far below subsistence. Much of the literature that supports globalization or equivocates between its positive and negative effects tends to ignore the acuteness of such pressures, and their systemic roots in the general as well as sector specific processes underlying globalization.

One of the key findings of the studies has been that despite the general impression that under globalization female employment in manufacturing increases relative to male employment, in India, inequalities between male and female employment have grown and during the period of opening up of the economy to international trade and capital flows. On this count, whereas in the garment industry a decline in female share of employment is apparent in the statistics, in electronics the small increase in female share is rendered inconsequential within the larger picture of the fall in both male and female employment and the stagnation in employment that appears in the dataset for manufacturing as a whole. Examination of official occupational wage data for both garments and electronics industries, has established a clear link between low and unequal wages as a factor determining the areas of expansion of women's employment, albeit unable to completely override the more generalized male bias in non-agricultural employment apparent in the national labour statistics. From these overarching national employment statistics which are discussed in Chapter 5, it appears that the process of marginalization of women in manufacturing remains an important feature, evidenced in the high proportions of solely subsidiary status employment and a decline in women's share of principal status employment. The evidence from the case studies on garments and electronics in this volume indicates that such a decline is partly explainable by the pressure of widespread and continuing loss of employment in several industries compelling sections of male workers to accept the lower levels of wages that might otherwise be offered to women by those employers whose profit maximization is based on lowering the absolute costs of labour. It is clear that the inequalities experienced by women in terms of both lower wages relative to men, as well as lower access to employment, can no longer be attributed merely to historically inherited social inequalities. Such inequalities have obviously been further moulded by the operation of market forces and aggravated by the policies of freeing of private capital from state regulation and the accompanying reluctance to impose restriction on the anti-social methods of profit maximization. In other words, the market fundamentalism that underpins the ideology of globalization operates as a counter force to the social project of equality for women.

But it is not only manufacturing employment that displays a continued bias against women workers. Even in service sector employment, where the share of women workers has remained lower than in agriculture or manufacturing, there has hardly been any increase in share of female employment. This is despite the fact that in 1999-2000, for the first time, the share of services overtook manufacturing within women's employment distribution. One of the reasons for the significant increase in numbers of women workers in the service sector at the time was the major and absolute losses in agricultural employment for women following from the effects of neo-liberal policies. By 2004, with the closure of viable employment in either services or manufacturing, large numbers of women were obviously being pushed back into crisis ridden agriculture as a form of residual reserve employment and three-fourths of the female workforce remained concentrated in agriculture. It appears that the absolute losses in women's employment in agriculture, and the ejection of many women workers from their jobs in manufacturing in the 1990s had brought over a million women crowding into the lower segments of petty retail trade, while simultaneously pushing large numbers of women out of the workforce. That such employment was unviable for many became apparent in 2004 when once again more women were crowded back into agriculture. In fact, one of the most significant developments in India through the 1990s that may be viewed as a crucial indicator of the effects of liberalization-enabled globalization on women workers in India, has been the fall in the work participation rates among women to all time lows in rural areas, but significantly even in urban areas women workers seem to be being pushed out to the workforce. Such a fall in work participation rates can only be taken to mean growing unemployment for women at a time when the findings of every survey at both macro- and micro-levels show a spreading and increasing urgency to the felt need for paid work among women. For such women, employment opportunities are obviously not available even in those segments of the service sector, where otherwise women's employment share has expanded. In such a context, the opening up of the much hyped new forms of employment in export-oriented IT-enabled services, which barely account for 0.06 per cent of total employment and 0.2 per cent of even service sector employment, can have only a limited significance and little relevance to the conditions and lives of the larger classes of women workers in the country.[14]

Finally, all the sector specific studies in this volume clearly indicate that it is primarily the interests of metropolitan capital that are being served by India's linking up with globalized production and market networks. In the process, workers thrown out of jobs by a degree of deindustrialization due to substitution of Indian manufactured products by imports as well as the retreat from public sector expansion are clearly not compensated by either the expansion of exports in other sectors or the infusion of FDI. The result of such deindustrialization has been an extreme reduction in the availability of sustained or viable employment for women in the manufacturing sector even in the most ill paid segments of the informal sector.

As has been shown in the case of garment exports, consolidation and centralization by monopoly retailers of the metropolitan capitalist economies has ensured that the shift from protective barriers in the United States and Europe (through quota-based restrictions on garment imports) to supposed free trade, has been marked by an enhanced domination of metropolitan retail capital over developing country exporters. The new trade regime under the aegis of the WTO has not reduced the inequalizing tendency in the relations between the importing capitalist core countries and the exporting developing countries in the global garment industry. On the other hand, the near monopoly over global markets established by the multinational retailers has in fact promoted a labour regime in India's garment export industry characterized by the use of casualization by Indian manufacturers as a wage-depressing mechanism, an intensification of the labour process, and an extension of the hours of work. The ongoing restructuring and consolidation within the Indian garment export industry in order to tailor it to the needs of globally centralizing retail capital has also led to major losses of jobs and a deterioration of the conditions of work and wages in the small scale unorganized segment of the garment export industry, including in the home-based segment.

In electronics manufacture the deindustrializing effects of accelerated import liberalization have been more acutely felt in the form of widespread closures of electronics factories and ensuing loss of employment, particularly after the Information Technology Agreement came into existence. The entry of multinational producers into this sector and their cornering of a large share of the Indian market from the latter half of the 1990s has not led to commensurate or compensatory growth of employment. Rather, the most recent employment data for 2004 indicates that there has been a substantial loss of employment in electronics manufacturing. Further, the retreat of the public sector has played the role of closing the options for better quality of employment of women workers in electronics, while the MNCs have been leading the way in introducing oppressive conditions and extension of hours of work. The facts also show that some MNCs too, alongside several Indian brand companies, have gone in for closures and outsourcing from captive units with more degraded conditions of work and wages.

But perhaps the most crippling effects of deindustrialization have been felt by home-based workers, as the closure of a range of small factories has added reduced work availability to the woes of low wage rates and social confinement. The flood of cheap imports into the domestic market in the wake of accelerating import liberalization through the 1990s has been an important precipitating factor in the closure of several factories. Through the 1980s and early 1990s these factories had provided more regular access to piece-rated work for home-based workers. As has been shown in the description and analysis of the social and economic relations that are coming to the fore in this segment of the informal sector, the scope for viable incomes from home work has shrunk even further, and only large traders are emerging as principal beneficiaries of the system of home-based production under the present dispensation.

On the other hand, in the much touted high-quality employment in export-oriented call centres or IT-enabled services (whose promotion has been based on the very same import liberalization policies that have led to the collapse of the electronic hardware manufacturing sector), a new breed of young, educated and hopeful workers are being offered the destiny of a lifetime of night-work with its attendant disturbances in their social life and health. Nevertheless, the fact that a significant proportion (but not the majority) of call centre workers are women, many of whom live independent of their families, signals a degree of aspiration for social independence among these sections of the young and educated. For such aspirations, the expansion of call centre employment (marked as it is by personal subordination through extreme levels of monitoring and supervision at a daily and hourly level, and characterized by a loss of identity and dignity through having to change their names, their accents and cultural 'stylisms'), has less potential than it has as a profit-maximization service for metropolitan capital and their Indian contractors.

New Developments and Shifts in Public Discourse

The euphoric zeal with which liberalization was pushed through in the 1990s had ensured that many of the experiences that have been detailed in this set of studies were kept out of sight, and the 1990s was a decade that saw a pronounced marginalization of the political voice of labour; however, particularly since the general elections of 2004, a number of other voices against the ill effects of the globalization regime on labour and employment have begun to be heard, and the present period seems to be opening up space for a somewhat enhanced level of political intervention by representatives of the working class in India. Even among the middle classes, there are signs of a growing realization that globalization has had severely adverse and sometimes catastrophic effects on the lives of the majority, particularly on those whose survival is more closely linked with the destiny of the production base of the

Indian economy.

Such a shift in the political mood came to the fore in 2004, when a high-pitched campaign based on a projection of 'India Shining' by the government of the day was rejected by the Indian electorate. Its effects can also be perceived in the enactment of the National Rural Employment Guarantee Act, 2005, that marks official acknowledgement of the acute and deepening distress and unemployment in rural India, and holds the promise of the government playing a more active role in expenditures towards such an employment guarantee.[15] In similar vein, the discussion on the need for substantial outlays by the government for providing some social security benefits to unorganized sector workers has also been gaining momentum.[16] And yet, given that the policy environment in relation to liberalization and globalization has not altered, the prospects of the government initiating measures to substantively alter the trajectories outlined in the set of studies here and towards a better deal for labour and women workers in particular, as yet look bleak. Instead, there seems to be a continuing and unrelenting pressure from financial and industrial circles for so called 'labour reform'. The reforms sought by liberalizers in the sphere of labour are essentially directed at dilution of the few employment and social security protections for workers that exist in the letter of the Indian law, and include moves to exempt small and medium sized enterprises and larger industries that are specially favoured by the government from the application of labour laws altogether.[17] Such pressures are of course being resisted by central trade unions, but as of now it is a relatively unequal public debate with the mainstream media (print and electronic) pitching strongly for liberalization's agenda of curtailment of labour rights. The adverse effects of such 'labour law reforms' on women workers have yet to acquire due prominence in any of the public discourses and require to be fore-grounded.

There are of course also a few outside government and business circles, who in the name of women workers' rights continue to proffer a line that argues that globalization should be welcomed and supported on the grounds that it offers greater employment opportunities to women workers. According to their understanding, employment opportunities are supposedly denied to women in the absence of global integration, and in fact greater scope for global organization is now made possible because of what they hold to be an inherent 'non-imperialist' agenda of globalization. The proponents of this line of globalization of 'labour standards' tend to see multilateral trade organizations such as the WTO as potential instruments for enforcing ILO's core labour standards for Indian workers on the basis of an illusion that 'globalization depends on real political autonomy among its participants'.[18] Such views continue to echo the views prevalent in first world dominated international fora, despite the accumulating evidence from third world countries of an advancing imperialist agenda at an economic as well as political level.

Fortunately such views that go against the grain of empirical realities in India—of low work participation rates among women and growing unemployment, have struck no chord with the principal organizations of workers in the country, who have maintained that international trade and labour standards should remain delinked. Their argument is that the already grim employment scenario is compounded by the entry of capital goods and import intensive (and therefore less labour employing) multinational corporations adding further weight to the trend of displacement from employment. Further, even the interests of the majority of middle-class service sector workers are better served by efforts to turn government policy and economic programmes towards a stronger and more effective investment and redistributive trajectory. As such, the trade union opposition to the liberalization policy programme more closely reflects the interests of women workers than is often realized even by some groups and organizations that work exclusively among women workers. Some of these exclusive women workers' organizations have scrupulously distanced themselves from the joint oppositional platforms of central trade unions in India in contrast to other mass organizations of women, who since 1993 have associated themselves with what is known as the National Platform of Mass Organisations (NPMO). The NPMO, in which the trade unions have played a leading role and which includes several of the large mass organizations of women, has become the largest united platform of workers, peasants and women in terms of mass-following in the country, not least because it has spearheaded opposition to liberalization and the adverse effects of globalization; however, even apart from the growing popular opposition to the liberalization programme, as our own investigations into the impact of globalization have shown, proposals for tying the action and agency of women workers to globalizing interests can only lead to subordination of their interests to the class interests of metropolitan capital. Globalization has only added more tiers to the layers of exploitation, forms of discrimination and inequality faced by women workers in India.

NOTES

1 WPR for Noida and Gurgaon calculated from urban worker and population figures in Tables of Total population, total workers, main workers, marginal workers and non-workers-India, States and Union territories and Districts: Census 2001.

2 It may be observed that the two southern cities of Chennai and Bangalore have the highest WPR for women, and apart from Varanasi, the northern cities of Kanpur, Lucknow, Ludhiana and Delhi are among the lowest.

3 See *Census of India 2001*, Delhi, Provisional Population Totals, Paper 1, figure 2 for sex ratio figures from 1901 to 2001. An important reason for the decline in Delhi's sex ratio is a sharp fall in the sex ratio of the 0–6 age group, but a part is also due to a reduced scope for fresh male migrants to bring their families for settlement in Delhi during this period.

4 The rural stretches of the districts of Gurgaon and Gautam Budhnagar (Noida), (not included in the above figures) are of course more prominent in terms of population compared to the urban, in contrast to Delhi where the situation is the opposite. In Gautambudhnagar, the rural population constitutes 63 per cent of the total population, while in Gurgaon their proportions are even larger at 78 per cent. In Delhi, on the other hand the rural population is less than 7 per cent of the population.

5 Source: Conceptual Plan, Delhi Urban Arts Commission, 1986, for number of migrants until 1981. The figures for 1981-1991 have been calculated from census data on population, and births and deaths in Delhi, from Delhi Statistical Handbook, and for 1991–2001 from *Census of India 2001*,Data Highlights, Migration Tables (D1, D1 (Appendix), D2 and D3 Tables).

6 *Census of India* Migration data compiled in V.B. Singh, Political profile of Delhi and support bases of parties: an analysis. In Dupont, V., E.

Tarlo and D. Vidal, eds., *Delhi, Urban Spaces and Human Destinies,* (New Delhi: Manohar, 2000).

7 In the first two decades after independence, the bulk of the migrants into Delhi (apart from partition refugees), were from the surrounding districts of Western Uttar Pradesh and Haryana. See Asok Mitra, *Delhi, the Capital City,* 1970. The increased presence of migrants from Bihar is commonly commented upon by workers in Noida and Gurgaon as well.

8 Report of the Census of Industrial Units in the Union Territory of Delhi,1969, Directorate of Industries, Delhi Administration.

9 Source: *Economic Survey of Delhi*, 2001–2002. Although the Delhi government does not have any up to date figures for distribution of the industrial units by product group, in 1988, textile products accounted for the maximum, around 20 per cent of all units, while electronics constituted around 3 to 4 per cent of all units.

10 The census count of women workers in 2001 was around 560,000 in Delhi, 20,855 for urban Gurgaon, and 20,502 for urban Noida.

11 Organized sector data from DG E&T, *Employment Review*, 2002.

12 Domestic service is obviously the single largest employment category of women workers in Delhi and within the NSS estimates, numbering well over 300,000, that is, around one-half of all women workers in Delhi, if one excludes agriculture.

13 Such resettlement colonies however, do not exist in Noida and Gurgaon, where the predominant pattern of working class residence is *jhuggies,* urban villages and unauthorized colonies.

14 Even the more statistically significant trend of increases in numbers of women employed in education (which is generally seen as falling within the relatively high-end services) could be seen as carrying within it a degradation of wage and working conditions since profit extraction oriented privatization and related private investment is a factor in the expansion of employment in education in this period, particularly in a context of lowering of profits in several sub-sectors in manufacturing and agriculture. Such degradation would also be a factor determining the increasing relative share of women workers in education.

15 Of course, in the case of the rural employment guarantee law provides for 100 days of employment by the government to only one member per household (with a proviso that one-third of the employment be earmarked for women), despite the unanimous recommendations of a parliamentary committee (that heard several depositions including from trade unions and women's organiations) that the guarantee of be extended to all adults.

Table A.1 (*continued*)

Rank in 2001	Urban Agglomeration/City (1,000,000+ Population	Population 2001 Persons	Males	Females	Sex Ratio
20.	Kochi	1,355,406	670,462	684,955	1021
21.	Visakhapatnam	1,329,472	674,080	6,55,392	972
22.	Agra	1,321,410	708,622	612,788	865
23.	Varanasi	1,211,749	644,922	566,827	879
24.	Madurai	1,194,665	604,728	589,937	976
25.	Meerut	1,167,399	624,904	542,495	868
26.	Nashik	1,152,048	619,962	532,086	858
27.	Jabalpur	1,117,200	588,556	528,644	898
28.	Jamshedpur	1,101,804	580,336	521,468	899
29.	Asansol	1,090,171	576,813	513,358	890
30.	Dhanbad	1,064,357	578,602	485,755	840
31.	Faridabad	1,054,981	580,548	474,433	817
32.	Allahabad	1,049,579	581,876	467,703	804
33.	Amritsar	1,011,327	543,638	467,689	860
34.	Vijayawada	1,011,152	531,084	480,068	904
35.	Rajkot	1,002,160	525,797	476,363	906
	Total	107,881,836	57,664,396	50,217,440	871

It is important to reiterate that the data presented in this Appendix is yet provisional as the same has not been subjected to the intensive checks and cross checks which are applied before finalizing the census data. Data users are requested to keep this limitation in mind while using the same.

References

Apparel Export Promotion Council, *Handbook of Export Statistics*, 1998-2001, Delhi.

Assaad, Ragui, Informalization and De-feminization: Explaining the Unusual Pattern in Egypt. Conference on Rethinking Labor Market Informalization: Precarious Jobs, Poverty, and Social Protection, 18-19 October 2002, Cornell University.

Banerjee, Nirmala, How Real Is the Bogey of Feminisation? in T. S. Papola and A. N. Sharma, eds., *Gender and Employment in India*, Delhi: Vikas,1999.

---, Something Old, Something New, in Swasti Mitter and Shiela Rowbottom, eds., *Women Encounter Technology*, New York: Routledge, 1995.

Bangasser, Paul E., The ILO and the Informal Sector: An Institutional History, Geneva: ILO Employment Paper 2000/9.

Batra, S. L., *Employment for Women: A Study of Export-Oriented Garment Industry*, Delhi: CSD, 1996.

Bhatia, Satinder, Indian Garments Industry in the Post-MFA period, Occasional Paper 7, IIFT 1997.

Bhavani, T. A., Technological Change in the Indian Small-Scale Industries. IDPAD Project Report, Institute of Economic Growth, Delhi, 2001.

Blunch, Niel-Hugo, S. Canagarajah, and Dhushyanath Raju, The Informal Sector Revisited: A Synthesis across Space and Time. Social Protection Discussion Paper, Washington, DC: World Bank, Social Protection Unit, July 2001.

Bombay Textile Research Association, In-depth Study of the Indian Apparel Industry with Special Reference to Steps to Increase Garment Exports, Textile Committee Report, 1991.

Bonacich, E. L., N. Cheng, N. Chinchilla, eds, *Global Production: The Apparel Industry in the Pacific Rim*, Philadelphia: Temple University Press, 1994.

Borrus, Michael, Left for Dead: Asian Production Networks and the Revival of US Electronics, in Barry Naughton, ed., *The China Circle: Economics and Technology in the PRC, Taiwan and Hong Kong,* Washington D.C.: Brookings Institution Press, 1997.

Borrus, Michael, and Stephen Cohen, Why Now? A New Translatlantic Initiative in Information Technology. BRIE Working Paper 119, 1998.

Braverman, Harry, *Labour and Monopoly Capital,* New York: Monthly Review Press, [1974] 1998.

Breman, Jan, *Footloose Labour,* Cambridge: Cambridge University Press, 1996.

—, *The Labouring Poor in India,* Delhi, Oxford University Press, 2003.

Burke, James, and Gerald Epstein, Threat Effects and the Internationalization of Production, in J. Ghosh and C. P. Chandrashekhar, eds., *Work and Well-Being in the Age of Finance,* Delhi: Tulika, 2003.

The BPO Status Report, *Businessworld,* 4 Aug 2003.

Byers, T. J., Structural Change, the Agrarian Question and the Possible Impact of Globalization in J. Ghosh and C. P. Chandrashekhar, eds, *Work and Well-Being in the Age of Finance,* Delhi: Tulika, 2003.

callcentres.net, The 2003 India Call Centre Industry Benchmark Study, ACA Research Pty Ltd, Sydney, Australia, 2003.

Cawthorne, Pamela, The Labour Process under Amoebic Capitalism: A Case Study of the Garment Industry in a South Indian Town, in I. S. A. Baud and G. A. de Bruijne, eds., *Gender, Small-Scale Industry and Development Policy,* London: Intermediate Technology Publications, London, 1993.

Chandrashekhar, C. P., The Imperialist War on 'Terror', *The Marxist,* 19, 3 (July-Sept 2003).

—, ITES and Hard Facts, *Frontline,* 4 July 2003.

—, Services and the New Capitalism, in J. Ghosh and C. P. Chandrashekhar, eds., *Work and Well-Being in the Age of Finance,* Delhi: Tulika, 2003.

—, The Diffusion of Information Technology: The Indian Experience, *Social Scientist,* 31, 7-8 (July-Aug 2003).

—, Behind the Agrarian Crisis of the 1990s, *People's Democracy,* 4 Jan 2004.

Chandrashekhar, C. P., and Jayati Ghosh, *The Market That Failed,* Delhi: LeftWord, 2002.

Chatterjee, S., and R. Mohan, India's Garment Exports, *Economic and Political Weekly* (henceforth *EPW),* 28, 35 (1993).

Chhachi, Amrita, Women Workers and Organizational Strategies, mimeo, The Hague: Institute of Social Studies; India: FREA.

Delahanty, Julie, The North-South Institute. A Common Thread: Issues for Garment Workers, paper for WIEGO, 1999, http://www.nsi-ins.ca/english/pdf/thread.pdf.

Delhi Urban Arts Commission, Conceptual Plan for Delhi, *1986*. Mimeo.

Elson, Diane. Appraising Recent Developments in the World Market for Nimble fingers, in Amrita Chhachhi and Renée Pittin, eds., *Confronting State, Capital and Patriarchy*, New York: St. Martin's Press, 1996.

Ernst, Dieter, From Partial to Systemic Globalization: International Production Networks in the Electronics Industry. BRIE, Working Paper 98, 1997.

Government of the National Capital Territory of Delhi, Economic Survey of Delhi, 2001-2002. delhiplanning.nic.in

Electronics and Computer Software Export Promotion Council, *Statistical Year Book of Indian IT and Electronics Industry,* 2000-2001.

Frobel, Folker, Jurgen Heinrichs, and Otto Krey, *The New International Division of Labour*, Cambridge: Cambridge University Press, 1980: 84.

Ghosh, Jayati, *Globalisation, Export-Oriented Employment for Women and Social Policy*, UNRISD: 2002. www.unrisd.org

—, Exporting Jobs or Watching Them Disappear, in J. Ghosh and C. P. Chandrashekhar, eds., *Work and Well-Being in the Age of Finance*, Delhi: Tulika, 2003.

Ghosh, Jayati, and C. P. Chandrashekhar, eds., Introduction, in *Work and Well-Being in the Age of Finance,* Delhi: Tulika, 2003.

Government of India, *Report of the Census of Industrial Units in the Union Territory of Delhi, 1969*. Delhi Administration, Central Secretariat Library.

—, *Towards Equality: Report of the Committee on the Status of Women in India,* Delhi: Ministry of Education, 1974.

—, *Integrated Policy Measures in Electronics*, Delhi: Department of Electronics. 1985.

—, *Occupational Wage Survey, Report on the Textile Garments Industry*, Third, Fourth and Fifth Rounds, 1977-79, 1987-88, 1994-95, Delhi: Ministry of Labour, Labour Bureau.

—, *Report on Textiles Garments Industry*, Delhi: Ministry of Labour, Labour Bureau, 1995-96.

—, *Annual Survey of Industries, 1999-2000,* vol 1. Delhi: Ministry of Statistics and Programme Implementation.

—, *Eighth Five year Plan, 1992-97*, vol 2, Delhi: Ministry of Finance.

—, Ninth Five-Year Plan, 1997-2002, Delhi: Department of Electronics.

—, Planning Commission, Report of the Working Group on Information

Technology Sector for the Tenth Five Year Plan.
—, *Guide to Electronics Industry in India,* Delhi: Department of Electronics, Data Bank and Information Division, 1999.
—,Discussion Paper on Home-Based Workers, Delhi: Ministry of Labour, 2000.
—, *Census of India, 2001*, Provisional Population Totals, Paper 1, Delhi, Registrar General of India.
—. *Census of India, 2001*, Migration Tables, Data Highlights, Delhi, Registrar General of India.
—, *Foreign Investment in India,* Delhi: Planning Commission, 2002.
.—. *Report of the National Commission on Labour,* vol 1, part 1, Delhi: Ministry of Labour, 2002.
—, *Report on Currency and Finance,* Mumbai: Reserve Bank of India, Directorate General, Employment and Training, Ministry of Labour, Employment Review, 2002.
Harrison, Bennett, and Barry Bluestone, *The Great U-Turn: Corporate Restructuring and the Polarizing of America*, New York: Basic Books, 1988.
Hart, K., Informal Income Opportunities and Urban Employment in Ghana, in R. Jolly, E. De Kadt, H. Singer and F. Wilson, eds., *Third World Employment: Problems and Strategy,* Harmondsworth: Penguin, 1973.
Hensman, Rohini: Globalisation, Women and Work. *EPW* (6 March 2004).
Hobsbawm, Eric, *The Age of Empire, 1875-1914,* New York: Vintage, 1987.
—, *Age of Extremes,* New York: Vintage, 1996.
ILO, *Labour Practices in Footwear, Leather, Textiles and Clothing Industries,* Geneva, 2000.
—,*Impact of Flexible Labour Market Arrangements on the Machinery, Electrical and Electronic Industries,* Geneva, 1998.
—, *Working Women's Rights in India: Issues and Strategies,* New Delhi, 1999.
—, *Life at Work in the Information Economy,* World Employment Report 2001, Geneva, 2001.
International Labour Conference, Decent Work and the Informal Economy. Report 6, Geneva, 2002.
Jhabvala, Renana, *Globalization, Liberalization and Women in the Informal Economy*, in Veena Jha, ed., *Trade, Globalisation and Gende: Evidence from South Asia,* Delhi: UNIFEM, 2003.
Joekes, Susan, *Trade Related Employment for Women in Industry and Services in Developing Countries,* UNRISD, 1995.
Klein, Naomi, *No Logo,* New York: HarperCollins, 2000.
Kleinecht, Alfred, and C.W.M. Naastepad, Much Ado about Nothing?

Growth, Productivity and Employment in the OECD's 'New Economy, in Jayati Ghosh and C. P. Chandrashekhar, eds., *Work and Well-Being in the Age of Finance*, Delhi: Tulika Books, 2003.

Krishnamurthy, Sujana, *Structure of the Garment Industry and Labour Rights in the Post-MFA Context: A Study*, Delhi: Centre for Education and Communication, 2003

Lenin, V. I., *Imperialism, the Highest Stage of Capitalism*. Lenin Selected Works, vol. 1, Progress Publishers, Moscow, USSR, 1970.

Lüthje, Boy, IT and the Changing Social Division of Labor: The Case of Electronics Contract Manufacturing, Frankfurt: Institute of Social Science Research, January 2003.

M. Vijaybhaskaran, Garment Industry in India, in Gopal Joshi, ed., *Garment Industry in South Asia, Rags or Riches*, ILO/SAAT, 2002.

Mazumdar, Indrani, EPZs and Their Workers in India: A Study of the NOIDA Export Processing Zone, in A. S. Oberai, A. Sivananthisan, C.S. Venkataratnam, eds., *Labour Issues in Export Processing Zones in South Asia: Role of Social Dialogue*; SAAT/ILO/IIRA, 2001.

—, *Unorganised Workers of Delhi and the Seven Day Strike of 1988*. NLI Research Studies Series, NOIDA: V.V Giri National Labour Institute, 2002.

Mazumdar, Indrani, Rewa Shankar Misra, and Aanchal Kapur, Equal Remuneration in India, Law and Practice on Gender Based Wage Differentials with Special Reference to the Banking Sector, Mimeo, Delhi: ILO, 2000.

Mazumdar, Indrani, and Indu Agnihotri, Labour in Times of Closure, in U. Kalpagam, ed., *Labour and Poverty in Uttar Pradesh*, Delhi: Segment Books, 2004.

Mitra, Ashok, *Delhi, the Capital City*. New Delhi: Thomson Press, 1970.

N. Neetha, *Gender and Technology: Impact of Flexible Organisation and Production on Female Labour in the Tiruppur Knitwear Industry*, NLI Research Studies, NOIDA: V.V Giri National Labour Institute, 2001.

National Association of Software and Service Companies Resource Centre, Industry Trends, 2005, www.nasscom.org,

———Factsheets, www.nasscom.org

National Commission on Self-Employed Women and Women in the Informal Sector, *Shramshakti* (1988). Government of India, Ministry of Human Resource Development, Department of Women and Child Development.

National Rural Employment Guarantee Act, 2005, Delhi, *The Gazette of India*, no 48, 7 Sept 2005.

National Sample Survey Organisation (NSSO), Unorganised Manufacturing

Sector in India 2000-2001, Employment, Assets and Borrowings. Report No. 479 (56/2.2/3), 2002.

—,Employment and Unemployment in India, for 1987-88 (Report No. 43/1) published in 1991; for 1993-94 (Report No. 50/409) published in 1997, for 1999-2000 (Report No. 55/455) published in 2002,

———Employment and Unemployment Situation in India January-June 2004 (60/506) published in 2006.

—,Employment and Unemployment Situation in Major Towns and Cities in India, 55/468 NSSO '99-00, 2001.

Panthaki, M. K., 'Have Quota Restrictions increased Garment Exports?' *Clothesline,* April, 2001.

Patnaik, Prabhat, On the Political Economy of Economic 'Liberalization', in his book *Whatever Happened to Imperialism and other essays,* Delhi: Tulika, 1995.

—, Political Economy of Underdevelopment, in *Whatever Happened to Imperialism,* Delhi: Tulika, 1995.

—, Globalization of Capital and the Theory of Imperialism, in *Retreat to Unfreedom,* Delhi: Tulika, 2003.

—, Imperialism and Diffusion of Development, in *The Retreat to Unfreedom,* Delhi: Tulika, 2003.

Patnaik, Utsa, India's Agricultural Development in the light of Historical Experience, in T. J. Byres, ed., *The State, Development Planning and Liberalisation in India,* Delhi: Oxford University Press, 1998.

—, On the Inverse Relation between Primary Exports and Food Absorption in Developing Countries under Liberalised Trade Regimes, in J. Ghosh and C. P. Chandrashekhar, eds., *Work and Well-Being in the Age of Finance,* Delhi: Tulika, 2003.

—, *Rural India in Ruins, Frontline,* 12 March 2004.

Petras, James, and Henry Veltmeyer, *Globalization Unmasked*, Delhi: Madhyam, 2001.

Pore, Kumud, Women at Work – A Secondary Line of Operation, in Nirmala Banerjee, ed., *Indian Women in a Changing Industrial Scenario,* Delhi: Sage, 1991.

Ramachandran, V. K., and Madhura Swaminathan, Financial Liberalization and Rural Credit in India, in J. Ghosh and C. P. Chandrashekhar, eds., *Work and Well-Being in the Age of Finance,* Delhi: Tulika, 2003.

Ramaswamy, K.V., and G. Gereffi, India's Apparel Sector in a Global Economy, *EPW*, 33, 3 (1998).

Ranadive, J. and I. Mazumdar, The Effect of an Urban Environment upon the lives of Women: A Case Study of Women Industrial Workers in Noida, Delhi: CWDS, mimeo, 1998.

Rao, Rukmini, and Sehba Husain, Invisible Hands: The Women behind India's Export Earnings, in N. Banerjee, ed., Indian *Women in a Changing Industrial Scenario*, Delhi: Sage,1991.

Remesh, Babu P., Insecurituies and Vulnerabilities of Non-Standard Work: A Case Study of Business Process Outsourcing, mimeo, Noida: V.V. Giri National Labour Institute. 2005.

Rastogi, Rajiv, Indian electronics Industry–Geographical Spread, *Electronics Information and Planning (henceforth EPIP)*, (Sept 2000).

—, Electronics and Information Technology Production Trends in 2001, *EPIP* (March-April 2002).

Rosen, Ellen Israel, *Making Sweatshops, The Globalization of the US Apparel Industry*, Berkeley, CA: University of California Press, 2002.

Roy, Tirthankar, Outline of a History of Labour in Traditional Small-Scale Industry in India, NLI Research Studies Series No. 015/2001, Noida: V. V. Giri National Labour Institute.date?

Sauve, Pierre, Trade Policy Implications of the New Economy: Preliminary Thoughts. OECD, 2001. Paper available on http://www.cid.harvard.edu/cidtrade/Papers/Sauve/sauvetpimp.pdf

Schwartz, Peter, and Peter Leyden, The Long Boom: A History of the Future, 1980-2020, *www.wired.com/wired/archive/5.07/longboom_pr.html*, 1997.

Sen, Abhijit, Globalization, Growth and Inequality in South Asia. in J. Ghosh and C. P. Chandrashekhar, eds., *Work and Well-Being in the Age of Finance*, Delhi: Tulika, 2003.

Sen Gupta, D.N., Effect of Policy on Export Competitiveness: The Case of the Indian Garment Industry, Conference presentation, IIM, Ahmedabad, 1994.

Singh, A., Global Economic Change, Skills and International Competitiveness, *International Labour Review* 133 (1994).

Singh, Kavaljit, *A Citizen's Guide to the Globalisation of Finance*, Delhi: Madhyam Books, 1998.

—, *Globalisation of Finance*, Delhi: Madhyam Books, 1998.

Singh, V. B., Political Profile of Delhi and Support Bases of Parties: An Analysis, in V. Dupont, E. Tarlo and D. Vidal eds., *Urban Spaces and Human Destinies*, Delhi: Manohar, 2000.

Somavia, Juan, *The Dilemma of the Informal Sector*, ILO Director General's report to the 78th session of the International Labour Conference, Geneva, 1991.

Standing, Guy, Global Feminization through Flexible Labor: A Theme Revisited, *World Development* 27, 3 (1999).

Stiglitz, Joseph, *Globalization and Its Discontents*, London: Allen Lane, 2002.

Story, Jonathan, The ICT Revolution, background paper for ILO's World Employment Report, Geneva: ILO, 2001.

Sundaram, K., Employment and Poverty in the 1990s, Further Results from NSS 55th Round Employment-Unemployment Survey, 1999-2000, *EPW* 36, 32 (11-17 Aug 2001).

Sussex, Edward, Trends in Telecommunication work, *Communications International* July 1998.

Tait, Niki, Indian Garment Exports, Moving towards 2005, *Clothesline*, April 2001.

Thiagarajan, Krishnan, Hardware: An Experiment in Globalisation, *The Hindu Business Line*, 5 May 2002.

UNCTAD E-Commerce and Development Report, 2002, 2003, www.unctad.org.

—, World Investment Report, 2002. www.unctad.org

UNDP, *Human Development Report 1999*.

United Nations, *1999 Survey of Women in Development, Globalization, Women and Work*, 2000. un.org/womenwatch/daw/public/

Unorganized Sector Workers (Social Security) Bill, 2005 (Draft) and Unorganized Sector Workers (Conditions of Work and Livelihood Promotion) Bill, 2005 (Draft) on http://nceuis.nic.in/.

Unni, Jeemol, Size, Contribution and Characteristics of Informal Employment in India, in *Bharat, Globalization and Its Impact on Women Workers in the Informal Economy*, December, UNIFEM and SEWA, Delhi: 2002.

Unni, Jeemol, and Uma Rani, Globalisation, Information Technology and Service Sector in India, *Indian J Labour Economics* 43, 4 (2000).

Vanamala, M. Informalisation and Feminisation of a Formal Sector Industry: A Case Study, *EPW* 20 June 2001.

Wadia, Behram, From Roots to Fruits: *Electronics, Outlook*, June 2002.

Website of World Socialist Workers, *Telephone call centres expand worldwide*, , 9 December 1998.

Womenspeak, United Voices Against Globalization, Poverty and Violence in India, March 2000.

World Bank, *Indian Cotton and Textile Industry: Reforming to Compete*, South Asia Rural Development Series, 1999.

—, Workers in an Integrating World,. *World Development Report*, Delhi: Oxford University Press, 1995.

WTO, *International Trade Statistics*, http://www.wto.org/english/res_e/statis_e/statis_e.htm.

Index